palgrave macmillan law masters

intellectual property law

Series editor: Marise Cremona

Business Law   Stephen Judge
Company Law   Janet Dine and Marios Koutsias
Constitutional and Administrative Law   John Alder
Contract Law   Ewan McKendrick
Criminal Law   Jonathan Herring
Employment Law   Deborah J. Lockton
Evidence   Raymond Emson
Family Law   Kate Standley and Paula Davies
Intellectual Property Law   Tina Hart, Simon Clark and Linda Fazzani
Land Law   Mark Davys
Landlord and Tenant Law   Margaret Wilkie, Peter Luxton and Desmond Kilcoyne
Legal Method   Ian McLeod
Legal Theory   Ian McLeod
Medical Law   Jo Samanta and Ash Samanta
Sports Law   Mark James
Torts   Alastair Mullis and Ken Oliphant
Trusts Law   Charlie Webb and Tim Akkouh

If you would like to comment on this book, or on the series generally, please write to lawfeedback@palgrave.com.

palgrave macmillan law masters

intellectual property law

tina hart

Principal Lecturer in Law, University of Huddersfield

simon clark

Head of Intellectual Property, Berwin Leighton Paisner

linda fazzani

Former Consultant, Berwin Leighton Paisner

Sixth edition

palgrave
macmillan

This edition first published 2013 by PALGRAVE MACMILLAN

Palgrave Macmillan in the UK is an imprint of Macmillan Publishers Limited, registered in England, company number 785998, of Houndmills, Basingstoke, Hampshire RG21 6XS.

Palgrave Macmillan in the US is a division of St Martin's Press LLC, 175 Fifth Avenue, New York, NY 10010.

Palgrave Macmillan is the global academic imprint of the above companies and has companies and representatives throughout the world.

Palgrave® and Macmillan® are registered trademarks in the United States, the United Kingdom, Europe and other countries.

ISBN-13: 978–0–230–36653–4   paperback

This book is printed on paper suitable for recycling and made from fully managed and sustained forest sources. Logging, pulping and manufacturing processes are expected to conform to the environmental regulations of the country of origin.

A catalogue record for this book is available from the British Library.

Contents

Preface

This edition once again includes substantial changes from the previous edition, reflecting the constant evolution of intellectual property law, particularly as a result of new challenges created by digitalisation and new media.

The chapters on trade marks highlight the issues connected with the use of the internet to shop for and advertise trade-marked goods. The chapter on Breach of Confidence takes account of the growing interplay between the tort and the relevant articles of the European Convention on Human Rights.

The past two years have surely been some of the busiest ever for developments in copyright law. Following the Hargreaves Review, the government has announced proposals to expand exceptions to copyright, whilst at the same time the duration of protection in sound recordings and copyright works is to be extended. These issues are discussed in the copyright chapters, together with some of the major copyright cases from the Court of Appeal, the Supreme Court and the European Court.

Similarly the database chapter and the design chapters feature several important new national and European Court decisions, whilst both the competition and copyright chapters cover in detail the *Football Association Premier League v QC Leisure* cases.

In this book we use the term 'ECJ' to denote the Court of Justice and not the term 'CJEU' as is sometimes used by others. This is because the Court of Justice of the European Union (CJEU) includes the Court of Justice, the General Court and the Civil Service Tribunal and 'ECJ' has typically been used to describe the Court of Justice. We have therefore chosen to maintain that naming convention here.

The authors have sought to state the law as at 1 January 2013.

Acknowledgements

Once more, we would like to thank the various people who have helped us in the production of this edition.

Tina would like to thank her children Martyn junior and Josephine for their continued love, support and patience with their mother.

Simon would like to thank the members of Berwin Leighton Paisner's Intellectual Property and Competition departments for their substantial contributions to the following chapters for this edition, namely Gavin Llewellyn and Jamie Drucker (copyright, designs and performance rights), with input from Richard Benn and William Priestly, Tamara Quinn (database rights), with input from Gavin Llewellyn, Andrew Hockley and Annabel Baxter (competition), Ian De Freitas, Gavin Llewellyn and Jamie Drucker for the new privacy section of the confidence chapter, and Emma Rumens for ensuring once again that it all stayed in the correct order!

Tina Hart
Simon Clark

Table of cases

Table of legislation

Chapter 1

Introduction

1.1 The subject matter

The aim of this book is to ground you thoroughly in intellectual property law. It is worth starting off with a brief overview of the central concepts and terms. This will give you an indication of the areas that the book will cover and help you to fit them all together as you continue through the book.

1.1.1 Patents

A patent is a monopoly right granted by the government through the Intellectual Property Office to an individual who has invented a product or process. The basic objectives for granting this right are: to inform the public through publication of details from the application of the latest technological advances; to provide an incentive for innovation and thereby stimulate economic activity; and to provide a reward for creative and innovative effort.

1.1.2 Copyright

This is an exclusive right to deal with original literary, dramatic, artistic and musical works. As well as protecting the fruits of creative effort, the legislation also protects those who have invested in those efforts by providing protection for sound recordings, films and published editions of literary work.

1.1.3 Database right

Information arranged in a methodical and systematic way, usually accessible by electronic means such as databases, was originally protected under copyright law. However, with the implementation of the EU Directive on the legal protection of databases by the Copyright and Rights in Databases Regulations 1997, a new database right was created.

1.1.4 Performers' rights

These are linked with copyright but are aimed at providing protection for the actual performance of copyright works as distinct from the copyright works themselves.

1.1.5 Trade marks

Trade marks are words or symbols used in relation to goods and services that distinguish the owner's goods and services from those of another. Current legislation allows for the possibility of distinctive smells and sounds also attracting protection. The law in this area restrains others from applying the owner's brand to their goods and services. The trade mark owner's rights are protected by statute, if registered, or by common law, where the rights in the trade mark are based on use and goodwill.

1.1.6 Designs

Designs which give visual appeal to mass-produced goods may be protected as registered designs, whereas designs which are merely functional are protected as unregistered designs. A child's toothbrush in the shape of a Walt Disney character is an example of the former, whereas an item of garden equipment is an example of the latter.

1.1.7 Confidential information

Equitable remedies are available to restrain the use of trade secrets and other confidential information without the owner's authority.

1.2 The protection provided

Legal recognition of intellectual property is provided by a negative form of protection. The legislation will usually describe the owner's right as 'exclusive', thus, by implication, giving the owner the right to restrain others from using his intellectual property without authority.

It can be argued that the protection given is purely economic as the intellectual property owner is being provided with the exclusive right to exploit that property. However, since 1988, there has also been a recognition of moral rights under the Copyright, Designs and Patents Act 1988. The author of a work can, among other things, protect the integrity of the work using his right to object to derogatory treatment of the work under section 80. By its very nature intellectual property requires protection on an international level. For example, the author Alice Walker is an American national whose work is produced in the United States of America. Her work is also popular in the UK and other countries. Thus to afford her protection in the United States alone would be of little benefit. There has been a number of international agreements in existence since the nineteenth century to protect intellectual property owners internationally, but on the whole their purpose was to harmonise and regularise the criteria for protection, as well as to provide for reciprocity. Intellectual property owners must still enforce their rights through national courts and thus rely on the differing methods of protection that each domestic court may utilise. Added to this, intellectual property owners may be operating in jurisdictions where the system of intellectual property protection is less than they would enjoy at home. Concerns about the lack of intellectual property protection in certain states led to the Agreement on Trade Related Aspects of Intellectual Property Rights (the TRIPS Agreement, 1994), one of the multilateral agreements signed to establish the World Trade Organization (WTO).

The Agreement is based on three principles. First, to establish minimum standards for the protection and enforcement of intellectual rights in all Member States. Second, each country must protect the nationals of other Member States by granting the rights set out in the Agreement. Third, members are required to provide the nationals of other states with protection that is 'no less favourable' than that provided to their own nationals. Added to this is the 'most favoured nation principle'. This is stipulated in article 4(1), which states:

> With regard to the protection of intellectual property, any advantage, favour, privilege or immunity granted by a Member to the nationals of any other country shall be accorded immediately and unconditionally to the nationals of all other Members.

The Agreement is administered by the WTO. It is sovereign states rather than individual intellectual property owners who will make use of the WTO's Dispute Settlement Body, to complain about the lack of intellectual property protection.

1.3 Justification

It would appear that the protection of intellectual property rights conflicts with policies in the European Economic Area (EEA) to maintain free competition. However, it can be argued that the market economy is stimulated by the fact that consumers are assisted in making choices from a selection of goods by the use of trade marks, for example, which distinguish one trader's goods from those of another. Further, because the trade mark informs the consumer about the quality of the owner's goods, there is an element of consumer protection. Granting patents encourages innovation so more goods are available on the market.

Competition within the EEA is protected by articles 34–36 of the Treaty on the Functioning of the EU (TFEU), which provide for the free movement of goods, and articles 101–102, which legislate for free competition.

Nationally, the abuse of intellectual property is checked using a variety of means, for example, licences of right for patents are provided during the last four years of the 20-year term, and compulsory licences are also available for unreasonable underuse of the patent by the patentee. Section 144 of the Copyright, Designs and Patents Act 1988 restrains anti-competitive licensing in relation to copyright and section 238 does the same in relation to unregistered design rights.

The recognition and protection of intellectual property is vital in a market economy and as such is kept under review. In 2005, the government set up a review of the intellectual property system in the UK under the *Financial Times* journalist Andrew Gowers. The remit of the Review was to: '[E]xamine all elements of the intellectual property system, to ensure that it delivers incentives while minimising inefficiency ...'.

We will consider the recommendations and conclusions of the Gowers Review where appropriate throughout the book.

1.4 Sources of law

Intellectual property law is mainly codified. Each of the main subjects of intellectual property is governed by statute and supported by delegated legislation. The following are the main statutory sources of law:

- Registered Designs Act 1949 (as amended);
- Patents Act 1977 (as amended);
- Copyright, Designs and Patents Act 1988;
- Trade Marks Act 1994;
- Copyright and Rights in Databases Regulations 1997;
- Council Regulation of 12 December 2001 on Community Designs; and
- Patents Act 2004.

Confidential information and passing off are creatures of common law. Intellectual property cannot be protected merely on a national level and international influences can be found within the above legislation, most of which was passed to enforce the international obligations of the UK as well as to update the law. For example, one of the objectives of the Trade Marks Act 1994 was to implement Council Directive 89/104/ EEC of 21 December 1988 to approximate the laws of the Member States relating to trade marks, and the Patents Act 1977 was passed, among other things, to give effect to provisions in the European Patent Convention (EPC).

More recent changes which have been made include Commission Regulation of 21 October 2002 implementing Council Regulation (EC) No. 6/2002 on Community Designs (2245/2002/EC), and the changes made to the Copyright, Designs and Patents Act 1988 by the Copyright Regulations, to implement the Directive of the European Parliament and the Council of the EU 2001/29/EC on the harmonisation of certain aspects of copyright and related rights in the information society.

A body of case law has developed on the interpretation of the above provisions by national courts and international bodies such as the European Patent Office (EPO). Common law also has a part to play in the areas of passing off and the law of confidence.

Intellectual property law is administered in the Chancery Division of the High Court, with appeals to the Court of Appeal and the Supreme Court . The Patents Court is also part of the Chancery Division and will hear cases regarding patents and registered designs. Since the passing of the Copyright, Designs and Patents Act 1988, there is also a Patents County Court.

As we have already indicated, the nature of the protection given for intellectual property is negative. The owners will usually go to court to restrain unauthorised use of their property by others. In some cases, the remedy sought is the interlocutory injunction. An interlocutory injunction is an order sought by the intellectual property owner as a first step in proceedings, before the substantive issues regarding ownership and infringement are considered. As a result, some of the case law that has developed has done so mainly from trial judges making a decision as to whether they are satisfied that the claimant has at least an arguable case, because that is all a claimant needs to show at the stage of seeking an interlocutory injunction.

Cases on intellectual property law are reported in specialist law reports as well as the standard reports. Students of intellectual property law can, therefore, also consult the Reports of Patent, Design and Trade Mark Cases (RPC) published by the Intellectual Property Office and the Fleet Street Reports (FSR) published by Sweet & Maxwell. Cases of the European Board of Appeal (EBOR) report on decisions concerning European patents. The *European Intellectual Property Review* (EIPR) is the main journal where academic work on the subject can be found.

Summary

▷ Intellectual property is a form of personal intangible property. The subject matter includes copyright, database right, registered and unregistered trade marks, patents, registered and unregistered designs, as well as the law of confidence.

▷ The legal protection is negative in the sense that the law can be used to stop others exploiting the intellectual property owner's property.

▷ The market economy is arguably stimulated by this legal incentive to create. Competition law exists in the EU and UK to discourage abuse of the rights granted to those who create.

▷ Intellectual property law is mainly a creature of statute but has also developed through common law and equity.

Useful websites

There is a wealth of material on intellectual property (as on other subjects) to be found on the internet. Below is a list of useful website addresses for those interested in pursuing the topics raised in this book in further detail.

American Intellectual Property Law Association: www.aipla.org
Copyright Licensing Agency: www.cla.co.uk
European Community cases: www.curia.europa.eu
European Patent Office: www.epo.org
Intellectual Property Law Server: www.intelproplaw.com
Intellectual Property Office: www.ipo.gov.uk
Intellectual Property Owners Association: www.ipo.org
International Trademark Association: www.inta.org
Internet Corporation for Assigned Names and Numbers: www.icann.org
Nominct, internet registry for domain names: www.nominet.org.uk
Office of the European Union: www.oami.europa.eu
World Intellectual Property Organization: www.wipo.org
World Trade Organization: www.wto.org

Part I

Patents and confidential information

Chapter 2

Patents

2.1 What is a patent?

Ibrufen, cats' eyes and bagless vacuum cleaners are examples of well-known inventions. In return for sharing the information about their ideas, the inventors of these products have been rewarded with patents by the state.

A patent gives the owner (the patentee) the exclusive right to exploit the invention. For up to 20 years (25 in the case of pharmaceutical patents), the patentee has the legal right to stop others producing the patented goods or applying the patented process by suing for infringement. This means that, for the duration of the patent, others cannot produce the patented product or use the patented process without the patentee's permission, and this is so even if a third party has come upon the patented product or process completely independently. The grant of a patent is, therefore, the grant of a monopoly right for a specified period.

2.2 Historical background

Patents were originally granted by the Crown exercising its Royal Prerogative. Letters Patent were a royal proclamation that the bearer had the Crown's authority to do whatever had been authorised within the Letters.

The earliest record of a granted patent dates from 1331, to a Flemish weaver who wanted to practise his trade in England. Most of the patents granted at this time were to encourage trade in general, rather than for new inventions. In many cases, the grant of a patent was the Crown's method of controlling trade, and towards the end of Elizabeth I's reign there were many abuses of the system. In *Darcy v Thomas Allen* (1602) Co Rep 84b, a monopoly granted to a merchant exclusively to import, make and sell playing cards was held to be void because it was contrary to the common law.

The Statute of Monopolies 1623 was passed to control or limit these abuses. Monopolies per se were excluded unless they came within the exception in section 6. Under section 6, a 14-year monopoly could be granted for any 'manner of new manufacture'. Whereas the section allowed for the grant of patents, the actual application procedure and enforcement of the monopoly right were still governed by the common law. The Patents Act 1835 was passed to deal with disclaimers and prolongations of claim, but the first comprehensive statute on the subject was the Patent Law Amendment Act 1852, which set up the Patent Office and Registrar of Patents. The Act also introduced the requirement that a 'specification' be filed with any application for a patent describing the nature of the invention.

In 1883, the Patents, Designs and Trade Marks Act was passed to enable the UK to satisfy its obligations of reciprocity under the Paris Convention for the Protection of Industrial Property. This Act required a full specification including detailed claims to be completed by the applicant and examined by the Patent Office before a patent would be granted. The case of *Nobel's Explosive Co Ltd v Anderson* (1894) 11 RPC 115 established that it was no longer possible to claim that the patent extended to matter contained in the specification where such matter was not in the 'claim'. This highlighted the use of claims to mark the legal boundaries of the patent.

At this point, the UK patent system was purely a deposit system, where applications were checked simply to make sure that they had been completed correctly. The need to prove that an invention was really 'new' did not come until the Patents Act 1907, which introduced the practice of checking applications for 'novelty', with searches being extended to cover patents granted over the previous 50 years. The grounds for declaring a patent invalid were codified in the 1907 Act. In the Patents Act 1919 it was stated that invalid claims within an application would not invalidate the whole application.

The entire patent system was overhauled by the Patents Act 1949. The modern law on patents is set down in the Patents Act 1977, which was passed to satisfy the UK's obligations under the European Patent Convention 1973 (EPC), the Community Patent Convention 1975 and the Patent Cooperation Treaty 1970. It contains sections outlining the procedures followed in the European Patent Office (EPO) and plans for the Community Patent. The 1949 Act was not completely repealed by the 1977 Act; only the parts that were in conflict with the EPC. The unaffected provisions now form part of the 1977 Act, which itself has been amended by EC legislation and the TRIPS Agreement. In 2004, further amendments were added by the Patents Act 2004. This was passed to implement changes agreed by the Diplomatic Conference to the EPC in 2000 and to introduce measures designed to assist with the enforcement of patent rights and the resolution of disputes.

2.3   Why are patents granted?

The ability to stop others using or manufacturing the patented product or process effectively stops competition for the 20-year period. One might ask: how can this be justified? First of all, in obtaining a patent, the patentee has publicised the invention. While others cannot use the patent during the patent period, they can certainly look at the details and learn from the technological advances made. The grant of the patent is the reward for sharing knowledge regarding new inventions. Second, the inventor who is rewarded in this way may be encouraged to make other useful inventions. The patent is thus an incentive to be more creative. A third possible justification for patents is that, as new products are invented, this stimulates the economy as there are more products for consumers to buy.

The patentee will have often spent a great deal of money on research and development of the product (or process) in question. Having the monopoly for a limited period allows that investment to be recouped before others come onto the market to compete. Further, without the grant of a patent, others who have not had to invest in research and development would be able to copy the invention, produce it more cheaply and still make a profit, thereby depriving the inventor of the ability to recoup the investment. According to Lord Neuberger in *Human Genome Sciences Inc v Eli Lilly and Co* [2011] UKSC 51:

> [I]t is worth remembering the purpose of the patent system, namely to provide a temporary monopoly as an incentive to innovation, while at the same time facilitating the early dissemination of any such innovation through an early application for a patent and its subsequent publication (at [99]).

To ensure that the patentee uses the monopoly only for the legitimate purpose of recouping the investment, and not for the purpose of purely blocking competition, there is provision for compulsory licences to be granted if the patentee has not commercially exploited the patent after a certain period. This is looked at in more detail in Chapter 5.

2.4   The patent system

2.4.1   The application

There are two main methods of obtaining a patent for the UK. The applicant can either apply for a domestic patent from the Intellectual Property Office in London, or for a European patent designating a number of Member States of the EPC, including the UK. If the EPO application is successful in respect of the UK, the patent in the UK will be governed by the Patents Act 1977. A further method is to apply under the Patent Cooperation Treaty (PCT) designating some or all of the contracting states.

The date on which an application is filed is called the 'priority date' and the duration of the patent is calculated from that date. Establishing the priority date is important for two reasons. First, matters such as novelty and inventive step are judged by considering the state of the art at that date, so details about the invention must not have been made available to the public prior to that date. Second, any person who in good faith had prior to that date been committing what would otherwise be an infringing act may continue to engage in those activities after the patent has been granted, although it is likely that such prior use would invalidate the patent application (see Chapter 3).

Under section 14, the application should be in the prescribed form and filed in the prescribed manner, accompanied by the prescribed fee. The application must include a 'specification', a 'claim' or 'claims' and any drawings that are referred to. The application should also include an abstract. It is possible, when filing an application, to claim as the priority date the date of an earlier application made within the previous 12 months, but only if the earlier application consists of or contains matter in support of the later application. Under section 16, the application will be published in the official journal of the Patent Office (unless the application is withdrawn) and it is only at this stage that the application is available to the public.

Within a year of the date of filing the application (the priority date), section 17 allows for the applicant to request a preliminary examination and search. This will be carried out by an official at the Patent Office, to make sure that the legal requirements have been complied with. There will also be a search of the prior art. A report of the search will then be sent to the applicant. The applicant will then request a substantial examination within six months. If the application succeeds, the patent will be granted, a notice will be published and the grant will take effect from the date of publication, although the duration of the patent runs from the date of the application.

A patent application may be amended after filing but before grant, either to correct any deficiencies in the application which are identified by the Patent Office or at the applicant's choice following receipt of the results of either the preliminary or the substantive search. It is a condition of these amendments that they do not result in any 'added matter' being included.

2.4.2   The specification

The specification is essentially a description of the invention and the best method of performing it. It should include drawings graphically representing the invention and how it is proposed to work. A good specification will describe the invention comprehensively, as any omissions will reduce the effectiveness of the patent. The specification must disclose enough detail so that a 'person skilled in the art' could perform or make the invention. If it does not, the patent could be subject to revocation for lack of sufficiency.

2.4.3   The claims

The claims form part of the specification. These are the legal parts of the application which a court will look at to determine whether there has been infringement. Section 14(5) states that the claims should:

- define the matter for which the applicant seeks protection;
- be clear and concise;
- be supported by the description; and
- relate to one invention or to a group of inventions which are so linked as to form a single inventive concept.

A failure to indicate fully all the invention's features will make it easier for third parties to engage in activities which fall outside the claims of a valid patent and thus avoid an action for infringement. On the other hand, a patent can be invalidated if the claims overstate the abilities of the invention. The claims will define and set out what is 'novel' and 'inventive' about the invention. These should act as boundaries to the patentee's property over which others should not trespass.

2.4.4   The abstract

The abstract is the part of the document that is directed to the technician. It will contain sufficient technical information for a skilled person in that area to study the science to see whether it goes beyond what already exists in the field.

2.5   The international patent system

The grant of a patent in the UK does not automatically provide international protection. However, whereas there is still no such thing as a worldwide patent, there are a number of international arrangements that make it possible to obtain protection in other jurisdictions.

2.5.1   Paris Convention for the Protection of Industrial Property 1883

Two basic principles emerge from the Paris Convention: the principle of reciprocity and the system of priority. Under the principle of reciprocity nationals of any one of the Member States are to be accorded the same rights in another Member State as nationals of that second Member State. The system of priority allows an application to be made in one Member State claiming an earlier date of application, if the earlier application was made in another Member State within the previous 12 months. The priority system also means that the earlier application will not defeat the second application for want of novelty.

2.5.2   Patent Cooperation Treaty 1970

The Patent Cooperation Treaty is administered by the World Intellectual Property Organization (WIPO) in Geneva. The objective behind the system is to eliminate the need to make applications in a number of countries. A national of a Member State can file an International Patent Application in a given patent office (known as the Receiving Office), designating the countries in which registration is being sought. This has the effect of filing the application in both the first country and also in the designated countries. The application is then transmitted to an International Searching Authority which will do the prior-art search and transmit the results to the individual patent offices of the designated states. From that stage, the further prosecution in each country is dealt with by the local patent office in accordance with its normal procedure. Regulations under the PCT came into force on 1 January 2004 and the UK Patent Act 2004 made minor changes to the 1977 Act to clarify the relationship between domestic patent law and the PCT.

2.5.3   European Patent Convention 1973

The European Patent Convention is an intergovernmental agreement among thirty-seven European states including all of the individual members of the European Union. The principles behind the EPC are similar to those of the PCT in that the applicant makes a single application designating particular European countries. The EPC established a procedure for obtaining a 'European patent', following a single application to the EPO. The Convention is administered by the EPO, with questions of interpretation being handled by the Boards of Appeal. In *Merrill Dow v Norton* [1996] RPC 76, the House of Lords said that courts in the UK must consider the decisions of the EPO on the interpretation of the Convention. By implication, this means that the approach of the EPO should be followed when interpreting sections of the Patent Act 1977. This point was reiterated by the Supreme Court in *Human Genome Sciences Inc v Eli Lilly and Co* [2011] UKSC 51, where it was stated that it was important that UK patent law was aligned so far as possible with the jurisprudence of the EPO, although it was recognised that national courts and the EPO could reach different conclusions because they had different evidence or arguments. The EPC was revised in 2000, following agreement by the Diplomatic Conference in November 2000.

2.5.4   Community Patent Convention 1975

Member States of what was then the European Economic Community (now the EU) established the Community Patent Convention, in order to set up a system where a single Community-wide patent could be granted. This would differ from a patent under the EPC in that the Community Patent system would be a unitary system granting patents which would take effect throughout the EU. The plans were that this system would also be administered by the EPO in Munich. Once in place, the European Community would be a signatory to the EPC (a patent application to the EPO would thus designate the EU). The patent granted would then take effect throughout the Community. Following a draft Directive to introduce a Community Patent, the hope was expressed in the fourth edition of this book that there would be a Community-wide patent by 2012. However, this is now uncertain.

2.6   The future of patents

The patent system was the first of the intellectual property systems to legislate for a truly harmonised and Community-wide system. The advances in patent law that are on the horizon relate not so much to harmonisation, but to how the system is to address advances in biotechnology, genetic engineering and computing. It is suggested that a further challenge is to finalise the arrangements for a Community Patent.

The future for patents: still no Community Patent!

According to David Bainbridge (2009), '[the] interest in the Community Patent flares up every now and again but it does not seem as if it is likely to come into being in the immediate future' (p 16). The European Council in Lisbon 2000 called for a Community-wide patent so that Community-wide patent protection in the Union would be as simple and inexpensive to obtain and as comprehensive in its scope as the protection granted by competitors. Further support comes from the Gowers Review of Intellectual Property which advises that the introduction of a single unitary European patent would have significant benefits (p 81).

Cornish and Llewelyn (2007) point out that 'The chief advantage of the single Community patent would be the ability to enforce it throughout the EU with a single main proceeding' (p 128).

So what is the problem?

The main issues appear to be that of translation and jurisdiction. While the official languages of the EPO are English, French and German, the EU has approximately 23 official languages and a majority of EU Member States have apparently insisted that upon grant a Community Patent must be translated into their national languages. This would prove quite expensive and outweigh any savings made in applying for a Community Patent. According to the European Commission:

> The cost of translating the patent into all the official languages of the Community would entail a risk of the entire Community patent project floundering, placing as it would too heavy a burden on inventors, above all small and medium sized enterprises.

The other main problem is one of jurisdiction. Once granted, EPC patents are subject to the national laws and enforced in the national courts of the countries designated. With regard to the Community Patent, the proposal is that the EPO would examine the applications and grant Community Patents, but disputes would be dealt with by the Community Patent Court, with appeals on questions of fact and law going to a specialised chamber of the Court of First Instance (CFI). There is an alternative proposal, namely, an integrated judicial system to deal with litigation concerning EPC patents. There is a draft European Patent Litigation Agreement (EPLA). The EPLA also proposes an EPC, with a court of appeal and a court of first instance. The EPLA would be open to accession by any contracting state of the EPC and possibly to the EU.

So who would have jurisdiction over the Community Patent?

The problem is that not all members of the EPC are members of the EU. It is therefore argued that all patents granted by the EPO should be subject to a uniform system so that they are treated in a harmonised way. According to Joanna Schmidt-Szalewski (in 'Europe, patents and dinosaurs'), this position either disregards or understates the fact that the EC Patent would be a new territorial patent subject to its own national (i.e. Community) law.

While all commentators appear to agree that it is in the interests of the EU to create its own patent, finding a compromise with regard to language and jurisdiction appears to be the main hurdles.

Further constitutional concerns

In 2007, the Commission presented a communication entitled 'Enhancing the patent system in Europe' to the European Parliament and the Council. The Commission proposed the creation of an integrated system for the European and the future Community Patent. The Community Patent would be granted by the EPO under the provisions of the EPC. It would have a unitary and autonomous character, producing equal effect throughout the European Union.

A further agreement was prepared which created a court with jurisdiction to hear actions related to the European and Community Patents. This court would be composed of a court of first instance and a court of appeal, which would hear appeals brought against decisions delivered by the court of first instance. The Council requested an Opinion from the Court of Justice (of the EU), asking whether the envisaged agreement creating a Unified Patent Litigation System was compatible with the provisions of the Treaty establishing the European Community *(Re Draft Agreement on a European and Community Patents Court* (Opinion 1/09) [2011] 3 CMLR 4 (ECJ)). The Court held that the proposed court was not part of the judicial system of the EU and was an organisation with a distinct legal personality under international law. The Court was therefore holding that the EU's participation in the negotiation of an international treaty relating to patent litigation was incompatible with EU law. Steve Peers raises the question of how this incompatibility might be cured. In his article, 'The Constitutional Implications of the EU Patent', the author identifies that the objections of the ECJ to the planned treaty regarding patent litigation needs to be addressed. As already indicated, the draft patent court agreement would have created a new court, comprising regional first instance chambers and an appeal court, with exclusive jurisdiction over key aspects of litigation over EU patents and European patents. The first instance chambers would have been able to send questions for a preliminary ruling on the EU law issues to the Court of Justice, while the appeal court would have been obliged to send such questions. The agreement would have been signed by the EU, its member states and any third states which are party to the EPC; it would have come into force once all EU Member.

States had ratified it. However, the proposed patent court was not part of the judicial system provided for in the Treaties and would be outside the institutional and judicial framework of the EU. The planned patent court would have extensive jurisdiction to interpret and apply EU patent legislation, as well as EU rules on free movement and competition, other EU rules on intellectual property and EU human rights rules. Member states could not divest their national courts of that jurisdiction and give it to an international court.

Summary

▶ A patent is a monopoly granted to the owner by the state in return for disclosing information about the invention.

▶ Regulation of the patent system dates back to the Statute of Monopolies 1623. The modern statute on patents is the Patents Act 1977.

▶ Patents are granted in return for information about technological advances. The monopoly is also justified as it allows the owner to recoup the investment in research and development before others can enter the market.

▶ The main part of the application is the specification that will include claims and an abstract.

Summary cont'd

▶ The UK's membership of a number of reciprocal international conventions has influenced the law on patents.

▶ The patent system will need to adapt to address advances in biotechnology and genetic engineering.

Exercises

2.1 What exactly does the owner of a patent obtain from the state?

2.2 Why should anyone be allowed to keep their competitors out of the market for up to 20 years?

2.3 Your client has developed a chemical compound to produce a fat-busting drug. She would like to apply for a patent. Advise her of the procedure.

2.4 What is the best way to achieve international protection for a patent?

Further reading and references

Arnull, 'Patent Failure?' [2007] EL Review 32(3), 293.

Bainbridge, *Intellectual Property Law* (8th edn, Pitman Longman, 2010).

Cornish and Llewelyn, *Intellectual Property Law* (6th edn, Sweet & Maxwell, 2007) pp 127–30 (paras 3.23–3.29).

MacQueen, Waelde and Laurie, *Contemporary Intellectual Property Law and Policy* (3rd edn, Oxford University Press, 2008) pp 367–73.

Parish, 'International Courts and the European Legal Order' EJIL, (2012), 23(1), 141–153.

Peers, 'The Constitutional Implications of the eu Patent' [2011] ECL Review 7(2), 229.

Schmidt-Szalewski, 'Europe, Patents and Dinosaurs' [2007] IIC 38(7), 757.

WTO Agreement on Trade-Related Aspects of Intellectual Property Rights, Including Trade in Counterfeit Goods' [1994] ILM 33, 81.

Chapter 3

Patentability: excluded matters

3.1 Introduction

Patent protection is available for products and processes which satisfy four basic requirements of patentability.

Patentability under the 1977 Act is based on articles 52–57 of the European Patent Convention (EPC), and it is the practice of English courts to take into account the spirit and purpose of the EPC in settling disputes which arise either on application or after a patent has been granted.

Section 1(1) of the 1977 Act states that a patent may only be granted if the invention in question:

(a) is new (or novel);
(b) involves an inventive step;
(c) is capable of industrial application; and
(d) is not excluded under s.1(2) or (3).

Before considering questions of novelty, inventive step and industrial application, one should make sure that the subject of an application does not fall within one of the exclusions.

3.2 Exclusions from patentability

If the subject of the application falls under one of the exclusions, there is no need to go any further. The exclusions are in sections 1(2) and (3) of the Patents Act. Section 1(2) states:

It is hereby declared that the following (among other things) are not inventions for the purposes of this Act, that is to say, anything which consists of:

(a) a discovery, scientific theory or mathematical method;
(b) a literary, dramatic, musical or artistic work or any other aesthetic creation whatsoever;
(c) a scheme, rule or method for performing a mental act, playing a game or doing business, or a program for a computer;
(d) the presentation of information

but the foregoing provision shall prevent anything from being treated as an invention for the purposes of this Act only to the extent that a patent or application for a patent relates to that thing as such.

Discoveries are not patentable under paragraph (a). However, if they lead to something tangible, they may be able to attract patent protection. For example, penicillin, a naturally occurring medicine, which was discovered in 1928, could not be the subject of a patent. However, 12 years on, drugs produced from it were patented. The importance of the last two words of section 1(2) ('as such') is illustrated by cases such as *Genentech Incorporation's Application* [1989] RPC 147. In that case, one of the questions that the court had to consider was whether the invention in question (a process for the production of human growth hormone in bacteria which would result in an enzyme capable of dissolving fibrin in blood clots) was excluded from patentability because it related to a discovery. It was stated that where an invention consists of more than excluded subject matter, the application should be looked at as a whole. In other words, if the application contains excluded subject matter, it should not be rejected simply on that basis. If an application consists of excluded subject matter, then the suggestion is that it does not contain any other subject matter. However, an application containing excluded subject matter can also contain other, 'included' subject matter. Thus whereas it is not permissible to patent a discovery, it is possible to patent an invention which embodies that discovery.

3.2.1 Computer-implemented inventions

The subject matter excluded from patentability by paragraph (b) is already capable of being protected under the law of copyright. The exclusion of computer programs, under paragraph (c), has been a source of frustration for the software industry. Although copyright is available to protect computer programs, as we shall see later, copyright, unlike patents, is not a monopoly right. The cases in this area either concern computer programs themselves or inventions that include a computer program. *Gale's Application* [1991] RPC 305, is an example of the former. The applicant discovered an improved method of calculating square root numbers using a computer. Instructions were placed into the electronic circuitry of a read-only memory (ROM) unit. However, outside the computer, the instructions did not represent a technical process, nor did they provide solutions to technical problems within the computer. The Court of Appeal was of the view that the subject of *Gale's Application* was essentially a computer program and, therefore, excluded from patentability. The fact that the invention was embodied in the form of a ROM, and thus technically hardware, was irrelevant and the application was dismissed.

A slightly different approach is taken where the invention includes a computer program but is not the program itself. If the machine in question meets the criteria for patentability, without the program, it can be patented. The Technical Board of Appeal in the European Patent Office (EPO) provided useful guidance on this point in *Vicom Systems Inc's Application* [1987] OJ EPO 14, when it stated that what would be decisive is the technical contribution that the invention makes to the known art. This decision influenced the Court of Appeal in *Merrill Lynch's Application* [1989] RPC 561. There, the application concerned a data-processing system for making a trading market in securities. This invention used a known computer system controlled by a program coded in any known programming language. The Court of Appeal defined 'technical effect' as some technical advance on the prior art in the form of a new result. Although the subject of the application met that requirement, it was really a method of doing business, which is also excluded from patentability under section 1(2). The applicants failed to prove that what they had produced was more than a computer program or that, if it was, it was anything more than a method of doing business 'as such'.

In *Fujitsu Ltd's Application* [1997] RPC 608; CA[1997] EWCA Civ 1174, the application was for a method and apparatus for modelling a synthetic structure for designing inorganic materials. It involved a computer programmed so that an operator could select an atom, a lattice vector and a crystal face in each of two crystal structures displayed by the computer. The computer then converted data representing the physical layouts of the crystal structure which would have been obtained by combining the original two structures in such a way that the two selected atoms were superimposed, the two selected lattice vectors were superimposed and the two selected crystal faces were superimposed. The resulting data were then displayed to give an image of the resulting combined structure.

The applicant argued that this was not merely a thought process or a program for a computer 'as such' but that the images displayed were a technical contribution to the manufacture of new inorganic materials. Laddie J, whose decision was followed by the Court of Appeal, disagreed. On the issue of exclusion, the court was interested in substance over form. Even if the program made the computer perform in a novel way, it was still necessary to look at precisely what the computer was doing. If all that was being done, as a matter of substance, was the performance of one of the excluded activities (for example, a discovery, a method of doing business), it still could not be protected as a patent.

So in following the above decisions, the question to be asked would be whether the invention in question makes a 'technical contribution' to the state of the art. If so, whether it would still be patentable, so long as the contribution is not solely within the realm of the excluded matter.

In *IBM's Application* [1999] RPC 861, which concerned computer programs which were engaged in window management and provided a system whereby information displayed on a junior window was rearranged so that the entirety of the information in that window was visible, notwithstanding that it was overlapped or obscured by a senior window, the Examining Division of the EPO found that the claims in question were directed to a computer program 'as such' and therefore not patentable.

On appeal to the Technical Board of Appeal, the following observations were made:

(a) There was no doubt that Article 52(2)(C) of the European Patent Convention 1973 provided that programs for computers should not be regarded as inventions and thus patents for them were not available. However, the exclusion was limited to claims for computer programs 'as such', which meant that not all programs for computers were to be excluded. Hence, where a claim was being made for something other than a computer program 'as such', then without other objections it would be patentable. Therefore the meaning of the words 'as such' was the key to determining the scope and limits of the patentability of computer programs.

(b) The exclusion of computer programs 'as such' should be construed as meaning that a computer program was considered to be a mere abstract creation which was lacking in technical character. Therefore, the main problem for the interpretation of the exclusion from patentability was to define the meaning of 'technical character'.

(c) Such a technical character could be said to be the effect of execution of the program where the software solved a technical problem. If such were the case, then the underlying computer program would be patentable. A patent could therefore be granted not only in the case of an invention where a computer program was employed to control an industrial process or a piece of machinery or the working of a piece of machinery, but in cases where the computer program was the only means, or one of the necessary means, of obtaining a technical effect, including a technical effect which was achieved by the internal functioning of the computer itself.

Since 2000, the EPO has taken what is referred to as the *'Pensions Benefit'* approach (after *Pension Benefit Systems/Controlling Pension Systems* [2002] EPOR 52). This related to a computer system which performed a number of pension-related tasks, including calculations, speculation and the control of the benefit system to ensure periodic payments to subscribers. This approach asks two questions:

(1) Does the claimed invention have any technical features? If there are no technical features at all, then the application should be rejected as not being an invention.
(2) Is the claimed invention old or obvious?

In deciding whether it is old or obvious, the examiner must ignore anything which is not a 'technical feature'. What is the difference between the Vicom 'technical contribution test' and the *Pensions Benefit* test? With the former, the subject matter of the application (for example, a business method) would be excluded before such stages as the novelty and inventive step were considered, while the *Pensions Benefit* test would involve an examination at the same stage. The question is: which approach should be followed? As stated in Chapter 2, the House of Lords in *Merrill Dow Pharmaceuticals Inc v HN Norton & Co Ltd* [1996] RPC 76 has stated that English courts should follow the decisions of the Technical Boards of Appeal in interpreting the EPC on which the 1977 Act is based. In *Merill Lynch [1989] RPC 561* and *Fujitsu*, the Court of Appeal followed the EPO decision in *Vicom*. It did seem that the *Pensions Benefit* approach was being endorsed by English practitioners. *CFPH LLC's Patent Applications* [2005] EWHC 1589; [2006] RPC 259 concerned whether an invention for reducing delays in online betting were unpatentable business methods within section 1(2) and *Halliburton Energy Services Inc v Smith International (North Sea) Ltd* [2005] EWHC 1623; [2006] RPC 25 concerned a computerised system for designing drill bits. In both cases the judges (Prescott QC in *CFPH* and Pumfrey J in *Halliburton*) were of the opinion that the *Pensions Benefit* test of considering novelty, obviousness and excluded matter should be adopted by courts in the UK. The UK Intellectual Property Office appeared to bring the UK in line with developments in the Technical Boards of Appeal of the EPO until the decision of the Court of Appeal in *Aerotel Ltd v Telco Holdings Ltd & Macrossan's Patent Application* [2007] RPC 117. This concerned two separate appeals heard together. The Aerotel patent was a telephone system allowing pre-payment from any available telephone. The Macrossan application was for a method for automatically acquiring the documents required for the formation of a company. Jacobs LJ reviewed the decisions of the Boards of Appeal of the EPO and the Court of Appeal in the UK. He then stated that he had no choice but to follow the previous decisions of the Court of Appeal. In doing so, he attempted to clarify the position using the structured approach put forward by counsel for the Comptroller of Patents:

1. Properly construe the claim.
2. Identify the actual contribution.
3. Ask whether the contribution falls squarely within excluded subject matter.
4. Check whether the contribution is actually technical in nature.

On identifying the 'contribution', Jacob LJ made the following point:

> ...it is an exercise in judgment, probably involving the problem said to be solved, how the invention works, what its advantages are. What has the inventor really added to human knowledge perhaps best sums up the exercise. The formulation involves looking at substance not form – which is surely what the legislator intended (at [43]).

He then held that the Aerotel patent was valid as it used a new contribution of existing apparatus and was not a business method as such. The alleged invention of the

Macrossan application, however, was an interactive system to do the work that would normally be done by a solicitor or a company formation agent. This was a business method 'as such' and also a claim to a computer program 'as such'.

The decision would appear to be at odds with practice at the EPO. Macrossan sought leave to appeal to the House of Lords, because of the difference between the approaches taken. It is suggested that a House of Lords statement on the matter would have been beneficial, but, unfortunately, leave was refused by the House.

The Intellectual Property Office (IPO) issued a Practice Statement on 2 November 2006, giving effect to the *Aerotel* decision (see *Practice Notice* (*Patents Act 1977: Patentable subject matter*) [2007] Bus LR 672).

Aerotel has been followed in *Cappellini's Application and Bloomberg LLP's Application* [2007] FSR 663.

In *Astron Clinica & ors v Comptroller General of Patents, Designs and Trade Marks* [2008] EWHC 85, the appellants appealed against the decision of the Hearing Officer in upholding the refusal to grant their patent applications relating to computer programs. Kitchin J held that, where as a result of applying *Aerotel/Macrossan*, claims to a method performed by running a suitably programmed computer or to a computer programmed to carry out the method were allowable, then, in principle, a claim to the program itself should also be allowable.

The English Court of Appeal and the IPO would now appear to be at odds with the practice of the Boards of Appeal at the EPO. However, note the comments of Lord Neuberger in *Symbian Ltd v Comptroller General of Patents* [2008] EWCA Civ 1066, covered later on in this chapter. The invention in question related to a method of accessing data held in a dynamic-link library within a computing device. It was also related to a computing device controlled by the method. Following *Aerotel*, the court held that the claimed invention did make a technical contribution. The program did not embody any of the items specifically excluded in that it was not: (a) a method of doing business as in *Merill Lynch*; (b) a mathematical method as in *Gale's Application*; or (c) a method for performing a mental act as in *Fujitsu*.

On the question of whether the invention in question makes a 'technical' contribution, Lord Neuberger stated that each case had to be decided by reference to its own particular facts and features.

In *ATT Knowledge Ventures LP v Comptroller of Patents*[2009] EWHC 343 Lewison J stated that it would be impossible to define the meaning of 'technical' but indicated that there were a number of signposts which he set out in the judgment. These were:

i) whether the claimed technical effect has a technical effect on a process which is carried on outside the computer;
ii) whether the claimed invention technical effect operates at the level of the architecture of the computer; that is to say whether the effect is produced irrespective of the data being processed or the application being run;
iii) whether the claimed technical effect results in the computer being made to operate in a new way;
iv) whether there is an increase in the speed or reliability of the computer;
v) whether the perceived problem is overcome by the claimed invention as opposed to merely being circumvented. (at [40])

He went on to decide that a computer software invention and a telecommunications network messaging service were devoid of 'technical effect' for the purposes of patentability.

It is now suggested that an invention that has none of the signposts referred to by Lewison J is unlikely to involve a technical contribution and is therefore excluded from patentability 'as such'.

In *Re Protecting Kids The World Over (PKTWO) Ltd* [2011] EWHC 2720, a patent application for an electronic monitoring system, which alerted parents by text or e-mail when their children were exposed to inappropriate communications amounted to a technical contribution to human knowledge and did not fall within the computer program exclusion. In coming to this decision, Floyd J noted firstly that although the concept in question related to electronic communications, it was a physical rather than abstract one. Secondly, the contribution of the relevant claim did not simply produce a different display, or merely rely on the output of the computer and its effect on the user. The effect as viewed as a whole, was an improved monitoring of the content of electronic communications. The monitoring was technically superior to that produced by the prior art.

To conclude, on the question of computer-implemented inventions, the courts in the UK continue to follow the guidance provided in *Aerotel*. Although it remains difficult to formulate a clear definition of 'technical', there are 'signposts' that the courts may use for guidance.

3.2.2 Biotechnology

There are further exclusions to patentability in section 1(3). This has been modified by the Patent Regulations 2000 (SI No. 2037), which implement Directive 98/44/EC (the Biotechnology Directive). Patents are not to be granted whose commercial exploitation would be contrary to public policy or morality. Morality must be something more than 'illegality' (s 1(4)). Schedule 2A to the Patents Act 1977 deals with biotechnological inventions. These are defined as:

(a) inventions concerning products consisting of or containing biological material; or
(b) processes by means of which biological material is produced processed or used (Schedule 2A, para 1).

'Biological material' is defined as any material containing genetic information and which is capable of reproducing itself or being reproduced in a biological system (para 2).

Paragraph 3 sets out the subject matter that is not allowed:

(a) the human body, at various stages of its formation and development and the simple discovery of one of its elements, including the sequence or partial sequence of a gene;
(b) processes for human cloning;
(c) processes for modifying the germ line genetic identity of human beings;
(d) uses of human embryos for industrial or commercial purposes;
(e) processes for modifying the genetic identity of animals which are likely to cause them suffering without any substantial medical benefit to humans or animals; and animals resulting from such processes;
(f) any variety of animal or plant or any essentially biological process for the reproduction of animals or plants, not being a micro-biological or other technical process or product of such a process.

For an interesting case concerning the issues, see *Harvard/Onco-Mouse* [2005] EPOR 31, where the Technical Board of Appeal of the EPO had to consider, among other things, the morality of creating a genetically altered mouse with susceptibility to cancer, as against the potential benefit in the possible discovery of a cure for cancer.

Article 53 of the EPC has been amended to take account of the Directive.

The patenting of computer software: the UK court of appeal versus the European patent office

The issue raised on this appeal requires us to consider the reach of the exclusion of 'programs for computers' from patentable inventions, a topic which is inherently difficult and on which there is apparently inconsistent authority domestically and in the European Patent Office (EPO).

So said Lord Neuberger in *Symbian Ltd v Comptroller General of Patents* [2008] EWCA Civ 1066. The wording of section 1(2) of the Patents Act 1977 is almost identical to that of article 52(2) and (3) which lists a series of items that are not patentable 'as such'. It can be argued that never have two words caused such controversy and diversity of opinion between English courts and the Boards of Appeal of the EPO. In *Aerotel Ltd v Telco Holdings Ltd & Macrossan's Patent Application* [2006] EWCA Civ 1371, Jacob LJ appears to have moved away from decisions such as *Pension Benefit Systems/Controlling Pension Systems* [2002] EPOR 52 (decided in the Technical Boards of Appeal in the EPO) in favour of decisions from the Court of Appeal. In *Symbian Ltd*, Lord Neuberger reviewed the authorities both in the UK and the EPO. His Lordship confirmed that *Aerotel* followed the decisions in *Merrill Lynch, Gale's Application* [1991] RPC 305 and *Fujitsu Ltd's Application* [1997] RPC 608; CA[1997] EWCA Civ 1174. He then went on to analyse whether there really was a significant inconsistency with decisions of the EPO. The *Aerotel* decision was considered by the Technical Board of Appeal of the EPO in *Dunns Licensing* T0154/04. The Board in *Dunns* stated that it was taking a different approach to the UK Court of Appeal and decided that 'any subject matter or activity having a "technical character" could be an invention'. Lord Neuberger, in *Symbian*, states that the two decisions can be reconciled, pointing out that there is a 'consistent thread that in order to be patentable a contribution must be technical or at least have technical features which contribute to the technical character of the invention' (see para 11). The decision in *Gameaccount* T1543/06 was also considered by his Lordship as consistent with both *Dunns* and *Aerotel*. Since *Aerotel*, the following have also come before the EPO: *Sharp* T1188/04; *File Method/Fujitsu* T1351/04. These follow the approach taken by *Pensions Benefit*, which, according to the Court of Appeal, are at odds with previous Board decisions. So what should the courts in the UK do? If there is a question of inconsistency between the Boards of Appeal, then it would appear that Jacob LJ was correct to follow the earlier Court of Appeal decisions. According to the Gowers Review of Intellectual Property, the UK should maintain its policy of not extending patent rights beyond their current limits. Until there is clear guidance from the EPO, it is suggested that the approach taken in *Symbian* is the correct one to take.

Developments in biotechnology

Developments in biotechnology are exciting, yet raise great concern. The possibilities, from treating serious illness to ending world poverty, signal the desire by governments and business to invest in this area of science. Yet the use of biological material for research leading to possible commercial gain raises a number of ethical issues. In their article, 'The importance of the morality exception under the European Patent Convention', Thomas and Richards, commenting on the *Onco-Mouse* (*Harvard/Onco-Mouse* [2005] EPOR 31) litigation outline two possible objections: concerns for animal welfare and objections on religious or other grounds to the patenting of life forms. Both are essentially matters of morality and as such are difficult to quantify. How is morality to be assessed? In *Plant Genetic Systems/Plant Cells (Opponent: Greenpeace)* [1995] EPOR 357, the Technical Board of Appeal stated:

> the concept of morality is one which is related to the belief that some behaviour is right whereas other behaviour is wrong, this belief being founded on the totality of the accepted norms which are deeply rooted in a particular culture which, in the case of the European Patent Convention, is the culture inherent in European society and civilization ([1995] EPOR 357 at page 366).

It is respectfully suggested that this in itself does not reveal much. Clearly, public opinion will be a factor but there is also the issue of how to solicit and assess that opinion. The Boards of Appeal have had to consider issues of morality in a number of cases. Perhaps the most well-known is the *Onco-Mouse*. Laboratory mice that had been genetically altered to increase their susceptibility to developing cancer were then used for research into anti-cancer drugs. Here the conflict is clearly between animal welfare and the possible alleviation of human suffering.

The Technical Board of Appeal adopted a two-stage test in *Onco-Mouse*:

(1) If there is likely to be suffering to animals from the application of the invention and no likelihood of substantial medical benefit to people or other animals, the patent must be refused.

(2) Even if there is substantial medical benefit as well as animal suffering, consider whether a patent should nevertheless be refused under the traditional article 53(a). In other words, a balance must be made between animal suffering and usefulness to human kind.

We suggest that the issues are complex, and more so when the issue concerns the use of human biological materials – see *Hormone Relaxin Opposition* [1995] OJ EPO 338. Linked to this has been the debate concerning research into human stem cells. According to Graeme Laurie:

> Research using the human embryo is ethically problematic for a number of reasons, all of which centre around the moral status of this organism. While some consider it to be a human being from conception and deserving of full respect, most people do not see it that way, and most legal systems accord the embryo a special status which falls short of conferring the protection of full legal human rights and privileges. But whatever view we might take of its status, most agree that the human embryo is somehow unique ....(See Laurie, 'Patenting Stem Cells of Human Origin' [2004] EIPR 26(2), 59 at page 60).

Yet such research can provide scientists with the means to repair or replace diseased or damaged cells in conditions such as Parkinson's disease, heart failure and injuries to the spinal cord. Even if such research is to be supported, should it lead to the grant of patents? Laurie suggests that a way forward is to separate the ethical objections to the scientific developments themselves from the ethical concerns about the scope of patent monopoly and the consequences of granting that monopoly. Consider the use of biological material to obtain a patent without the donor's consent. In *Moore v Regents of the University of California* [1990] (793P 2d.479), Moore suffered from hairy-cell leukaemia and was treated at the defendants' hospital. He authorised the surgical removal of his spleen as part of his treatment. The defendants conducted research on cells derived from Moore's spleen and established a cell-line from the T. lymphocytes. They applied to patent the cell-line and negotiated commercial exploitation agreements with third parties. When he found out, Moore took legal action claiming the tort of conversion for the use of his body cells without permission. The case centred on the ownership of body cells. As other common law jurisdictions, the Supreme Court in the United States does not recognise the ownership of body cells. The patented cell-line was said to be factually and legally distinct from the cells taken from Moore's body. The defendants therefore had the right to the patent.

Summary

▶ To obtain a patent, the product or process must be new, involve an inventive step, be capable of industrial application and not be excluded under sections 1(2) or 1(3).

▶ Whereas computer programs 'as such' are excluded from patentability, a product containing a program may be patented if it makes a technical contribution to the science.

▶ The EPO and the EU recognise that some forms of software will be patentable.

Exercises

2.1 What are the basic requirements for obtaining a patent?

2.2 What is the significance of the words 'as such' in relation to the patentability of computer programs? Outline the arguments for allowing software to be patented.

Further reading and references

Bainbridge, *Intellectual Property Law* (7th edn, Pitman Longman, 2009) pp 431–35.

Laurie, 'Patenting Stem Cells of Human Origin' [2004] EIPR 26(2), 59.

Schertenleib, 'The Patentability and Protection of DNA-Based Inventions in the European Patent Office and the European Union' [2003] EIPR 25(3), 125.

Thomas and Richards, 'The Importance of the Morality Exception Under The EPC' [2004] EIPR 26(3), 97.

Van Hoorebeek, 'Chromophores and Proteomes: *Astron Clinica* (2008) Delivers Judgment on Computer Program Claims within UK Patents' [2007] *Student Law Review* (54), 44.

Chapter 4

Patentability: novelty, inventive step and industrial application

4.1 Novelty and publication

As the grant of a patent provides the patentee with a monopoly for up to 20 years, it would seem only fair that one of the conditions for such a grant is that the subject of the application is 'new', in other words, something that has never been done or made before.

Under section 2(1) of the Act, an invention is new if 'it does not form part of the state of the art'. This means that the subject matter should not have been available to the public before the date of the application. Section 2(2) goes further:

> The state of the art in the case of an invention shall be taken to comprise all matter (whether a product, a process, information about either, or anything else) which has at any time before the priority date of the invention been made available to the public (whether in the United Kingdom or elsewhere) by written or oral description, by use or in any other way.

Cases decided under this section cover a number of issues. They concern, for example, information found in journals, information in previous (but, at the relevant time, unpublished) applications, prior use of the invention claimed and the inventor's own disclosure. Before considering these issues in turn, let us consider the question of 'availability to the public'.

Material is available to the public if it is available anywhere in the world. Published material is clearly available to the public. This is defined by section 130(1), which states:

> 'published' means made available to the public (whether in the United Kingdom or elsewhere) and a document shall be taken to be published under any provision of this Act if it can be inspected as of right at any place in the United Kingdom by members of the public.

So, even if the relevant information is contained in a journal shelved at the University of Buea, it will be deemed available to the public if it is possible to gain access to it. In *Quantel Ltd v Spaceward Microsystems Ltd* [1990] RPC 83, one of the issues was whether the subject matter of an infringement action had been anticipated by demonstrations at various institutions in the United States and elsewhere. Although Falconer J held that the invention satisfied the test of novelty, it was made clear that prior use (including in a demonstration) would amount to anticipation. Returning to our example, Buea is not in the United States and few people may know that it is in the West African state of Cameroon. Common sense has to prevail and one must consider how readily available the information is. In *General Tire & Rubber Co v Firestone Tyre & Rubber Co Ltd* [1972] RPC 457, Sachs LJ suggested that the state of the art will not include matter which would not have been discovered during the course of a diligent search. This seems a reasonable test.

If a 'diligent search' results in a discovery of documentary information concerning the subject matter of the proposed patentee's application, then the product or process prima facie lacks novelty. In order for prior-documentary information, or indeed any 'prior art', to invalidate a patent on the grounds that it lacks novelty, that information must amount to a clear disclosure of the invention. Traditionally the courts have approved the 'planting the flag' test set out in the Court of Appeal's judgment in *General Tire*, namely that:

> To anticipate the patentee's claim the prior publication must contain clear and unmistakable directions to do what the patentee claims to have invented ... A signpost, however clear, upon the road to the patentee's invention will not suffice. The prior inventor must be clearly shown to have planted his flag at the precise destination before the patentee (at 485).

In *Qualcomm Inc v Nokia Corp* [2008] EWHC 329, Qualcomm claimed that Nokia's sale of headsets for mobile telephones infringed their European patents. The first patent was for a complete system of apparatus comprising a base station which affected the transmission timing. The inventive concepts in the second patent were the radio circuit and corresponding power correction and limitation methods. In response Nokia argued that the claim in issue of the first patent was completely anticipated by an earlier publication and a Japanese patent. Floyd J found the first patent invalid for lack of novelty and obviousness. The earlier publication comprised a signal sent between a base station and a mobile in order to change modes, while the Japanese patent also included the sending of signals between a mobile and a receiver. Thus such information was sufficient to anticipate the claim in issue.

In order for information to 'anticipate' a claim, that information must amount to what the courts refer to as 'enabling disclosure'. This was reinforced by the House of Lords in *Asahi Kasei Kogyo KK's Application* [1991] RPC 485, where Lord Oliver said:

> I do not see how an invention can be said to have been made available to the public merely by a published statement of its existence, unless the method of working is so self-evident as to require no explanation (at 539).

It is not possible to create a 'mosaic' of documents to challenge an application on novelty. If several documents are to be read together for the purposes of challenging a patent application on the grounds of novelty, the documents must be such that they would naturally be read together (for instance, because they cross-refer to one another). This principle is confirmed in the European Patent Office Guidelines.

In *Bristol-Myers Squibb Co v Baker Norton Pharmaceuticals* [2001] RPC 1, a lecture given by the patentee's Director of Research before the priority date on use of the drug taxol to treat ovarian cancer over a shorter infusion period amounted to 'enabling disclosure'. Aldous LJ (at 46) said that using the information from the lecture, members of the public could carry out the procedure without the need for any further information from the patent. The lecture contained 'clear and unmistakable directions' to carry out what was being claimed in the patent. See also *Actavis Ltd v Janssen Pharmaceuticals NV* [2008] EWHC 1422, where one of the reasons why the patent was lost was the fact that one of the patent holder's employees had discussed the subject matter of the patent in a lecture given at a scientific conference before the patent had been registered.

4.2 Novelty and earlier application

The 'state of the art' referred to in section 2(2) includes information contained in other patent applications with earlier priority dates. This is confirmed in section 2(3), which states:

> The state of the art of an invention to which an application for a patent or a patent relates shall be taken also to comprise matter contained in an application for another patent which

was published on or after the priority date of that invention, if the following conditions are satisfied, that is to say:

(a) that matter was contained in the application for that other patent both as filed and as published; and
(b) the priority date of that matter is earlier than that of the invention.

To an extent, this puts the applicant at a disadvantage, as the applicant will have no means of knowing the contents of other applications until they are published. Yet those details may jeopardise his or her application. The applicant's claim would be invalidated by information that is not technically 'available to the public'.

This reinforces the importance of the priority date. As stated in Chapter 2, it is possible to file a skeleton application and then file a fuller application within the next 12 months claiming the priority date of the earlier application. So it is not unusual to have the following scenario: A puts in an earlier application with sufficient details to satisfy the requirements of the Patents Act. B then puts in his application. A then files a fuller application which contains information which would anticipate B's claim and, because of the earlier priority date, it does anticipate and, therefore, invalidate B's claim.

However, the possible inequity of this is mitigated by the practice of interpreting section 2(3) in the same way as section 2(2). Information contained in the earlier application must be 'enabling information'. In *Asahi Kasei Kogyo KK's Application* [1991] RPC 485, a major issue was whether the application in suit lacked novelty because of an earlier application. The application in suit described and claimed a physiologically active polypeptide (human tissue necrosis factor) produced by genetic engineering and useful in treating human tumours. A competitor's application was actually filed after the priority date of the application in suit, but it claimed priority from an earlier application. That earlier application disclosed the polypeptide but did not describe any method of preparing it. The House of Lords held that the earlier disclosure had not been an 'enabling disclosure' and there was, therefore, no anticipation. Passages from Lord Oliver's judgment indicate the unfairness of deciding otherwise. He says:

> No doubt the claim is 'matter contained' in an application but the claimant may in fact not even know whether the compound can be produced in practice. If nothing further is added … the application must fail and be refused. It would be a most unreasonable result that this failed application should nevertheless be capable of being cited as an anticipation of a subsequent application on the basis of the priority of an invention which it was never in a position successfully to claim (at 542).

On the face of it, *Asahi* appears to conflict with section 5(2) of the Patents Act.

Section 5(2) allows for the filing of applications from which a later, fuller application, filed within 12 months of the applicant's first application, can claim priority and not be anticipated by an intervening, otherwise anticipatory, application. Section 5(2) is useful for researchers who may have found a solution to a particular problem, but need time to pursue it further. They can be rewarded for being the first to come up with the solution, even if they cannot immediately specify how the solution works, provided that they can disclose the full story within the statutory 12 months. However, to avoid possible injustices where applications are filed merely to block competitors, the first application must disclose the elements of the later application in suit. In *Asahi*, Lord Jauncey felt that for the purposes of section 5(2), information in the earlier application should also be 'enabling'. He states:

> an invention is only supported by prior matter for the purposes of paragraph [5(2)(a)] if the earlier relevant application not only describes the invention but also contains an enabling disclosure (at 457).

In *Synthon BV v SmithKlineBeecham plc* [2005] UKHL 59, the House of Lords appears to have made adjustments to the principles laid down in *Asahi*. In giving the leading judgment, Lord Hoffmann separated disclosure from enablement. In assessing whether a prior-art document anticipates a claimed invention, he said first one had to look at what the prior-art document disclosed (to the skilled man):

> the matter relied upon as prior art must disclose subject matter which, if performed, would necessarily result in an infringement of the patent (at [22]).

Second, one had to look at whether that disclosure enabled the claimed invention to be performed (by the skilled man):

> Enablement means that the ordinary skilled person would have been able to perform the invention which satisfies the requirement of disclosure ... (at [26]).

4.3 Novelty and use

Prior use of the invention in question is also considered part of the state of the art. This is based on the principle that a monopoly should not be granted to stop individuals from doing what they had been doing legitimately before the date of the application. This principle dates back to the Statute of Monopolies 1623 and is best summed up by Lord Denning's question in *Bristol/Meyers (Johnson)* [1973] RPC 157:

> If this patent were granted, would it stop the prior user from doing what he was doing before? (at 164)

From a number of cases, it is also clear that for prior use to anticipate, it must be 'enabling use'; in other words, the use must give information as to how the invention works.

In *Windsurfing International Inc v Tabur Marine (GB) Ltd* [1985] RPC 59, the plaintiffs were the owners of a patent on a sailboard which featured a Bermuda rig with a wishbone spar. In an infringement action brought by the plaintiffs, the defendants argued that there had been an anticipation ten years before the patent had been granted. This involved the use in public by a 12-year-old boy, who had built his own sailboard and used it for two summers off the coast of Hayling Island. The booms of that sailboard differed slightly in that they were straight (whereas those of the plaintiffs were curved) but, while in use, they were flexible enough to bend like those of the plaintiffs. The prior use was held to have anticipated the plaintiffs' patent and the patent was declared invalid. This can be contrasted with *Quantel Ltd v Spaceward Microsystems Ltd* [1990] RPC 83 where it was held that use during demonstrations did not anticipate, because in that case the use did not show how the invention worked.

In *PLG Research Ltd v Ardon International* [1995] RPC 287, Aldous J said that prior use only forms part of the state of the art if it discloses the necessary information about the invention in question. The Technical Board of the European Patent Office (EPO) appears to favour this principle, making it possible in some cases to obtain a patent for a new use of an existing patent. In *Mobil/Friction Reducing Additive* [1990] EPOR 73, the claimed invention was for the use of compounds as friction-reducing additives in lubricant compositions. A prior document disclosed the use of the same compounds as additives in engine oil to inhibit rust. The question was whether the friction-reducing properties of the claimed compounds had been made available to the public by the prior disclosure. The Technical Board of Appeal did not think so. In its view, 'available' meant more than just knowledge of the patent. All the technical features of the claimed invention must be communicated to the public, or laid open for inspection. In other words, the prior document or use must communicate its technical features to the public.

It seems that *Mobil* confirms that it is possible to claim a new use for an old patent, as long as the new use has a new technical effect, and the prior use did not disclose or enable the public to understand that new technical effect. It is suggested that this approach allows patent holders to extend the term of their monopoly.

What effect has *Mobil* had on English courts? In *Merrill Dow v Norton* [1996] RPC 76, the House of Lords said that courts in the UK must have regard to the decisions of the EPO on the construction of the European Patent Convention (EPC) on which the Patents Act 1977 is based. In *Merrill Dow*, the plaintiff was a pharmaceutical company which had patented an anti-histamine drug called terfenadine. Unlike other anti-histamines, this did not cause drowsiness. The patent was obtained in 1972 and expired in 1992. Other companies were then allowed to make and market terfenadine. The plaintiff had researched terfenadine and discovered that it worked by forming an acid metabolite in the liver. The plaintiff company analysed its chemical composition, then produced and patented its own acid metabolite in 1980 for anti-histamine drugs. It claimed that the sale of terfenadine by other companies infringed its patent for the acid metabolite because acid metabolite is automatically produced in the liver when terfenadine is swallowed. The sale of terfenadine, it was claimed, was an infringement because it involved knowingly supplying consumers with the means of producing the patented acid metabolite.

To deal with the issue of infringement, the House of Lords had to consider the issue of novelty. It was claimed as a defence that there had been anticipation of the acid metabolite patent by use and disclosure. The anticipation by use had taken place when the terfenadine was made available to, and used by, volunteers in clinical trials between 1977 and 1978. Acid metabolite had been produced in their livers and they had experienced its anti-histamine effects. Anticipation by disclosure was claimed in the specification of the terfenadine patent. According to Lord Hoffmann:

> An invention is a piece of information. Making matter available to the public within the meaning of s.2(2) therefore requires the communication of information. The use of a product makes the invention part of the state of the art only so far as that use makes available the necessary information (at 86).

This confirms that prior use will only anticipate if that use illustrates how the invention works. So each case will depend on the workings of the invention in question. If the mechanics are simple, as in *Windsurfing*, then use anticipates, but if they are very technical or, indeed, cannot be seen, even on close inspection, then use is less likely to anticipate. In *Merrill Dow*, Lord Hoffmann made the following observation about the 'infringement test' from *General Tire & Rubber Co v Firestone Tyre & Rubber Co Ltd* [1972] RPC 457:

> Acts done secretly or without the knowledge of the relevant facts, which would amount to infringements after the grant of the patent, will not count as anticipations before (([1996] RPC at 86).

Such use as there was, did not amount to 'enabling use', so there was no anticipation by use. There was, however, anticipation by disclosure. After *Merrill Dow*, on anticipation and use, see *Evans Medical Ltd's Application* [1998] RPC 517. This concerned a patent for pertactin, a surface antigen of the whooping cough bacterium Bordatella pertussis. At the priority date, Takeda's vaccine was already on the market. This must have contained pertactin, although at the time no one appreciated this. Relying on comments made in *Merrill Dow*, the proprietor therefore argued that the prior use in Takeda's vaccine did not invalidate the patent because no one knew that the pertactin was present. Laddie J, however, made a distinction. In *Merrill Dow*, the patients in question were never in possession of a product containing the acid metabolite, whereas in *Evans*, the Takeda vaccine was a product within the claims.

In a similar case but with a different result to that of *Mobil*, the patent owner in *Actavis UK Ltd v Janssen Pharmaceutical NV* [2008] EWHC 1422 (Pat), lost the patent. The patent in question was concerned with a substance used to increase the effectiveness of blood pressure-reducing agents. Janssen also held an earlier patent concerned with a compound designed to be used in the manufacture of various pharmaceutical compositions aimed at preventing disorders of the cardiovascular system. Applying the test from *Synthon BV v SmithKlineBeecham plc* [2005] UKHL 59, the court held that several claims in Janssen's patent were anticipated by its own prior patent, which comprised a pharmaceutical composition having all the same features. The same technical effect underlay both the old use and the new use and was therefore for the same purpose.

One interesting type of anticipation is by the inventor himself. This is illustrated by *Fomento v Mentmore* [1956] RPC 87, where the plaintiff had a patent for making a particular type of improved ballpoint pen. It was claimed that the patentees themselves had anticipated their application by providing the public with pens, which were the subject of the invention, before the priority date. The Court of Appeal held that, as the pens came into the hands of those who were free at law and equity to do whatever they liked with them, they anticipated the invention claimed in the application. However, as with other types of anticipation, providing goods to the public in this way will only anticipate if it is easy to understand how the patent works by using it. Further, if the inventor has made it clear that the invention is being shown for purely experimental purposes, or is disclosed on a confidential basis, the invention will not be anticipated by their prior use or the disclosure. In *Pall Corp v Commercial Hydraulic* [1990] RPC 329, the patentee's delivery of membrane samples, in confidence, to those who were aware that the samples were being supplied for experimental purposes and on a secret basis did not constitute making the invention 'available to the public'. This underlines the importance for inventors of only disclosing inventions to those who are under an obligation of confidentiality; this obligation may be implied in certain fiduciary relationships (such as between a solicitor and client or patent agent and client) or imposed by a contractual agreement (see Chapter 7).

Sections 2(4)–(6) define specific types of disclosure which will not anticipate a patent application. These include information obtained unlawfully, information disclosed through a breach of confidence and disclosure at a recognised international exhibition. Prior use to treat humans and animals will not invalidate for lack of novelty.

In particular, section 2(6) makes clear that just because a substance or composition is part of the state of the art, that does not stop its being patentable as an invention if the particular use which is applied for is a method of treatment of a human or animal body which was not part of the state of the art. This section of the Act has been interpreted as allowing patents for the first discovered medical use of a known substance, but not second and subsequently discovered medical uses of the same substance. However, the EPO has been willing to entertain applications for second (and further) medical uses when they are presented in the form approved by the Swiss Patent Office, namely, 'an application' for use of the substance for the manufacture of a medicament for the treatment of a particular condition. This has become known as the 'Swiss form'.

4.4 Inventive step

Even after satisfying the test of novelty, the application must involve an inventive step. This means that it must move the science on and not be merely something that would be 'obvious' to anyone skilled in the art if he or she had put their mind to it (see *Pfizer Ltd's Patent* [2002] EWCA Civ 1). Section 3 states:

> An invention shall involve an inventive step if it is not obvious to a person skilled in the art, having regard to any matter which forms part of the state of the art.

This is based on the philosophy, similar to that in novelty, that the public should not be prevented from doing anything that is merely an obvious extension or workshop variation of what was already known. Unlike novelty, it is possible to make a 'mosaic' of documents or information, in other words, put together documents or pockets of separately available information and claim that the invention is obvious. However, the documents must be in the same field, and the 'mosaic' will only establish prima facie obviousness. It is still possible to argue that the combination of the documents has resulted in an unexpected technical advantage and that there has, therefore, been an inventive step.

The question to ask is: to whom must the invention be obvious? In *Technograph Printed Circuits Ltd v Mills & Rockley (Electronics) Ltd* [1972] RPC 346 at 355, Lord Reid suggested the 'skilled but unimaginative worker' test. If the product or process would have been obvious to someone with some knowledge of the technology or science within which the invention lies, then it is obvious. In *Rockwater Ltd v Technip France SA* [2004] EWCA Civ 381, the skilled but unimaginative worker is described as 'a nerd but not an android' (see paras 7, 10 and 11). If the invention is not obvious to even skilled and inventive technicians, it must involve an inventive step. The definition of the skilled technician will depend on the type of science or industry. If the work involves high levels of research, it may be that a researcher with a Ph.D. is the skilled technician; in which case even though the invention may not be 'obvious' to the average technician, it will still fail the inventive step test if obvious to others in the industry having that type of qualification (*Genentech Incorporation's Application* [1989] RPC 147). In *Minnesota Mining & Manufacturing Co v ATI Atlas Ltd* [2001] FSR 514, Pumfrey J said that it could also be a person with a practical interest in the development of the invention. For further guidance on the skilled addressee, see *Mayne Pharma (2)*, *Mayne Pharma plc v (1) Debiopharm SA* [2006] EWHC 1123.

A product may be satisfactory and useful, but that will not make it inventive. See *Rocky Mountain Traders Ltd v Hewlett Packard GmbH & ors* [2002] FSR 1.

For 1949 Act patents, the steps to be taken to establish whether an invention is obvious were suggested by Oliver LJ in *Windsurfing International Inc v Tabur Marine (GB) Ltd* [1985] RPC 59. He stated that to answer the question of obviousness, one had to follow four steps:

(1) identify the inventive concept embodied in the patent;
(2) import to a normally skilled, but unimaginative, addressee what was, at that date, common general knowledge in the art at the priority date;

(3) identify the differences, if any, between the matter cited and the alleged invention; and

(4) decide whether those differences, viewed without any knowledge of the alleged invention, constituted steps that would have been obvious to the skilled man or whether they required any degree of invention. (at 73–74)

This was confirmed as a useful test for 1977 Act patents by the Court of Appeal in *Mölnlycke AB v Procter & Gamble Ltd (No 5)* [1994] RPC 49. See also *Union Carbide Corp v BP Chemicals* [1999] RPC 409, where the patent in question related to a continuous heating process for the production of polymers. According to the invention, the recycled gases were cooled to below the dew point of the gas stream to produce a two-phase gas-liquid mixture before reintroduction to the reactor. It had been thought necessary to keep the temperature of the reactor gas above the dew point of the recycled gases in order to prevent the introduction of liquid. This invention provided the advantages of a cooler recycled gas stream and cooling from the latent heat of evaporation of the liquid.

In an action for infringement, the defendants claimed the invention was obvious in view of a disclosure referred to as 'Mitsui'. This described a similar polymerisation process in which the recycled gases were cooled to condense and separate the liquid, but did not say how the separated liquid was introduced into the reactor.

The Court of Appeal held, on the issue of obviousness:

> To decide whether the claim in question was obvious, the first step was to identify the inventive concept embedded in the patent. In this case, this was the introduction into the reactor of the two-phase mixture of gas and entrained liquid, not limited to a place where the reintroduction took place or to a requirement that the gas consisted of recycled gases rather than make-up monomer. 'Mitsui' nowhere suggested entrainment of liquid with gas to provide a two-phase gas-liquid mixture, and there was nothing in 'Mitsui' that would make that obvious (see Aldous LJ in *Union Carbide Corp v BP Chemicals* [1999] RPC at 423–424).

4.4.1   Does the Windsurfing test always apply?

Davina Wheatley v Drillsafe Ltd [2001] RPC 133 concerned a patent that claimed an improved method for drilling a new threaded hole in the lid of underground tanks. In reversing the decision of Ferris J, the Court of Appeal maintained that *Windsurfing* sets out the structured approach to be followed in deciding whether a patent is obvious. The second limb of the test requires the court to adopt the mantle of the notional unimaginative skilled addressee and impute to him what, at the priority date, was the common general knowledge in the art in question. Aldous LJ went on to point out that Ferris J did not follow the *Windsurfing* test in his judgment and this failure led him 'into the trap of hindsight reasoning'.

In *Sabaf SpA v MFI* [2005] RPC 10, the court considered the relevance of *Windsurfing*. It concerned a patent for a burner for gas cookers and hobs. In particular the issue was whether one or two inventions were being claimed. The stated features were:

(1) the drawing of primary air in from above the hob unit; and

(2) the use of a flow path under the flame spreader in which a Venturi effect would be present.

At first instance, Laddie J, applying the law of collocation, stated that both inventive features were obvious in the light of the prior art. In doing so, he referred to *Windsurfing* but considered that the law of collocation did not fit easily into its structural approach and, given the obviousness of the subject matter, did not see the need to apply it.

The Court of Appeal held that where a case involved a 'mere collocation' of two known concepts, the question was whether it would be obvious to the skilled person to combine the concepts. Peter Gibson LJ considered that Laddie J had taken a 'dangerous short cut' in not directly applying the *Windsurfing* structural approach.

The House of Lords reversed the Court of Appeal's finding that, although there was no exception to section 3, it was necessary to decide whether there was one or more inventions before applying section 3. The judge had been correct to find that there were two alleged inventions and correct in finding that there was virtually no difference between the relevant prior art and the invention.

In *Pozzoli SpA v BDMO SA* [2007] FSR 872, it was suggested by Jacob LJ that the *Windsurfing* test should be restated as follows:

1. (a) Identify the notional 'person skilled in the art';
   (b) Identify the relevant common knowledge of that person;
2. Identify the inventive concept of the claim in question or, if that cannot readily be done, construe it;
3. Identify what, if any, differences exist between the matter cited as forming part of the 'state of the art' and the inventive concept of the claim or the claim as construed;
4. Viewed without any knowledge of the alleged invention as claimed, do those differences constitute steps which would have been obvious to the person skilled in the art or do they require a degree of invention?

The four-stage *Windsurfing/Pozzoli* test does not have an equivalent in the EPO. Instead a number of approaches are taken, the most used being the problem–solution approach. The House of Lords had the opportunity to consider whether *Windsurfing/Pozzoli* is valid in *Conor Medsystems Inc v Angiotech Pharmaceuticals* [2008] UKHL 49. Conor attacked a European patent for lack of inventive step in the Netherlands and the UK. The invention itself was a stent coated with taxol to treat or prevent stenosis. The alleged inventiveness lay in the claim that the product had a particular property. The question for the House of Lords was whether to claim inventive step; it was necessary for the specification to show that the invention worked or how it works. In holding that the invention was inventive, Lord Hoffmann stated that the invention is the product specified in a claim and the patentee is entitled to have the question of obviousness determined by reference to his or her claim and not to some 'vague paraphrase based upon the extent of his disclosure in the description'. No reference was made to *Windsurfing/Pozzoli*. According to Otto Swens (2008), the Lords were more interested in stressing the importance of the facts and circumstances in each case rather than adhering to a particular approach.

The main problem for inventors in this area is one of hindsight. Once something has been done, it may appear to have been obvious. It is quite easy to think 'I could have thought of that'. This will be the case, particularly, if there have been pockets of information in the field and the inventor appears to have simply put them together. The courts have never really favoured this argument, particularly when it is advanced by competitors. In *British Westinghouse Electric & Manufacturing Co Ltd v Braulik* (1910) 27 RPC 209, Fletcher-Moulton LJ made the following statement:

> I confess that I view with suspicion arguments to the effect that a new combination bringing with it new and important consequences in the shape of practical machines, is not an invention because, when it has once been established, it is easy to show how it might be arrived at by starting from something known, and taking a series of apparently easy steps. This ex post facto

analysis of invention is unfair to the inventors and, in my opinion, it is not to be countenanced by English patent law.

In *Technograph Printed Circuits Ltd v Mills& Rockley (Electronics) Ltd* [1972] RPC 346, Lord Reid said that, rather than considering what is obvious to the court in hearing a dispute, one has to look at what was obvious at the date of the application. This view was further stated by Kitchin J in *Abbott Laboratories Ltd Evysion Medical Devices UCL* [2008] EWHC 800 (Pat):

> It is particularly important to be wary of hindsight when considering an obviousness attack based upon the general common knowledge... . It is all too easy after the event to identify aspects of the general knowledge which can be combined together in such a way as to lead the court astray. The question is whether it would have been obvious to the skilled but uninventive person to take those features, extract them from the context in which they appear and combine them togther to produce the invention (at [180]).

One way of dealing with the issue of hindsight is to ask: if the product or process was obvious, why had it not been done before, particularly if it satisfies a 'long-felt' need? In *Lux Traffic Controls Ltd v Pike Signals Ltd* [1993] RPC 107, it was claimed that some of the plaintiff's patents in traffic control signals were invalid because they were obvious. One of the patents in question was for a means of varying the 'inter-green' period (that is, the safety period between the lights in one direction changing to red before the lights in the other direction change to green). The court held that, although simple, the invention represented an advance and technical contribution to the art. If the process had been obvious, it would have been proposed before.

Likewise, in *Parkes Cramer Co v GW Thornton & Sons Ltd* [1966] RPC 407, where the invention was a method of cleaning floors between rows of textile machines, made up of an overhead vacuum cleaner which moved back and forth between the textile machines, with a long vertical tube attached to it. It was argued that this was obvious because every competent housewife knows that dust can be removed from a floor using a vacuum cleaner. This argument was rejected. There had been many unsuccessful attempts to find a satisfactory solution, but none of them had actually worked. The fact that the invention was also a commercial success once it entered the market demonstrated that it satisfied a long-awaited need which would have been met long before had the plaintiff's invention been so 'obvious'. Of course, if an invention is not a commercial success, this does not mean that it was obvious.

The problem–solution approach was also considered in *Haberman & Another v Jackel International Ltd* [1999] FSR 683. Mrs Haberman had the patent for the ANYWAYUP Cup, a trainer cup for toddlers. The plaintiff's cup had a valve fitted to the lid, which would open when the baby sucked and close when it stopped, thereby solving the problem of leakage. The cup was an immediate commercial success. The defendants produced and launched a rival product, 'Super-Seal'. In an action for infringement, the defendants claimed that the plaintiff's patent was invalid on the grounds of 'obviousness'. Laddie J found that, even although the invention in question only involved a 'very small and simple step', it was sufficiently inventive to deserve the grant of a patent. The invention itself was quite simple but it had solved a problem to which many had sought a solution, that is, leakage in infant trainer cups. While its commercial success could have something to do with other factors, such as marketing, it also demonstrated that this was a problem to which a solution had been sought. It satisfied a need. The success of the product was found to be attributable to the solution it gave to the long-felt need for a spill-proof cup.

The decision in *Dyson Appliances Ltd v Hoover* [2001] EWCA Civ 440, suggests that the response, or lack of it, to the patent holder's solution, at the priority date, is also important. The dispute between the parties has been well documented in the press. Dyson invented a bagless vacuum cleaner, whose use of cyclones rids the air of dirt. Before the priority date no vacuum cleaner manufacturer had commercially sold or proposed a bagless vacuum cleaner. According to Sedley LJ:

> The vacuum-cleaner industry was functionally deaf and blind to any technology which did not involve a replaceable bag (at [89]).

In *Biogen Inc v Medeva plc* [1997] RPC 1, the plaintiff had obtained a patent for recombinantly-produced DNA molecule coding for the hepatitis B virus (HBV). At the priority date, HBV DNA had not been sequenced, nor had the viral proteins been expressed. It was claimed that the step taken was one that was 'obvious to try', in the light of a paper published by an expert in the field. Aldous J held that Biogen had taken the initiative and attempted something uncontemplated by others. This demonstrated that its approach was not obvious and demonstrated an inventive step. Sadly this decision was overturned by the Court of Appeal (and the Court of Appeal decision was upheld in the House of Lords). In the view of the Court of Appeal, the step taken was based on a commercial decision to pursue an identified goal by known means. To spend time and money on a project, where others would have regarded the odds against success as too long to justify the investment, was a business judgment rather than an inventive step. In the House of Lords, Lord Hoffmann (at 44) felt that reference to a commercial decision was less than helpful. In his view there was no reason why a chosen experimental strategy should not involve an inventive step simply because it had been adopted for commercial reasons. His Lordship went on to state that the inventiveness in this particular case was of a very unusual kind. It was said to consist of attempting something, which a man less skilled in the art might have regarded as obvious, but which the expert would have thought so beset by obstacles as to be not worth trying. The House of Lords found the invention to be inventive but invalid for want of sufficiency.

The Court of Appeal's decision may be justified on the grounds that the plaintiff merely took a gamble, which paid off, when others were not prepared to take the risk. However, there are surely many inventions that are the result of a lucky discovery.

The Court of Appeal has stated that 'obviousness' is a jury-type question for a judge at first instance who has heard all the technical evidence. The Court of Appeal should therefore be slow to come to a different conclusion from that of the judge when the conclusion was one to which he was entitled to come. See *Raychem Corp's Patents* [1999] RPC 497 at 516.

In *David J Instance Ltd v Denny Bros Printing Ltd* [2001] EWCA Civ 939; [2002] RPC 114, it was stated that the Court of Appeal should only interfere with a judge's conclusion on obviousness if he had erred in principle (see para 16). The trial judge in *Apimed Medical Honey Ltd v Brightwave Ltd* [2012] EWCA Civ 5 was held to have erred in that he had not correctly identified the differences between the state of the art and the inventive concept of the patentee's claim. As a consequence he had failed to identify correctly whether the differences constituted steps which would have been obvious to the person skilled in the art or whether they required any degree of invention. The Court of Appeal found that the judge had erred in finding that a patent for a medical dressing comprising gelled honey was invalid on the ground of obviousness. He had misconstrued an article written before the priority date and taken the wrong approach to obviousness based on the common general knowledge.

4.4.2   Inventive step and sufficiency

As indicated in Chapter 2, section 14(4) of the Act provides that an application for a patent will be refused or the patent revoked if the specification fails to disclose enough detail for a 'person skilled in the art' to perform or make the invention. Thus, there should be clear and unmistakeable instructions, in other words, enabling disclosure. In order to determine whether there is sufficiency, it is suggested that a helpful comment comes from the House of Lords in *Kirin-Amgen Inc & ors v Hoechst Marion Roussel* [2004] UKHL 46:

> The first step is to identify the invention and decide what it claims to enable the skilled man to do. Then one can ask whether the specification enables him to do it (per Lord Hoffmann at [112–13]).

If the specification effectively claims too much for the invention, then the application or patent will be invalid for insufficiency. This was the case in *Biogen Inc v Medeva plc* [1997] RPC 1 and *Kirin-Amgen*. In *Haliburton Energy Services Inc v Smith International (North Sea) Ltd & ors* [2006] EWCA Civ 1715, the Court of Appeal held that the patent for a rotary cone drill bit was invalid for insufficiency because it required too much work from the skilled person to reproduce the various features of the invention. If a patent involves an unreasonable amount of work in light of all the relevant circumstances, then it would be regarded as not containing an enabling disclosure. In *Biogen*, the inventor was the first to succeed in producing a recombinant genetic technology, a DNA molecule which could express the antigens of the hepatitis B virus in a host cell. He would not have been able to claim the DNA molecule, since it exists naturally in individuals suffering from hepatitis B. Rather, he had invented a process for making it. According to Lord Hoffmann (see *H. Lundbeck A/S v Generics and ors* [2003] EWCA Civ 311, at [32–33]), the inventor in *Biogen* clearly thought that he would not gain a monopoly in the process alone as the science was advancing rapidly and other ways would be found to make the antigens outside of any process that he would claim. Instead he tried to patent a product by-process claim that would provide the widest monopoly. The House of Lords therefore interpreted the claim as being to a class of products which satisfied the specific conditions, one of which was that the molecule had been made by recombinant technology. That interpretation meant that the claim did not accord with the law of sufficiency in both the UK and EPO, which states that a class of products is only enabled if the skilled man can work the invention in respect of all members of the class; so the patent was declared invalid for lack of sufficiency. It is suggested however that *Biogen* should be considered on its own set of facts. In *Lundbeck*, Lord Hoffmann suggested that *Biogen* should be limited to that particular form of claim, and not be extended to an ordinary product claim. Thus *Lundbeck* holds that where the invention claimed is a product, as such, it is sufficiently enabled if the patent specification discloses at least one way of making it.

4.5   Industrial application

Even if the invention satisfies sections 2 and 3, under section 4 it will only be patentable if it can be manufactured and is marketable in any industry, including agriculture. For this reason, methods of treatment for people or animals are not covered under section 4A(1), which states that an invention which consists of a method of treatment (by surgery or therapy) or a method of diagnosis cannot be patented. But any drugs produced for treatment are capable of industrial application and are, therefore, patentable if the other conditions are satisfied (see s 4A(2)). This links with section 2(6) on novelty, which states that prior use to treat humans and animals will not invalidate a patent for want of novelty. See *Bristol-Myers Squibb Co v Baker Norton Pharmaceuticals* [2001] RPC 1.

A useful explanation of how the requirement for industrial application will be applied can be found Kitchen J's decision of *Eli Lilly & Co v Human Genome Sciences Inc* [2008] EWHC 1903 (later reversed by the Supreme Court [2011] UKSC 51). The defendant's patent disclosed the nucleotide and amino-acid sequence of a novel member of the anti-tumour (TNF) ligand superfamily which it called Neutrokine-a. This was a protein which acted as an anti-cellular mediator in inflammation and immune responses. The Neutrokine-a had been found using 'bioinformatics' or 'computational biology', rather than by the traditional laboratory techniques. H applied for and was granted a patent, which included a long description of N's activities and its uses. However, the description was not supported by any data and was essentially a prediction based on what was known about other members of the TNF superfamily. The claimant challenged the patent on the grounds that, among other things, the patent specification failed to disclose an invention which was capable of industrial application. In deciding that the claims in the patent were invalid for lack of industrial applicability, Kitchen J reviewed decisions of the EPO, the United States and the UK ([2008] EWHC 1903; see paras 180–225). He noted that the notion of industry would include all manufacturing, extracting and processing activities which were carried out continuously, independently and for commercial gain. However, the activities did not have to be conducted for profit: a product which was shown to be useful in curing a rare disease might be considered capable of industrial application even if it were not intended to be used in any trade at all. The skilled person should be able to derive the capability of industrial application from the description, so read. It should disclose a practical way of exploiting the invention in at least one field of industrial activity. Whilst the guidance provided by Kitchen J is comprehensive and the decision followed by the Court of Appeal, the Supreme Court held that his approach was not consistent with that adopted by the Boards of Appeal of the European Patent Office [2011] UKSC 51 (at [106]). From a line of EPOR decisions, Lord Neuberger listed the principles as follows:

▶ the patent had to disclose a practical application and profitable use which could be expected to lead to some commercial benefit;
▶ a concrete benefit had to be derivable directly from the description and the common general knowledge;
▶ a speculative use would not suffice;
▶ the skilled person had to be able to exploit the invention without undue burden;
▶ the patent had to demonstrate a real possibility of exploitation;
▶ identifying the structure of a protein, without suggesting a practical use, was insufficient;
▶ the absence of experimental activity of the protein was not fatal;
▶ a plausible use could suffice;
▶ plausibility could be assisted by later evidence;
▶ a plausible and specific possibility of exploitation could be at the biochemical, cellular or biological level;
▶ if all family or superfamily members of the protein had a role in controlling cells, assigning a similar role to the protein could suffice;

- the problem to be solved in such a case could be by isolating a further member of the family;
- if disclosure was important to the pharmaceutical industry, disclosure of the sequences of the protein could suffice, even though its role had not been clearly defined;
- the position could be different if there was evidence calling membership of the family into question;
- the position could also be different if the family members had different activities. (at [107])

In light of the above principles the Supreme Court held that the patent should have satisfied article 57 on which section 4 is based.

The need for consistency in the interpretation of the European patent convention

In his judgment in the case of *Conor Medsystems Inc v Angiotech Pharmaceuticals Inc* [2008] UKHL 49, Lord Hoffmann made the following observation:

There is still no European Patent Court. A European patent takes effect as a bundle of national patents over which the national courts have jurisdiction. It is therefore inevitable that they will occasionally give inconsistent decisions about the same patent. Sometimes this is because the evidence is different. In most continental jurisdictions, including the European Patent Office (EPO), cross-examination is limited or unknown. Sometimes one is dealing with questions of degree over which judges may legitimately differ. ... But when the question is one of principle, it is desirable that so far as possible there should be uniformity in the way that national courts and the EPO interpret the European Patent Convention.

In Chapter 2, the difficulties involved in establishing a European patent were noted. The apparent difference in approach between the UK and the EPO as to whether a computer program is excluded 'as such' has also been noted. Further examples may also be found in Chapter 6 on infringement. It is suggested that some of the inconsistency might be removed if there were an EC Directive establishing a Community Patent. It is now the practice that questions of interpretation in relation to trade marks are referred to the Court of First Instance or the European Court of Justice (ECJ). If the same were the case for patents, 'the ECJ would interpret European patent law in a more harmonised way' (de Ranitz and Swens, 2008). It would also be more difficult for a national court to ignore an ECJ decision. At present, members of the EPC can look to the Boards of Appeal. However, it is claimed that while most of continental Europe looks to the EPO, the courts in the UK have not always followed its approach. De Ranitz and Swens (2008) point out that the UK courts have taken a slightly different approach in the way that inventive step is determined; while the continental courts and the EPO adopt the 'problem–solution' method, the UK has adopted the four-step approach from *Windsurfing/Pozzoli*. Differences also occur in deciding whether the claims include 'sufficient' information to work the patent. The authors claim that the UK has been considered one of the most patentee-unfriendly jurisdictions in Europe. However, it was noted in *Symbian Ltd v Comptroller General of Patents* [2008] EWCA Civ 1066 (discussed in Chapter 3) that the decisions of the Court of Appeal can be reconciled with some of the decisions of the EPO on the question of computer programs. De Ranitz and Swens do also point out that the decisions in *H. Lundbeck A/S v Generics and ors* [2003] EWCA Civ 311, *Conor* and *Merck v Actavis*, 28 May 2008, align the UK courts more closely to the European approach.

Summary

▶ Information about material parts of the invention which is available on or before the priority date can defeat a patent application for want of novelty, if it can be discovered following a diligent search.

▶ Information in earlier, but unpublished, applications can affect the application but only if it is 'enabling information'.

▶ Prior use will also defeat a patent application, but only if it is 'enabling use' in the sense that it allows the user to determine how the patent works.

▶ To be patentable the invention should not be obvious to the skilled but unimaginative technician.

▶ That the invention is capable of industrial application should be evident to the skilled person reading the description.

Exercises

4.1   In 1997, A invented a formula for use in drugs to control weight gain. It works by breaking up fat tissue in the body. In 1993, a research student at the University of Benin had written about the need for a fat-busting drug to fight obesity. How will this affect A's patent application?

4.2   What exactly is 'enabling disclosure'?

4.3   A's formula and compound for reducing weight is patented as obsetabolite. A discovers that, when mixed with stomach juices, it produces a substance called X-it which breaks up fat tissue. A has found a method of producing X-it in the laboratory. Advise her of the likelihood of obtaining a patent for X-it.

4.4   What is the 'skilled but unimaginative worker test'? Is it a realistic test?

4.5   Many things may seem 'obvious' once invented. How can inventors overcome the problem of hindsight when their patents are challenged?

4.6   A doctor develops a revolutionary method of treating cancer of the colon. Is it fair that she cannot obtain a patent for that method?

Further reading and references

Antcliff and Hopewell, 'United Kingdom: Patents – the United Kingdom Supreme Court Finds Industrial Application in a Biotechnology Patent' [2012] BSLR 12(2), 66.

Batteson and Karet, 'Lundbeck v Generics – "Biogen insufficiency" Explained' [2009] EIPR 31(1), 51.

Ranitz, de and Swens, 'UK Patent Law Crosses the Channel' [2008] EIPR 30, 389.

Sharples, 'Industrial Applicability, Patents and the Supreme Court: Human Genome Sciences Inc v Eli Lilly' [2012] EIPR 34(4), 284.

Thorne and Priestley, 'Sweet Success for Patent Holder: Gelled Manuka Honey Medical Dressing Non-Obvious', JIPLP (2012), 7(11), 778–779.

Chapter 5

Ownership

5.1 Introduction

The person to whom the patent is granted (the proprietor) is the only person entitled to manufacture, use, sell or import the product or process. If the proprietor does not wish to work the patent, the licence can be assigned to another. An assignment gives the assignee full rights in the patent, whereas the terms of a licence might only allow the licensee to do certain things.

Since the proprietor is the individual with rights over the patented invention, it is crucial to determine who is entitled to apply for and claim the patent. This is not always as straightforward as it might seem.

Section 7 of the Patents Act 1977 provides that 'any person can apply for a patent'. This would imply that there are no conditions as to nationality of the applicant or the country where the invention was made, unlike the position in copyright law. Section 7(2) states that patents can be granted to: (a) the inventor and joint inventor; (b) other persons entitled to property in the invention; or (c) successors in title. Sections 8 and 9 deal with disputes regarding the ownership of patents and section 10 provides guidance on how disputes between joint applicants are to be handled.

5.2 Who can apply?

Whereas section 7(2)(a) states that a patent may be granted primarily to the inventor or joint inventors, section 7(2)(b) recognises that others may have a legal claim to the patent. A patent can be granted to:

> any person or persons who by virtue of any enactment or rule of law, or any foreign law or treaty or international convention, or by virtue of an enforceable term of any agreement entered into with the inventor before the making of the invention was or were at the time of the making of the invention entitled to the whole of the property in it other than equitable interests in the United Kingdom.

The inventor may have been engaged as a consultant to solve a problem for a firm and under the terms of the consultant's contract it may have been expressly provided that any resulting invention would belong to the firm. Alternatively, the 'inventor' may be an employee and any inventions made will belong to the employer by virtue of section 39 of the 1977 Act. Without this section, the inventor would have to apply for and then assign or license the patent to the employer. While assigning and licensing of patents takes place, the inventor is often not able to afford the cost of making an application. Further, if the invention is made under a consultancy agreement or in the course of employment, the rightful owners should be able to apply and register their property interest from the outset.

5.3 The inventor

In any dispute concerning the right of ownership, the first step must be to decide who was the inventor or inventors of the claimed invention (per Lord Hoffmann in *Yeda*

Research & Development Co Ltd v Rhone-Poulenc Rorer International Holdings Inc and ors [2007] UKHL 43, at [19]).

The inventor is defined under section 7(3) as the 'deviser of the invention'. As there is no further explanation of what is meant by the 'deviser' and no definition of the word 'invention' within the Act, we have to rely on common sense; the inventor will be the person who has worked out the subject matter of the patent application through his own efforts, or as stated by Laddie J, in *University of Southampton's Applications* [2005] RPC 220, at 234, the natural person who 'came up with the inventive concept'. Simply making a contribution to the claims will not be enough. In *Markem Corp v Zipher Ltd* [2005] EWCA Civ 267, an employee of Markem Corporation left and went to work for Zipher. Both companies made thermal transfer printing machines. The employee concerned left with a great deal of know-how about thermal transfer printing, but no trade secrets (as found by the Court of Appeal). While working for Zipher, he came up with an inventive concept for improved machines for which the company took out a number of patents. Markem claimed entitlement to the patent on the ground that it used information which the employee had obtained while working for them. However, the Court of Appeal found that although that information may have contributed to the claims, the inventive concept had been devised entirely by the employee while working for Zipher. The decision in *Markem* was confirmed as correct by the House of Lords in *Yeda Research & Development Co Ltd v Rhone-Poulenc Rorer International Holdings Inc and ors*, although the reasoning was deemed to be incorrect. In *Markem*, the Court of Appeal had stated that a person claiming to be an inventor had to rely on some other rule of law, such as breach of confidence. Rather, all that was required was that the proprietor was the actual deviser of the invention, or was entitled under section 7(2) or (3) (per Lord Hoffmann at [24]). See also *IDA Ltd v University of Southampton* [2006] EWCA Civ 145.

As already indicated, the inventor will not always be the person applying for the patent. Even so, the inventor has the right to be named as the inventor under section 13(1). Inventors are also, to some extent, protected by section 13(2). Section 13(2) states that any person, other than the inventor, who is making an application must identify the inventor and state the grounds on which the applicant is entitled to the patent. Failure to comply with this section could result in the application being refused.

As section 7(1) states, an application can be made either by an individual alone or jointly with another. Any disputes between inventors as to the prosecution of the application are handled by the Comptroller-General under section 10.

Each individual inventor is entitled to be named on the patent by virtue of section 13(1). However, there may be cases where an individual inventor feels that the other's contribution was so insignificant that he is the only one entitled to be mentioned. When this happens, he can make an application under section 13(3) to have the other inventor's name removed. However, as shown by *Staeng Ltd's Patents* [1996] RPC 183, the onus is on the applicant to prove his right to sole ownership.

5.4 Employee patents

Most ownership disputes are between employee-inventors and their employers. The law on ownership of patents for inventions devised by employee-inventors is set out in sections 39–43 of the Patents Act 1977.

In settling disputes about employee inventions, the starting point is to confirm that the inventor is actually an 'employee'. Traditionally, a number of factors determined whether there was an employer–employee relationship between the inventor and alleged owner of the invention. These could include: responsibility for the deduction of income tax and national insurance contributions; provision of any equipment used; and the supervision and control of the inventor's activities. Section 130 of the Patents Act 1977 defines an employee as someone 'who works or has worked under a contract of employment or in employment within a Government department, or serves or has served in the navy, military or air forces of the Crown'.

Once it is settled that the inventor can be classified as an employee, the next step is to determine whether the invention belongs to the inventor or the employer. Before the 1977 Act, the court would analyse the inventor's contract of employment for an indication of whether it was the employee's responsibility to invent. In *Electrolux Ltd v Hudson* [1977] FSR 312 decided under the 1949 Act, which did not have equivalent provisions to sections 39–43), Hudson was employed as a senior storekeeper for the electrical manufacturers, Electrolux. In his spare time, Hudson and his wife invented an adaptor for a vacuum cleaner taking disposable bags.

Electrolux, whose products included vacuum cleaners, claimed to be the owners of the resulting patent. The claim was based on a term in Hudson's contract of employment that stated that anything invented, or any process ascertained or discovered, in relation to any of Electrolux's products in the UK or elsewhere, had to be disclosed to Electrolux, and any such invention or process would belong to Electrolux. Dismissing the claim, Whitford J was of the opinion that the clause was too wide even to cover a person employed to research and invent and, on common law rules of restraint of trade, was more than was necessary to protect the employer's legitimate business interests. In his view, the validity of any clause concerning patent ownership would depend on the type of work done by the employee. Hudson was employed as a storekeeper. It was not his responsibility to invent.

Section 39(1) of the Patents Act 1977 is quite specific about the ownership of an employee patent. A patent resulting from an invention devised by an employee belongs to the employer if:

(a) it was made in the course of the normal duties of the employee or in the course of duties falling outside his normal duties, but specifically assigned to him, and the circumstances in either case were such that an invention might reasonably be expected to result from the carrying out of his duties; or

(b) the invention was made in the course of the duties of the employee and, at the time of making the invention, because of the nature of his duties he had a special obligation to further the interests of the employer's undertaking.

An interpretation of section 39(1) was attempted in *Re Harris Patent* [1985] RPC 19. Harris was employed as a manager in the wey valve department for company R, which operated under licence from a Swiss company, S. R had no research facilities and never undertook any creative design activity. Major problems were referred to company S. Harris's primary duties were to sell valves made by R under the licence from S and to use his specialist knowledge to assist his employer's customers. During the period of his redundancy notice, Harris invented a slide valve. His employer claimed ownership of the patent.

In the Patents Court, Falconer J held that an employee's duties in section 39(1)(a) were the normal duties which he was employed to perform. The 'circumstances' referred to were the circumstances under which the particular invention in suit was made, rather than the circumstances in which any invention whatsoever might be made. Harris's employer never took it upon itself to solve the design problems in the valves, so it could never have been part of any of its employees' normal duties to invent. And the invention had not been made under circumstances such that an invention might reasonably be expected to have resulted from the carrying out of Harris's normal duties. On section 39(1)(b), Falconer J was of the opinion that the nature and extent of an employee's obligation to further the interests of the employer's undertaking depended on the employee's status, with its attendant duties and responsibilities. Harris's only real obligations were to sell valves and provide after-sales services to customers.

In *Staeng Ltd's Patent* [1996] RPC 183, the court stated that in applying section 39(1), one should first decide what constituted the employee's normal duties, then decide whether the circumstances were such that an invention might reasonably be expected to result from the execution of those duties.

Section 39(1) was also applied in *Greater Glasgow Health Board's Application* [1996] RPC 207. A junior doctor was employed as a Registrar by the Health Board in the Department of Ophthalmology. His job description stated that his responsibilities were mainly clinical but indicated that he was also expected to participate in undergraduate and postgraduate teaching, although the latter were not described as duties. He was also expected to avail himself of the research facilities provided. While revising for fellowship examinations at home, he invented a device for examining the retina. The Health Board claimed ownership. In the Patents Court, Jacob J followed the approach taken by the Court of Appeal in earlier copyright cases concerning ownership of copyright in employees' work. He held that, whereas the device was a useful accessory to the doctor's contracted work, it was not an integral part of it. A factor which might have persuaded the court was the fact that, in evidence, the inventor's manager stated that the junior doctor would not have been failing in his duties if he had not invented anything. This is a useful guide in interpreting section 39(1)(a). Would the employee in question have been failing in his duties had he not sought to invent? That test is equally relevant to section 39(1)(b), which is concerned more with the status of the employee, which indicates a general duty to further the interest of the employer, and which does not necessarily require a duty to invent. This may arise where the employee concerned is considered a rising star within the organisation or indeed an 'ideas man'. The contract of employment may be said to evolve as the responsibilities increase. In *LIFFE Administration and Management v Pavel Pinkava* [2007] EWCA Civ 217, Dr Pinkava worked for LIFFE which operated the London Futures Market. While working for LIFFE, he invented a system of electronic trading for financial instruments not previously traded. Knowing that they were unpatentable in the UK, because of section 1(2)(c) of the Patents Act, he applied for patents in the United States. LIFFE claimed ownership of the patents. While a duty to invent was not specifically stated within the terms of his contract, the Court of Appeal stated that because it was usual for employment contracts to evolve over time, regard must be had to how the contractual duties evolved over time by a process of continual variation. The majority of the Court of Appeal also adopted a subjective test to section 39, taking account as it did of the particular employee's abilities. Jacob LJ disagreed on that point, stating that he could not accept that ownership depended on whether the individual employee is 'thick or brilliant'. Why should the unimaginative get the invention because no one expected him to come up with it, as opposed to the 'Edison', who in exactly the same position must hand it over to his employer?

5.5   Employee compensation

If it is agreed or determined that the patent belongs to the employer under section 39, section 40 allows an employee to claim compensation if he can show that *either the invention*, patent or both is of 'outstanding benefit' to the employer, taking into account the employer's size and type of business.

Benefit means 'benefit in money or money's worth' (s 43(7)) and Patent Office practice is to consider the actual rather than the potential benefit to the employer; potential benefit is only relevant to decide the level of compensation if it is to be awarded.

In practice, it proved difficult to succeed in a claim for an section 40 award. There appears to be no recorded case where an employee has successfully claimed the award. The words in italics were added by the Patents Act 2004, to try to redress the balance. A selection of cases below indicates the difficulties encountered by employees.

In *GEC Avionics Ltd's Patent* [1992] RPC 107, the Patent Office read section 40 in the context of section 39 and reached the view that if it is agreed that the employee is employed to invent, then he already receives a reward for inventive activity in the form of salary. Hence the need for the 'benefit' to the employer to be 'outstanding' if an additional award is to be made. In *Elliot Brs' Patent* SRIS 0/47/89, it was held that 'outstanding' means something out of the ordinary and not such as would be expected to arise from the duties that the employee is paid for.

Another factor is the level of investment by the employer in the project. As section 40 refers to the size and nature of the employer's undertaking, an inventor working for a business with high turnover and profits will find it difficult to prove 'outstanding benefit'. This is illustrated by *British Steel plc's Patent* [1992] RPC 117, where the patent concerned an outlet valve for vessels containing molten material. It was regarded as a great technological advance in its field and the annual benefits to British Steel were worth up to £500,000. However, because this represented no more than 0.01 per cent of the company's annual turnover and 0.08 per cent of its profits, the employee's claim for compensation under section 40 failed.

In *GEC Avionics Ltd's Patent* [1992] RPC 107, the patent in question related to an optical system for providing a 'head-up display' (HUD) in an aircraft cockpit. Whereas the inventor's employers had secured a contract worth $72 million involving the patent, they had previously secured contracts worth $75 million for HUDs not involving the patented system. Again, the Patent Office refused the employee's claim. The Patent Office's approach appears to be that if the employer is habitually involved in contracts worth many millions, an employee's contribution is not 'outstanding' or 'out of the ordinary' even if it also attracts contracts worth many millions.

If there was evidence of previous dealings with a particular customer, irrespective of the patent in question, the inventor's task in making a section 40 claim is even more onerous. In *Memco-Med Ltd's Patents* [1992] RPC 403, the patent in question concerned units to detect a person near lift doors, the idea being to prevent the doors from closing on people. The employers had previous contracts to build lift-door detector units for O Elevator Co. Ltd. Sales of their products had gone to O Elevator in the past. The history of the business relationship between Memco and O Elevator supported the view that it would have continued whether or not a patent had been granted for the invention. Accordingly, the employee's invention had not been of outstanding benefit. *Memco* also suggests that, even where an employee-inventor can show a substantial increase in sales of his employer's product, the onus is on him to demonstrate that the increase was due to the patent and not other factors, such as the price, marketing or quality of the employer's general product range.

Although the employee-inventor's task may seem onerous in claiming section 40 compensation, the employer has quite a heavy burden in surpassing section 39. Additionally, it can be argued that an employee who is contracted to invent will no doubt draw a salary whether he invents or not. The employer bears the cost and effort of trying to realise the initial concept. For every successful patent, there will have been many discarded attempts and the project can take years to develop. Meanwhile the employee draws a salary without the risks.

Prior to the 2004 amendment, there were no recorded cases of employees successfully claiming section 40 compensation. It appears that this was due to the original wording of section 40 which drew a distinction between the 'patent' and the 'invention' in the assessment of outstanding benefit. This made it difficult for an employee to show that the benefit was derived from the patent rather than the invention. Section 40 was therefore amended by the Patents Act 2004 to include section 40(1)(b), which refers to 'the invention and/or the patent'.

The modification introduced by the Patents Act 2004 is not exactly radical. The onus will still be on the employee to prove that the invention or patent is of outstanding benefit. The first reported case of an employee succeeding in an application for compensation is that of *Kelly and Another v GE Healthcare* [2009] EWHC 181, decided under section 40 before the 2004 amendment. The claimants were two research scientists who co-invented a radioactive cardiac imaging agent which was marketed under the trade mark Myview. The product was very successful, achieving sales exceeding £1 billion. The value of the benefit which their employer could be said to have derived from the patents was based on a number of factors, including the finding that patent protection would strengthen the company's bargaining position when it came to corporate deals. Floyd J valued this as in the region of £50 million. It was held that the patent had provided an outstanding benefit. In calculating the amount that was just, the judge decided that three per cent of the value of the benefit (£50 million) was just and made compensation orders totalling £1.5 million.

It is suggested that following the decision in *Kelly*, as well as the 2004 amendment, it will be prudent for employers in research industries to introduce employee-inventor incentive schemes.

5.6 Dealings in patents

Patents and patent applications are personal property and accordingly may be assigned, mortgaged and transferred as part of a person's estate. These transactions must be in writing and signed by both parties (except in the case of transfers on death, where only the personal representatives need to sign). Where there are joint owners, all must sign for a transaction to be valid. Different provisions apply to Scotland (s 31).

When a patent has been transferred, the new owner should register his interest on the Patents Register. Failure to register the interest could result in the new owner losing his rights to a third party who subsequently acquires rights in the same patent without knowledge of the earlier transaction.

Where the patent is owned by two or more persons, each of them is entitled on his own behalf to do any of the acts in respect of the patent which would otherwise be an infringement.

The owner or owners of the patent may also license others to work the patent. Licensees in these circumstances will be limited to activities covered within the licence agreement. Under section 46, the owner may also apply for an entry to be made in the register that licences as of right are available. This is useful to a proprietor who discovers, after the patent has been granted, that she is not in a position to exploit the patent effectively.

After a patent has been granted for three years, any person may apply for a compulsory licence to work the patent, or apply for an entry on the register that licences are available as of right. Generally such applications are made if it is felt that the patentee is either not making full use of the patent or refusing to grant licences on reasonable terms. The exact grounds are listed in section 48(3). These are:

(a) The patent is capable of being commercially worked but is not being worked to its fullest potential as far as is reasonably practicable.
(b) The demand in the United Kingdom for the patented product is not being met on reasonable terms, or is being met to a substantial extent by importation.
(c) The patent is capable of being commercially worked in the United Kingdom and such work is being prevented or hindered.
(d) The proprietor's refusal to grant a licence on reasonable terms has resulted in:
    (i) a market in the export of the patented product made in the United Kingdom not being supplied, or
    (ii) the working or efficient working in the United Kingdom of any other patented product which makes a substantial contribution to the art is prevented from or hindered, or
    (iii) the establishment or development of commercial activities in the United Kingdom is unfairly prejudiced.
(e) The terms imposed by the proprietor in licence agreements are unfairly prejudicial to commercial or industrial activities in the United Kingdom.

As stated in Chapter 2, these provisions redress the balance against allowing a patentee to abuse the monopoly granted.

Summary

▶ The Patents Act 1977 allows an individual inventor, joint inventor, other persons entitled to the invention and successors in title to apply for a patent.

▶ If the applicant is not the actual inventor, she must justify ownership, and the inventor is entitled to be named.

▶ The inventor is the person who devised the subject matter of the application.

▶ An employee's invention will only belong to the employer if it was part of the employee's duty to invent or the employee has special responsibilities to further the interests of the employer's business.

▶ Although it is possible for an employee to obtain compensation for a patentable invention of 'outstanding benefit', in practice this is difficult if the employers habitually secure profitable contracts irrespective of the invention.

Exercises

5.1   How is the actual inventor protected against others making a false claim on his invention?

5.2   A is a senior member of the research team at B Pharmaceutical. B have been developing a non-habit-forming drug to aid restful sleep. It contains the compound dormalite. A, who is a keen gardener, makes up the formula at B's laboratory and takes it home to try on her weak plants. The formula works as a very effective fertiliser and A decides to apply to patent this use on plants. Advise B Pharmaceutical.

Further reading and references

Howell, 'Extra Compensation for Inventive Employees: Is Our System Equitable, Unbiased and Motivating?', IPQ, 2011, 4, 371–389.

Hull, 'Ownership of Rights Created in Sponsored Academic Collaborations – A Note on the *IDA*, *Statoil* and *Cyprotex* Decisions' [2007] EIPR 29(1), 6. An interesting article which discusses the implications of research collaborations between industry and academia. The author stresses the importance of having clear contractual terms on ownership at the start of the process.

Odell-West, '*Kelly v GE Healthcare Ltd*: Employee Innovation in Health Care: Deciphering Ownership and the Alchemy of "Outstanding Benefit"' [2010] EIPR 32(9), 449.

Chapter 6

Protecting the patent

6.1 Introduction

The whole point of obtaining a patent is to gain a monopoly in the invented product or process. Thus once a patent has been granted, the proprietor (the patentee) has the right to stop others from manufacturing, using, selling or importing the subject of the patent for 20 years from the priority date. The patentee may protect his interest by suing for infringement. An exclusive licensee also has rights against infringers (s 67), as long as his interest has been registered (33). Where there are joint owners of a patent, any of the owners may commence infringement proceedings but must notify the other owners.

The general right to take action and obtain remedies for infringement is covered by sections 60 and 61. There are risks in commencing infringement actions. Section 70 creates a right to claim damages and other remedies for groundless threats, and many claims for infringement are defended by a challenge to the validity of the patent (72).

6.2 Acts of infringement

A patented product is infringed under section 60(1) by the following activities in the UK: making the product, disposing of it, offering to dispose of it, using or importing it or keeping it (whether for disposal or otherwise), all without the patentee's consent. A patented process is infringed by its use, or offer for use, in the UK, in circumstances where the infringer knows, or it is obvious to the reasonable person, that such use without the patentee's consent is an infringement. It is also infringement of a patented process to do any of the acts that would be an infringement of a patented product in respect of any product 'obtained directly by means of that process'. What is meant by a product 'obtained directly by means of that process' was considered in the case of *Pioneer Electronics Capital Inc v Warner Music Manufacturing Europe GmbH* [1997] RPC 757. The case involved a patent for a process to manufacture masters for optical discs. The defendant had manufactured and sold optical discs, but three further stages were introduced between the manufacture of the master disc and the manufacture of the discs that were made by the defendants. The Court of Appeal approved the decision of the High Court that the defendant's products were not obtained directly from the patented process.

For a brief discussion of how the English courts' approach to the protection of a product from a process differs from that of the rest of the European Patent Office (EPO) members, see *Kirin-Amgen Inc and ors v Hoechst Marion Roussel Ltd & ors* [2004] UKHL 46, at paragraphs 89–91.

Section 60(2) states that it is an infringement for anyone, other than the patentee, to provide others with the means to make a patented product or use a patented process. This amounts to 'indirect infringement', so the wrongdoer in this case must know, or the circumstances must be such that it is obvious to the reasonable person that sufficient means are being provided to put the invention into effect in the UK. Section 60(3) allows the supply of a 'staple commercial product', even if covered by a patent, provided that product is not being supplied for the purpose of inducing the person supplied to commit one of the infringing acts under section 60(1).

It is possible to infringe even if part of the infringing apparatus is located overseas. See *Menashe Business Mercantile Ltd v William Hill Organisation Ltd* [2003] 1 All ER 279 (CA).

6.3 The significance of the claims

The extent of an invention is set out in the claims (see Patents Act 1977, s 125; European Patent Convention 1973 (EPC), art 69). In any action for infringement, the court will therefore start by considering the claims within the specification. The claims map out the extent of the patentee's monopoly. According to Lord Russell in *Electric & Musical Industries Ltd v Lissen Ltd* (1939) 56 RPC 23:

> The function of the claims is to define clearly and with precision the monopoly claimed, so that others may know the exact boundaries of the area within which they will be trespassers. Their primary object is to limit and not extend the monopoly. What is not claimed is disclaimed.

According to Laddie J, in *Merck & Co v Generics (UK) Ltd* [2003] EWHC 2842 [2004] RPC 31:

> The purpose of a patent is to convey to the public what the patentee considers to be his invention and what monopoly he has chosen to obtain. These are not necessarily the same. The former is primarily to be found in the specification and the latter is primarily to be found in the claims ... It is his duty to communicate his invention and his assertion of monopoly to the public in language it will understand ... (at [38]).

For this reason, claims need to be drafted very carefully. A specification containing broad claims covering every possible variation may be rejected, but one drafted too narrowly allows competitors to add insignificant modifications and escape infringement actions.

6.4 Interpretation of the claims

There appears to be a difference in the approach to the interpretation of claims across Europe. In Germany, for example, the claims were treated simply as a guide to determine the scope of the protection. By contrast, English case law suggests that, English judges have found it difficult to move away from the traditional approach adopted in interpreting statutes and other legal documents. Judges will either take a strict literal approach or, where there is some ambiguity, a purposive approach. The former approach is said to be justified for statutes because it is up to Parliament to correct any discrepancies. In patent law, this approach is justified on the grounds that the patentee was given the opportunity to map out his monopoly when he drafted the specification. In *C van der Lely NV v Bamfords* [1963] RPC 61, Viscount Radcliffe said:

> After all, it is [the patentee] who has committed himself to the unequivocal description of what he claims to have invented, and he must submit in the first place to be judged by his own action and words.

Although English judges are more at home with a literal approach, it has been argued that such an approach is inappropriate for patent specifications. In *Rodi & Wienenberger AG v Henry Showell Ltd* [1969] RPC 367, in a dissenting judgment, Lord Reid said:

Claims are not addressed to conveyancers: they are addressed to practical men skilled in the prior art, and I do not think that they ought to be construed with that meticulousness which was once thought appropriate for conveyancing documents (at 378).

Instead it is recommended that judges study the specification and what the alleged infringer has done. If the defendant's activities fall within the claims, then there is infringement. If there are variations, the court should determine whether these are fundamental differences between the patentee's invention and what the alleged infringer has produced. This is referred to as the 'pith-and-marrow' approach to the interpretation of patent claims. It involves looking at each element or section of the claim (the 'integers') and considering how many integers have been taken by the defendant, and the extent to which those integers are vital to the working of the invention.

Even with the pith-and-marrow approach, competitors have been able to avoid infringement by making cosmetic modifications. In *C van der Lely NV v Bamfords*, the plaintiff had a patent for a mechanical hay-rake with movable wheels at the back ('hindmost'). The defendant's machine had movable wheels at the front ('foremost'). The court decided that it could not regard 'hindmost' in the plaintiff's claims as the same as 'foremost', and the plaintiff's action for infringement, therefore, failed. *Rodi & Wienenberger AG v Henry Showell Ltd* concerned a patent for expanding metal bracelets for wrist watches. The House of Lords held that the defendant's replacement of two U-shaped bows with a single C-shaped bow meant that its product did not infringe the plaintiff's patent. The court decided that the U-shaped bow was an essential integer. Lord Pearce (who dissented) felt that it was not enough to say that the U-shaped bow was an essential integer and that the defendant's bracelet did not infringe by having a C-shaped bow. As far as he was concerned, both connected to adjacent sleeves by a bridge between two parallel limbs that lay in the sleeves and pivoted in the spring. The differences were not essential.

6.5   Has there been infringement?

The leading case on patent infringement is *Catnic Components Ltd v Hill & Smith Ltd* [1982] FSR 60. The plaintiff had a patent for load-bearing steel lintels, which had a rear support member, described in the claims as 'vertical'. The defendant made a similar lintel but the rear support member was inclined between six and eight degrees from the vertical. This meant that its load-bearing capacity was slightly less than that of the plaintiff but not enough to make a significant difference in its practical use. The plaintiff had described another part of its lintel as 'substantially horizontal', and the defendant claimed that, as the reference to the 'vertical' support had not been qualified in the same way, the defendant's lintel would have to be exactly vertical to infringe. The House of Lords rejected this argument and held that the patent had been infringed.

According to Lord Diplock, the real question was whether persons skilled in the art would understand that strict compliance with a particular descriptive word or phrase was intended by the patentee to be an essential requirement of the invention, so that any variant would fall outside the monopoly, whether or not it had any material effect on the way that the invention worked. This introduced a purposive approach to the interpretation of claims.

Catnic concerned a 1949 Act patent. There has been a debate about whether this is appropriate for patents granted under the 1977 Act and, indeed, whether this is compatible with the Protocol adopted at the Munich Conference (which established the EPC) on the Interpretation of article 69 of the EPC. The Protocol was a compromise between the perceived differences of approach across the Member States, the UK and German approaches being at the two extremes. It states that the interpretation of a claim should combine fair protection for the patentee with a reasonable degree of certainty for third parties. *Catnic* appears to be compatible with that objective and the actual wording of the Protocol. The protocol was replaced by the EPC 2000 which incorporates its principles.

The approach suggested by *Catnic* is to follow a process involving three main questions:

(1) Does the variant have a material effect upon the way the invention works? If 'yes', a variation will not infringe; if 'no', the second question is considered.
(2) When the specification was published, would it have been obvious to the skilled reader that the variant had no material effect? If 'no', the variant does not infringe; if 'yes', consider the final question.
(3) Would the skilled reader understand that the patentee intended that strict compliance with the claim was essential? If 'yes', the variant does not infringe; if 'no', there is infringement.

This process was apparently followed by Hoffmann J in *Improver Corp v Remington Consumer Products Ltd* [1990] FSR 181. The plaintiff had a European patent for a hair-removing device called 'Epilady'. This removed hair by a helical spring, which rotated to pluck out the hairs. The defendant brought onto the market a similar device called 'Smooth and Silky', which removed hair by an elastomeric rod with slits to pluck out hair. In what have become known as the *'Improver* questions', Hoffmann J stated:

(1) Does the variant have a material effect on the way the invention works? If 'yes', the variant is outside the claim. If 'no':
(2) Would this (i.e. that the variant had no material effect) have been obvious at the date of the publication of the patent to a reader skilled in the art? If 'no', the variant is outside the claim. If 'yes':
(3) Would the reader skilled in the art nevertheless have understood from the language of the claim that strict compliance with the primary meaning was an essential requirement of the invention? If 'yes', the variant is outside the claim.

His Lordship went on to decide that there was no infringement. In his view, the variant had no material effect on how the invention worked, but on the third question, he felt that because the claim referred to a helical spring, it could not be interpreted broadly to include a rubber rod.

It is our view that to reach this decision, Hoffmann J applied the literal interpretation approach, criticised by Lord Reid in *Rodi & Wienenberger AG v Henry Showell Ltd* [1969] RPC 367 and by Lord Diplock in *Catnic*. As a point of interest, the same parties appeared before a German court, concerning the same patent. In the German courts, where a more purposive approach was applied, the defendant's device was held to infringe the 'Epilady' patent.

In *PLG Research Ltd v Ardon International* [1995] RPC 287, Millett LJ in the Court of Appeal was of the opinion that, if the *Catnic* test was the same as the Protocol, it was no longer necessary and, if it differed, its continued use would be dangerous. However, Lord Hoffmann in *Kirin-Amgen Inc & ors v Hoechst Marion Roussel Ltd & ors* [2004] UKHL 46, specifically disagreed. The test, he said, was:

precisely in accordance with the Protocol. It is intended to give the patentee the full extent, but no more than the full extent, of the monopoly which a reasonable person skilled in the art, reading the claims in context, would think he was intending to claim (at [48]).

In *Assidoman Multipack Ltd v The Mead Corp* [1995] FSR 225, Aldous J decided to continue to follow *Catnic*. The purposive approach recommended by Lord Diplock in *Catnic* was also followed in *Kastner v Rizla & Another (No 1)* [1995] RPC 585, which concerned a patented method and machine for interleaving and severing paper used, in particular, in relation to cigarette papers. In deciding whether the defendant's machine infringed the plaintiff's patent, Aldous LJ (as he became) in the Court of Appeal adopted a purposive approach to the whole of the patent specification. In *Catnic*, Lord Diplock had merely stated that the purposive approach should be used to interpret 'a particular descriptive word or phrase appearing in a claim'. The purposive approach was given far broader application by the Court of Appeal in *Kastner*.

In *Consafe Engineering (UK) Ltd v Emitunga UK Ltd* [1999] RPC 154, Pumfrey J held the question to be decided was whether, on a true construction of the claim in its context in the specification, the patentee had intended that strict compliance with any particular descriptive word or phrase was an essential requirement of the invention, so that any variant would fall outside his monopoly even if the variant would have had no effect upon the way that the invention worked and a skilled man would have appreciated that to be so. This question was conveniently approached by way of Hoffmann J's questions in *Improver* designed to result in a fair protection for the patentee with a reasonable degree of certainty for third parties.

See also *Auchinloss v Agricultural & Veterinary Supplies Ltd* [1999] RPC 397, where the Court of Appeal held, inter alia, that the patent with its claims must be construed as a whole according to the guidelines given in the Protocol on the Interpretation of article 69 of the EPC. The purposive construction was therefore the correct approach.

In *Union Carbide Corp v BP Chemicals* [1999] RPC 409, the Court of Appeal held that the ambit of the monopoly lay between the extremes of literal construction and the use of the claims only as a guideline, and was to be interpreted as defining a position which combined fair protection for the patentee with a reasonable amount of certainty for third parties. To find that position, the court should apply a purposive construction in accordance with the guidance given in *Catnic* and explained in *Improver*.

See also *Davina Wheatley v Drillsafe Ltd* [2001] RPC 133 and *Amersham Pharmacia Biotech AB v Amicon Ltd* [2001] EWCA Civ 1042.

In *Kirin-Amgen Inc & ors v Hoechst Marion Roussel Ltd & ors* [2004] UKHL 46; [2005] RPC 9, Lord Hoffmann was able to confirm the *Catnic* test as compatible with the Protocol (see above). At paragraph 33, he stated that the skilled reader:

...reads the specification on the assumption that its purpose is to both describe and demarcate an invention – a practical idea which the patentee has had for a new product or process. ... [34]...it must be recognised that the patentee is trying to describe something which he at any rate in his opinion, thinks is new...

In *Virgin Atlantic Airways Ltd v Premium Aircraft Interiors Group* [2009] EWCA Civ 1062, Jacob LJ stated:

One might have thought there was nothing more to say on this topic (at [5]).

Yet the issue again arose as to the approach to be taken in interpreting the claims. In that case, a patent concerning an aircraft seating system for flat-bed seats was held to be valid and infringed by a company that had been manufacturing aircraft seating. In reaching the decision, Jacob LJ restated the Catnic/Kirin-Amgen principles but in so doing used the terminology to be found in the EPC 2000. His Lordship went to state that the skilled reader would be taken to suppose that the patentee knew some patent law – that his claim is for the purpose of defining the monopoly (see [13]).

6.6   Defences

When faced with an action for infringement, the alleged infringer has a number of options available.

First, he can challenge the validity of the claimant's patent, using sections 72 and 74. The grounds upon which a patent can be challenged are:

(a) the invention was not patentable in the first place (*Windsurfing*);
(b) the patent was granted to someone who was not entitled to it (although this is only available during the two years after the grant of the patent, unless the patentee knew at the time of the application that he was not entitled);
(c) the specification does not disclose the invention with sufficient clarity and fullness for it to be performed by a person skilled in the art;
(d) what is disclosed in the specification extends beyond what was disclosed in the application for the patent as filed; or
(e) the protection conferred by the patent has been extended by an amendment which should not have been allowed.

A successful challenge will result in the patent being revoked or amended.

It is also possible to argue that there has been no infringement, because the defendant's activities vary sufficiently from what is contained in the claims. Cases like *Improver Corp v Remington Consumer Products Ltd* demonstrate this. A defendant can accordingly also apply to the courts under section 71 for a declaration of non-infringement.

Section 60(5) lists the general statutory defences, which are:

(a) the infringing activity took place privately and was not for commercial purposes;
(b) the infringing activity took place for experimental purposes;
(c) the activity involved the extemporaneous preparation in a pharmacy of medicine for an individual in accordance with a registered medical or dental practitioner's prescription;
(d) use of the invention was in relation to certain ships, aircraft or vehicles temporarily or accidentally in or crossing the United Kingdom.

A further defence is that of 'exhaustion of rights' under EU competition law. Apart from the above, there is protection for the bona fide prior user in section 64. This states that acts done in good faith before the priority date are allowed to continue. This maintains the principle that a monopoly should not be granted to stop individuals from doing what they were legitimately doing before the grant.

Anti-competitive practices are discouraged by the statutory defence in section 44. This refers to certain restrictive practices, such as requiring licensees of patents to take non-patented products as a condition of the licence. Such agreements are void and section 44(3) provides a defence against infringement of a patent if, at the time of the alleged infringement, such an agreement was in force in respect of the patent with the consent of the plaintiff. The effects of this provision were felt by Chiron Corporation in *Chiron Corp v Murex Diagnostics Ltd (No 12)* [1996] FSR 153.

Government departments are exempt from infringement action under section 55, if the use of the patent is for the use of the Crown, subject to payment of a royalty.

At common law, there is an implied licence to use or resell a patented product acquired through ordinary purchase of that product (as illustrated by *Betts v Will-mott* [1871] LR 6 Ch App 239) and an implied licence to repair patented goods even if that involves an activity that would otherwise infringe the patent (as illustrated by *Solar Thomson Engineering Co Ltd v Barton* [1977] RPC 537). In *Solar Thomson* the defendant had to repair part of a patented product supplied to it by the plaintiff. The defendant replaced a part of the patented product with one that it had manufactured, which had an identical design to the plaintiff's product. The Court of Appeal held that it was permissible to carry out repairs without infringing the patent covering the repaired product, provided the work of repair did not amount to the manufacture of a new article (but note *United Wire Ltd v Screen Repairs Services & ors* [2001] RPC 439).

As with all equitable remedies, a failure on the part of the patent holder to take immediate action against infringers might prevent him from obtaining certain remedies.

6.7 Remedies

If successful in an infringement action, the patentee is entitled to the following remedies under section 61:

(a) an injunction restraining the defendant from any apprehended act of infringement;
(b) an order for the defendant to deliver up or destroy any patented product which relates to the infringement;
(c) damages in respect of the infringement;
(d) an order for an account of the profits made from the infringement; and
(e) a declaration that the patent is valid and has been infringed.

Remedies (c) and (d) are alternatives and will not both be awarded.

In the case of *Gerber Garment Technology Inc v Lectra Systems Ltd* [1997] RPC 443, the court agreed with the plaintiff that damages for patent infringement could be based not only on lost sales of products covered by the patent, but also on other related sales and supplies which the patent owner might have made if it had not been for the infringer's activities. In that case, the plaintiff successfully claimed damages in respect of loss of sales on spare parts for the patented product, loss of income for servicing the patented product and the so-called springboard damages in respect of sales which could have been made after expiry of the patent.

For further guidance on assessing accounts of profits, see Laddie J in *Celanese International Corp v BP Chemicals Ltd* [1999] RPC 203.

6.8 Criminal offences

The Patents Act 1977 creates some criminal offences attracting criminal penalties, but these are not related to acts of infringement. The specific offences are: falsification of the Patents Register; misrepresenting a connection with the Patent Office; falsely representing oneself as a patent agent or patent attorney; falsely claiming that a product is patented; and falsely claiming that a patent has been applied for. Obviously, there may be situations where an applicant has prepared goods having the word 'patented' applied to them in expectation of obtaining the patent or without expectation that the patent will be revoked. In such a case, a reasonable period is allowed to prevent the commission of further offences by having the articles in question amended. It is also a defence to prove that due diligence had been exercised by the person charged to prevent continuance of the offence.

As with other criminal offences under intellectual property statutes, where the offender is a corporate body and the act was done with the consent, knowledge or connivance of an officer, the officer may also be found personally guilty of the offence.

6.9 Groundless threats of infringement

Section 70 of the 1977 Act introduced protection against groundless threats made against alleged defendants which did not exist in the 1949 Patents Act. The provision is there to prevent patentees from threatening unwarranted legal action. Infringement actions are quite complex and expensive to defend. Patentees are aware of this and some may be tempted to threaten legal action on the weakest of cases, knowing that the other party will cease the alleged infringing activity without a fight. The section, which has been significantly amended by the Patents Act 2004, provides that where anyone, by whatever means, threatens another with infringement proceedings, anyone aggrieved by the threats may claim relief against the person making the threats. The courts will consider threats which are both express and implied. The test is an objective one, assessing whether the language used would convey to the reasonable man an intention to bring infringement proceedings (see *Jaybeam Ltd v Abru Aluminium* [1976] RPC 308). The 'person aggrieved' is defined in broad terms to include anyone whose 'commercial interests are likely to be adversely affected in a real, as opposed to a fanciful or minimal way' (see *C&P Developments Co (London) v Sisabro Novelty Co* (1953) 70 RPC 277). A good explanation of section 70 both prior to and following the 2004 amendment can be found in Nettleton and Cordery, 'Walking the groundless threats minefield' (JIPLP (2005) vol. 1(1): 51). There, the authors point out that prior to 2005 (when the amendment took effect), the section did not apply to alleged primary infringements that involve making or importing products or using a process. The provision is intended to protect the potentially innocent middle party who is merely selling or using a product covered by the patent and who might, on receipt of such a threat, cease selling the product regardless of the validity of the action. However, the patentee's position is strengthened slightly in that permitted threats now cover all threats made to primary infringers. This will affect the decision in *Cavity Trays Ltd v RMC Panel Products Ltd* [1996] RPC 361 concerning the meaning of section 70(4), which is the provision that removes the right to bring a threats action where the threat of proceedings was in respect of making or importing a product for disposal or in respect of using a process. In *Cavity Trays*, the threat of proceedings made against the plaintiff, who was the manufacturer of the allegedly infringing products, was in respect of the acts of manufacture, promotion, marketing, advertisement and sale. The defendant argued that section 70(4) was aimed at removing the right to bring a threats action from primary infringers (that is, manufacturers) and was intended to protect secondary infringers further along the chain of supply. The court did not agree. Section 70(4) clearly provided an exception in respect of threats made about certain acts, and not in respect of threats made against types of person.

Accordingly, since the defendant had threatened proceedings for infringements in respect of activities other than manufacture and importation of a product or use of a process, the plaintiff was entitled to its remedies under section 70. This is now not good law.

It is still a defence to a claim for unjustified threats that the threats were justified – this involves proving that the acts complained of were indeed infringements of a valid patent. Where the patent was found to be invalid, the defence was not available. The case of *Patrick John Brian v Ingledew Brown Bennison & Garrett and Riso National Laboratory* [1996] FSR 341 underlines the risk of making threats of patent infringement on the basis of a patent application (as opposed to a granted patent). In that case, the threats were made at a time when the patent in question was an application being considered by the EPO. The EPO refused the application and sent it to the Examining Division for consideration. However, the court agreed with the plaintiff that it was entitled to an early decision on the threats action and that it should not have to wait for final determination on the validity of the patent. The defence of justification has now been widened to the extent that the patentee can avoid liability if he can show that he did not know and had no reason to suspect that the patent would be held invalid.

Summary

▶ Once a patent is granted, the owner of the patent has the right to stop others dealing in the invention without his consent.

▶ Making the invention, using it, or otherwise dealing with the invention all amount to acts of infringement.

▶ To determine whether there has been infringement, the court will consider whether the defendant's activities fall within the claimant's claims.

▶ English judges are being encouraged to adopt a more purposive approach to interpreting patent claims.

▶ Slight modifications to the patent will still amount to infringement if there is no material difference in the working of the invention.

▶ The general statutory defences are listed in section 60(5). A defendant can also claim that because of modifications made to the patent, there is no infringement. There is also the risk that a defendant will challenge the validity of the patent.

▶ The general intellectual property remedies apply in respect of patent infringement and are listed in section 61.

▶ The criminal offences under the Patents Act 1977 relate to false claims about whether a patent has been applied for and granted. It is also a criminal offence to misrepresent a connection with the Patent Office. Infringement of a patent is not a criminal offence.

Exercises

6.1 If the applicant has had the opportunity to prepare a patent specification, why should it not be interpreted literally for infringement purposes?

6.2 What exactly is the *Catnic* approach? Assess its validity for 1977 patents.

6.3 In 1980, A Toys obtained a patent for 'Josie the storytelling elephant', a cuddly toy whose voice is activated when her tummy is squeezed. B Toys have begun making 'Marty lullaby bear'. He is activated to play soothing music when a baby starts crying. Advise A Toys.

6.4 C acquired a licence to make and sell 'Josie the storytelling elephant'. Under the terms of the licence they agreed the following:

(a) not to produce a similar toy for five years after the expiry of A's patent;

(b) to purchase the materials to make Josie from sources recommended by A Toys; and

(c) not to challenge the validity of the patent for the term of the licence agreement.

6.5 C has produced 'Charlie the chatty chipmunk'. His voice is activated by a cuddle from a child or adult. He automatically switches off after five minutes to save the batteries. The idea for C's design came from a member of staff who remembered having a soft cuddly doll in the 1970s which sang when her tummy was squeezed. Advise A Toys, the owner of Josie.

Further reading and references

Bainbridge, *Intellectual Property* (9th edn, Pearson, 2012) chapter 14.

O'Sullivan, 'Case Comment on *Virgin Atlantic Airways Ltd v Premium Aircraft Interiors UK Ltd*' EIPR 2010, 32(8), 415–420.

Chapter 7

Breach of confidence

7.1 Introduction

This area of law has developed through the common law and equity. It is aimed at protecting secrets, and should not be confused with laws available in other countries providing a right to privacy (see *Kaye v Robertson* [1991] 2 All ER 599); although it has been argued that in '*Campbell v. Mirror Group Newspapers* [2004] UKHL 22, English law took a significant step closer to the protection of privacy as such' (Brazell, 2005: 405–11). Invasions of privacy can be dealt with under the Human Rights Act 1998 and their Lordships in *Campbell* unanimously acknowledged that the values of privacy and free speech set out in the European Convention on Human Rights (ECHR) now form part of the cause of action for breach of confidence.

Breach of confidence complements other aspects of intellectual property, as an obligation of confidence can arise even before the work in question is tangible. So, for example, whereas the idea for a television programme cannot attract copyright protection until it is recorded in some way, the person to whom the idea is disclosed can be prevented from publicising that idea to others or exploiting the idea by the use of an action for breach of confidence. In *Fraser v Thames Television Ltd* [1984] 1 QB 44, three actresses and a composer devised an idea for a television series based on the story of three female rock singers who formed a band. They discussed the idea with Thames Television and offered Thames first option on the idea, subject to the three actresses being given the parts of the three rock singers.

A dispute arose, and Thames made the programme without engaging the actresses. The plaintiffs claimed for breach of confidence. The defendant argued that the idea disclosed was not entitled to protection unless it was a developed idea that had been recorded in some permanent form. The court did not agree – those requirements were more relevant to the issue of copyright protection – and accepted the plaintiffs' argument of breach of confidence. Hirst J did, however, state that to be capable of protection by the law of confidence an idea must be 'sufficiently developed, so that it would be seen to be a concept … which is capable of being realised as an actuality'.

The law of breach of confidence also protects the applicant for a patent by allowing him to impose an obligation of confidence on those who are in a position to know, or who need to know, the details of the invention before a patent application is filed. This is important because if the details of an invention are made public before the patent application is made, as we have seen, it could fail for lack of novelty. Section 2(4)(b) of the Patents Act 1977 states that publication made in breach of confidence will not invalidate the patent application.

The law here is not limited to commercial or industrial situations. The obligation of confidence has been enforced to protect secrets between husband and wife (*Argyll v Argyll* [1967] Ch 303), secrets between friends (*Stephens v Avery* [1988] 1 Ch 457), drawings by members of the Royal family (*Prince Albert v Strange* [1849] 1 Mac & G 25) and state secrets (*A-G v The Observer Ltd* [1989] AC 109), as well as details in a journal kept by a member of the Royal family (*HRH Prince of Wales v Associated Newspapers* [2006] EWCA Civ 1776).

7.2 Historical background

Since the mid-nineteenth century, the law has recognised that an obligation of confidence can exist, although the action was not necessarily referred to as breach of confidence. In *Prince Albert v Strange* [1849] 1 Mac & G 25, the Prince Consort was able to prevent the exhibition of prints taken from etchings he had produced of Queen Victoria. The House of Lords recognised a proprietary interest in the prints but stated that the plaintiff would have been equally protected if the etchings had been disclosed by actions for breach of trust, confidence or contract.

Another case from this period is that of *Morison v Moat* (1851) 9 Hare 492. Morison invented 'Morison's Universal Medicine' and entered a partnership with Moat senior to market and sell it. The recipe was given in confidence to Moat senior. Before his death, Moat senior appointed his son as his successor in the partnership. Morison and his family believed that Moat senior had not passed the recipe on to Moat junior but, in fact, he had. On termination of the partnership agreement, Moat junior went into business on his own account, using Morison's recipe. The plaintiff was successful in restraining Moat junior from using the recipe. Turner vc felt that the disclosure by Moat senior to his son amounted to a breach of faith, as well as a breach of contract. This case also illustrates that it is possible to obtain protection for a longer period by relying on the obligation of confidence rather than the patent system. 'Morison's Universal Medicine' had not been patented. We know from the previous chapters that the details of patents are published and can be inspected by members of the public and it is possible for a competitor to work the patent after the patent has expired. However, where there has been no patent application, provided the details of the invention are kept secret by the owner, and by anyone to whom it is disclosed, it cannot be inspected in the same way, thus maintaining the invention's secrecy.

7.3 The basic requirements

The conditions for imposing an obligation of confidence were stated in Megarry J's decision in *Coco v AN Clark (Eng) Ltd* [1969] RPC 41. The plaintiff, who had designed an engine for a moped, entered into negotiations with the defendant company to discuss manufacture of the engine. All the details of the design were disclosed during these discussions. The parties subsequently fell out and the defendant decided to make its own engine, which closely resembled the plaintiff's. The plaintiff failed in his attempt to get an injunction to stop the defendant manufacturing his engine. Instead, the court required the defendant to deposit royalties on sales of the engines into a joint account until the full hearing. According to Megarry J, to be able to claim breach of confidence, a plaintiff needed to satisfy three conditions. First, the information must have the necessary quality of confidence. Second, the information must have been imparted in circumstances importing an obligation of confidence. Third, there must be unauthorised use of the information. In *Coco v Clark* the court felt that the plaintiff could only satisfy the second condition. Let us consider each requirement in detail.

7.4 The necessary quality of confidence

The first condition is that the information must have the necessary quality of confidence. In other words, it should not be in the public domain. In a commercial or industrial context, this might be a trade secret. But what is a trade secret? Obviously it will cover technical information, like the mechanics of an invention that is yet to be the subject of a patent application. Price lists, customers' names and addresses and delivery routes might also be covered. In *Vestergaard Frandsen S/A v Bestnet Europe Ltd* [2011] EWCA Civ 424, a database with the ingredients used to make a product was protected. A useful (but not conclusive) test is provided by Lord Parker in *Herbert Morris Ltd v Saxelby* [1916] 1 AC 688. If the information is so detailed that it cannot be carried in the head, then it is a trade secret, but if it is simply a general method or scheme that is easily remembered, it is not.

Even where the information is not a trade secret, it can be classified as information of a confidential nature if it has 'the necessary quality of confidence about it, namely it must not be something which is public property and public knowledge' per Lord Greene MR in *Saltman Engineering Co v Campbell Engineering Co* [1963] 3 All ER 413, at 415. The question is: how do we tell whether the information has the 'necessary quality of confidence about it'? According to Megarry VC in *Thomas Marshall (Exports) Ltd v Guinle* [1979] 1 Ch 227 there are four elements that should be taken into account. First, the owner must believe that the release of the information would be injurious to him or of advantage to his rivals. Second, the owner must believe that the information is confidential or secret. Third, the two first beliefs must be reasonable. Finally, the information must be considered taking into account trade practice. This would appear, initially, to be a subjective test, in that it considers what the owner of the information believes. However, such belief must be reasonable suggesting an objective element (see Holyoak and Torremans, 2005).

The important point is that the owner of the information has not placed it in the public domain. Confidential information can come into the public domain in a number of ways, including by applying for a patent, as discussed above. When a patent is applied for, details of the patent application are published on the Patents Register and, as a result, come into the public domain. In *Mustad (O) & Son v S Allcock & Co Ltd and Dosen* [1963] 3 All ER 416, Mustad took over a business that had formerly employed Dosen. Dosen had acquired knowledge of the business's trade secrets but had been advised that he was no longer under an obligation of secrecy. He passed his knowledge onto his new employers. Mustad, who had acquired the trade secrets with the business, applied for a patent to protect one of the business's inventions and sued to restrain Dosen from passing on the trade secrets connected with it. The House of Lords held that, as the essential parts of the invention had been disclosed through publication of the patent application, the information was no longer confidential. The defendant must know that information is confidential (see *PCR Ltd v Dow Jones Telerate* [1998] FSR 170) and it must be possible to isolate the information that is claimed to be confidential (see *Inline Logistics Ltd v UCI Logistics Ltd* [2001] EWCA Civ 1613).

7.4.1 Disclosure and the 'springboard' doctrine

Although general disclosure or publication of the information in question generally removes the obligation of confidence, a person under an obligation of confidence may nevertheless be held to that obligation for a certain period of time after the general disclosure or publication. This is referred to as the 'springboard' doctrine. The following two cases are examples of this doctrine in practice.

In *Terrapin Ltd v Builder's Supply Co (Hayes) Ltd* [1967] RPC 375, the defendant made prefabricated portable buildings designed by the plaintiff. During the period of their agreement, the plaintiff disclosed details of its designs to the defendant in confidence. After the agreement ended, the defendant produced its own buildings, which were similar to those designed by the plaintiff. At this stage the information was not confidential because the buildings could be inspected by any member of the public, but Roxburgh J granted an injunction on the basis that the defendant should not be in the position where it could make use of information gained in confidence from the plaintiff to compete with the plaintiff. As Roxburgh J said in that case:

> A person who has obtained information in confidence is not allowed to use it as a springboard for activities detrimental to the person who made the confidential communication, and springboard it remains even when all the features have been published or can be ascertained by actual inspection by any member of the public.

In *Cranleigh Precision Engineering Ltd v Bryant* [1964] 3 All ER 289, the defendant was the managing director and inventor for the plaintiff company, which made above-ground swimming pools. Before leaving the plaintiff company, the defendant was informed of another type of pool for which there was a patent (the Bischoff patent). This information was not disclosed to his employers. The defendant left the plaintiff company and set up business in competition, having acquired the Bischoff patent. He used the Bischoff patent, incorporating features from the plaintiff's pools. The plaintiff company applied for an injunction to prevent the defendant from making use of information about the plaintiff's pools. Although details of the Bischoff patent were available for inspection, the injunction was granted. The defendant's position had placed him at an unfair advantage. The information acquired as an employee meant that he could 'springboard' when setting up his own business.

In *Vestergaard Frandsen S/A (MVF3 APS) v Bestnet Europe Ltd* [2011] EWCA Civ 424, two former employees of the claimant decided to compete using information kept in its database. Vestergaard manufactured insecticidal fabrics. The defendants produced an anti-mosquito product using the ingredients and required properties obtained from the company's database. A restraining injunction on the first version of their product was held to be appropriate, even though they had only used the information to get a head start in the market.

These cases illustrate the principle that, even if the information becomes available to the public, those previously under an obligation of confidence in respect of the information should not have an unfair advantage as a result of having previously obtained that information.

7.4.2 What is confidential?

Apart from the 'springboard' doctrine, once the information is available to the public, it ceases to be confidential. Thus a group of celebrities were unable to stop the publication of details of their extra-marital activities in *Woodward v Hutchins* [1977] 2 All ER 751, because a number of those activities took place in public places and were well known. Further, the Court of Appeal felt that the plaintiffs had been quite happy to court publicity that portrayed them in a positive light, while attempting to suppress information that displayed their true characters. According to Lord Denning MR, it was in the interests of the public to know the truth. In *A-G v The Observer Ltd* [1989] AC 109, the House of Lords refused an injunction against the serialisation of *Spycatcher*, a book written by Peter Wright, an ex-member of MI5, because the book's publication abroad meant that its contents were no longer secret. However, just because a secret is disclosed to another person does not necessarily place it in the public domain. This is illustrated by *Stephens v Avery* [1988] 1 Ch 457. In that case, the plaintiff confided to a friend that she had been involved in a lesbian relationship with the deceased wife of a known criminal. The 'friend' disclosed the information to a Sunday newspaper, claiming that the disclosure to her meant that the information ceased to be confidential. Sir Nicholas Browne-Wilkinson did not agree:

> The mere fact that two people know a secret does not mean that it is not confidential. If, in fact, information is secret, then in my judgment it is capable of being kept secret by the imposition of a duty of confidence on any person to whom it is communicated. Information only ceases to be capable of protection as confidential when it is in fact known to a substantial number of people.

It is clear then that if a person is told something as a secret that person will be under an obligation of confidence. *Stephens v Avery* involved a secret told to one person. The question is: how many people can be told the secret before a 'substantial number' know of it and it ceases to be confidential? We suggest that a court will take the objective view and consider what is reasonable in each case. In *A v B* [2003] QB 195, a so-called kiss and tell case, Lord Woolf CJ stated that a duty of confidence will arise whenever a person is in a situation where he knows or ought to know that the other person can reasonably expect his privacy to be protected. As previously stated, the enactment of the Human Rights Act 1998 has perhaps reinforced the protection. In *Douglas v Hello! Ltd* [2005] EWCA Civ 595, the Court of Appeal held that when considering what information should be protected as confidential, the courts are required as a result of the Human Rights Act 1998 to adopt and develop the law of breach of confidence in such a way as to give effect to the competing rights of privacy and freedom of expression. In the lower court, Hello! had argued that the photographs taken could not be considered private information as the claimants had agreed to sell photographs of their wedding to a rival publication. Lindsay J stated that the fact that the photographs could be sold was what gave them the necessary element of confidentiality. They were a valuable commercial asset, just like a trade secret (see also *OBG v Allan* [2007] UKHL 21). Private information includes personal information not intended to be made public (see also *Campbell v Mirror Group Newspapers* [2004] UKHL 22).

Even if a large number of people have been told the information, if they have all been bound to an obligation of confidence, the information is clearly not in the public domain. For instance, a software company may allow its licensees to have access to the computer source code (the human-readable coding, rather than the machine-readable code, known as object code) for the purposes of error correction and development, subject to obligations of confidentiality. Even if the software is licensed to a large number of people, provided the obligations of confidentiality are imposed on and enforced against all the licensees, the source code will remain confidential information. Note also that although the information may be disclosed to an individual for a specific purpose, it can remain confidential for other purposes. So in *HRH Prince of Wales v Associated Newspapers* [2006] EWCA Civ 1776, where information from a journal kept by the Prince of Wales was disclosed to his biographer, the press could be restrained from using it.

7.5 The obligation of confidence

The second condition from *Coco v AN Clark (Eng) Ltd* [1969] RPC 41 is that the information must have been 'imparted in circumstances importing an obligation of confidence'. Here we are looking at the relationship between the person imparting the information and the person who receives it. This relationship may be based on contract, trust, friendship or, even, marriage.

7.5.1 Contractual relationships

This is the most straightforward. The parties to a contractual agreement may have express terms of confidence in their agreement. Even if there are no express terms, an obligation of confidence might be implied. See *Saltman Engineering Co v Campbell Engineering Co* [1963] 3All ER 413. *Coco v AN Clark (Eng) Ltd* [1969] RPC 41 confirms that the obligation extends to pre-contractual disclosures, even if no contract materialises.

The law has imposed an obligation of confidence on a variety of contractual relationships. In *Tournier v National Provincial & Union Bank of England* [1924] 1 KB 461, it was held that a bank was under an obligation of confidence to its customers, unless required to disclose information by law. Partnership agreements also impose duties of confidentiality on all the partners concerned (as illustrated by *Morison v Moat* (1851) 9 Hare 492), as do agreements between directors and the companies that they represent (cases such as *Cranleigh Precision Engineering Ltd v Bryant* [1964] 3 All ER 289 and *Thomas Marshall (Exports) Ltd v Guinle* [1979] 1 Ch 227 illustrate this). The above contracts also give rise to fiduciary relationships where the law will also impose a duty of confidence.

What would be the position if the owner of the information wrongfully repudiates the contractual relationship? In *Naomi Campbell v Frisbee (Vanessa)* [2002] EWCA Civ 1374, the defendant had been employed by the claimant, a well-known catwalk model. The latter sued when the defendant disclosed details of her personal life to a national newspaper. In deciding the effect that the claimant's wrongful repudiation of contract would have on any obligation of confidence, the Court of Appeal held that the principles were not clearly defined.

7.5.2 Contracts of employment

The obligation of confidence is also part of the contract of employment (although there is no duty to keep a secret about the employer's wrongful or unlawful act: see *Initial Services v Putterill* [1968] 1 QB 396). The duty imposed on employees is illustrated by *Hivac v Park Royal Science Instruments Ltd* [1946] 1 All ER 350. Park Royal, the plaintiff's competitor, was restrained from employing Hivac's employees. The employees had been working for the defendant in their spare time and, although there was no proof that confidential information had been disclosed, the Court of Appeal accepted that there was a risk that this could happen. For an employee's obligation of confidence, see also *Polymasc Pharmaceutical plc v Stephen Alexander Charles* [1999] FSR 711 and *SBJ Stephenson Ltd v Mandy* [2000] FSR 286.

In *FSS Travel & Leisure Systems Ltd v Johnson* [1999] FSR 505, it was stated that it is critical to distinguish the trade secrets that the employer could claim as his property from the skill, experience, know-how and general knowledge that the employee could regard as his property, as only the former could be subject to an obligation.

The obligation of confidence can continue even after the contract of employment has been brought to an end. However, this is subject to quite a stringent test. In *Faccenda Chicken Ltd v Fowler* [1987] 1 Ch 117, the plaintiff, who sold fresh chickens from refrigerated vans, applied for an injunction to restrain two former employees from using their knowledge of sales, prices and customers' details, when they set up a competing business. Neill LJ said that in deciding whether the former employees owed a duty of confidence in respect of this information a number of factors should be considered:

(1) The nature of the employment. Was confidential information habitually, normally or only occasionally handled by the employee?
(2) The nature of the information itself: only trade secrets or information of a highly confidential nature would be protected.
(3) Whether the employer impressed upon the employee the confidential nature of the information.
(4) Whether the relevant information could be isolated easily from other information that the employee was free to use or disclose. (at 137–38)

While Fowler (one of the former employees) was still employed, there was information that could be regarded as confidential and could not be disclosed by him or used for any other purpose, as he would be in breach of contract. However, when the contract of employment ended, such information that had become part of his own skill and knowledge ceased to be confidential and the employee was entitled to make use of that information and those skills.

Independent contractors, while not under a contract of employment, are usually under a duty of confidence by virtue of terms expressed or implied by law in a contract for services.

7.5.3 Non-contractual relationships

The obligation of confidence is not restricted to contractual relationships. *W v Edgell* [1990] 1 Ch 359 shows that it does apply to fiduciary relationships such as that between doctor and patient, subject to the public interest defence. *Stephens v Avery* [1988] 1 Ch 457 confirms that even a secret disclosed to a friend gives rise to an obligation based on the relationship of trust. What ties the different types of relationship together is that, as stated by Megarry J in *Coco v AN Clark (Eng) Ltd* [1969] RPC 41:

> the circumstances are such that any reasonable man standing in the shoes of the recipient of the information would have realised that upon reasonable grounds the information was given to him in confidence (at 48).

However, in *Carflow Products (UK) Ltd v Linwood Securities (Birmingham) Ltd* [1996] FSR 424, the judge applied a different test to decide whether, in the absence of a contractual agreement, any confidentiality obligation could be implied. The judge applied a 'subjective test': what obligations did the parties intend to impose and accept? In that case, because both parties wanted to invalidate a third party's registered design right by showing that it had previously been available in the public domain, both parties agreed that they did not intend the information to be treated as confidential. The judge also described an objective test (which could have been used if the subjective test had not answered the question). This test was the same test used in *Coco v Clark*. The interesting point about the *Carflow* case is that the judge felt that, in the circumstances of the case, the reasonable bystander would have realised that the design in question would be protected by intellectual property rights and would, therefore, not assume that the information was disclosed in confidence. We think this attributes a degree of knowledge about intellectual property rights that most bystanders would not possess.

In any event, even if other intellectual property rights were available to protect the information, as we have already said, obligations of confidentiality can provide additional and potentially unlimited protection, whereas most intellectual property rights expire after a period of time.

7.5.4   The position of third parties

The obligation will extend to a third party if it is obvious (to that party) that the information is of a confidential nature. So, as with cases such as *Stephens v Avery* [1988] 1 Ch 457, the media are also under an obligation not to publish information of a confidential nature passed on by the recipient. Similarly, where an ex-employee is under an obligation of confidence, his new employer will also be held to an obligation of confidence in respect of the matters covered by the employee's obligation. In *Morison v Moat* (1851) 9 Hare 492, Turner vc suggested that a third party would only escape the obligation of confidence if he were a purchaser for value of the secret without notice of the obligation. In other words, if the information is acquired by a third party who has paid for that information and who has no reasonable grounds to suspect that it is confidential, there is no obligation of secrecy. In *Susan Thomas v Pearce* [2000] FSR 718, the first defendant kept a list of the clients of her former employer, which she gave to the second defendant, who used it. The Court of Appeal stated that the correct test was whether the third party had acted honestly. Behaviour that is considered careless, naive or stupid is not enough. The third party must have acted dishonestly with conscious knowledge of the breach or at least deliberately closed his or her mind to it. The test would appear to be very similar to that used for holding a third party liable for assisting in a breach of trust.

This would appear to cover another interesting possibility. The third party may be unknown to both the person confiding the information and the person to whom he is disclosing it. For example, the information may be disclosed in a telephone conversation to which another party is listening in. Is that party also under an obligation of confidence? Technically, that third party owes no such obligation. Is it possible to owe an obligation to a person who does not know you exist? Turner vc's guidance is helpful here because a third party obtaining information from listening in on a telephone conversation is not, in our view, a 'purchaser for value'. This view is not, however, supported by the decision in *Malone v Metropolitan Police Comr (No 2)* [1979] 1 Ch 344. In that case, the plaintiff was charged with handling stolen goods. The prosecution case was based on information obtained by the tapping of the plaintiff's telephone conversations with the authority of the Home Secretary. The plaintiff sought an injunction to prevent use of the information. Megarry J refused to grant the injunction. In his view, anyone using a telephone to disclose confidential information had to accept the risk of being overheard. We think it would have been better if his Lordship had decided the issue on the question of public interest alone. Clearly, in this case, permission had been given by the Home Secretary, the objective being the detection and prevention of crime. To decide that, because of faults on the line, we take a risk when we disclose information on the telephone is less than satisfactory.

Malone was distinguished in *Francome v Mirror Group Newspapers Ltd* [1984] 2 All ER 408. Here the information concerned had also been obtained by telephone tapping. The plaintiff was a well-known jockey, the defendant the proprietor and journalists of a tabloid newspaper. The defendant obtained information that suggested that the plaintiff had taken part in illegal activities. This information had come from an unknown source who had illegally tapped conversations from the plaintiff's telephone. Here the Court of Appeal held that the plaintiff had the right to protect the confidentiality of his telephone conversations. The distinguishing factor between the two cases appears to be that in *Malone* the tapping took place legally, whereas in *Francome* it did not. Megarry J's view in *Malone* was not followed here.

7.5.5 No pre-existing relationship

Cases such as *Campbell v Mirror Group Newspapers* [2004] UKHL 22 do not appear to rely on the second requirement from *Coco v AN Clark (Eng) Ltd* [1969] RPC 41. A pre-existing relationship of confidence is no longer essential. In *Campbell v Mirror Group Newspapers*, the claimant was a well-known supermodel who was photographed in the street leaving a Narcotics Anonymous meeting. The House of Lords stated that an obligation of confidence could extend to strangers, if the information and/or activities observed are private. In reaching this decision, reference was made to a statement of Lord Goff in *A-G v Guardian Newspapers Ltd (No 2)* [1990] AC 109.

> A duty of confidence arises when confidential information comes to the knowledge of a person ... in circumstances where he has notice, or is held to have agreed, that the information is confidential, with the effect that it would be just in the circumstances that he should be precluded from disclosing the information (at 281).

In *Campbell*, Lord Hoffman (at [50]) stated that the enactment of the Human Rights Act 1998 has served to 'identify private information as something worth protecting as an aspect of human autonomy and dignity'.

In his article, 'Rethinking surreptitious takings in the law of confidence', Chris Hunt questions this development. He states:

> Rather remarkably, we have thus arrived at a place where obligations of confidence may be imposed on complete strangers, based on nothing more than their constructive knowledge that the information is 'private' ... or 'confidential'.

It is suggested that *Campbell* and *Douglas v Hello!* [2005] EWCA Civ 595, together with the Human Rights Act 1998, have created a new tort called 'misuse of private information'. This requires a two-stage rather than three-stage test, the two stages being:

1. Did the claimant have a reasonable expectation of privacy with respect to the information disclosed? If so
2. Is the person's right to privacy under article 8 of the European Convention on Human Rights more important in the circumstances, than someone else's right to freedom of expression under article 10?

These cases are discussed in further detail later in this chapter.

7.6 Unauthorised use of the information

Megarry J's third condition in *Coco v AN Clark (Eng) Ltd* [1969] RPC 41 was that the information has been used without the owner's authority. Within an agreement involving obligations of confidence, there will be implied as well as express terms. It will be clear that certain information is confidential. However, it may be necessary to disclose the information to others not directly party to the agreement. Where one party is engaged to manufacture the subject of the agreement, employees on the shop floor will need to have access to the information covered by the agreement in order to produce the end product, as will subcontractors. The authority to disclose in this instance will be implied into the agreement, even if not expressly contained.

Disclosure of the information includes using it to produce goods in order to compete with the person owning the information, as well as disclosing it to others. In *Seager v Copydex (No 1)* [1967] 2 All ER 415, the plaintiff and defendant had discussed the plaintiff's design for a stair carpet grip. Sometime later the defendant designed its own carpet grip, which inadvertently incorporated the plaintiff's idea. The Court of Appeal held this to be a case of unconscious copying and use of the plaintiff's idea and found in favour of the plaintiff. As shown by this case, the state of the defendant's mind is irrelevant when determining liability, but it will be relevant when the court determines the plaintiff's remedy.

There is some doubt as to whether the disclosure or use of the information has to be detrimental to the plaintiff for the claim of breach of confidence to succeed. In *Coco v Clark*, Megarry J suggests that it is part of the definition. If this is so, detriment must be proved in order for the plaintiff to succeed. We suggest that in most cases the detriment can be implied or assumed, even if it is not obvious or proven. Where the information is of a commercial nature, then disclosure to the plaintiff's competitors is bound to have an effect on his trade. The competitor will, for example, be able to use the information to produce competing goods without the investment costs incurred by the plaintiff and, therefore, sell those goods at a lower price. Even disclosure of personal information can lead to detriment. For example, the plaintiff in *Stephens v Avery* [1988] 1 Ch 457 would have suffered emotionally from unwanted media attention.

In *Drummond Murray v Yorkshire Fund Managers Ltd and Michael Hartley* [1998] FSR 372, the concern was whether a co-owner of information can prevent its use by the other co-owners.

The plaintiff was a marketing expert involved in the purchase of companies. He joined a team of five for the purpose of a management buy-in–buy-out of a company. The team created a business plan to attract venture capitalists. The business plan and the price to be paid for the assets was highly confidential information. Each member of the team was a co-author of the business plan with equal rights in it. But there was no agreement between the team members as to how this confidential information would be used.

The team approached the defendants as potential investors. The business plan and the price to be paid for the assets were discussed. The first defendant was interested in investing in the company but questioned the plaintiff's involvement as managing director and the team, other than the plaintiff, agreed to the latter being replaced by the second defendant. The plaintiff sued for breach of confidential information, contending that the confidential information was given to the defendants for the purpose of deciding whether to invest. The second defendant was therefore not entitled to use that information for any other purpose and had breached this obligation by using the information for the purpose of replacing him as managing director. The Court of Appeal held that the confidential information was incidental to the relationship between the team members. The confidential information ceased to be the plaintiff's property once this relationship was dissolved. He could not, therefore, prevent the other team members from using it as they pleased. As there had been no agreement concerning the relationship between the team members, the plaintiff could not prolong that relationship once he ceased to be a team member.

7.7   Defences

7.7.1   Confidential information and the public interest

The only real defence to this form of action is that disclosure of the information is in the public interest. For example, in *Lion Laboratories Ltd v Evans & ors* [1984] 2 All ER 417, the plaintiff company made and supplied the police with intoximeters which were used to test the breath of drivers for the presence of alcohol under section 12 of the Road Traffic Act 1972. The defendants had been employed as technicians in developing the device and were aware of information which questioned its reliability. Concerned that the police were making use of an inaccurate and unreliable device, the defendants decided to pass the information on to a newspaper. The plaintiff sought an injunction to stop them. In the Court of Appeal, the defendants argued that it was in the public interest to disclose the possible unreliability of a device from which results were used as evidence against an individual charged with a criminal offence. The court agreed. The defence of public interest was available if it was in the public interest to publish the information. The Court of Appeal stated that it had to weigh up the public interest in maintaining secrecy in the plaintiff's documents against the public interest in the accuracy and reliability of an approved device that was used to determine whether a defendant facing a drink-driving charge should be convicted and suffer a penalty possibly as serious as imprisonment.

In the earlier decision of *Hubbard v Vosper* [1972] 2 QB 84, the Court of Appeal refused to grant an injunction to the leader of the Church of Scientology, L. Ron Hubbard. Vosper had agreed, on joining the Church, to keep certain aspects of the Church's activities secret. When he left, he wrote a book about its activities using material from Hubbard's book and certain other confidential information. The Church applied for an injunction to prevent publication of the book. The Court of Appeal considered that it was in the public interest that details of the activities of the Church be published.

Public interest as a defence also succeeded in *W v Edgell* [1990] 1 Ch 359, which concerned the release of a report on a mental health patient considered a danger to others. The Court of Appeal held that there was certainly a duty of confidence between a doctor and patient, but this duty had to be balanced against the public interest in protecting others from possible violence.

In limited circumstances, confidence may be breached in the prevention of crime. See *Hellewell v Chief Constable of Derbyshire* [1995] 1 WLR 804, where the police circulated photographs of the plaintiff, who had previous convictions for theft. The photographs were circulated to local shopkeepers as part of a neighbourhood watch scheme. Laws J held that where the photograph was being used for the prevention and detection of crime, the police had a public interest defence to any action for breach of confidence. However, not all information collected by the police can be disclosed on the basis of this defence. In *Marcel v Comr of Police* [1991] 1 All ER 845, it was held that information seized by the police under the Police and Criminal Evidence Act 1984 could not be disclosed to a third party for use in civil proceedings. Where the information is commercially sensitive, the need to protect it will be balanced against the public's right to know, as was the case in *London Regional Transport v Mayor of London* [2001] EWCA Civ 1491.

Where the information concerns the personal details of a public figure, the courts will now consider the interplay between article 8 and article 10 of the European Convention on Human Rights. Article 10 concerns freedom of expression. In analysing public interest, the court will discuss whether the information is something that is in the public interest or whether it is something that the public is interested in. This is discussed further later in the chapter.

7.8   Remedies

Damages for breach of confidence will generally be calculated on the basis of compensating the claimant for the conversion of property, although Holyoak and Torremans (2005) make a distinction between whether the breach is contractual or non-contractual. They suggest that for a contractual breach, damages should be assessed on the basis of contractual principles. That would appear to be logical. Where the breach is non-contractual, several commentaries appear to agree with Lord Denning in *Seager v Copydex (No 2)* [1969] RPC 250. His Lordship suggested considering the value of the information in question. If there is nothing particularly special about the information, such that it could have been obtained by employing a competent consultant, then damages should be assessed on the basis of the cost of hiring such a consultant. If, on the other hand, the information is special, perhaps involving an inventive step, then damages should reflect the price that a willing buyer would pay for the information on the open market. In *Indata Equipment Supplies Ltd v ACL Ltd* [1998] FSR 248, the Court of Appeal stated that damages should be assessed on a tortious basis, that is, such sum as would have put the claimant into the position he would have been in had it not been for the tort, or breach of confidence.

As with infringement of other intellectual property rights, the claimant may request an account of profits where the information has been used commercially. This is an equitable remedy that is at the court's discretion, as is an order for the delivery-up and destruction of goods made using the confidential information.

As this area of law is concerned with secrets, the most usual remedy that the claimant seeks is an injunction preventing disclosure of the information. To restrain publication by an interlocutory injunction, the claimant has had to satisfy a particularly high threshold test since the enactment of the Human Rights Act 1998. Under section 12, an interlocutory injunction should generally only be granted if the claimant can show that they are likely to prove a breach of confidence at trial. See *Cream Holdings Ltd v Bannerjee* [2005] 1 AC 253, where the House of Lords stated that this would usually mean that the injunction should be granted if the claimant can prove that it was likely that they would win at trial (but see also *Browne v Associated Newspapers* [2008] QB 103 discussed in Section 7.17).

A number of special injunctions have been referred to recently by the media. A 'super-injunction' stops the publication of any details of a news story, including the identities of those involved. It also prevents the press from mentioning that an injunction exists. An 'anonymised' injunction is where the name of the claimant is kept secret and is referred to by randomly chosen initials. These are discussed further in Section 7.18.

If the information is already in the public domain, an injunction is impractical and will not be granted, as illustrated by *A-G v The Observer Ltd* [1989] AC 109, where publication abroad of Peter Wright's book, *Spycatcher*, made it impractical for the House of Lords to restrain British newspapers from publishing extracts. The 'springboard' doctrine is, however, an exception to this. As already stated, an individual under an obligation of confidence can be held to it even after general disclosure of the information, if it is felt that previous knowledge of the information places him at an unfair advantage over the claimant's other competitors.

7.9   Privacy: introduction

In England, the law relating to the publication of information about individuals had traditionally been dominated by the law of defamation. In simple terms, this protects a party from attacks by the media (as well as from businesses or individuals) that consist of allegations that are untrue and damage the party's reputation.

However, since the introduction of the European Convention on Human Rights directly into English law in 2000, there has been a growing body of case law conferring what might be termed 'privacy rights' on individuals. Much of the focus of this case law has been on the relationship between the media and famous individuals. However, the phone-hacking scandal that first came to prominence in 2011 has demonstrated that it is not only famous people who are affected by the media's activities.

This new case law has shifted the balance of power in favour of celebrities in that it has created a new remedy to prevent the circulation of true but private material about an individual. It has now extended to allegations that are true but private. It is also a more effective right than that offered by defamation law in that interim injunctions are available as a remedy in privacy cases preventing the publication of the information pending a full trial, whereas in defamation claims interim injunctions are not generally available.

There have also been perhaps more surprising results as the development of this right has given celebrities (and the media that they enter into contracts with) greater control over how fame is exploited. Celebrity has effectively been recognised as a tradable asset, which, when added to extended passing-off rights, has created a right close to what is commonly termed 'image rights'.

7.10   Background to the development of a law of privacy

The Human Rights Act brought the European Convention on Human Rights ('the Convention') into direct effect in the UK. This has been the catalyst for developing a privacy law. The foundation of the privacy right is set out in article 8 of the Convention. This provides that everyone has the right to respect for his private and family life. However, within article 8, a balance is struck because it also provides that this right can be interfered with where it is necessary in a democratic society for the protection of the rights and freedom of others.

Article 10 of the Convention deals with the main competing right of freedom of expression. It provides that everyone has the right to freedom of expression. This right includes the freedom to hold opinions and to receive and impart information and ideas without interference by a public authority (e.g. a court). However, once again a balance is being struck because article 10 also provides that the exercise of these freedoms carries with it duties and responsibilities. So, the right may be subject to restrictions necessary for the protection of the reputation or rights of others or for preventing the disclosure of information received in confidence.

The English courts have been involved in a process of balancing these rights and responsibilities. In the course of this process there has been much discussion as to whether there is a new legal right to privacy, something that has not been recognised in terms before. In reaching a conclusion on these matters, the courts have made rulings that have had a profound effect on the way in which the media operates and the way in which people in the public eye can seek to protect or exploit their reputation.

The approach that the English courts have taken is to fit the new developing law into the existing law of breach of confidence, previously mainly used in relation to the unlawful disclosure or use of trade secrets. The English courts have consistently said that there is no free-standing right to privacy per se, preferring instead to label it a right not to have one's private information misused.

The test used by the court is to first ask whether a person has a reasonable expectation of privacy. If the answer to this is yes, then the court goes on to consider whether that right is overridden by other rights, principally the article 10 rights of the media or those who wish to disclose information using the media. This has been described by the courts as involving 'an intense focus' between the competing positions and is very fact-specific to each case. This balancing exercise means that editorial decisions about whether to publish and how much to publish have become increasingly difficult. One of the best illustrations of this is in the leading case of *Campbell v MGN* [2004]2 AC 457.

7.11 Campbell: a new model for privacy

This case involved the model, Naomi Campbell. The Daily Mirror newspaper produced a series of articles and photographs reporting that Naomi Campbell was a drug addict and was attending Narcotics Anonymous meetings. In order to understand the decision in this case, it is important to appreciate the effect of various concessions that Ms Campbell made in bringing her claim. She conceded that the Daily Mirror was entitled to publish that she was a drug addict and was receiving treatment for her addiction. This was because Ms Campbell recognised that, as a result of her previous pronouncements that she did not take drugs, it was legitimate for the newspaper to put the record straight.

However, Ms Campbell still made a claim for breach of confidence for those sections of the articles that additionally reported that she was receiving therapy from Narcotics Anonymous and for publication of the photographs of her entering and leaving Narcotics Anonymous meetings. The Court of Appeal dismissed her claim in respect of the photographs because they said they were of a public street scene and did not convey any information that was in itself confidential. That information was in fact conveyed by the written material. The Court of Appeal also decided that information that Ms Campbell was receiving therapy from Narcotics Anonymous could not be equated with the disclosure of clinical details of medical treatment (often seen by the courts as particularly private and sensitive information) and so declined her claim in that respect as well. The Court of Appeal said that when the articles legitimately referred to Ms Campbell being a drug addict and receiving treatment, it was no more than peripheral to add that she was attending Narcotics Anonymous meetings.

Ms Campbell appealed this decision to the House of Lords who decided by a majority of 3:2 to overturn the Court of Appeal's decision and restore the judge's award of damages to Ms Campbell of £3,500. The five Law Lords were unanimous in respect of the test to be applied.

The House of Lords based their decision on the following principles. Applying the earlier House of Lords judgment in *Wainwright v Home Office* [2003] 3 WLR 1137, there is no right to privacy per se in England. However, the introduction of the Convention directly into English law means that the courts have to have regard to the provisions of the Convention when determining cases. In particular, the law as to breach of confidence has been given greater strength and breadth by article 8 of the Convention in that everyone has the right to respect for their private and family life. In this way, an action for breach of confidence is effective to determine cases such as the one involving Naomi Campbell. The width of this duty of confidence is illustrated by previous case law adopting the test that a duty of confidence will arise whenever the party subject to the duty is in the situation where he either knows or ought to know that the other person can reasonably expect his privacy to be protected. Finally, in determining whether a publication involves a breach of confidence the court engages in a two-stage test: is the information confidential (is article 8 engaged?); if it is, is publication justified in any event (based on article 10)?

The Law Lords also made reference to the European Court of Human Rights' (ECtHR) decision in *Peck* [2003] 36 EHRR 41. This case involved CCTV footage of Mr Peck apparently engaged in an attempted suicide in a public place. The CCTV footage was broadcast on television. The Law Lords commented that the taking of the footage itself did not infringe Mr Peck's rights, but re-utilising the footage in a public broadcast did constitute an infringement of his rights. Therefore, the fact that an individual may be engaged in a particular activity in a public place is not necessarily confidential but if that information is then re-utilised in a way that the individual would not expect then that may well constitute an infringement.

The majority in the House of Lords found that the disclosure of information in the newspaper that Ms Campbell was receiving treatment from Narcotics Anonymous, about what that treatment involved and of the photographs of her leaving Narcotics Anonymous meetings was not justified.

This decision had profound implications for the media. For example, while this decision may not prevent the publication of the basic fact of a celebrity's extra-marital affairs where the celebrity has made a virtue of their status as coming from a stable family background, it may prevent the publication of the details of the sexual activity, depriving a story of much of its 'appeal' for many of its readers because, on the House of Lords' ruling, that is going too far in providing detail that is not necessary for the story.

7.12 Exploiting privacy

As the action based upon a right to respect for private information has its roots in breach of confidence claims traditionally protecting trade secrets, there has been a strange and unexpected development in the law that has granted celebrities much greater rights over how their fame can be exploited. This was established during the very long-running litigation between Catherine Zeta-Jones and Michael Douglas and *Hello!* magazine (*Douglas v Hello!* [2003] EMLR 31).

This case involved claims by the actors Michael Douglas and Catherine Zeta-Jones and Northern & Shell Plc (publishers of *OK!* magazine) against the magazine *Hello!* Limited and various other parties. The Douglas' wedding took place at the Plaza Hotel in New York on 18 November 2000. Prior to the wedding the Douglases had signed an exclusive deal with *OK!* magazine to allow *OK!* to publish approved photographs of the wedding. However, rival magazine *Hello!* obtained and published unofficial photographs.

The Douglases brought claims against *Hello!* for a breach of confidence, a breach of their rights to privacy and a breach of the Data Protection Act. In addition, the Douglases and *OK!* brought a claim for breach of confidence in a commercial or trade secret.

In relation to the claim for breach of confidence in a commercial or trade secret, *Hello!* was held liable to all three claimants. The judge treated the Douglases' rights to exploit their image as a valuable trading asset which would be diminished in the hands of all three claimants if a third party encroached on those rights by taking or publishing unauthorised photographs.

However, simply because that right was protected by the law of confidence did not necessarily mean that a remedy would be granted by the court. The judge referred to the balance to be struck between competing rights under articles 8 and 10 of the European Convention on Human Rights. In particular, regard should be had to *Hello!*'s rights to freedom of expression. The judge recognised that if he granted substantial damages then this could have a chilling effect on freedom of expression.

The judge struck the balance in favour of the confidentiality rights. He said that no public interest was claimed in the unauthorised pictures. He said that there was clearly an intrusion into the individuals' private lives without consent, a wedding being an exceptional event to any bride and groom. He said that although *Hello!* were not held by him to have authorised that intrusion they must have been taken to have known about it and that it was not justified.

The judge specifically rejected a defence by *Hello!* that in seeking to exploit their images and their wedding, the Douglases had forgone any rights to confidentiality. He accepted the Douglases' evidence that they wished to keep their wedding private but at the same time they recognised that it was going to be difficult to do that unless they struck an exclusive deal with a particular publisher. Both *Hello!* and *OK!* magazines bid for the rights. Although *Hello!* bid more, *OK!* was successful with their bid. In effect, the judge decided that by taking steps to control the way in which these matters were reported, the Douglases added to their confidentiality rights by elevating those rights beyond a personal right to a trading right.

In relation to the Douglases' claim for breach of confidence, in the absence of any commercial confidence, the judge said that a defence on the basis that the Douglases had forgone any right to confidence because they intended to release photographs of the event to the public had greater force. Despite this, the judge decided that the right to personal confidence weighed more heavily in the balance than *Hello!*'s right to freedom of expression.

In relation to the claim for breach of a right to privacy, the judge rejected the Douglases' claim. Echoing the *Wainwright* decision, he held that there is no right to privacy in English law as such. He said that there was no need for such a right in this case because the Douglases had been protected by the law of confidence.

At a separate hearing, [2004] EMLR 2, the judge awarded *OK!* magazine £1,033,156 mainly for lost sales as a result of the competing *Hello!* edition. He awarded the Douglases £3,750 each for distress arising out of the publication of the unauthorised photographs and a further £7,000 for the expenses that the Douglases incurred dealing with the issues after it became clear that *Hello!* would be publishing unauthorised photographs.

These rulings were significant for the following reasons:

▶ They strengthened the hand of celebrities in controlling the manner in which their images are dealt with and confirmed that their images are exploitable assets. However, the judge was careful to point out that where someone has fostered an image which is not a true one then there can be a public interest in correcting it. The judge also indicated that where someone creates or 'hypes' an event simply for the purposes of attracting publicity that again may be fair game for the media despite attempts to maintain exclusivity.

▶ The judge recognised that in balancing the rights between confidence and freedom of speech, the courts need to have regard to the 'chilling effect' of awards of damages. It is not simply the threat of an injunction that can mean the media might be reluctant to publish.

▶ When assessing the public interest, the judge said that the fact that the public are interested is not to be confused with there being a public interest.

The case was appealed to the Court of Appeal [2005] EMLR 28. They agreed with the judge that the Douglases' wedding was a private occasion which they had the commercial right to exploit if they so wished. So, the fact that they sold the exclusive rights to publish photographs of their wedding to *OK!* magazine did not destroy their rights. Instead it was merely a confirmation that they had rights to sell and which they could protect. In essence, the Douglases had a right just like any other commercial trade secret. However, the Court of Appeal disagreed with the finding of the judge who had awarded *OK!* magazine just over £1 million for the lost profit they suffered due to the publication of photographs by *Hello!* magazine. They ruled that *OK!* could not benefit from the Douglases' privacy rights, which only they had the right to protect. *OK!* appealed this ruling to the House of Lords.

By a 3:2 majority, the House of Lords ruled in favour of *OK!* and upheld their claim for compensation [2007] EMLR 12. Giving the main judgment for the majority in the House of Lords, Lord Hoffman decided that the Douglases had the right to sell the exclusive images of their wedding and that covered any photographs taken at the wedding, not just the authorised ones. He said that the rights that the Douglases sold to *OK!* were just like any other trade secret and both the Douglases and *OK!* were entitled to stop *Hello!* interfering with those rights.

Douglas v Hello! therefore represents a landmark case. Over the course of the six and a half years that it took to conclude the litigation, it has established that:

▶ Celebrities have a right to trade in their fame. The courts consider that there is no difference in this respect between a trade secret held by a commercial organisation and what occurs at a private function held by a celebrity.

▶ In consequence, celebrities have a right to prevent others from interfering with commercial contracts through which they exploit this fame.

▶ Damages are very limited for the distress caused by infringement of privacy. They are measured in thousands of pounds.

▶ However, damages for the interference with commercial arrangements with an authorised publisher could be very substantial.

This case has far-reaching implications for the media. A lot of the media feeds off 'celebrity'. The rulings in *Douglas v Hello!* represent a powerful shift in favour of celebrities in their dealings with the media. The rulings also represent a very great incentive to the media to formalise their relationships with celebrities through 'exclusive' deals in order to protect their position against other publishers.

This right to use private information in a commercial context may appear controversial. However, when viewed against the fact that we have a celebrity industry it seems less so. In modern times it is perhaps uncontroversial to say that 'celebrity' is a tradable asset. If so, then why should the party to whom it is traded (the authorised publisher) not also be entitled to protect it? Giving the leading judgment in the House of Lords, Lord Hoffman said that *OK!* had paid £1 million for the benefit of the obligation of confidence which was imposed on all those attending the wedding in respect of any photographs taken. He said that the obligation of confidence had been imposed for the benefit of both the Douglases and *OK!* and there was no reason to stop *OK!* from relying on that obligation.

However, perhaps more controversial is the finding that these rights survive the publication of authorised photographs. In a dissenting judgment in the House of Lords, Lord Nicholls said that if the basis of the right is the law relating to trade secrets, then once the authorised photographs are published the secret is out and there could be no breach of confidence in publishing the unauthorised photographs thereafter. Lord Hoffman responded by saying that the unauthorised reproduction of authorised photographs would not attract a claim for breach of confidence because that information would already be in the public domain (although a breach of copyright claim would almost certainly arise). However, the publication of any other unauthorised photographs would be a breach of confidence. He said that those unauthorised photographs convey something else of value, otherwise *Hello!* would not have gone to the trouble of paying for them. That something else must be different information. He concluded that this information is a trade secret and it remains so because it has not been published before.

7.13 Testing the balance

The case of *McKennitt and ors v Ash and another* [2006] EWCA Civ 1714 highlights the extent to which the opposing Convention Articles now form the heart of the tort of misuse of private information.

Loreena McKennitt, a famous folk musician, brought a claim for breach of confidence against the defendant for writing a book about her which contained personal and private information, including details about her personal and sexual relationships, her emotional state and matters relating to her health and diet. She applied for an injunction preventing further publication of a significant part of the book and Mr Justice Eady granted it on the basis that the claimant's article 8 rights outweighed the defendant's article 10 rights. The defendant's appeal was unsuccessful. The Court of Appeal said the ECtHR's decision in *Von Hannover v Germany* (59320/00 24 June 2004) extended the reach of article 8 beyond what had previously been understood. In *Von Hannover*, a case relating to the publication of pictures of the Princess of Monaco with her family, the ECtHR said that article 8 is intended to ensure, without interference, an individual's development of his personality in his relations with other people. The Court of Appeal in this case said that it was open to Mr Justice Eady to interpret the term 'reasonable expectation of privacy' in light of the *Von Hannover* principle.

In relation to the article 10 rights, the defendant argued that Mr Justice Eady should have followed the decision of the Court of Appeal in *A v B plc* [2002] EWCA Civ 337, a case relating to publication of details of a Premier League footballer's extra-marital affairs, rather than *Von Hannover*. In *A v B*, the court held that public figures must expect their actions to be more closely scrutinised by the media and that a public figure may hold a position where higher standards of conduct would be expected by the public. This apparently contrasts with the decision in *Von Hannover* on article 10, where the

ECtHR held that a distinction needs to be drawn between reporting facts capable of contributing to debate in a democratic society and reporting details of an individual's private life where they do not exercise official functions. It went on to say that in order for article 10 to apply to the reporting of an individual's private life, there must be special circumstances in play. The two authorities were therefore difficult to reconcile.

The Court of Appeal in *McKennitt* applied the rule in *Von Hannover* in preference to the rule in *A v B*. The rationale for this was that *A v B* did not rule definitively on the content and application of article 10, but instead addressed the balancing exercise in domestic breach of confidence terms. Therefore, *A v B* could not act as a binding authority on the interpretation of the articles 8 and 10 balancing act.

In light of the facts, the Court of Appeal dismissed the defendant's appeal and maintained the grant of the injunction. What is clear from this case is that the jurisprudence of the ECtHR must form part of the interpretation of articles 8 and 10 and that it has become a fundamental part of ruling on the tort of misuse of private information.

7.14   Interim privacy injunctions

The decisions reached by Mr Justice Eady in *Mosley v News Group Newspapers* [2008] EWHC 687; [2008] EWHC 1777 demonstrate how the media can initially avoid the consequences of infringing privacy yet still face sanctions in the end.

The *News of the World* newspaper published an article exposing Max Mosley's liaison with five prostitutes (at the time Mosley was the president of the FIA (Fédération Internationale de l'Automobile)). Not only did the newspaper print the story with accompanying still photographs but it also produced an on-line version of the article. This included edited video highlights showing Mr Mosley engaging in what were described in court by the judge as 'S&M' activities. Mr Mosley challenged the continuing publication of these video highlights. He sought an interim injunction against the *News of the World* banning it from further displaying the material pending a full trial. Mr Justice Eady refused to grant Mr Mosley the interim injunction. The judge found that by the time the application came before him the video had received approximately 1.4 million 'hits' in a period of 24 hours. On this basis the judge said that it would be pointless to ban the *News of the World* from continuing to publish the video given the number of people who had already seen the material and the fact that other websites had now copied it and were making it available as well.

However, Mr Mosley persevered and took his case to a full trial. His arguments were partly based upon existing case law that has consistently found that the display of photographs or videos of people engaging in private acts are particularly intrusive. Modern case law has held that writing about or describing such activities may be a legitimate exercise of the right to freedom of expression which is not trumped by the article 8 privacy right. However, publishing photographic material is often unnecessary and disproportionate to the exercise of that right to freedom of expression, as was held in *Campbell*. A similar decision was reached in *Theakston v MGN Ltd* [2002 EMLR 22]. Here the television presenter, Jamie Theakston, obtained an injunction to stop the publication of still photographs of his activities in a brothel (but not written descriptions of those activities). However, Mr Mosley went further and said that sexual acts carried out on private premises between consenting adults were private and should not be disclosed whether by way of photographs or a written description.

The judge ruled in Mr Mosley's favour and awarded him damages of £60,000 and legal costs reported to be in the region of £500,000. He said that the activities were undoubtedly private in nature. He also found that there were no Nazi overtones to the activities, as alleged by the newspaper, or anything which involved any significant breach of criminal law and so there was no public interest in the publication of the articles or the photographic material.

This appears to leave the slightly odd position that if a publisher gets its material out quickly and effectively to the mass market then the target of the publication is less likely to obtain a speedy injunction to stop it. This seems to encourage greater publication, flooding media channels with the material so that the media's position in fighting off a speedy injunction application is strengthened. The media does then face the prospect of very expensive litigation to a full trial. However, if this case were to be re-run today, the application for an interim injunction might well be decided differently, particularly in light of the rulings in *CTB v Newsgroup Newspapers Ltd* [2011] EWHC 1232, where the widespread naming of a footballer on the social media website Twitter did not lead to the lifting of an injunction preventing the media from reporting his name.

Following his successful breach of confidence claim, Max Moseley took his case to the ECtHR to argue that article 8 required Member States to legislate to prevent newspapers publishing stories about a person's private life without first notifying that individual of the story (*Moseley v UK*, 10 May 2011). Whilst the court was sympathetic to Moseley, it rejected this proposed 'doctrine of notification' and held that the domestic law of the United Kingdom already provided sufficient protection against such newspaper conduct.

7.15 Celebrities' families

In *Murray v Big Pictures (UK) Ltd* [2008] EWCA Civ 446, a photograph of the author J. K. Rowling's one-year-old son was taken and published in the *Sunday Express* newspaper. It showed the boy sitting in his pushchair in an Edinburgh street. His parents, on his behalf, brought a claim for infringement of his privacy. We referred earlier to the ruling of the ECtHR involving Princess Caroline of Monaco where it had found that photographs taken of her in a public place going about her day-to-day activities infringed her privacy (*Von Hanover v Germany* [2004] 40 EHRR 1). So, it might be thought that photographs taken of a child sitting in a pushchair would also be similarly protected. Mr Justice Patten disagreed and he struck out the claim without a trial taking place. However, the Court of Appeal overruled him. They decided that the claim was arguable on privacy grounds and ordered that it should go to a full trial (strongly hinting that the claim would be successful if the claimants could establish all of the facts). In particular, they emphasised that a child might have a higher expectation of privacy in these circumstances than an adult.

The decision gives further guidance on the taking and publication of photographs of celebrities and their families in public places, in particular, on whether the publication of photographs of celebrities undertaking routine acts, like visiting a shop, attracts a reasonable expectation of privacy. The Court of Appeal drew a distinction between merely photographing someone in a public place and then publishing that image to the world at large. The former activity might be lawful, but the latter would have to be scrutinised more carefully.

7.16 Special relationships and confidentiality agreements

Another development in the area of privacy emphasises the importance of entering into non-disclosure agreements. The courts give great weight to pre-existing relationships which have express or implied terms of confidentiality when deciding whether to allow former employees or acquaintances to reveal information about what they have learned in their dealings with their employer or friend.

This was made clear in *Prince of Wales v Associated Newspapers* [2008] Ch 57. The Prince of Wales maintained diaries recording his thoughts on the foreign official visits that he undertook. One such diary related to his visit to Hong Kong during the handover of sovereignty from Britain to China in the summer of 1997. A former employee in Prince Charles' private office copied some of the diaries (including the Hong Kong diary) and provided them to a newspaper, *The Mail on Sunday*. The newspaper published extracts from the diary. The Prince sued the newspaper for breach of confidence.

At first instance, the judge gave summary judgment (without a full trial) to the Prince. The newspaper appealed. The Court of Appeal upheld the judge's decision, but did so primarily on the basis of reasoning that was different from that used by the judge. The judge approached the case on the usual basis weighing up the importance of the right to respect for private life with the right to freedom of expression for the media and others. The judge found in favour of the Prince of Wales on this basis.

The Court of Appeal agreed with the judge's finding for the Prince, but said that the decision should really have rested on a more fundamental point. The former employee, who had handed a copy of the Hong Kong diary to *The Mail on Sunday*, had entered into an express obligation of confidence with the Prince that any information in relation to the Prince that was acquired during the course of her employment was not be disclosed to any unauthorised person. The Court of Appeal said that there is an important public interest in upholding express duties of confidence owed by one person to another. Even if disclosure of information is in the public interest, the Court of Appeal said it also has to weigh up whether it is in the public interest to allow a breach of confidence to occur. The Court of Appeal said that when adding this factor to the judge's reasoning, the Prince's claim against *The Mail on Sunday* became overwhelming. In summary, when looking at a case involving an express obligation of confidence, it is likely to be very difficult to justify publication in breach of that obligation unless the public interest in allowing it is overwhelming.

A similar conclusion was reached by the Court of Appeal in the case of *McKennitt and ors v Ash and another* [2006] EWCA Civ 1714, which we referred to earlier. The Court of Appeal upheld the judge's finding that there was a pre-existing relationship between the parties which imposed an obligation of confidence.

7.17 Business information

In *Browne v Associated Newspapers* [2008] QB 103, the court considered, amongst other things, whether business information could be subject to privacy protection. Lord Browne was the group Chief Executive of British Petroleum. Following the breakdown of their relationship, Lord Browne's former partner disclosed information to *The Mail on Sunday* which included: that Lord Browne had allegedly offered access to BP's resources for his former partner's personal use; the fact of the relationship between the two men;

and the fact that Lord Browne discussed BP's confidential business affairs with his former partner (although not specifically identifying what they were).

Lord Browne applied for an interim injunction to stop publication pending a full trial. One of the main issues was the interpretation of section 12 of the Human Rights Act 1998 which provides that, where issues of freedom of expression are involved, before a court grants an interim injunction it has to be satisfied that the claimant is likely to establish at a full trial that publication should not be allowed. In *Cream Holdings v Banerjee* [2008 1 AC 253], the House of Lords said 'likely' meant 'more likely than not', a higher threshold than the test usually applied to determine whether an interim injunction should be granted, which is whether the applicant has a 'real prospect' of success at trial. The House of Lords also recognised, however, that even if the 'more likely than not' threshold has not been satisfied, there can be reasons why an interim injunction should still be granted, e.g. the adverse consequences of disclosure are very grave, such as where someone's life might be put in danger.

In *Browne*, the court applied the established test, first, addressing whether article 8 is engaged, and second, balancing this with the article 10 rights. Finally, it considered whether the claimant could show that he was more likely than not to succeed at a full trial given that an interim injunction was being sought.

The Court of Appeal refused to restrain the publication of the allegations about use of BP resources. There was no reasonable expectation of privacy in that respect, so article 8 was not engaged and, even if it was, article 10 was likely to trump it such that the claimant could not show that he was more likely than not to succeed at a full trial. As to the fact of discussion of confidential business affairs between Lord Browne and his partner, the Court of Appeal reached the same conclusion. However, it made clear that information could be private and engage article 8 even though it related to business affairs discussed between partners. For example, someone coming home and letting off steam to their partner about what was going on at work might reasonably expect that not to appear in the media. As to the fact of the relationship, the Court of Appeal decided that this needed to be disclosed to put the other matters in context.

7.18 Anonymised and super-injunctions

As part of the growth of the law in the area of privacy, procedural rules have also been devised leading to the use of 'anonymised' and 'super' injunctions. These are both forms of interim injunction which restrict publishing and reporting on various facts relating to the case and the terms of the court orders. In old confidence cases, the reporting of the names of the parties was never a major issue – it was the information itself which needed to be protected. The position has developed in privacy cases as it is often the names of the parties themselves which require protection. The obtaining of an interim injunction to prevent publication of private information would become worthless if the names of the parties to the proceedings were freely reportable.

An anonymised injunction is a form of interim injunction where a person is not permitted to publish information relating to the applicant, or alternatively all the parties. A super-injunction goes further than this in that persons are also not permitted to publicise or inform others about the allegations or the court order itself.

The use of these types of order has been controversial as it is a derogation from the concept of open justice. Open justice is the fundamental and long-standing constitutional principle that judgments should be given in public. Article 6 of the

European Convention on Human Rights also enshrines this principle. However, it is not an absolute principle and article 6 also makes provision for restrictions on open justice for several reasons including 'the protection of the private life of the parties ... or [to] the extent strictly necessary in the opinion of the court in special circumstances where publicity would prejudice the interests of justice'. There have been several instances where such a restriction has been used.

In *RJW v Guardian News and Media Ltd* [2009] EWHC 2540 (QB) (the 'Trafigura' case), the *Guardian* was prevented from reporting not only the name 'Trafigura', but also the very existence of the interim injunction. Another example of a super-injunction was in *Terry v Persons Unknown* [2010] EWHC 119 (QB), where England footballer John Terry was initially granted a super-injunction preventing newspapers from reporting alleged extra-marital affairs. The injunction was rescinded a week later, however, when the court determined that Mr Terry was using the proceedings essentially to protect his commercial interests rather than his and others' rights to privacy.

However, more recent cases have shown a trend towards openness rather than anonymity. In *JIH v News Group Newspapers* [2011] EWCA Civ 42, the court set out a number of factors which must be considered prior to the grant of an anonymity order. These include a requirement for close scrutiny of the application and a consideration of whether there is a more acceptable alternative which can be employed to protect the efficacy of the order but still allow a degree of openness. The court also held that an order providing for anonymity could not be made by consent of the parties as the parties could not waive the public's right to open justice.

The *Report of the Committee on Super-Injunctions*, commissioned following public interest in the matter, states that such derogations from open justice may only be used 'where, and to the extent that, they are strictly necessary in order to secure the proper administration of justice'.

Summary

- ▶ The law of confidence can be used to impose secrecy in a variety of relationships.

- ▶ The basic requirements for a successful action are to be found in Megarry J's judgment in *Coco v Clark*.

- ▶ To be protected, the information must be of a confidential nature. In other words, it must not have reached the public domain unless the 'springboard' doctrine applies. The court will also consider whether it is in the public interest that the information is disclosed.

- ▶ The obligation of confidence may arise from a number of relationships from contractual to relationships of trust and confidence.

- ▶ Use of the information must be unauthorised but it is questionable whether use must be detrimental to the claimant.

- ▶ The normal intellectual property remedies apply to breach of confidence actions.

- ▶ The law of confidence has been reinforced to some extent by the Human Rights Act 1998.

Further reading and references

Brazell, 'Confidence, Privacy and Human Rights, English Law in the 21st Century' [2005] EIPR 27(11), 405.

Foster, 'The Public Interest in Press Intrusion into the Private Lives of Celebrities: The Decision in Ferdinand V MGN Ltd,' Comms L 2011, 16(4), 129.

Holyoak and Torremans, *Intellectual Property Law* (4th edn, Oxford University Press, 2005).

Hunt, 'Rethinking Surreptitious Takings in the Law of Confidence' IPQ 2011, 1, 66.

Singer and Scott, 'The 21st Century Journalist' [2006] Ent LR 17(2), 55.

Part II

Trade marks and passing off

Chapter 8

Trade marks

8.1 Introduction

The following chapters are concerned with trade names and devices which have been registered under the Trade Marks Act 1938 or the Trade Marks Act 1994. Unregistered trade names and devices might be protected by means of a common law action for the tort of passing off and, in some cases, by copyright.

The Trade Marks Act 1994 harmonised the trade mark law of the UK with that of the rest of the European Union and implemented the First Council Directive (89/104/EEC) to approximate the laws of the Member States relating to trade marks. The government used the new Act as an opportunity to bring the law in this area up to date with current business practices.

8.2 What is a trade mark?

A trade mark can be described as a sign or symbol placed on, or used in relation to, one trader's goods or services to distinguish them from similar goods or services supplied by other traders. Section 1 of the Trade Marks Act 1994 defines a trade mark as any sign capable of being represented graphically which distinguishes the goods or services of one business from those of another.

The 1938 definition of a trade mark did not provide adequately for the registration of shapes of goods or their packaging, even though shape is as good an identifier of one trader's goods as any other type of trade mark. This was illustrated in *Coca-Cola Trade Mark Applications* [1986] 2 All ER 274 in which Coca-Cola filed an application to register the shape of the distinctive Coca-Cola bottle as a trade mark. Coca-Cola's application failed because, the Registrar said, it was trying to register 'the thing itself' as a trade mark. The Registrar and the court took the view that the definition of a trade mark in the 1938 Act required the mark to be 'something distinct from the thing marked'. The House of Lords was also concerned that by granting a trade mark in respect of the bottle itself, it would be allowing an undesirable monopoly in containers to develop.

The 1994 Act allows for the registration of words, designs, letters, numerals and the shape of goods or their packaging. In theory it is even possible for sounds and smells to be registered, although in practice this has proved difficult for applicants.

8.3 Possible functions of trade marks

A trade mark may satisfy a number of functions. Its main function is indicated in the definition given above, namely, to differentiate one trader's goods or services from those of another. As mass production and self-service in the wholesale and retail markets have replaced limited product ranges and personal service, the trade mark allows the consumer to distinguish between similar products.

A good trade mark can be an essential tool for selling goods. As such, it is invaluable to the producer. In a market swamped by competing goods, the trade mark is a shorthand description for the product. Without a trade mark it would be necessary, each time a purchase is contemplated, to compare products by reference to ingredients, function and consumer experiences, which would be very long-winded. The trade mark is useful to the consumer as she will choose goods based on personal or vicarious experiences of a product and the trade mark allows easy identification of the product which previously gave satisfaction, thus leading to repeat purchases. This leads to another possible function of the trade mark: its guarantee function. Once a customer has tried a product with a particular name and found it satisfactory, repeat purchases of goods bearing that name will guarantee repetition of that satisfaction.

Equally, where a consumer has had a bad experience with a product, the trade mark can act as a warning against further purchases. Traders thus have an interest in protecting the good name of their mark by only attaching it to quality goods. Provided that the mark is imbued with this good reputation, the trader can use it to increase and generate sales by investing in promotions and advertising, and by using the mark.

The European Court of Justice (ECJ), in *SA CNL-Sucal v Hag GF AG* [1990] 3 CMLR 571, 608, at paragraphs 13 and 14, described the essential function of a trade mark as giving the consumer or the ultimate user 'a guarantee of the identity of the origin of the marked product by enabling him to distinguish, without any possible confusion, that product from others of a different provenance'.

In *Philips Electronics NV v Remington Consumer Products* [1999] RPC 809, the Court of Appeal stated:

> The function of a trade mark is to identify the trade origin of goods and services. That function is important to protect both traders and consumers. It is a requirement of a trade mark under European law just as much as it has been under UK law (at 815).

Thus in legal terms the main function of a trade mark is to identify the source of the goods and services to which it is attached; according to Lord Nicholls, in *Scandecor Developments AB v Scandecor Marketing AV & ors* [2001] UKHL 21, at paragraph 16, it is a 'badge of origin'. His Lordship elaborated further in paras 18 and 19. Use of the trade mark would encourage producers of the goods or services to which they are attached to set and maintain quality standards. Consumers would then rely on the quality of goods not because there is a legal guarantee of quality but rather because 'the proprietor has an economic interest in maintaining the value of his mark'. The guarantee of origin function was confirmed by the ECJ in Case C-206/01, *Arsenal Football Club v Reed* [2002] ECR I-10273. In *Interflora Inc v Marks & Spencer plc* (C-323/09), the Court of Justice (ECJ), identified three functions: the origin function, namely that the goods and services originate from the proprietor of the mark or an undertaking economically connected to it; an advertising function; and finally an investment function to acquire or preserve a reputation capable of attracting customers and retaining their loyalty.

8.4 Historical background

From the earliest times, traders have distinguished their goods by marking them. According to the Mathys Committee Report 1974, goods have been marked in various ways since Greek and Roman times. By the nineteenth century it was clear that marks applied to goods that had become distinctive had an intrinsic value and were worthy of some form of legal protection. Such protection was available through the use of Royal Charters and court action.

Protection from the courts came through two forms of action. First, a manufacturer could seek an injunction and damages against another person who was passing off his goods as those of the manufacturer. The basis for such an action was the plaintiff's reputation acquired by use of the mark. The second form of action was for infringement of a trade mark, an action developed by the courts of Chancery, which viewed the trade mark as a form of property. The main difficulties with this second form of action were that each time the plaintiff had to prove title to the mark the court had to resolve the problem of what exactly constituted a trade mark.

The Trade Marks Registration Act 1875 was passed to overcome the difficulties encountered in such infringement actions. The Act established a statutory Register of trade marks that is still in use today. The Register provides the trade mark owner with evidence of legal title to, and exclusive rights of use of, the trade mark for the goods in respect of which it is registered. Entry of a mark on the Register is prima facie evidence that the proprietor has property in the mark and is entitled to prevent its unauthorised use by third parties. The Act of 1875 also laid down the essentials of a trade mark, giving practitioners and the courts the criteria for determining what could legally amount to a trade mark and, therefore, benefit from registration.

There then followed a number of repealing and amending Acts including the Patents, Designs and Trade Marks Act 1883, the Trade Marks Act 1905 and the Trade Marks Act 1919. Each Act moved the law relating to the registration of trade marks forward in line with changes in commercial practice, culminating in the 1938 Trade Marks Act. Apart from amendments made by the Trade Marks (Amendment) Act 1984 (which introduced the registration of service marks – trade marks used in relation to services rather than goods) and the Copyright, Designs and Patents Act 1988 (which made forgery of a trade mark a criminal offence), the 1938 Act governed trade mark law in the UK for nearly 60 years – until the Trade Marks Act 1994 came into force.

8.5   Background to the Trade Marks Act 1994

The need to reform trade mark law had been perceived in the UK for some time. In 1972, the Mathys Committee met to examine the state of British trade mark law and practice. Its report of 1974 made a number of recommendations for amending the law, but apart from the introduction of registration for service marks as a result of the Trade Marks (Amendment) Act 1984, none of these recommendations was implemented.

Certain aspects of the Trade Marks Act 1938 led to a great deal of judicial frustration. The Act lacked clarity for interpretation purposes and it failed to cater for modern commercial activities, such as character merchandising (as illustrated by the Holly Hobbie case, discussed below). The impetus for change to trade mark law in the UK finally came from the EC and the international stage.

In December 1988, the Council of the EC adopted EC Directive 89/104/EEC, which aimed to harmonise, as far as possible, trade mark law throughout the EC. While leaving individual Member States to determine certain procedural details of application, revocation and infringement proceedings, the Directive sought to harmonise the criteria for registrability and to minimise any differences in law between Member States which might affect the free movement of goods. The Directive prescribes what can and cannot be registered as a trade mark, the extent of the trade mark right, certain mandatory grounds for revocation and the means of licensing trade marks. It also confirms the obligation to use a trade mark to avoid cancellation of the mark.

In December 1993, the Council also adopted Commission Regulation 40/94/EEC, which was aimed at the creation of a Community Trade Mark, a single trade mark which would apply throughout the EC. Meanwhile, there was also pressure on the international stage for the UK to ratify the Protocol to the Madrid Agreement and various provisions of the Paris Convention. While legislating to enable the UK to fulfil its obligations under EC law (that is, to implement Council Directive 89/104/EEC) and various international conventions, the government identified other areas in need of reform. It recognised, for example, that statutory amendments to the 1938 Act, and case law on that Act, had made the legislation complicated to interpret and administer. Another specific problem with the 1938 Act, which had resulted in many commercially contradictory decisions, was the definition of a trade mark (under s 68), which limited the scope of what could amount to a trade mark. Distinctive shapes, smells and sounds could not be registered, while in other cases trade marks comprising distinctive colour combinations were allowed. The 1994 Act neither specifically allows nor excludes the registration of marks consisting of shapes, smells or sounds, but allows for a trade mark to be any sign that is capable of being represented graphically, and that distinguishes the goods or services of one undertaking from those of another. It goes on to state that a trade mark may consist of words (including personal names), designs, letters, numerals or (subject to a few limitations) the shape of goods or their packaging. This places the onus on a trader to convince the Registrar that the subject of the application can function as a trade mark, without placing any technical barriers in the way once that has been proved.

The Trade Marks Act 1938 also failed to cater for a number of common business practices. For example, under section 3, registration of a mark had to be for particular goods within one of the 42 internationally standard classes of goods. This meant that a trader wanting to register a mark in respect of goods falling within several classes had to file a separate application for each class, which was inconvenient and expensive. It is now possible to make a single application to cover goods and services in several classes at a reduced cost. So a mark can be registered to cover, say, drinks (Class 32) and sweets (Class 30) without the need for two separate applications. There is a small additional cost for each additional class.

Additionally, section 28(6) of the 1938 Act was a particular irritant for those engaged in the practice of licensing fictional characters and celebrities, as it stated that:

> The Registrar shall refuse an application ... if it appears to him that the grant thereof would tend to facilitate trafficking in a trade mark.

The full effect of this provision was felt in *American Greetings Corp's Application* [1984] RPC 329 (known as the 'Holly Hobbie' case). The applicants were an American greetings card company, wanting to register 'Holly Hobbie', a mark comprising a drawing of a little girl called Holly Hobbie in a distinctive dress. The applicants' intention was to license others to use the mark on various items, including stationery and bedding, and with that intention they filed applications in numerous classes. Registration was refused on a number of grounds, but in particular because of section 28(6). The House of Lords upheld the Registrar's refusal to register, holding that the applicants were attempting to deal in the trade mark as a commodity in its own right and not for the purpose of identifying or promoting merchandise in which they were interested. The feelings of the business community and practitioners at that time were best summed up by Lord Bridge, who said:

> though I can find no escape from s.28(6) of the Act of 1938, I do not hesitate to express my opinion that it has become a complete anachronism and that the sooner it is repealed the better.

Section 28(6) has been repealed by the 1994 Trade Marks Act.

A further change introduced by the 1994 Act relates to the Register itself. Since 1919, the Trade Marks Register has been divided into two parts, Part A and Part B. To be registered in Part A a mark had to be 'adapted to distinguish' the applicant's goods or services, while for Part B it was sufficient that it be, or had become, 'capable of distinguishing' the goods or services, for instance, as a result of long use. The criteria for registration in Part B were less onerous but offered less protection against infringement. A great deal of time was spent in considering whether a mark should be registered in Part A or Part B of the Register. The 1994 Act has resulted in the two parts being combined into a single Register with the same requirements of distinctiveness and the same level of protection.

8.6 The international trade mark system

8.6.1 Introduction

Trade marks, like all other intellectual property rights, are national rights. This means that a trade mark, once registered, only offers protection against unauthorised use by third parties within the country of registration. Unlike copyright, there is no automatic extension of a national trade mark to other countries.

There are, however, a number of international conventions and arrangements that give some international recognition to national trade marks. These are the Paris Convention, the Madrid Agreement and the Protocol to the Madrid Agreement (commonly known as the Madrid Protocol). There is also a Community Trade Marks System that creates a trade mark that gives rights throughout the European Union (EU).

8.6.2 Paris Convention

The Paris Convention was established in 1883 to create some interaction and recognition between various countries of each other's national intellectual property rights. For all intellectual property rights of a registerable nature, this was achieved by the concept of priority.

Priority recognises the first filing date for a particular intellectual property right in any Convention country as the filing date for all other filings in any Convention country in respect of the same intellectual property right by the same proprietor made during the priority period. The period of priority differs from intellectual property right to intellectual property right, but in the case of trade marks the period is six months. This has given a level of international protection for trade marks, because the first to file a trade mark application is, in most countries, the person with the better claim to a trade mark.

This is not the case in the UK, because rights in passing off can be built up through sufficient use of a trade mark without registration, and those rights can act as an obstacle to any subsequent application to register the trade mark by a third party.

Another provision of the Paris Convention relevant to trade marks is article 6bis, which gives international protection to 'well-known' trade marks. A person can own a 'well-known' mark in registered or unregistered form even in countries where the action of passing off does not exist. Ownership of a well-known mark will prevent a third party from applying to register the same or a very similar mark in any other Convention country that has implemented article 6bis into its national laws and allows cancellation of an existing registration for such an identical or similar mark during the first five years after registration on the application of the owner of the well-known mark to the relevant authority.

This international recognition of national trade marks is of limited application because it only applies to trade marks that have become 'well-known' in other Convention countries. The Paris Convention gives no definition of the phrase 'well-known' and therefore countries of the Paris Union have devised their own guidelines from case law. The World Intellectual Property Organization (WIPO) has commented that this is unsatisfactory for a provision having international effect.

8.6.3   Madrid Agreement

In 1891, the Madrid Agreement was implemented to simplify the procedure for filing trade mark registrations in many countries. Up until that point, anyone wanting to obtain trade mark registrations in, say, ten countries, had to file ten separate applications at the ten separate national trade mark registries in accordance with the ten different procedural requirements.

The Madrid Agreement allows anyone established or domiciled in a Madrid Agreement country, with a trade mark registration in his or her country of establishment or domicile, to file one international application which can be extended to one or more other Madrid Agreement countries as specified. The central international application is filed with WIPO in Geneva, designating to which countries it is to be extended. WIPO then takes responsibility for passing the application on to each of the designated national registries, where the application proceeds according to the national laws and procedures of each country.

The UK did not sign the Madrid Agreement because the procedures that the Trade Marks Registry would have had to apply in dealing with Madrid Agreement applications are in conflict with the established procedures used by the Trade Marks Registry. This method of filing registrations is therefore not available to anyone who is established or domiciled only in the UK (or only in countries that are also not party to the Madrid Agreement).

8.6.4   Madrid Protocol

As a number of key countries (for example, the UK, the United States, Canada, South Africa) had been unwilling to sign the Madrid Agreement, discussions began in the mid-1980s (around the time of the discussions on general harmonisation of trade mark laws in the EC) on how to make the Madrid Agreement system more palatable. The result was the Protocol to the Madrid Arrangement which was adopted in 1989.

The Protocol is based on essentially the same structure as the Madrid Agreement. It is open to anyone with a pending application in a Protocol country which is their home country. This is the first advantage of the Protocol system over the Madrid Agreement system – namely, the possibility of filing an application and immediately filing a Protocol application with WIPO to extend the protection to designated Protocol countries. The other differences, which have led to the UK signing up, are that:

(1) the examination period can be extended at each country's choice to 18 months; and
(2) although central attack still applies, all cancelled applications/registrations can be re-filed nationally with the same priority date as the original Protocol application.

8.6.5 Community Trade Mark system

A Community Trade Mark (CTM) is a registration for a single trade mark that is valid in all of the countries of the EU.

The CTM is legislated for in Council Regulation 40/94, with amendments from Council Regulation 422/2004 and Commission Regulation 1042/2005. Each Member State is required to implement the Regulations into national law. An application can be filed direct with the Office for the Harmonisation of the Internal Market (Trade Marks and Designs) (OHIM) in Alicante, Spain, or at the national trade mark office in any EC country which will pass the application to the Community Trade Mark Office.

Once filed, the application will be examined to make sure that it meets all the basic conditions of registrability. These conditions will be similar to those applied in most of the national trade mark offices of the EU. Appeals against a refusal to register can be made to one of the Boards of Appeal. From there, further appeals on the interpretation of the Regulation will go to the General Court (formerly the European Court of First Instance), and ultimately to the Court of Justice of the European Union (ECJ).

8.6.6 The Agreement on Trade Related Aspects of Intellectual Property Rights 1994 (TRIPS)

This sets out requirements for trade mark registration and protection that are similar to those found in the legislation of the UK and the EU. Section 2, articles 15–21 of the Agreement deal with trademarks. Although the TRIPS Agreement cannot be said to have direct effect, it was confirmed in Case C-245/02 *Anheuser-Busch Inc v Bude˘jovi-cky Budvar Narodni Podnik* [2000] RPC 906 that since the EU is a party to the Agreement, it is under an obligation to interpret trade mark legislation, so far as possible in the light of the wording of the Agreement (para 42).

8.7 Conclusion

International obligations and the desire to administer trade mark law more efficiently, taking account of current trade practice and the decisions in numerous trade mark cases, finally led to the enactment of the Trade Marks Act 1994. The Act was brought into force by statutory instrument on 31 October 1994 and applies to all trade marks registered under the 1938 and 1984 Acts. In the following chapters we look at the registration, protection and enforcement of trade marks under the 1994 Act.

Summary

▶ A trade mark is a sign distinguishing the goods and services of one trader from those of another.

▶ If consumers are able to identify goods by reference to a trade mark, this will allow for repeat purchases and, equally, avoidance of low-quality products. In this way trade marks can be seen to add value to the goods and services to which they are applied.

▶ The 1994 Trade Marks Act has resulted from the EC Directive on harmonisation of trade mark laws and the needs of modern commerce, and has also enabled the UK to ratify the Madrid Protocol and to implement the Community Trade Mark registration system.

▶ The CTM is aimed at consolidating the single market from a trade mark perspective. The unitary nature of the right is intended to support the free movement of goods doctrine and is intended to work against the creation of national borders.

Chapter 9

Registration of trade marks

9.1 Introduction

The scope of what can be registered as a trade mark would appear to be quite broad. The definition of a trade mark is not limited to being in any particular form, as long as it can be graphically represented and as long as it functions as a trade mark.

The producer of the goods or services to which the mark will be applied, or the person who designed the mark, can apply to register by virtue of section 32. Section 23 recognises joint ownership and section 30 recognises the interests of licensees. Licensees can also sue for infringement if their interests have been registered under section 25. For the first time, the interests of a mortgagee in a trade mark are recognised, with the possibility under section 25 of registering security interests on the Register.

9.2 The application process

Section 32 requires the following documents for registration of a trade mark:

(a) request for registration;
(b) information about the identity and address of the applicant;
(c) a statement about the goods and/or services in respect of which the mark is being registered;
(d) a graphic representation of the mark;
(e) payment of the appropriate fees (although payment can be delayed);
(f) a statement from the applicant that she is using the trade mark, or that it is being used with her permission, in relation to goods or services, or that she has a bona fide intention to do so.

Once the application is received at the Trade Marks Registry, it will be examined as required by section 37 to make sure that the rules and requirements of the legislation have been satisfied. If it is accepted, it will be published in the *Trade Marks Journal* (s 38), so that interested parties have the opportunity to oppose the trade mark within a specified period (three months from the date of publication).

If no opposition is filed, or an opposition is unsuccessful, the mark will be registered under section 40.

Each separate trade mark must be the subject of a separate application. Applications can be filed for a series of marks if they are sufficiently similar so as not to be considered as different marks by the Registrar.

Under the 1938 Act it used to be possible to associate marks that were similar or identical and that were registered for similar goods and/or services. Associated marks were useful, as use of one associated mark counted as use of all other associated marks (for the purposes of non-use challenges). The disadvantage was that once associated, such marks had to be held by the same owner, unless special procedures were followed. The 1994 Act does not provide for association of marks.

9.3 What is a registrable trade mark?

Section 1(1) defines a trade mark as:

> any sign capable of being represented graphically which is capable of distinguishing goods or services of one undertaking from those of another.

Under the 1938 Act, before a trade mark could be registered in Part A, it had to consist of or contain one of the 'essential particulars' listed in section 9. These particulars were names, signatures, invented words, words having no direct reference to the goods or services in question and any other distinctive mark. This more restrictive definition was seen not to admit trade marks which consisted purely of shape, sound or smell.

Section 9 of the 1938 Act also expressly prohibited the registration of geographical names and surnames. Names that were words in ordinary usage as well as being, coincidentally, geographical names could be registered (if they passed all other registrability tests). Surnames were held unregistrable in Part A of the Register if they appeared more than twice in the English telephone directory and unregistrable in Part B if they appeared more than five times in the English telephone directory. This Registry practice for determining whether a surname was common or not was strictly adhered to by the Registry. It is obvious that this test had its limitations – a truly 'common' surname could be registered if people with that name did not possess telephones or were ex-directory. This practice, which has survived the Act of 1994, has been criticised by the European Court of Justice (ECJ) in *Nichols plc v Registrar of Trade Marks* (Case C-404/02) [2005] RPC 12.

The position has changed under the 1994 Act because the absolute bar on geographical names and other names indicating type, origin and so on (s 3(1)(c)) is subject to a proviso if the name has acquired a secondary meaning.

9.3.1 So what is included?

9.3.1(a) Colours

Whilst a colour can be registered as a trade mark, registration is not straightforward. As well as the ability to distinguish, there is the question of whether a colour can be represented graphically as required by section 1(1). This has been the subject of debate for both national and Community Trade Mark (CTM) officials. According to Charlotte Schulze:

> Unless a colour mark is clearly defined, it is impossible to assess the exact scope of protection, i.e. the degree of monopoly use of a colour or colours (2003: 55–67).

In Case R7/97–3, *Orange Personal Communications Ltd's Application* [1998] ETMR 460, the mark was simply described by the applicant as 'orange'. This was judged as not sufficiently precise to be a representation of a colour. The Third Board of Appeal of the Community Trade Mark Office observed that:

> An uncountable number of different colour shades, ranging in the specific case from dark to light and from the yellowish to the reddish tones, are conceivable which would fall under the wide generic term 'orange'.

On its own, the mark as represented was vague and did not provide enough information to tell others what the mark to be protected actually was.

There is also a need for interested parties to be able to determine what is actually being protected, without having to engage in a complicated exercise to find out what the trade mark is.

On the other hand, an application could fail where the information is so detailed that it could leave interested parties confused as to what the mark actually is.

In *Ty Nant Spring Water Ltd's Application* [2000] RPC 55, the applicant applied to register a trade mark for a selection of bottled waters. The application defined the trade mark in terms of characteristic optical properties represented in the following terms:

> A blue bottle of optical characteristics, such that if the wall thickness is 3 mm the bottle has, in air, a dominant wavelength of 472 to 474 nanometres, a purity of 44 to 48%, an optical brightness of 28 to 32%.

The sign in question consisted of a blue bottle of any shape or size made from any material which would, if the wall thickness of the bottle was adjusted to 3 mm, be found to produce readings within the ranges specified when its ability to absorb and reflect white light was measured with the aid of a spectrophotometer. The colour presented to the eye by light radiating within the ranges specified is known as cobalt blue.

A number of problems were identified with the application, in particular the fact that those reading the application would need to take further steps, such as using a spectrophotometer to obtain the necessary readings to determine whether a bottle was of a particular hue. The representation had not mentioned the colour cobalt blue, nor had it included a graphic example of the relevant colour. To overcome the problem of graphic representation for colours, David Bainbridge (2002: 642–3), suggests two possibilities. The first is to include the colour or colours as a sample, the second is to use a well-known referencing system such as the Pantone system. Where a sample is used, the applicant must ensure that it matches the colour described. See *Calor Gas (Northern Ireland)Ltd's Application*, No 2154261 (Lawtel 16 January 2007), where the colour was described as yellow but the sample supplied was orange.

Following the decision in Case C-273/00, *Ralf Sieckmann v Deutsches Patent-und Markenaml* [2002] ECR I-11737 (discussed later), an unconventional sign can be registered if it is 'clear, precise, self-contained, easily accessible, intelligible, durable and objective'.

A single colour sign will also have the problem of establishing distinctiveness as required under section 3.although the proprietor of the sign in question can meet this hurdle if it has acquired distinctiveness through use. This was the case in *Application by Cadbury Ltd to Regsiter a Shade of the Colour Purple for Goods in Class 30; Opposition by Société des Produits Nestlé SA, 0–358–11, 20 October 2011.*

9.3.1(b) Slogans

Applications to register slogans do not encounter the same difficulties as those concerning other non-traditional marks, since the graphic representation requirement can easily be satisfied. There is, however, still the issue of whether slogans can function as trade marks in the sense that consumers can distinguish the goods or services to which they are applied. There is also the need to ensure that a monopoly is not gained in phrases that other legitimate traders would want to use. So in *Fieldturf v Office for Harmonisation in the Internal Market (OHIM)* T.216/02, the Court of First Instance (CFI) upheld the refusal to register the phrase 'looks like grass … feels like grass … plays like grass' for synthetic lawns and related services. (See also T.281/02, *Mehrfürlhr Geld*, 'more for your money'.) However, lack of imagination in the slogan selected does not necessarily amount to lack of distinctiveness (see Case C-64/02P, *OHIM v ErpoMöbelwerk GmbH*). In Case C-353/03, *Société des Produits Nestlé SA v Mars (UK)Ltd*, the main issue was whether Nestlé could register the words 'Have a break' as a trade mark without the rest of the well-known phrase used in its advertising. The ECJ had to consider whether that part of the phrase had acquired distinctive character. In Advocate General Kokott's opinion, the reflex reaction from relevant consumers ('… have a KitKat') would not be sufficient (see para 34). The court agreed with this but went on to hold, taking into account the factors it had identified in *Windsurfing Chiemsee Produktions v Huber* [1999] ETMR 585 (*Windsurfing Cheimsee*) on acquired distinctiveness, that such a mark may acquire distinctiveness through the use made of it (see Section 9.5).

9.3.1(c)   Shapes

Before 1994, the registration of shapes was hampered by a statement of Lindley LJ in *James v Soulby* [1886] 33 Ch D 392:

> A mark must be something distinct from the thing marked. A mark itself cannot be a mark of itself.

Coca-Cola Trade Mark Applications [1986] 2 All ER 274 concerned an application to register the famous Coca-Cola bottle as a trade mark. The House of Lords held that the legislation was there to protect marks, and not the article marked. The mark should distinguish the goods rather than be the goods themselves. Lord Templeman was concerned about granting a monopoly in respect of containers. He felt that rival manufacturers should be free to use any container of a similar shape provided it was labelled and packaged differently. This was an interesting conclusion, given that Coca-Cola would undoubtedly have had good grounds for an action in passing off if anyone else had used a bottle of the same shape. This is confirmed by the House of Lords' decision in *Reckitt & Colman Products Ltd v Borden Inc (No 3)* [1990] 1 All ER 873, which we shall discuss in Chapter 11.

The decision in Coca-Cola has effectively been overruled by the second part of section 1(1), which states:

> A trade mark may, in particular, consist of words … designs, letters, numerals or the shape of goods or their packaging.

The Trade Marks Registry has now accepted the shape of the Coca-Cola bottle as a trade mark. It has also accepted many other containers, and even the shape of a peppermill, as trade marks. It is questionable whether all of these shapes do, in fact, function as trade marks – but, for now, they are getting onto the Register. However, not all shapes will be registrable. Section 3(2) states that a sign will not be registered if it consists exclusively of the shape that gives substantial value to the goods or is necessary to obtain a technical result. It also prohibits the registration of shapes which result from the nature of the goods themselves. In *Procter & Gamble Co's TM Application* [1998] RPC 710 to register a three-dimensional mark for soap, the Registry gave some helpful statements in relation to the registrability of shape marks. The Hearing Officer in that case said that a shape was only likely to be held as functioning as a trade mark if 'the shape in question immediately strikes the eye as different and therefore memorable' and that if a shape was held by the public to be serving a functional purpose, operating as a convenience feature or having a purely decorative or aesthetic purpose, then it would be 'unlikely to be regarded as performing a trade mark function'. See also *SwizzelMatlows Three Dimensional Trade Mark Application* [1999] RPC 879 (love heart sweets) and *Bongrain SA's Trade Mark Application* [2005] RPC 306 (shape applied to cheese).

9.3.1(d) Sounds and smells

These are potentially registrable, but the question is: how will they satisfy the condition that they should be represented graphically? It has been suggested that an application could include musical notation for sounds and a chemical equation for smells. However, will this allow interested parties to know what the trade mark is? A suggested method of representing an olfactory mark is to describe it. However, the description should provide information which is so clear and precise that anyone reading it has 'an immediate and unambiguous idea of what the mark is' when used in connection with the goods or services to which it is applied. This certainly appears to be the approach taken by the Office for the Harmonisation of the Internal Market (formerly the Community Trade Marks Office).

The case of *Venootsschaponder Firma Senta Aromatic Marketing's Application* [1999] ETMR 429 concerned an application to register 'the smell of fresh cut grass' to tennis balls. In considering whether the application complied with article 4 of the Community Trade Mark Regulation (equivalent to 1994 Act, s 1(1)), the Second Board of Appeal of the Community Trade Marks Office made the following observations:

> The question then arises whether or not this description gives clear enough information to those reading it to walk away with an immediate and unambiguous idea of what the mark is when used in connection with tennis balls.

> The smell of freshly cut grass is a distinct smell, which everyone immediately recognises from experience. For many, the scent or fragrance of freshly cut grass reminds them of spring, or summer, manicured lawns or playing fields, or other such pleasant experiences.

> The Board is satisfied that the description provided for the olfactory mark sought to be registered for tennis balls is appropriate and complies with the graphical representation requirement of Article 4 of the CTMR.

This now has to be considered in light of the ECJ's decision in Case C-273/00, *Ralf Sieckmann v Deutsches Patent- und Markenamt* [2002] ECR I-11737, which was that although a trade mark can consist of a sign which is not of itself capable of being perceived visually, a smell could not be registered as a trade mark by means of a chemical formula, a description in words or the deposit of an odour sample (para 73). The applicant had applied to register an olfactory mark at the German Patent and Trade Mark Office. The application contained a chemical formula and was accompanied by an odour sample of the scent. It was also described as 'balsamically fruity with a slight hint of cinnamon'. The court accepted the submission from the UK and the EC Commission that a chemical formula does not represent the odour of a substance, but the substance as such, and nor is it 'sufficiently precise' (at [69]). While the description was 'graphic', it was not sufficiently 'clear, precise and objective' (at [70]). The deposit of a sample did not constitute a graphic representation. In what are now referred to as the '*Sieckmann* criteria', non-visual marks will have to be 'clear, precise, self-contained, easily accessible, intelligible, durable and objective'.

It will be difficult to register olfactory marks on the basis of the above decision. Clearly samples and chemical formulae are unacceptable. Owners of such marks will have to find a way to describe the scent in a way which satisfies the above criteria.

The Registry issued a practice notice on sound marks in the *Trade Marks Journal*, giving examples of musical notations which have been accepted (prima facie) and also specifying the following examples as not acceptable without further evidence of factual distinctiveness: children's nursery rhymes for children's goods or services, national anthems, songs commonly used as chimes for ice-cream vans such as 'Greensleeves'). In Case C-283/01, *Shield Mark BV v Joost Kist* (Trading as Memex) (Case C-283/01) [2004] RPC 315, the ECJ stated that sounds could be registered if the *Sieckmann*criteria are met. Further for CTMs, Regulation3(6) has been added to the Regulation that implements the Community Trade Mark (2868/95). This allows the filing of sound files in an electronic CTM application together with a graphic representation. In *Metro-Goldwyn-Meyer Lion Corp's Application* R781/1999–4 [2004] ETMR 34, it was stated that the roar of a lion was registrable in principle if supported by a suitable spectrogram. Case R708/2006–4 *Edgar Rice Burroughs Inc v OHIM* (27 September 2007), concerned an application to register the sound of Tarzan's jungle yodel as a CTM. The relevant part of the application stated:

> The mark consists of the yell of the fictional character TARZAN, the yell consisting of five distinct phases, namely sustain, followed by ululation, followed by sustain, but at a higher frequency, followed by ululation, followed by sustain at the starting frequency …

Although the mark was ultimately rejected, the OHIM issued a press release in November 2007, indicating that the yell was already registered as a mark following a second application which combined a spectrogram and an MP3 sound file.

It is suggested that now that the *Trade Marks Journal* in the UK is available in electronic form, it should be possible to file a sound in digital form so that it can be played by accessing the file by computer.

9.4 Conditions for registration

These are the matters which the Examiner will consider under section 37. Section 1(1) establishes two basic conditions for registrability. The mark must be:

(1) capable of being represented graphically; and
(2) capable of distinguishing one trader's products from those of others.

9.4.1 Graphic representation

The objective here is to make it possible for interested parties to judge the monopoly given. Bentley and Sherman (2002: 770) identify three main functions of the graphic representation requirement. These are the property function, to determine exactly what sign is protected; the administrative function, to assist the trade mark authorities in dealing with the sign; and the information or publicity function, where third parties can search the *Trade Marks Journal* not only to be aware of the trade mark owners' rights but also to determine whether a fresh application conflicts with earlier marks. As stated above, the *Sieckmann*criteria will also apply. Words and symbols will pose no problems and a two-dimensional drawing can represent a three-dimensional shape. However, as highlighted earlier, there are some interesting cases for sounds and smells.

9.4.2 Capable of distinguishing

Under previous law, to obtain superior trade mark protection under Part A of the Register, the mark had to be inherently distinctive. That is to say, it had to convey no meaning to the consumer except in the context of the applicant's goods or services, for example, an invented word like KODAK.

Lesser protection through registration in Part B of the Register was granted to trade marks which were 'factually distinctive'. These could be common words or symbols which had been used so extensively by the applicant that consumers recognised the sign as identifying the applicant's goods or services. However, strict judicial interpretation led to situations where even proof of factual distinctiveness failed to provide applicants with even the basic protection provided by Part B registrations. In *York Trailer Holdings v Registrar of Trade Marks* [1982] 1 All ER 257, the applicant tried to register a mark which consisted of the word 'YORK' in white block capital letters on a black rectangular background with a maple leaf drawn inside the letter 'O'. There was evidence to show that the applicant's use in this way was distinctive of their products. There would have been a strong case in passing off, if others had used the mark. Nevertheless, the House of Lords refused the application. 'Capable of distinguishing', in their view, meant 'capable in law'. In other words, the House of Lords were looking for inherent distinctiveness.

Contrast this with the attitude of the Irish judges in *Waterford Trade Mark* [1984] FSR 390, who were satisfied that the extensive use of 'Waterford' on crystal had made it 'capable of distinguishing' and allowed the registration.

Section 3(1)(c) of the 1994 Act states that a trade mark designating a geographical origin is not capable of registration, unless the mark has acquired a distinctive character through use. The proviso has the effect of overruling *York Trailer*. The wording of section 1(1), and the qualification at the end of section 3(1) on absolute grounds of refusal, suggest that factual distinctiveness will be sufficient under the Trade Marks Act 1994.

Even if a mark appears to satisfy section 1, it could fail to achieve registration because of section 3 and/or section 5. Section 3 covers absolute grounds for refusal and section 5 covers relative grounds.

9.5   Absolute grounds for refusal

These are to be found in section 3(1), which states:

The following shall not be registered:

(a) signs which do not satisfy the requirements of s.1(1),
(b) trade marks which are devoid of distinctive character,
(c) trade marks which consist of signs or indications which may serve in trade to designate the kind, quality, quantity, intended purpose, value, geographical origin, the time of production of goods or of rendering of services, or other characteristics of goods or services,
(d) trade marks which consist exclusively of signs or indications which have become customary in the current language or in the bona fide and established practices of the trade.

Provided that a trade mark shall not be refused registration by virtue of paragraph (b), (c) or (d) above, if before the date of registration, *it has in fact acquired a distinctive character as a result of the use made of it.* (our italics)

9.5.1   Signs which do not satisfy section 1 (1)

These will be signs that cannot be represented graphically or are not able to distinguish the goods of one trader from those of another. In *Healing Herbs Ltd v Bach Flower Remedies Ltd* [2000] RPC 513, BACH and BACH FLOWER REMEDIES were among marks registered by Bach Flower Remedies (BFR) for homeopathic products made according to the teachings of Dr Edward Bach. Healing Herbs (HHL), who also made products following the Bach method, applied under section 47 for declarations that each of the marks had been registered in breach of each of the paragraphs of section 3(1). On section 3(1)(a), the Court of Appeal held that as the words Bach and Bach Flower Remedies were commonly used to describe such products, the marks failed to satisfy section 1(1) of the Trade Marks Act 1994, in the sense that they did not distinguish goods produced by BFR from similar goods produced by other undertakings. As such they failed under section 3(1)(a). See also 1–800 *Flowers Inc v Phonenames Ltd* [2001] EWCA Civ 721.

9.5.2 Trade marks devoid of any distinctive character

In *AD2000 Trade Mark* [1997] RPC 168, Geoffrey Hobbs, sitting as the Appointed Person, stated that to avoid refusal under this heading a trade mark had to be 'distinctive by nature or have become distinctive by nurture', in other words, inherently distinctive as discussed earlier or made distinctive through use. See also *Procter & Gamble's TM Application* [1999] RPC 673. The shape of the bottle in *Yakult's TM Application* [2001] RPC 753 for yogurt drinks had been described as 'pretty ordinary' by the Registrar. Laddie J agreed. In his view it lacked inherent distinctiveness and had failed to acquire any distinctiveness through use.

Traditionally it was felt that trade marks which are descriptive of the goods or services to which they are applied cannot be distinctive and therefore cannot be registered. In *H. Quennel Ltd's Application* [1954] 72 RPC 36, the mark 'Pussikin' for cat food was considered directly descriptive of cat food. As such it was inherently incapable of distinguishing it. A useful test was put forward by Lloyd-Jacob J – would other traders in good faith legitimately want to use the word in the course of business? If the answer is 'yes', the applicant should not get a monopoly of the word. This would suggest that the requirement for distinctiveness has also a public policy function. Public perception as to whether the mark has acquired distinctiveness will therefore be taken into account, where the words appear to be descriptive. For example see *Procter & Gamble v OHIM* (Trade Marks and Designs) (Case C-383/99P). This concerned an application to register the words 'Baby Dry' as a CTM for disposable nappies. The Examiner refused registration, as did the First Board of Appeal. On appeal to the CFI, that court stated that since the purpose of nappies was to be absorbent, in order to keep babies dry, the term 'Baby Dry' merely conveyed to consumers the intended purpose of the goods without exhibiting any additional feature to render the sign distinctive (para 7). However the ECJ took a different view. First of all, to determine whether the word combination 'Baby Dry' is capable of distinctiveness, the court stated that one had to place oneself in the position of an 'English-speaking consumer'. From that point of view, it was necessary to determine whether the word combination is the normal way of referring to the goods in question. The ECJ held that while the word combination alluded to the function the goods in question were meant to fulfil, it should not be disqualified. While each of the two words did form part of expressions of everyday speech to designate the function of babies' nappies, 'their syntactically unusual juxtaposition is not a familiar expression in the English language, either for designating babies' nappies or for describing their essential features' (para 43). This tended to suggest that even descriptive words might be registered, provided they have acquired a secondary meaning. In other words, to the average consumer they serve to identify the applicant's goods and services.

However in Case C-191/01P, *Wrigley Jr Co v OHIM* [2004] ETMR 9, when Wrigley applied to register 'Doublemint' as a CTM for chewing-gum, the application was refused as the mark was said to lack distinctiveness. The OHIM was of the opinion that the word was descriptive of the product and that other legitimate traders may want to use the words. The CFI allowed Wrigley's appeal, stating that the ambiguity over whether the sign meant that the gum was flavoured by two types of mint, or that it was twice as minty, was enough to make the sign not exclusively descriptive. The CFI's judgment was annulled by the ECJ. A sign is unregistrable if at least one of its possible meanings designates a characteristic of the relevant goods or services. This has been followed in *Francis Geoffrey Bignell (t/a Just Employment (A Firm)) v Just Employment Law Ltd* [2007] EWHC 2203 (Ch). The claimant had an established employment law practice in Guildford under the name 'Just Employment'. The name was chosen to indicate both that the practice dealt mainly in employment law and that employment should be fair. He registered 'Just Employment' as a trade mark. Just Employment Law Ltd (JEL) was a Scottish company which had an office in London. In an action for trade mark infringement and passing off, JEL counterclaimed that Just Employment should not have been registered in the first place, as it was descriptive and therefore lacked inherent distinctiveness. It was further argued that it had not acquired distinctiveness through use. Englehart QC held that a mark had to be tested by reference to the reaction of an ordinary member of the public to the words. The most obvious reaction would be that the goods or services in question related to any employment matters. The words in question lacked inherent distinctiveness and were simply descriptive of the nature of the goods or services in question. Although the word 'Just' could have two connotations, it was enough to preclude registration if one of the possible meanings was descriptive of the goods or services in question.

Note that if the mark in question is made up of descriptive words but together the combination creates something which has secondary meaning, the sign should be judged as a whole. See Case C-363–99 *Koninklijke KPN Nederland NV v Benelux-Merkenbureau* [2004] ETMR 771 and Case C-273/05P *OHIM v Celltech R&D Ltd* [2007] ERC-1–2883.

For the position on the registration of surnames, see *Nichols plc v Registrar of Trade Marks* (Case C-404/02) [2005] RPC 12, where Nichols plc applied to register the company name 'Nichols' for vending machines and the food and drink that they contained. Trade Mark Office practice in the UK was to test for distinctiveness of surnames by consulting the London telephone directory. As the name appeared 483 times, it was classed as a common surname and devoid of distinctive character for use on the products but not for the vending machines. In response to a reference from the High Court, the ECJ stated that there was nothing to justify adopting different tests for different types of mark. Consulting the London telephone directory was applying a further test which was radically different from the rest of the European Union (EU). All marks were to be given the opportunity to demonstrate distinctiveness through use following the test from *Windsurfing Chiemsee Produktions v Huber* [1999] ETMR 585 (*Windsurfing Chiemsee*) – see Section 9.5.3(a). What is the relationship between sections 3(1)(a) and 3(1)(b) with regard to distinctiveness? We suggest, like others (for example, Bainbridge), that the intention must have been to add a further requirement for applicants. In *AD2000 Trade Mark*, the applicants appealed against the Registrar's refusal to register the mark AD2000 as devoid of distinctive character. They argued that having accepted that the mark was a sign 'capable of distinguishing goods' for the purpose of section 1(1), the Registrar was precluded from finding that it was devoid of distinctive character under section 3(1)(b). Dismissing the appeal, Geoffrey Hobbs QC held that 'capable' in section 1(1) meant that the mark was not 'incapable' of distinguishing goods or services from one undertaking from those of others. Even if section 1(1) was satisfied, a sign had to be 'distinctive by nature or become distinctive by nurture'. Since the year 2000 was significant for trading purposes, the onus was on the applicants to show that their sign was incapable of fair and honest application to the goods and services of anyone else. See also Jacob Jin *British Sugar plc v James Robertson & Sons Ltd* [1996] RPC 281. In *Philips Electronics NV v Remington Consumer Products* (Case C-299/99) 18 June 2002 [2003] RPC 2, the ECJ considered articles 2 and 3, the equivalent to sections 1(1) and 3. On the relationship between the provisions, the ECJ stated that if a sign is distinctive through either nature or use, then it would be treated by definition as 'capable of distinguishing' the goods as required in section 3(1)(a). Section 3(1)(a) and the other paragraphs should be read together (see paras 37 and 38).

9.5.2(a)   Marks excluded under section 3(1)(c)

As section 3(1)(c) states, signs or words which tend to describe certain attributes of the products or services to which they are attached will not be registered. In *LG Electronics Inc's Application (2460895) (4 June 2010)*, the Trade Marks Registry upheld the refusal to register the mark 'INTELLIGENT SENSOR' for goods that included televisions and mobile phones, as the mark simply described a characteristic of the goods in question. Similar wording can be found in article 7 of the Community Trade Regulation. In *LizEarleBeauty Co Ltd v OHIM (T-307/09)* [2011] ETMR 16, the General Court upheld the OHIM decision that the sign 'NATURALLY ACTIVE' consisted of two ordinary English words that indicated the characteristics of the relevant cosmetic products.

The proviso to sections 3(1)(b)–(d) states:

> Provided that, a trade mark shall not be refused registration by virtue of paragraph (b), (c) or (d) above, if before the date of registration, *it has in fact acquired a distinctive character as a result of the use made of it.* (our italics)

What will be required to bring an applicant or trade mark owner within the proviso? Important guidance was given by the ECJ in *Windsurfing Chiemsee Produktions v Huber* [1999] ETMR 585 (*Windsurfing Chiemsee*). This concerned registration of a geographical place name for use on sportswear. The ECJ stated that for such words to become distinctive through use, such use must serve to identify the product as originating from a particular undertaking, thus distinguishing its products from those of other undertakings. The geographical designation must have gained a new significance and its connotation must no longer be descriptive to justify its registration as a trade mark. What is particularly useful about the ECJ's decision is that it indicated other matters that could be taken into account, such as:

> the market share held by the mark; how intensive, geographically widespread and long-standing use of the mark has been; the amount invested by the undertaking in promoting the mark; the proportion of the relevant class of persons who, because of the mark, identify goods as originating from a particular undertaking; and statements from chambers of commerce and industry or other trade and professional associations.

To demonstrate that the mark in question has acquired a secondary meaning, in the words of Jacob J in *British Sugar plc v James Robertson & Sons Ltd* [1996] RPC 281, it must be shown that its original meaning has been 'displaced' (at 302). The claimants in *Premier Luggage & Bags Ltd v The Premier Co (UK) Ltd* [2002] EWCA Civ 387; [2001] FSR 461 were able to do this. Although the word 'Premier' could be described as an ordinary word, or descriptive and laudatory, the claimants were able to demonstrate that customers recognised that luggage bearing that mark was of a certain quality. The claimant had achieved a reputation for reliability, quality and value for money.

For community trade marks, similar considerations apply but the sign in question must have acquired distinctiveness throughout the EU. In *Audi AG v OHIM (T318/09)* [2011] ETMR 61, Audi appealed against the refusal to register TDI as a community trade mark. The sign was an acronym for 'Turbo Diesel Injection' or 'Turbo Direct Injection'. The main issues were whether the mark was devoid of distinctive character under article 7(1)(b) of the Community Trade Mark Regulation; or whether it was descriptive under article 7(1)(c); and if so, whether it had acquired distinctiveness through use under article 7(3). The General Court stated that to determine whether a mark had acquired distinctive character through use, the competent authority had to make an assessment of the evidence that the mark in question had come to identify the product as originating from a particular undertaking. The following factors could be taken into account:

▶ Market share
▶ How intensive, geographically widespread and long-standing the use of the mark had been made
▶ The amount invested by the undertaking promoting the mark
▶ The proportion of the relevant class of persons which because of the mark, identified the goods as originating from a particular undertaking
▶ Statements from chambers of commerce and industry or other trade and professional associations as well as consumer surveys.

In the instant case, the sign 'TDI' was inherently descriptive throughout the EU and the acquisition through use had to be proved in respect of each member state. Thus Audi lost its appeal.

9.5.3 Shapes that cannot be trade marks

Section 3(2) is based on article 3(1)(e) of Directive 89/104/EEC. Section 3(2)(a) does not allow registration of a shape 'which results from the nature of the goods themselves'.

This excludes shapes dictated by the actual function of the goods in question. This would make sense, for to allow registration would result in prohibiting other legitimate traders from using shapes that are inherent in the goods in question. Examples include the shape of footballs, shoehorns and keys. For similar reasons, the shapes of goods necessary to obtain a technical result are also not permitted under section 3(2)(b).

In *Philips Electronics NV v Remington Consumer Products* (Case C-299/99) 18 June 2002 [2003] RPC 2, the ECJ explained that the rationale behind the provision was to:

> prevent trade mark protection from granting its proprietor a monopoly on technical solutions or functional characteristics of a product, which a user is likely to seek in the products of competitors.

The ECJ went on to add that trade mark protection should not be used as an obstacle to prevent competitors from freely dealing in products incorporating such technical solutions or functional characteristics in competition with the owner of the trade mark. The reference from the Court of Appeal to the ECJ concerned the registration of a three-headed rotary electric shaver by Philips. When Philips sued Remington for infringing its mark by selling and offering to sell three-headed rotary razors, Remington claimed that the mark should not have been registered as it breached each of the paragraphs in section 3(1), as well as section 3(2). Confirming the decision of both the High Court and Court of Appeal, the mark was declared invalid. See also *Bang & Olufsen A/S v OHIM* Case T-508/08 where an application to register the three-dimensional shape of a loud speaker was refused.

We believe section 3(2)(c) will be the cause of much litigation, because it is not clear what the section is seeking to prohibit. It states that a sign will not be registrable if it consists exclusively of a 'shape which gives substantial value to the goods'.

> At this stage we can only speculate that, in interpreting this paragraph, courts will look to the consumer's motive for buying the product. Potentially it will cover products as diverse as luxury designer goods and biscuits shaped in the likeness of a Walt Disney character.

9.5.3(a) Trade marks offending public morality and good taste

Section 3(3) states that:

> A trade mark shall not be registered if it is:
>
> (a) contrary to public policy or to accepted principles of morality, or
> (b) of such a nature as to deceive the public (for instance as to the nature, quality or geographical origin of the goods or service).

In *ReH N Brock* [1910] Ch 130, one of the reasons why the Court of Appeal refused registration of the word 'orlwoola' was that, phonetically, it sounded like 'all wool' and would be deceptive if the goods to which it was applied were not made entirely of wool. In *Re Hallelujah Trade Mark* [1976] RPC 605, it was held that the religious connotation of the word 'Hallelujah' made it inappropriate as a trade mark for clothing.

Likewise in *Ghazilian's Trade Mark Application* [2002] RPC 628, Simon Thorley QC upheld the Registrar's decision to refuse an application to register 'TINY PENIS' for clothing. The correct anatomical term for parts of the human body should be 'reserved for serious use and not be debased by use as a smutty trade mark for clothing'.

Similar provisions apply for the Community Trade Mark. Article 7(1)(f) of the CMTR provides that:

> trade marks which are contrary to public policy or to accepted principles of morality, shall not be registered.

In *PAKI Logistics GmbH v OHIM* Case T-526/09, the word 'Paki' was refused registration. The Board of Appeal found that English-speaking consumers of the EU would interpret the term as a racist, derogatory and insulting term for people from Pakistan or more generally the Indian sub-continent.

9.5.4 Trade marks prohibited by enactments and emblems

Section 3(4) is intended to stop the registration of marks whose use is prohibited in the UK by any enactment or rule of law or by any provision of EU law. This would include use of the Red Cross symbol, for example, which is protected in another part of the Act or the inappropriate use of the word 'champagne', which would contravene EC Regulation 823/87. See *Taittinger SA v Allbev Ltd* [1993] FSR 641.

Specially protected emblems are covered in section 3(5) which complements section 4. Section 4 protects certain national and international emblems including Royal Arms, national flags and emblems of Paris Convention countries, as well as those of certain other international organisations. None of these is registrable without the consent of the relevant authorities.

9.5.5   Bad faith applications

An application made in bad faith is prohibited by section 3(6). A definition of bad faith was given by Lindley J in *Gromax Plasticulture Ltd v Don and Low Nonwovens Ltd* [1999] RPC 367; 'bad faith'

> includes dishonesty and, as I would hold includes also some dealings which fall short of the standards of acceptable commercial behaviour observed by reasonable and experienced men in the particular area examined.

Examples of bad faith include registering a trade mark with no bona fide intention to use in order to stop its use by other legitimate traders as in *Imperial Group Ltd v Philip Morris & Co Ltd* [1982] FSR 72 , or registering a trade mark in the knowledge that another may have a claim to it. In *Peter Byford v Graham Oliver & Another* [2003] EWHC 295 Ch, registration of SAXON, the name of a 1970s heavy metal band, was declared invalid. Former band members had obtained registration even though they had no title and had done so for the purpose of interfering with the rights of the others who did. Section 5(4), which we discuss later, also applied because passing off proceedings could prevent use of the word SAXON alone. See also *Harrison's Trade Mark Application* [2004] EWCA Civ 1028; [2005] FSR 10, where an employee of an established nightclub called 'China white' disclosed information about a cocktail to be named 'China White' to Harrison who then proceeded to apply for a trade mark in the name. The Court of Appeal held that the application had been made in bad faith.

9.6   Relative grounds for refusal

Even if the applicant gets past the absolute grounds for refusal in section 3, she still has to jump the hurdle of section 5. The aim of section 5 is to protect prior rights of third parties. Generally speaking, under section 5 the Registrar should not allow registration of a mark which is the same as, or similar to, an earlier mark. An earlier mark is defined in section 6(1) as:

(a) a registered trade mark, international trade mark (UK) or Community trade mark which has a date of application for registration earlier than that of the trade mark in question, taking account (where appropriate) of the priorities claimed in respect of the trade marks,

(b) a Community trade mark which has a valid claim to seniority from an earlier registered trade mark or international trade mark (UK), or

(c) a trade mark which, at the date of application for registration of the trade mark in question or (where appropriate) of the priority claimed in respect of the application, was entitled to protection under the Paris Convention as a well-known trade mark.

Section 5(1) states that a trade mark which is the same as an earlier mark and is for the same goods or services will not be registered. Under section 5(2), a mark is not registrable if it is likely to cause the public confusion, where the mark is identical to an earlier mark and is for similar goods or services, or if it is similar to an earlier mark and is for identical or similar goods or services. An old authority provides us with an example. In *Aristoc v Rysta* [1945] AC 68, the defendant repaired stockings manufactured by the plaintiff. The defendant decided to apply the mark 'RYSTA' to repaired stockings and the stockings that they manufactured. They were not allowed to do this as 'RYSTA' was phonetically too similar to 'ARISTOC'. If an applicant can show that the goods to which its mark will be applied are sold in different markets from those in which the goods to which the conflicting marks are applied, he may obtain registration.

In considering the likelihood of confusion for section 5(2), the viewpoint of the average consumer could be taken into account. In *Esure Insurance Ltd v Direct Line Insurance plc* [2008] EWCA Civ 842, Esure applied to register an image of a computer mouse on wheels for insurance and financial services. The application was opposed by Direct Line on the basis of its use of an image of a red telephone on wheels for similar services. The judge had reversed the Hearing Officer on the issue of confusion but had upheld the opposition on the basis of section 5(3). On appeal to the Court of Appeal, the Hearing Officer's decision was reinstated. According to Arden LJ, the Hearing Officer had been correct to base his decision on what he believed the average consumer would have thought of the two marks and whether they had confused him. The products offered by both companies were identical and of a kind familiar to members of the public (see para 56). Both her Ladyship and Jacob LJ were of the opinion that the Direct Line brand was so striking that the evidence of an expert witness was not required to prove the likelihood of confusion (see paras 70–4).

In considering the likelihood of confusion, factors such as the imperfect recollection of consumers, the type of products and the likely target consumer are relevant. In *Imperial Tobacco Ltd v Berry Bros& Rudd Ltd* (2001) (Opposition Number 47290), Patents Court, 31October 2001, the respondent's trade mark 'CUTTYSARK' was said to be a highly distinctive mark that must have had a significant reputation in the UK. Its opposition to the appellant's mark based on section 5(2)(b) was therefore upheld.

Section 5(3) states that an identical or similar mark will not be registrable if the earlier mark has gained a reputation, even in respect of different goods, if it would lead to taking unfair advantage of the earlier mark or would cause detriment to the earlier mark's distinctive character. So, for example, Rolls-Royce applied to burger bar services is unlikely to be allowed. *Oasis Store Ltd's Trade Mark Application* [1998] RPC 631 concerned an application to register 'EVEREADY' for contraceptives and condoms. Ever Ready plc, the owner of numerous 'EVER READY' words and device marks for batteries, torches, plugs and smoke alarms, opposed this. It opposed under section 5(3) that the mark would take unfair advantage of its reputation. Ever Ready also claimed that use of the 'EVEREADY' mark on contraceptives and condoms was contrary to section 5(4)(a) of the Trade Marks Act 1994, on the ground that it would succeed in a passing off action against the applicant if the mark were put to use in relation to the goods for which registration was sought. It was held that the burden of establishing an earlier right under section 5(4)(a) rested on the opponent. The fact that the parties were trading in different fields added to the opponent's burden of establishing a real risk of confusion and deception. In this case the fields of activity were so far removed that it could not be assumed that even if a small amount of confusion did arise it would be damaging to the opponent. Thus the opposition under section 5(4)(a) failed. Opposition under section 5(3) also failed. Simply being reminded of a similar trade mark with a reputation for dissimilar goods did not necessarily amount to taking unfair advantage of the repute of that trade mark.

Contrast this with *CA Sheimer (M)SdnBhd's TM Application* [2000] RPC 484, where Visa International, the proprietor of the VISA financial services brand, successfully opposed an application to register VISA for condoms under section 5(3). According to Geoffrey Hobbs QC:

The bringing to mind of the VISA mark for financial services, which had a strong distinctive character in the United Kingdom, when consumers were faced with the VISA mark on condoms was substantially detrimental to the distinctive character of VISA International's trade mark.

Solicitors Rowe and Maw (1999: 13) suggest that the difficulty for Ever Ready plc, in the earlier case, was that it is difficult to establish 'unfair advantage' when the mark consists of ordinary dictionary words.

See also *Inlima SL's Application for a 3-Dimensional Trade Mark* [2000] RPC 661, where the applicant's use of stripes similar to those used on Adidas sportswear was refused.

In *Intel Corp v Kirpal Singh Sihra* [2003] EWHC 17 (Ch), an application to register 'INTEL-PLAY' as a trade mark for toy puzzles was refused, since the applicant's intended use of it would take advantage of and be detrimental to the character and repute of INTEL's mark which was internationally recognised in the field of computer technology.

Finally, section 5(4) states that a mark will not be registered if its use could be prevented by passing off or the enforcement of some other earlier right, unless the proprietor's consent is obtained and there is no likelihood of confusion. See *Peter Byford v Graham Oliver & Another* [2003] EWHC 295 (Ch), referred to earlier.

A further requirement for opposition under section 5(4) is that the opponent must still retain sufficient goodwill at the relevant time. See *Minimax Gmbh & Co v Chubb Fire Ltd* [2008] EWHC 1960 (Pat), where Floyd J held that Chubb Fire Ltd had not made sufficient use of the mark 'MINIMAX' or established the necessary goodwill to oppose the registration of the same name by Minimax Gmbh.

Since the Trade Marks (Relative Grounds) Order 2007, sections 5(1)–(4) will only prevent a mark being registered if the proprietor of the earlier mark, or other earlier right raises an objection in opposition proceedings which is more in line with other European countries. This now places the onus on trade mark owners and those with goodwill to study the *Trade Marks Journal* to make sure that marks that are identical or similar to theirs are not registered.

9.7 Maintaining registration

If the application satisfies all the requirements in sections 1–7, the mark will be registered and the registration will last for a period of ten years (s 42(1)), and can be renewed indefinitely for further periods of ten years (s 43). After registration, a proprietor needs to take care to maintain the registration so that it does not lapse or is not open to challenge. As with patents, it is usual for a defendant in an infringement action to challenge the validity of the plaintiff's trade mark. Of course, a proprietor may decide of his own accord to surrender the trade mark in certain circumstances.

Under the 1938 Act, marks were registered in either Part A or Part B of the Register. Marks in Part A were protected from revocation (except on grounds of fraud) once they had been on the Register for seven years. When the 1994 Act came into force, the Register was consolidated for past and future marks. This means that all marks (including all Part A marks) are now open to revocation at any time.

9.7.1 Surrendering the trade mark

Section 45 allows the proprietor to surrender the trade mark in respect of some or all of the goods and/or services for which it is registered. It may be expedient to do this in the face of revocation or invalidity proceedings. If an identical CTM registration has been obtained, there is no longer the need to retain the national registration so it may be surrendered by the proprietor.

9.7.2   Revocation and invalidity

Under sections 46 and 47, any person can apply to have a trade mark revoked or declared invalid.

Under section 46, there are three grounds on which a trade mark registration can be revoked.

The first is where the mark has not been used in the UK for a period of five years or more without good cause. A registration cannot be attacked under this provision before it is five years old (the period being counted from the date of registration, not the date of application) even if the proprietor never had a bona fide intention to use the mark and has never used the mark. Any use of the mark within three months before the application for revocation is filed will be disregarded, unless the proprietor can show that he had made preparations to make genuine use of the trade mark before he became aware that an application for revocation might be made. 'Genuine use' can be defined as 'substantial and genuine use judged by ordinary commercial standards'. See *Imperial Group Ltd v Philip Morris & Co Ltd* [1982] FSR 72.

A trade mark may also be challenged for non-use if the mark in question has been used in a way which differs in some essential element from the mark as registered. In the case of *United Biscuits (UK) Ltd v Asda Stores Ltd* [1997] RPC 513, United Biscuits' registered marks of pictures of penguins were revoked for lack of use since the designs of penguins used on the Penguin packaging were different from those covered by the registration. As a result, the United Biscuits' claim of trade mark infringement against Asda for use of a representation of a puffin in relation to chocolate biscuits failed (although United Biscuits did succeed with their claim in passing off).

The second ground for revocation is where the mark has become generic. A trade mark can be challenged under section 46(1)(c) if it has become common 'in the trade' for the product or service for which it is registered by reason of the acts or inactivity of the proprietor. Famous examples include ASPIRIN and ESCALATOR. The party challenging must show that the mark has become 'generic' because of the proprietor's action or lack of action. To avoid marks becoming generic, proprietors should be vigilant and make good use of section 10 to stop the use of their mark on the same or similar goods to those for which the proprietor's mark is registered. Proprietors should also avoid using the trade mark as a noun to describe the product or service in question. For example, 'personal stereo' should be used instead of 'Walkman'. Rank Xerox have had to work against the peculiarly US practice of referring to 'xeroxing' instead of 'photocopying'.

The final ground for revocation is 'misleading use'. This is where the proprietor's use, or use with his consent, is likely to mislead the public as to the nature, quality or geographical origin of the goods or services to which the mark is applied.

In *Scandecor Developments AB v Scandecor Marketing AV &ors* [2001] UKHL 21, the House of Lords had to consider among other things whether the use of two SCANDECOR trade marks used by two associated enterprises had become liable to mislead the public because of the use made of them. The proprietor of the mark was not the origin of the goods using the mark and had no quality control over goods bearing them. Their Lordships had to consider whether the grant of a bare exclusive licence was 'inherently likely to deceive potential customers'. Lord Nicholls of Birkenhead suggested that a trade mark should not be regarded as liable to mislead if the origin of the goods is a bare exclusive licensee. One of the major advantages of the 1994 Act over the 1938 Act is the provision made for licensing and sub-licensing. According to Bainbridge, his Lordship's opinion accords with 'modern business practices'. To decide otherwise would, in our opinion, be a step backwards.

A trade mark registration may be declared invalid under section 47 if the trade mark application should have failed under one or more of the absolute conditions listed in section 3, for instance, an application made in bad faith as in *Imperial v Philip Morris*. Once the registration is declared invalid, the mark is treated as though it had never been registered. In *British Sugar plc v James Robertson & Sons Ltd* [1996] RPC 281, the mark 'TREAT', for dessert and ice-cream topping, was taken off the register after the owner brought an infringement action against the defendant for use of the mark in relation to their new spread. Jacob Jwas of the opinion that, as a descriptive word, it should never have been allowed registration because it did not function as a trade mark. See also *Bignall v Just Employment* discussed earlier.

Bearing in mind the apparently lax attitude of the Registry to some of the more ingenious trade mark applications, it is likely that a large number of trade marks will suffer the same fate if their owners ever try to exert their trade mark rights.

Community Trade Marks are subject to the same rules with regard to revocation and declarations of invalidity under the Regulation. Thus once a CTM registration has been granted, it can still be revoked on the application of an owner of a prior conflicting right (CTM or national) for up to five years after the owner of the prior right becomes aware of the use of the CTM, and also by anyone on grounds of non-use (after five years of non-use) or by anyone at any time if the mark becomes generic or misleading. Since a CTM can be maintained by use in any part of the European Union, it is clearly possible for the owner of a prior national right to be unaware of a conflicting CTM for many years. Since the existence of a CTM will be a matter of public record, the test of awareness may develop into a concept of constructive awareness – in other words, in future it may be held that if a CTM is on the Register, third parties will be fixed with constructive knowledge of its existence.

If a CTM is challenged and removed from the CTM register, the owner of the CTM can re-file national applications in all countries of the EU other than the country or countries in respect of which the challenge was made. These national applications will have the same application date as the CTM application.

9.8   Special marks

9.8.1   Collective marks

The collective mark was introduced by the Trade Marks Act 1994. Section 49 states:

> A collective mark is a mark distinguishing the goods or services of members of the association which is the proprietor of the mark for those undertakings.

A collective mark is a mark that can be used by anyone who is a member of the association in whose name the mark is registered. It differs from other marks in that the proprietor is a body of persons rather than an individual or company. The rules that apply to collective marks are set out in Schedule 1 of the Trade Marks Act 1994.

9.8.2   Certification marks

Certification marks guarantee that the goods to which they are attached have been certified as being of a particular material (such as the woolmark), method of manufacture, quality, accuracy or origin (s 50). Such marks are a testament to the quality or origin of the goods or services to which they are attached (see *Stilton Trade Mark* [1967] RPC 173). The rules that apply to certification marks are set out in Schedule 2 of the Trade Marks Act 1994. See also *Legal Aid Board's Application* (2114581) 3 October 2000.

Signs of the times: developments in the wake of the Trade Marks Act 1994

The enactment of the Trade Marks Act 1994 was met with a great deal of academic and professional excitement. Section 1(1) seemed to suggest that anything was possible, when it came to what could be registered. Susan Singleton (1994) noted that distinctive packaging like the famous Coca-Cola bottle would be capable of registration for the first time. Julian Gyngell (1994) stated that all manner of distinctive trade marks were eligible for registration and protection:

> it may be now possible to register a distinctive sound … a distinctive product design or packaging …, as well as the distinctive layout, arrangement or decoration of retail premises. It will also be easier to register colours …

In practice the registration of non-traditional marks has proved difficult because of the requirement for graphic representation as well as the ability of the mark to distinguish the goods. Indeed it could be argued that to allow the registration of shapes, sounds and smells, when the proprietor can register the name and symbols, is to allow an increase in the protection afforded, which may not be justified. But if proprietors have invested so much into creating goodwill in the colours, sounds or smells of their products and/services that they can attract common law protection, then it could be argued that proper registration should be permitted. The following case law notes on the Trade Marks Directive and the Community Trade Mark Regulation indicates that registration will not be straightforward.

Case notes

▶ **C-273/00, *Ralf Sieckmann v Deutsches Patent- und Markenamt* [2002] ECR I-11737**

Sieckmann wanted to register an olfactory mark at the German patent and trade mark office. The application contained a chemical formula and was accompanied by an odour sample of the scent. It was also described as 'balsamically fruity with a slight hint of cinnamon'. The ECJ stated that a smell would not be adequately graphically represented by a verbal description because it would not be 'sufficiently precise'. Depositing the sample was not sufficiently durable or stable; and the chemical formula would not be sufficiently clear or precise.

▶ **C-104/01, *LibertelGroep BV v Benelux-Merkenbureau* [2003] ECR I-3793**

An attempt was being made to register the colour orange for telephone books. A–G Leger was of the opinion that colours per se were not capable of graphic representation. While the ECJ rejected that view, it stated that the colour sample was not sufficiently durable. The *Sieckmann*criteria would apply. The court also suggested that an internationally recognised identification code (Pantone) may, in combination with a verbal description and colour sample, be acceptable.

▶ **C-49/02, *Heidelberger Bauchemie GmbH* [2004] ETMR 99**

Heidelberger Bauchemie brought proceedings against the German Patent and Trade Mark Office for its refusal to register the colours blue and yellow in respect of goods for the building trade. In its reference to the ECJ, the German Federal Patent Court referred the following questions:

(1) Are colours per se or other of their combinations distinctive for the purposes of article 2?
(2) If so, under what circumstances?

The ECJ's response was that, for registration, colours would have to satisfy the following:

(1) must be a sign;
(2) must be capable of graphic representation; and
(3) must be distinctive.

To meet these criteria, the marks must be 'precise, unambiguous, and durable'. Abstract colours without contours would need to be 'systematically arranged by associating [them] in a predetermined and uniform way'. The mere juxtaposition of two or more colours without shape or contours would not satisfy the criteria.

▶ **C-283/01, *Shield Mark BV v Joost Kist* (Trading as Memex) [2004] RPC 315**

This application was to register the first nine notes of 'Für Elise' and the Dutch equivalent

of the onomatopoeic sound 'cock-a-doodle-doo', said to be registrable in theory if the *Sieckmann* criteria are met. The problem was the linguistic differences in representing the sound of a cockerel across the EU. Following the initial refusal to register the sound of Tarzan's jungle yodel, the press office of the OHIM reminded applicants of the ability to include a digital recording of a sound mark following implementation of Regulation 3(6) which has been added to the Regulation that implements the Community Trade Mark (2868/95). This allows the filing of sound files in an electronic CTM application together with a graphic representation. See Case R708/2006–4 *Edgar Rice Burroughs Inc v OHIM* (27 September 2007). As stated earlier, since the *Trade Marks Journal* is available in electronic form, this should now also be possible for registration at the Intellectual Property Office. For olfactory marks, the challenges remain!

Summary

▶ In theory, the Trade Marks Act 1994 makes it possible to register a range of matter as trade marks, provided they can be represented graphically and function as trade marks.

▶ On receipt at the Registry, the application is examined, then published and registered if no reasonable objection has been raised within three months after publication.

▶ Colours, shapes, sounds and smells are potentially registrable if they function as trade marks; the problem has been to find a suitable method to graphically represent non-traditional marks.

▶ To obtain registration, the mark should be represented graphically and be capable of distinguishing the applicant's goods or services.

▶ The grounds on which an application can be refused outright are listed in section 3. These are mainly linked to the fact that the mark lacks distinctiveness.

▶ Under section 5, the Registrar can refuse a registration which interferes with a prior third-party right unless the prior owner consents.

▶ Even after registration the mark may be challenged as invalid under section 47 or revoked under section 46. A trade mark owner may also decide to surrender registration under section 45.

Further reading and references

Bainbridge, *Intellectual Property Law* (5th edn, Pitman Longman, 2002) pp 16 and 371.

Bentley and Sherman, *Intellectual Property Law* (2nd edn, Oxford University Press, 2002).

Grant, 'Bad Faith-Requirement of Dishonesty' [2005] EIPR 27(1), N14.

Gyngell, 'Trade Marks – Good News for Business' [1994] *NLJ Practitioner*,18 November.

Jenkins, 'Perils of a Weak Mark In *Just Employment*' (available at<www.jenkins.eu/mym-spring-2008/perils-of-a-weak-mark-in-just-employment.asp>).

Middlemiss and Badger, 'Nipping Taste Marks in the Bud' [2004] EIPR 26(3), 152.

Pinto, 'Application for "TDI" –Audi's Arguments Fail to Impress' JIPLP 2011, 6(12), 849.

Rowe and Maw, *Intellectual Property Newsletter* [1999] autumn/winter, 13.

Schulze, 'Registering Colour Trade Marks in the European Union' [2003] EIPR 25(2), 55.

Singleton, 'Full Marks for the New Law?' [1994] *Solicitors' Journal* 7 October.

Yavorsky, 'Ministry of Sound-OHIM and the Tarzan Yell' [2008] Ent LR, 19(3), 63.

Chapter 10

Protection of trade marks

10.1 Rights of the trade mark owner

Section 9 of the 1994 Act confirms the trade mark owner's exclusive rights. Exercise of those rights by anyone else, without his consent, amounts to infringement. In the case of co-owners, each owner is entitled to exercise the exclusive rights in relation to the trade mark without the consent of the other co-owner(s). However, all co-owners must consent to the exercise of those rights by a third party. The rights of the owner date from the filing date of the trade mark application, but an action for infringement cannot be commenced until the registration has been granted. Section 14 provides the owner with the authority to sue, based purely upon ownership of the registered trade mark. Unlike passing off, there is no need to establish trade use or reputation.

Where a trade mark is owned by more than one person, any of the co-owners may commence proceedings for infringement, but cannot continue with the proceedings without joining with all the other co-owners as co-claimants or defendants.

Licences of registered trade marks must be in writing and signed by the licensor. A licence may be general or limited, exclusive or non-exclusive. Section 29 defines an exclusive licence as one that authorises the licensee to use the trade mark to the exclusion of all other persons (including the licensor). Unless the licence states otherwise, it will be binding on any successor of the licensor. If the licence says so, the licensee will be entitled to grant sub-licences; this suggests that in the absence of an express right to sub-license, the licensee would not be entitled to grant sub-licences.

Section 30 sets out the rights of exclusive trade mark licensees in respect of infringements of the licensed trade mark. Broadly speaking, the licensee can, unless the licence says otherwise, call on the trade mark owner to bring infringement proceedings, and, if the owner refuses to do so, or fails to do so within two months of the request, the licensee may bring proceedings in his own name. The exact scope of the rights of an exclusive licensee are governed by sections 30 and 31, unless contractually varied.

10.2 When is the trade mark infringed?

The activities that can amount to an infringement are covered in section 10 of the Trade Marks Act 1994 and article 5 of Directive 89/104/EEC.

Section 10(1) states that it is an infringement of a registered trade mark to use, in the course of trade, an identical mark on the same goods or in respect of the same services for which that mark is registered. In *British Sugar plc v James Robertson & Sons Ltd* [1996] RPC 281, Jacob J said that if the defendant's use of the mark is in the course of trade, it does not need to be used in the trade mark sense to establish infringement. So it is possible to succeed in an infringement action, even if the claimant's symbol has not been used as a trade mark. The claimant needs only to prove that it was used in the course of trade. Use in the course of trade excludes use for a party political broadcast. See *Unilever v Griffin* [2010] EWHC 899.

The mark is used in the 'course of trade' if it can be said that such use takes place in a commercial context, with a view to economic advantage. See Case C-206/01, *Arsenal Football Club v Reed* [2002] ECR I-10273.

A defendant may try to defend an infringement action under section 10(1) by adopting a narrow interpretation of the goods or services to which the claimant has attached trade marks. This was the case in *Thomson Holidays Ltd v Norwegian Cruise Line Ltd* [2002] EWCA Civ 1828, where Norwegian Cruise Line Ltd had offered a range of holiday services under the name 'FREESTYLE CRUISES'. Thomson was the registered proprietor of trade mark 'FREESTYLE', which it applied to a range of package holidays aimed at the 18- to 30-year-old age group, which included cruises. The defendants argued that there had been no use of the claimant's mark on cruise holidays and that Thomson's use of the trade mark would be perceived as applied to land-based holidays, or holidays excluding cruises, so on that basis there was no infringement under section 10(1). The Court of Appeal rejected that argument. There was no evidence to show that there was a distinct category of holiday described as land-based. Although the tourism industry consisted of distinct segments, it did not follow that the claimant's services would not be referred to by a more general description, such as package holiday. On that basis, the defendant's use of the mark was in relation to services that were identical to those for which the claimant's mark had been registered.

10.2.1 Use on the internet

The growing use of the internet to shop for trade-marked goods and the resulting inevitable expansion of advertising through the internet have led to the need to assess the responsibility of search engine providers and analyse the meaning of the words 'use in the course of trade'. When the user, looking up information of any kind, enters a word or phrase into the search engine, it will display a list of 'natural' results. These are websites algorithmically ranked in order of relevance to the search terms used. Free search engines such as Google support this service with income that they earn from AdWords, where an advertiser 'bids' a cost per click against a desired AdWord. In *Google France SARL and Google Inc v Louis Vuitton Malletier SA (and ors)* Joined Cases C-236/08-C-238/08, Louis Vuitton, the manufacturer of luxury goods, discovered that Google had displayed advertisements of websites selling imitations of its products. This occurred when internet users keyed in Louis Vuitton's trade mark as a key word. The issue was whether as the service provider, Google had 'used' Louis Vuitton's trade mark. The European Court of Justice (ECJ) stated that search engine operators who allowed customers to exploit key words identical to third-party trade marks were not themselves 'using' those trade marks. Slightly different guidance was given in *L'Oreal SA (and ors) v eBay International AG Case C-234/09*. The company eBay operates a global internet market place where individuals and businesses can buy and sell goods and services. eBay bought advertising keywords to attract and direct new customers to its platform. These included well-known marks from paid referencing services. L'Oreal accused eBay of being involved in trade mark infringements committed by sellers on its websites, in that by buying key words corresponding to L'Oreal's trade marks, eBay directed internet users to infringing goods offered for sale on its website. Here there were two issues. First, the use of key words to promote eBay's own online market place. This, according to the ECJ, was not use in the trade mark sense. The second issue was the use of key words to promote the goods that its customers were marketing with its assistance. If such goods were counterfeit, this would amount to use, as eBay's advertisements of such goods created an obvious association between the trade-marked goods and buying those goods through eBay.

10.2.2 What is 'identical'?

The protection provided in section 10(1) is stronger than that of section 10(2) in that there is no need to prove 'confusion'. But the claimant must show that the two marks are identical as are the goods or services to which they are applied. In *Reed Executive plc & Another v Reed Business Information Ltd and ors* [2004] EWCA Civ 159, Jacobs LJ stated that the trade mark proprietor must show two things:

(1) use of a sign which is identical to his registered mark; and
(2) use for goods or services which are identical to those for which the mark is registered. (at [20])

The question is: to what extent would a slight variation take the action from section 10(1) to section 10(2)? In *Origins Natural Resources Inc v Origin Clothing Ltd* [1995] FSR 280, the addition of the letter 's' to the word 'Origin' was held not to be identical.

In Case C-291/00, *Société LTJ Diffusion v Sadas Vertbaudet SA* [2003] FSR 34, the ECJ had to consider this very question under article 5.1(a). The dispute concerned two French companies. The claimant's mark was a device which consisted of the word 'Arthur' written in ornamental script in the form of a signature. This was applied to clothing. The defendant operated a mail order business which included a range of children's clothing called 'Arthur et Félicie'. The defendant applied to register its mark as both a French trade mark and a Community Trade Mark (CTM). In addressing the claimant's opposition, the French court referred the following to the ECJ:

Whether the prohibition in article 5(1)(a) covered only identical reproduction, without addition or omission of the sign or signs constituting a mark or whether it could extend to

(1) Reproduction of the distinctive element of a mark composed of a number of signs?
(2) Full reproduction of the signs making up the mark where new signs were added?

In response the ECJ stated:

The criterion of identity of the sign and the trade mark must be interpreted strictly. The very definition of identity implies that the two elements compared should be the same in all respects (see paras 50–51).

This would appear straightforward. We suggest that on its own, this statement is clear. However, the ECJ then went on to state that the perception of identity had to be made globally taking account of the average consumer, bearing in mind that the latter rarely had the opportunity to make a side-by-side comparison of the mark and the sign but must rely on his own imperfect recollection of them. That being the case, insignificant differences between the sign and the trade mark may go unnoticed by the average consumer. Thus the court held:

the answer to the question referred must be that Article 5(1)(a) of the Directive must be interpreted as meaning that a sign is identical with the trade mark where it reproduces without any modification or addition, all the elements constituting the trade mark or where, viewed as a whole, it contains differences so insignificant that they may go unnoticed by an average consumer.

This reasoning was described by Jacobs LJ as 'opaque' in *Reed*. In *Reed*, the Court of Appeal held that Reed Business Information was not identical to the mark 'Reed'. The words 'Business Information' would not go unnoticed by the average consumer.

On the question of 'use' of the trade mark, see Case C-48/05 *Adam Opel AG v Autec AG* [2007] ECR I-1017. The claimant objected to the use of its 'Opel' trade mark, which was registered for motor vehicles and toys by a manufacturer of toy cars. The ECJ ruled that the 'use' in question could infringe if that use affects or is likely to affect the function of the trade mark in guaranteeing to consumers the origins of the goods.

Section 10(2) covers protection against the use of similar marks or identical marks attached to similar goods and states:

> A person infringes a registered trade mark if he uses in the course of trade a sign where because
>
> (a) the sign is identical with the trade mark and is used in relation to goods or services similar to those for which the trade mark is registered, or
> (b) the sign is similar to the trade mark and is used in relation to goods or services identical with or similar to those for which the trade mark is registered,
>
> there exists a likelihood of confusion on the part of the public, *which includes the likelihood of association with the trade mark.* (our italics)

This is where trade mark infringement has become broader, covering use of a trade mark on similar goods and services. Some commentators have said that because of this section, the action of passing off will become a thing of the past. This is not likely to be the case unless and until suppliers begin to register packaging and colour schemes more widely so as to have a registered trade mark that can be infringed in this broader sense. In the case of supermarket 'look-alike' products, it is usually the overall colour scheme and 'get-up' that are copied, and passing off is still, in most cases, the only available action.

The words 'likelihood of association' suggest a broader interpretation of section 10(2). In *Wagamama Ltd v City Centre Restaurants plc* [1995] FSR 713, the plaintiff operated a successful chain of Japanese-style restaurants under the name WAGAMAMA. They also owned trade marks of that name. The defendant opened a restaurant, with an Indian theme, under the name RAJAMAMA. This was changed to RAJA MAMA when the plaintiff objected but, in the plaintiff's view, that also amounted to infringement. The plaintiff claimed infringement in the classic sense, but also argued that the words at the end of section 10(2) suggested the introduction into English trade mark law of a new and enlarged basis for infringement. The plaintiffs argued that, as well as confusion in the classic sense, mere association between marks could amount to infringement, even if there was no possibility of a misunderstanding as to the origin of the goods or services in question. In other words, the mark would be infringed if, on seeing the alleged infringing sign, the registered trade mark would be called to mind.

The wording of section 10(2) comes directly from Directive 89/104/EEC to approximate the laws of the Member States relating to trade marks. The plaintiffs argued that the wording was introduced into the directive on the insistence of the Benelux countries whose case law had developed to the extent that infringement included situations where there was mere association between marks, without confusion. Laddie J was not prepared to give section 10(2) such a broad interpretation. In his view, to do so would create a new type of monopoly, which related to the trade mark itself and not the proprietor's business. The defendant was, nevertheless, found liable for trade mark infringement on the narrower interpretation and in passing off.

The approach taken in *Wagamama* has been endorsed by the ECJ in *Sabel BV v Puma AG, Rudolf Dassler Sport* [1998] RPC 199. This concerned an application by a Dutch company to register in Germany its trade mark, which consisted of a spotted cheetah running above the word 'Sabel', for clothing, jewellery and various fashion accessories. The application was opposed by Puma, which had prior registration for two device marks consisting of a black silhouette of a puma respectively running and leaping without any words, registered for the same goods. Puma's opposition was partially successful in the German Trade Marks Registry and, on appeal, the German Federal Court referred the following question to the ECJ:

> What is the significance of the wording of the Trade Mark Directive, according to which the risk of confusion includes the likelihood that a mark may be associated with an earlier mark?

The court stated that the reference to 'association' in article 4(1)(b) could have been intended simply to make it clear that the concept of confusion is not limited to confusion in the narrow sense, that is, the consumer mistakes one product for another, but extends to confusion in the broad sense, that is, the mistaken assumption that there is an organisational or economic link between the undertakings marketing the two products. The 'association' had to be linked with confusion.

Thus the mere association which the public might make between two trade marks as a result of their analogous semantic content is not in itself a sufficient ground for concluding that there is a likelihood of confusion within the meaning of the provision. See also *Canon Kabushiki Kaisha v Metro-Goldwyn-Mayer Inc* [1999] FSR 332 and *Lloyd Schufabrik Meyer & Co GmbH v Klijsen Handel BV* (Case C-342/97) [1999] ETMR 690.

In *Lloyd Schufabrik Meyer & Co GmbH v Klijsen Handel BV*, the ECJ stated that the wording of article 5(1)(b) of the directive, from which section 10(2) is taken, shows that the perception of marks in the mind of the average consumer of the category of goods or services in question would play a decisive role (para 25). It went on to add:

> the average consumer of the category of products concerned is deemed to be reasonably well informed and reasonably observant and circumspect (at [26]).

This certainly influenced the ECJ in *Société LTJ Diffusion*, but note that the ECJ was interpreting article 5.1(a) not 5.1(b). According to Isaac and Joshi (2005), the boundary between the two will become blurred.

To interpret section 10(2), Jacob J had suggested, in *Origins Natural Resources Inc v Origin Clothing Ltd* [1995] FSR 280, at 284, that the court should assume that the plaintiff's mark is used in a normal and fair manner in relation to the goods for which it is registered, and then assess a likelihood of confusion in relation to the way the defendant uses the mark, discounting any added matter or circumstances.

Jacob J provided detailed guidance on the interpretation of section 10(2) in *British Sugar plc v James Robertson & Sons Ltd* [1996] RPC 281. Here, the plaintiff's products included a syrup for pouring over ice cream and desserts called 'Treat'. Supermarkets usually placed the plaintiff's product in the sections for desserts and ice cream topping. The trade mark was registered for desserts, sauces and syrups. The defendant used the mark 'Robertsons' for a range of jams and preserves. In 1995, they launched a new toffee-flavoured sweet spread in a jar labelled 'Robertson's Toffee Treat'. In supermarkets it was shelved with jams and preserves. The plaintiff took action for infringement.

Jacob J said that section 10(2) was asking two questions: whether the goods were similar and, if so, was there likelihood of confusion? In his view, merging the two questions together, without the need to prove similarity, meant that strong marks would attract protection for a wider range of goods than weaker marks. In order to judge whether the goods in question were similar, a number of factors should be taken into account:

(a) the respective uses of the respective goods or services;
(b) the respective users of the respective goods or services;
(c) the physical nature of the goods or acts of service;
(d) the respective trade channels through which the goods or services reach the market;
(e) if the goods are sold in a self-serve environment, their respective positions within that environment – in other words, whether they are shelved together;
(f) the extent to which there is competition between the respective goods or services (at 296–97).

Taking all of the above together, the court held that the spread should not be regarded as similar to the dessert and, therefore, there was no infringement.

In *European (The) Ltd v The Economist Newspaper Ltd* [1998] FSR 283, the plaintiff published a weekly newspaper. The masthead featured its registered device mark incorporating the words 'The European'. The defendant's weekly newspaper used a masthead, which included the words 'European Voice'. The plaintiff sued under section 10(2) for use of a similar trade mark in relation to identical goods but disclaimed any monopoly in the word 'European'. The Court of Appeal was of the view that for infringement under section 10(2), the question was whether there was a likelihood of confusion because of the similarities between the defendant's sign and the plaintiff's registered trade mark. In this case there was no evidence of confusion.

Section 10(3) deals with the unauthorised use of a mark with a reputation in the UK by use of an identical or a similar mark on totally different goods. It is an infringement if such use would harm, or take unfair advantage of, the original proprietor's trade mark. This section would clearly be available to marks such as Rolls-Royce, Microsoft or Virgin. In addition, under section 56 of the 1994 Act, the owner of a well-known mark (as defined under the Paris Convention) can obtain an injunction to prevent use of a mark that is the same as, or similar to, his mark, in relation to the same or similar goods where that use is likely to cause confusion. This section implements into English law the protection offered by the Paris Convention to well-known marks. This right is also available to persons who only carry on business or only have a registration outside the UK, provided that the reputation of the trade mark is known in the UK.

In some cases even where the goods on the face of it may seem dissimilar, the court will be influenced by the impression created. For example, in *Pfizer Inc v Eurofood Link (UK) Ltd* [2000] ETMR 187, the claimant's trade mark in VIAGRA for a pharmaceutical product to treat a form of impotence was held to be infringed by the defendant's use of the mark VIAGRENE on a herbal beverage. The court was influenced by the defendant's marketing of the drink, which suggested that it was an aphrodisiac. The claimant also succeeded under section 10(3), discussed below.

The availability of an action under section 10(3) appears to make up for the fact that the use of defensive registration is no longer possible under the 1994 Act. In *Eastman v Griffiths* [1898] 15 RPC 105, the proprietor of the KODAK trade mark was able to stop the mark being used by another proprietor on bicycles in a passing off action because the court held that the trades in cameras and bicycles were similar. However, following that case (and a number of others) the Goschen Committee recommended the introduction of defensive registration for well-known marks so that in the Kodak situation a registration for the name could be obtained even in respect of goods in which the owner was not trading. Under the 1994 Act, Kodak would probably have a remedy under section 10(3) for unauthorised use of the Kodak name on other goods (including dissimilar goods).

Section 10(3) was considered in *Baywatch Production Co Inc v The Home Video Channel* [1997] FSR 22. This case concerned the popular television programme *Baywatch* and a programme on an adult television channel called *Babewatch*. The plaintiff, who was the producer of the *Baywatch* series and proprietor of the trade mark BAYWATCH in several classes, including Class 9, brought an action against the producer of the adult channel for trade mark infringement and passing off. The trade mark infringement claim was brought under sections 10(2) and 10(3). The plaintiff claimed that use of the name BABEWATCH was intended to take advantage of the reputation and distinctive character of the BAYWATCH mark and in addition would tarnish the reputation of the plaintiff's mark. In considering whether there had been section 10(3) infringement, the court considered the plaintiff's argument that confusion was not necessary to establish infringement. Section 10(3) applies where the goods or services of the plaintiff and defendant are not similar but where the mark used by the defendant is identical with or similar to the plaintiff's mark. The judge decided that 'the use of the concept of similarity in section 10(3) introduces in my judgment the ingredient of a likelihood of confusion on the part of the public'. As there was no evidence of actual or likely confusion between the two marks, the court dismissed the plaintiff's application. In passing, the judge referred to an unreported case, *BASF plc v CEP (UK) plc*, 26 October 1995, in which Knox J had commented that, in the absence of confusion, there was no basis for finding unfair advantage.

But in *Premier Brands UK Ltd v Typhoon Europe Ltd & Another* [2000] FSR 767, Neuberger J pointed out that while the need for confusion is stated in section 10(2), it is not in section 10(3). He confirmed that confusion is not a requirement for section 10(3). There the claimant held the trade mark Ty Phoo for tea and other kitchen goods, which were usually given away as free gifts. They objected to the defendant's use of the mark 'TYPHOON' on kitchenware. Neuberger J stated that dilution could be by 'blurring' where the distinctiveness of a mark is eroded as illustrated in the passing off case of *Taittinger SA v Allbev Ltd* [1993] FSR 641 or by the 'tarnishing' of the mark's reputation. The stronger the distinctive character and reputation of the mark, the easier it would be to establish detriment. In this particular case the claimant had failed to demonstrate that either 'blurring' or 'tarnishing' would occur. See also *DaimlerChrysler AG v Javid Alavi (t/a Merc)* [2001] RPC 813.

Rulings from the ECJ also suggest that section 10(3) can be used against defendants attaching their signs to goods and services that are the same or similar. See Case C-292/00, *Davidoff & Cie SA v Gofkid* [2003] 1 CMLR 35 and Case C-408/01, *Adidas AG v Fitness World Trading Ltd* [2004] 1 CMLR 448. This would give the owners of such marks the possibility of using section 10(3) in combination with either section 10(1) or section 10(2), with the added benefit in the latter case of not having to prove confusion.

10.2.3 Unfair advantage on the internet

The use of key words and AdWords has already been discussed in relation to section 10(1). The High Court has also sought guidance from the Court of Justice of the

EU in relation to article 5(2) of the directive, which is equivalent to section 10(3). The facts from *Interflora v Marks and Spencer plc C-323/09* clearly demonstrate the practice whereby an advertiser 'bids' a cost per click against a desired word, in this case a competitor's trade mark. Interflora is a well-known trade mark associated with the delivery of flowers. Behind the mark is a network of florists that allow customers to purchase flowers and have them delivered. An online search for Interflora will reveal the network's online store. But a search for the name also displays advertisements for competitors, in this case Marks and Spencer. This is because the latter had 'bid' on Interflora's name as a key word. So anyone searching Interflora would also see advertisements offering Marks and Spencer floral delivery services. The question for the European Court was whether this practice takes advantage of the trade mark owner's reputation. The ECJ's response stated that the wording of article 5(2) covered either dilution, tarnishment or free-riding. Tarnishment was not discussed. On the question of dilution, the ECJ stated that the mark was not diluted if a reasonable user could tell from the Marks and Spencer's sponsored results that its service was independent of Interflora. This left 'free-riding': 'taking unfair advantage of the distinctive character or repute of the trade mark'. On this the court stated:

Where a competitor of the proprietor of a trade mark with a reputation selects that trade mark as a keyword in an internet referencing service, the purpose of that use is to take advantage of the distinctive character and repute of the trade mark.

The court went on to add:

When internet users having studied the competitor's advertisement purchased the product or service offered by the competitor instead of that of the proprietor of the trade mark to which their search originally related that competitor derives a real advantage from the distinctive character and repute of the trade mark.

This would suggest that article 5(2) had been satisfied. However, the selection of the trade mark as a key word would have to be 'without due course' as stated in the article itself. On that point the issue was referred back to the UK court to determine on the facts.

Other activities that amount to infringement include: affixing the mark to goods; importing and exporting trade-marked goods; and using the mark on business papers or advertising (s 10(4)). A trade mark can also be infringed orally, for example in a radio advertisement criticising a rival product. Under section 10(5), persons other than the actual infringer can be liable. Those who apply a registered trade mark to material that is intended to be used for the labelling or packaging of goods, as business paper (for example, letterheads) or for advertising goods or services, will be treated as a party to infringement if they knew, or should have known, that use of the mark was not authorised.

10.3   Comparative advertising

Comparative advertising is the practice of advertising by comparing the merit of the product or service being advertised with that of a rival, using the rival's brand name. Under the 1938 Act, use of a Part A mark in this way, no matter how truthful the comparison, amounted to infringement (as 'importing a reference'); see *News Group Ltd v Mirror Group Ltd* [1989] FSR 126. Section 10(6) of the Trade Marks Act 1994 now appears to allow the practice. It states:

Nothing in the preceding provisions of this section shall be construed as preventing the use of a registered trade mark by any person for the purpose of identifying goods or services as those of the proprietor or a licensee.

But any such use otherwise than in accordance with honest practices in industrial or commercial matters shall be treated as infringing the registered mark if the use without due cause takes unfair advantage of, or is detrimental to, the distinctive character or repute of the trade mark.

The question to ask is: who will decide whether an advertiser's use is 'otherwise than in accordance with honest practices in industrial or commercial matters'? Or whether the use 'without due cause takes unfair advantage of, or is detrimental to, the distinctive character or repute of the trade mark'? In the White Paper which preceded the 1994 Act, the government stated that it was committed to allowing comparative advertising in the interests of better consumer awareness, provided advertisers and traders did not take a free ride on the back of the competitor's trade mark. Further, during the passage of the Trade Marks Bill, Lord Strathclyde, its sponsor, stated that the government had been persuaded that there was no harm in comparative advertising, provided it made use of a competitor's registered mark to inform the public. Section 10(6) does not come from Directive 89/104/EEC, on which the rest of the Trade Marks Act 1994 is based. Rather, the wording of section 10(6) is a combination of article 10bis of the Paris Convention, which deals with unfair competition, and articles 4 and 5 of the Directive. Since the passing of the 1994 Act, there has been a Directive on Comparative Advertising (Directive 97/55/EC), which the UK has since implemented (Control of Misleading Advertisements (Amendment) Regulations 2000, SI 914 of 2000).

The wording of section 10(6) was criticised by the courts for its lack of clarity. In *Barclays Bank plc v RBS Advanta* [1996] RPC 307, Laddie J said of the subsection:

It is a mess. The first part of the subsection allows comparative advertising. Its meaning is clear. However the second half beginning with the words 'But any such use ...' is a qualifying proviso and its meaning is far from clear (at 313).

However, Laddie J went on to decide, effectively, that the onus will be on the trade mark owner to establish that the use is not in '*accordance with honest practices in industrial or commercial matters*' (our italics).

The defendant, RBS Advanta, was launching a new credit card. It sent out pamphlets listing the 15 ways in which its card was allegedly better than other cards. On one of the pages, it listed the cards of six competitors, including Barclays. Barclays tried to obtain an injunction on the grounds that this use amounted to trade mark infringement. Laddie J held that, as the primary objective of section 10(6) was to allow comparative advertising, the proviso should not be construed in a way that would effectively prohibit all comparative advertising. The onus was on the plaintiff to demonstrate that the factors indicated in the proviso existed. In that case, the judge decided that Barclays had not shown that RBS's use fell within the proviso, because it was unlikely that any reasonable reader of the RBS advertisement would take the view that it was not honest when read as a whole. A similar decision was reached by the court in the case of *Vodafone Group plc v Orange Personal Communications Services Ltd* [1997] FSR 34, where the defendant's claim in its advertising that 'On average, Orange users save £20 every month' was held to be objectively honest and not misleading to the ordinary reader. On comparative advertising, see also *Macmillan Magazines Ltd v RCN Publishing Co Ltd* [1998] FSR 9 and *Cable and Wireless plc v British Telecommunications plc* [1998] FSR 383.

A rather surprising interpretation of section 10(6) was adopted in *British Airways plc v Ryanair Ltd* [2001] FSR 541. British Airways sued Ryanair for malicious falsehood and trade mark infringement when the latter advertised its services and prices with the following headings: 'EXPENSIVE BA ... DS' and 'EXPENSIVE BA', making price comparisons which the claimant felt were unfair. The first advertisement was withdrawn after a complaint to the Advertising Standards Authority However, Jacob J held that the fact that the advertisement was offensive did not mean that it fell outside the proviso of section 10(6), although the defendant claimed that their flights to Frankfurt were five times cheaper than the claimant's when they were in fact only three times cheaper. It was also claimed that like was not being compared with like as the defendant's flights were to a different airport in Frankfurt. Nevertheless, Jacob J held that the average consumer would not find the price comparison misleading. In his view the advertisements were true in substance and there had been honest use of British Airways' trade mark. It would be interesting to see whether a similar case would now be decided in the same way.

Regulation 2(2A) of the Control of Misleading Advertisements (Amendment) Regulations defines comparative advertising as:

> an advertisement is comparative if in any way, either explicitly or by implication, it identifies a competitor or goods or services offered by the competitor.

Regulation 4A (based on Directive 84/450, art 3a) then sets out the conditions under which comparative advertising will be permitted. The following is an outline:

(a) the advertisement should not be misleading;
(b) it compares goods and services meeting the same needs or intended for the same purpose;
(c) it objectively compares material;
(d) it does not create confusion;
(e) it does not discredit or denigrate the mark or trade name of the competitor;
(f) for products with designation of origin, it relates in each case to products with the same designation;
(g) it does not take unfair advantage of the reputation of a trade mark; and
(h) it does not present goods or services as imitations or replicas of goods or services bearing the protected trade mark or trade name.

We believe that even taking section 10(6) on its own, it is not fair and honest to state that your service is five times cheaper than a competitor's, when it is only three times cheaper. Hazel Carty (2002) suggests that the decision in *British Airways v Ryanair* reflects the fact that consumers are seen as streetwise, 'aware of the hyperbole and massaging of facts in advertising'. In making a reference to the ECJ for a ruling on *O$_2$ Holdings Ltd (2) O$_2$ (UK) Ltd v Hutchinson 3G Ltd* [2006] EWCA Civ 1656; [2007] RPC 16, Jacobs LJ has suggested that disparaging use of a trade mark would not be in accordance with 'honest practices', even if non-misleading. To that extent he stated that his decision in *Ryanair* had been wrong (see paras 56–8).

The ECJ has held that the conditions laid down in the Comparative Advertising Directive should be interpreted in the way that is most favourable to comparative advertising. See Case C-112/99, *Toshiba Europe GmbH v Katun Germany GmbH* [2002] FSR 39 and Case C-44/01, *Pippig Augenoptik GmbH & Co KG v Hartlauer Handelsgesellschaft GmbH ECR I-3095* (see Case notes at end of this chapter).

O₂ Holdings Ltd (2) O₂ (UK) Ltd v Hutchinson 3G Ltd [2008] RPC 33 concerned a comparative advertising campaign by the defendant which featured the use of bubbles similar to those registered by the claimants and used in a variety of ways in the claimants' advertisements. Lewison J held that while the claimant's trade mark was validly registered and infringed, the defendant was covered by the defence under the directive.

In the Court of Appeal, the following questions were referred to the ECJ:

1. Where a trader, in the advertisement for his own goods or services, uses a registered trade mark owned by a competitor for the purpose of comparing the characteristics (and in particular the price) of goods or services marketed by him with the characteristics (and in particular the price) of the goods or services marketed by the competitor under that mark in such a way that does not cause confusion or otherwise jeopardise the essential function of the trade mark as an indication of origin, does this use fall within either (a) or (b) of Art 5(1) of Directive 89/104 [infringement provisions]?

2. Where a trader uses, in a comparative advertisement, the registered trade mark of a competitor, in order to comply with Art. 3a(1) of Council Directive 84/450 must that use be 'indispensable' and if so what are the criteria by which indispensability is to be judged?

3. In particular, if there is a requirement of indispensability, does the requirement preclude any use of a sign which is not identical to the registered trade mark but is closely similar to it?

In response the ECJ has stated that the use by Hutchinson of the bubble images to indicate that its services were cheaper did not give rise to a likelihood of confusion on the part of consumers and did not suggest that there was any form of commercial link between O2 and Hutchinson 3G. As a whole the advertisement was not misleading. The advertisement therefore did not fall within either (a) or (b) of article 5(1) of the directive. In responding thus to the first question, the court did not feel the need to address questions 2 and 3. (See Case C-533/06 *O₂ Holdings Ltd v Hutchinson 3G Ltd* [2008] RPC 33.) See also *Specsavers International Health Care Ltd v ASDA Stores Ltd* [2012] EWCA Civ 24.

For a case on section 10(6) which does not concern comparative advertising, see *Primark Stores Ltd & Another v Lollipop Clothing Ltd* [2001] FSR 637. Here the defendant had acquired clothing, which had been made for the claimant, from the claimant's supplier, bearing the claimant's trade mark. In response to an action for infringement, the defendant claimed section 10(6), namely, that the mark merely identified the clothing as that of Primark. However, John Martin QC held that in order for the goods to be identified as the claimant's goods for the purposes of section 10(6), it was not enough that they were made to the claimant's specification; they must have been adopted by the claimant as its goods. Without that, the claimant could not be said to be the source of the goods for trade mark purposes.

10.4 Remedies

The general remedies for trade mark infringement are in section 14. These include damages, injunctions and an account of profits. A claimant cannot claim both damages and an account of profits. As with actions in tort, the purpose of damages is to place the claimant in the position in which he would have been had the wrong not been committed. The court will, therefore, take into consideration revenue from lost sales.

If infringement is proved, the defendant is liable to pay damages even if the act was committed innocently (see *Gillette UK Ltd v Edenwest Ltd* [1994] RPC 279). If the claimant claims an account of profits, the defendant has to hand over all the profits made from infringement. Account of profits is an equitable remedy, which means it will only be granted at the judge's discretion and is not available in cases of innocent infringement. An injunction prohibiting further use of the trade mark may also be granted. This is also an equitable remedy and where the claimant is seeking an interlocutory injunction, the conditions set out in *American Cyanamid Co v Ethicon Ltd* [1975] AC 396 apply.

Courts are also given the discretionary power under section 15 to order that an infringing sign be erased, removed or obliterated from any infringing goods (defined in section 17). Under section 16 an infringer can be ordered to deliver up to the trade mark owner any infringing goods, materials or articles. This must be specifically requested by the trade mark owner. Under section 19, the trade mark owner can apply to have the goods destroyed on delivery. The court must consider other remedies, and should take into account the interests of others in relation to the goods, for example, a person who has an interest under a retention of title clause or an interest in other intellectual property rights comprised in the infringing goods (for example, copyright or patent rights).

10.5 Exceptions and defences

An effective defence will remove the defendant's liability. The general defences are outlined in section 11. First of all, it is not an infringement to use the same mark as that of the claimant, if the defendant's mark is also registered. This is a form of statutory honest concurrent use. However, this should be read in the light of section 47 (discussed in Chapter 9), where the latter mark can be declared invalid if it should not have been registered in the first place because of the presence of the earlier mark.

The use of a person's name or address is not an infringement under section 11(2)(a), provided such use is consistent with 'honest practices in industrial or commercial matters'. In *Scandecor Developments AB v Scandecor Marketing AV & ors* [2001] UKHL 21, Lord Nicholls has suggested that a limited company can be a person for this purpose. This was followed in *Euromarket Designs Inc v Peters & Another* [2002] FSR 288 and confirmed by Jacobs LJ in *Reed Executive plc v Reed Business Information Ltd* [2004] EWCA Civ 159, at paragraph 116. Now see Case C-245/02 *Anheuser-Busch Inc v Bude'jovicky Budvar* [2004] ECRI-10989. However, in *Asprey & Gerrard Ltd v WRA (Guns) Ltd* [2001] EWCA Civ 1499; [2002] FSR 30, the Court of Appeal held that the own name defence is not available to a new company. So a Mr Paul Smith would not get away with opening a shop called 'Paul Smith' selling designer menswear. This subsection also allows the use of a trade mark to indicate the kind, quality or origin of goods, as well as use to indicate the purpose of the goods or service in question. So, for example, if a supplier is selling goods that have been manufactured using a material that is produced and sold by another supplier under a trade mark, the first supplier can state that his goods are made from the other supplier's material and use the other supplier's trade mark in doing so. And if a trader's goods are intended for use with the claimant's goods (for example, as accessories), the trader can use the claimant's trade mark to indicate that connection. However, all these uses must be in accordance with honest practices to fall within section 11(2).

Where a defendant can show that he had an established reputation in respect of his use of the mark in question in a particular locality pre-dating the claimant's registration, he can benefit from the defence in section 11(3). 'Locality' is not defined. To have such an 'earlier right', the right must be capable of protection by some other rule of law (including passing off).

One particular defence is the exhaustion of rights defence, which is set out in section 12. This section provides that, once goods bearing the claimant's trade mark have been legitimately put into circulation in the European Economic Area (EEA), the use of the trade mark in relation to those goods cannot be prevented elsewhere in the EEA by means of a claim of trade mark infringement. There is an exception to this, namely, where the goods have subsequently been tampered with in a way that could impair their quality.

It is also not an infringement of a trade mark to use only a part of the trade mark that is the subject of a disclaimer. A disclaimer is given for any part of a trade mark that does not satisfy the requirements of registrability and is necessary to ensure that the trade mark owner is not given a monopoly over a common word or other identifier. Under the 1938 Act, disclaimers had to appear on the face of the registration – this is not the case under the 1994 Act. A first step for any defendant should be to check whether any part of the infringed trade mark is disclaimed.

10.6 Groundless threats

The 1994 Act introduced a remedy for defendants in receipt of groundless threats of infringement (s 21), which is along the same lines as the corresponding section in the Patents Act 1977. This remedy is not, however, available to anyone who has actually applied the trade mark to goods or packaging, or who has imported the goods so trade-marked, or who is supplying services under the mark. The aim of this section is to protect traders who have not themselves instigated the act of trade mark infringement but who are just trading in goods or in some other way involved in dealing in the marked goods or services so that they might be targeted by a plaintiff. Attacking others in the chain of supply is a tactic often used by claimants when trying to reach the true primary infringer. See *Best Buy Co Inc v World Wide Sales Corp Espania SL* [2011] EWCA Civ 618.

10.7 Criminal offences

There are a number of criminal offences under the 1994 Trade Mark Act. First, to catch those persons who make a business of blatantly producing and selling counterfeits, section 92 makes it a criminal offence to commit any of the acts that amount to trade mark infringement with a view to gain for the offender or with intent to cause loss to another person. However, *R v Johnstone* [2002] EWCA Crim 194, *The Times*, 12 March states that for a successful prosecution under section 92, the Crown must prove that the defendant's acts amounted to civil infringement of the trade mark in question. Specific enforcement rights are given to the local weights and measures authority (that is, Trading Standards Officers). Other offences under the Act include:

(a) falsifying an entry on the Register of Trade Marks;
(b) falsely representing a trade mark as being registered when it is not (by including the ® against the mark before it is registered – ™ should be used instead);
(c) falsely representing that a registered mark is registered in respect of goods or services for which it is not registered; and
(d) unauthorised use of Royal Arms in such a way that suggests that such use has been duly authorised.

As with the Copyright, Designs and Patents Act 1988, where a company is found guilty of an offence, any officers with whose consent or connivance the offence was committed will also be guilty of an offence (s 101).

Sections 89 to 91 give trade mark owners the right to give notification to Customs and Excise of expected importation of infringing goods so that Customs and Excise can seize such goods at the point of entry. Customs and Excise only have power to seize goods but they can pass on information to the relevant weights and measures authority to enable any offences to be prosecuted.

10.8 Dealings in trade marks

A registered trade mark is capable of assignment or transmission and may also be charged like other personal property to provide security for, say, a loan.

Under the 1938 Act, special procedures had to be followed if a registered trade mark was to be assigned without the goodwill relating to the mark. Under the 1994 Act there are no such requirements, but if the trade mark is split from the business and goodwill to which it relates, there is a risk of the mark opening itself up to a possible challenge if the mark becomes deceptive. Registered trade marks may also be assigned in respect of only some of the goods covered by the registration or in respect of a particular locality only.

To be effective, an assignment must be in writing and signed by the assignor. All transactions in registered trade marks can be entered on the Register at the request of the person interested. If a transaction is not registered, a subsequent acquirer of interests in that mark who is not aware of the transaction would be entitled to treat the transaction as if it had not taken place. Failure to register a licence means the licensees do not have the rights in respect of infringements of the trade mark which are otherwise conferred by sections 30 and 31 of the 1994 Act. Someone who becomes the owner or licensee of a trade mark should register the transaction within six months, otherwise, in any infringement action, he will not be able to claim for an account of profits for the period between the transaction and registration of the transaction. These provisions concerning assignment of registered trade marks also apply to applications for trade marks. The position on unregistered trade marks is that, as they arise as a result of the generation of goodwill, they can only pass with the associated goodwill (normally as part of a business sale).

What is comparative advertising?

Comparative advertising is the practice of advertising by comparing the merit of the product or service being advertised with that of a rival, using the rival's brand name. Regulation 2(2A) of Control of Misleading Advertisements (Amendment) Regulations 2000, SI 914 of 2000, defines comparative advertising as:

> an advertisement is comparative if in any way, either explicitly or by implication, it identifies a competitor or goods or services offered by the competitor or goods or services offered by a competitor.

The main argument in favour of this practice is that in an open market, consumers should have all the available information and that comparative advertising facilitates this. The main argument against is that the advertiser will be selective in the way in which the products or services are compared in order to portray his own goods and/or services in the best possible light. According to Cornish and Llewelyn (2008: para 17.103):

> Some argue that no comparative advertising by one trader against another […] can be regarded as an honest practice … Those who take this view either treat it as self-evident or else claim that the advertising will inevitably be selective in content (and so distortive) so as to favour the advertiser.

The above is certainly the view of some EU Member States. In Germany and the Benelux countries, comparative advertising was prohibited prior to Directive 97/55/EC. In France, only comparisons of price were permitted. And in Denmark, advertisers had to make comparisons between all the relevant features, not just those favourable to the advertiser.

In the UK, the activity is regulated in a number of areas. For example, there is the British Code of Advertising which is administered by the Advertising Standards Authority, a self-regulatory system. According to Bentley and Sherman: 'the Code is based on the premise that comparative advertising should be allowed in the interests of vigorous competition and public information' (2006: 922). The interpretation of section 10(6) of the Trade Marks Act 1994 also reinforces the view that there is a liberal attitude in the UK, in contrast to Germany which is perhaps more paternalist, believing its citizens to be in need of consumer protection. According to Jacobs J (as he was), German unfair competition law is protective of 'even the stupid or careless' (*British Airways plc v Ryanair Ltd* [2001] FSR 541, at 552). British consumers, on the other hand, are regarded as somewhat streetwise in their attitude towards advertisements. According to Hughes, the decision in *British Airways v Ryanair*, discussed in Section 10.3, 'highlights the view that the general public are used to the ways of advertisers and that they expect hyperbole …'. Note that the decision should now be considered in the light of statements made by Jacob LJ in the O_2 reference to the ECJ.

Case notes

Cases where the ECJ have responded to references on the interpretation of Directive 97/55/EC suggest that a more liberal approach is to be encouraged within the internal market.

▶ **C-112/99, *Toshiba Europe GmbH v Katun Germany GmbH* [2002] FSR 39**

Katun had placed the reference numbers that Toshiba used for Toshiba's products alongside Katun's own product codes. This was done to allow consumers to identify the equivalent Toshiba products. The ECJ was asked:

(1) Was Katun's use of Toshiba's product numbers to be regarded as comparative advertising?
(2) If so, did the display of Toshiba's code alongside Katun's constitute a permissible comparison of goods?

In responding to the questions, the ECJ took account of the objectives as stated in the Preamble to the Directive. This indicated the importance of advertising in the establishment and furtherance of the internal market and the need to stimulate it. It therefore responded that the new directive should be interpreted in the way that was most favourable to comparative advertising.

▶ **C-44/01, *Pippig Augenoptik GmbH & Co KG v Hartlauer Handelsgesellschaft GmbH* ECR I-3095**

Hartlauer ran an advertising campaign in which leaflets directly compared Pippig's prices for spectacle frames with Zeiss lenses with Hartlauer's prices in respect of the same frames but with Optimed lenses. Television and radio broadcasts featured the same price comparison but did not state that the lenses were different brands and showed a Pippig shop front. The questions referred to the ECJ concerned whether a distinction could be made between those parts of the advertisements which could be considered comparative and those that could be considered non-comparative, with the latter being subject to national law on misleading advertisements. As with *Toshiba*, the ECJ was of the opinion that the new directive should be interpreted in the way that was most favourable to comparative advertising. Further, as the objective is the 'exhaustive harmonisation' of the conditions under which comparative advertising is deemed lawful, the ECJ ruled that the new directive precludes national legislation governing misleading advertising from applying to comparative advertising 'as far as the form and content of the comparison is concerned' (para 56).

▶ C-50/05, *Siemens AG v VIPA Gesellschaftfür Visualisierung und ProzeBautomatisierung mbH*

Siemens manufactures and distributes programmable controllers under the name 'Simatic'. In 1983 it introduced a system of order numbers for the controllers and their add-on components, which consists of a combination of capital letters and numbers. VIPA manufacture and sell components that are compatible with 'Simatic' controllers. From 1988 it used an identification system that was almost identical to that used by Siemens,

replacing the first group of characters of the Siemens' order number with VIPA, for example 6ES5 928–3UB21 became VIPA928–3UB21. In its catalogue it added: 'Please check the order number of the memory modules you require in the handbook for your module or call us. The order numbers correspond to those of Siemens' programmable modules.'

Siemens claimed VIPA was taking unfair advantage of the reputation of its products. According to the ECJ:

An advertiser cannot be regarded as taking unfair advantage of the reputation of the distinguishing marks of his competitor if effective competition on the relevant market is conditional upon a reference to those marks (para 15).

Comparative advertising is designed to enable consumers to make the best possible use of the internal market, given that advertising is a very important means of creating genuine outlets for all goods and services throughout the Community (para 22).

The purpose of comparative advertising is also to stimulate competition between suppliers of goods and services to the consumers' advantage (para 23).

The ECJ went on to hold that VIPA did not take unfair advantage of Siemens' reputation. The decision in *O₂ Holdings v Hutchinson 3G Ltd* [2008] RPC 33 further adds to the view that provided there is fair and honest use of the mark and no likelihood of confusion, comparative advertising is permitted.

Summary

▶ A trade mark is infringed if a person other than the owner makes use of it without his consent. Licensees also have a right to protection against infringement, which they can enforce if the trade mark owner fails to do so.

▶ Whereas it is obviously infringement to apply the same or a similar trade mark to the same or similar goods, it is also an infringement to apply a trade mark to dissimilar goods if the mark in question has acquired a reputation.

▶ Judges appear to be adopting a liberal interpretation of section 10(6) and Directive 97/55/EC to allow comparative advertising.

▶ Section 11 outlines a number of defences that remove the defendant's liability.

▶ A number of criminal offences have been introduced to stop the production and sale of counterfeit goods.

Further reading and references

Bainbridge, *Intellectual Property Law* (7th edn, Pitman Longman, 2009) pp 722–25.

Bentley and Sherman, *Intellectual Property Law* (2nd edn, Oxford University Press, 2002) pp 916–23.

Carty, 'Registered Trade Marks and Comparative Advertising' [2002] EIPR 294.

Clark and Shubert, 'Odysseus between Scylla and Charbdis? The ECJ rules in *L'Oreal v eBay*' JIPLP (2011) 6(12), 880.

Cornish and Llewelyn, *Intellectual Property Law* (5th edn, Sweet & Maxwell, 2008) para 17.103.

Cornthwaite, 'Say It with Flowers: The Judgment of the Court Of Justice of the European Union in *Interflora v Marks and Spencer*', 2012 EIPR 34(2), 127.

Fletcher, Fussing and Indraccolo, 'Comparisons and Conclusions: Welcome Clarification from the European Court of Justice on the Interpretation of the Comparative Advertising Directive' [2003] EIPR 25(12), 570.

Hughes 'Trade and Service Marks – Comparative Advertising – Whether Infringement' [2001] Ent LR 12(4), N34 35.

Isaac and Joshi, 'What Does Identical Mean?' [2005] EIPR 27(5), 184.

Smith and Silver, '*L'Oreal v eBay*: a Warning to on Line Market Place Operators' JIPLP (2011) 6(11), 765.

Stephenson 'Comparative Advertising And Intellectual Property Rights'[2006] EIPR 28(3), 182–191.

Chapter 11

Passing off

11.1　Introduction

The practice of passing off involves one trader giving consumers the impression that his goods are those of another trader who has an established goodwill. It also occurs where one trader indicates that his goods are of the same quality as those of another trader or where one trader creates the impression of association with another trader. Where an existing trader has a reputable and popular product or service, another trader will hope to take advantage of the goodwill that has been established in that product or service, by confusing consumers into purchasing his goods instead of those of the first trader. The first trader suffers lost sales as consumers buy goods from the trader who is passing off, believing them to be the same (or of the same quality) as those of the genuine trader. Where the second trader's goods are not of the same standard, there is added damage as consumers will assume that the substandard goods come from the first trader. There is, therefore, a loss of sales coupled with a loss of reputation.

Honest traders are protected against such activities by the law of passing off. Passing off is a tort. It provides common law protection of brand names and 'get-up'. This form of action is used either where the mark is an unregistered mark, or where the mark is unregistrable. For registered marks, the proprietor can bring an action for passing off as well as trade mark infringement. In court, the issues will be the same, namely, there must be a balance between protecting the proprietor's goodwill, and protecting the interests of other legitimate traders. The interests of consumers must also be considered.

11.2　The difference between trade mark infringement and passing off

Once a trade mark is registered, protection against infringement is automatic. Trade marks are a form of personal property and their use by another without the proprietor's authority is interference with his property right. The proprietor need prove nothing more. On the other hand, the claimant in a passing off action must demonstrate the presence of goodwill in order to have a right of action. The common law protects the goodwill of a business associated with a trade name or get-up, while trade mark legislation protects rights in the actual name. The protection provided in passing off is potentially broader. Business goodwill can cover the name of the goods or services in question, business methods, get-up and marketing styles.

Two cases sum up the difference in the protection provided. In *Coca-Cola Trade Mark Applications* [1986] 2 All ER 274, the House of Lords refused to allow the registration of the shape of the famous Coca-Cola bottle, because it was concerned about the creation of a monopoly in containers. Yet the same court, in *Reckitt & Colman Products Ltd v Borden Inc (No 3)* [1990] 1 All ER 873, restrained the defendant's use of a plastic container resembling the plaintiff's plastic lemon in a passing off action. Registration of shapes as trade marks is now allowed under the Trade Marks Act 1994.

By way of further example, the registration of single colours was refused in *Wyeth (John) Coloured Tablet Trade Mark* [1988] RPC 233, but in *White Hudson & Co Ltd v Asian Organisation Ltd* [1964] 1 WLR 1466, the plaintiff was able to claim protection in passing off for red cellophane sweet wrappers. Again, single colours are now being passed for registration under the Trade Marks Act 1994. So the protection given in passing off would appear to be wider, although it has proved difficult to use for protecting advertising campaigns (see *Cadbury-Schweppes Ltd v Pub Squash Co Ltd* [1981] 1 All ER 213).

11.3 Historical background

The traditional form of passing off is where the defendant gives the consumer the impression that the goods sold are actually those of the claimant. In other words, where the defendant passes off his goods as those of the claimant. A defendant may also be found to be passing off one quality of the claimant's goods as goods of another quality. In *Spalding (A G) & Bros v Gammage (A W) Ltd* (1915) 84 LJ Ch 449, the plaintiffs manufactured 'Orb' footballs. They applied their mark to two types of ball, and sold the inferior type to waste-rubber merchants. The defendant bought these inferior products and sold them in such a way as to imply that they were the higher-quality 'Orb' footballs. It was held that, as the plaintiffs had established a reputation in the quality of their footballs, the defendants were passing off the plaintiffs' goods of inferior quality as those of the higher quality.

In *Bollinger v Costa Brava Wine Co* [1960] Ch 262, the producers of French champagne took action against the producers of 'Spanish champagne'. The plaintiffs argued that they were the only people entitled to use the word 'champagne' as it was the name of a product from a particular region. This argument succeeded on the basis that use of the word in this way could lead to dilution of the word 'champagne'. See also *Taittinger SA v Allbev Ltd* [1993] FSR 641. Further, passing off can be used to ensure that goods are manufactured to the quality indicated by the name. In *Erven Warnink Besloten Vennootschap v J Townend & Sons (Hull) Ltd* [1979] AC 731, the plaintiff made a high-quality spirit-based drink called advocaat. The defendant produced 'egg flip' made from dried egg powder and fortified wine and called it 'Keeling's Old English Advocaat'. The defendant's product was an inferior, but cheaper, drink, which took away some of the plaintiff's custom. The plaintiff's main objection was that, in making the product incorrectly, a misrepresentation was being made to customers. Using the name 'advocaat' should mean that the drink was made to the same high quality as the plaintiff's product. The same also applies to the production and alcohol content of vodka. See *Diageo North America Inc & Anr v Intercontinental Brands Ltd & ors* [2010] EWCA Civ 920.

However, once a defendant has established goodwill in his own product using the plaintiff's name, it will be very difficult to restrain him. In *Vine Products Ltd v Mackenzie & Co Ltd (No 3)* [1969] RPC 1, Spanish producers of sherry tried to stop the use of the sherry name on wines produced from regions other than the Jerez region in Spain. However, producers in other countries were able to show that they had already established goodwill in their 'sherry'. As a result, the court held that they were entitled to continue to use the name, with the country of origin as a prefix. In each of these drinks cases, the goodwill in the relevant name was shared between any number of producers of the legitimate product.

11.4 The requirements of a passing off action

Traditionally, the minimum requirements for a successful action in passing off were laid down by Lord Diplock in *Erven Warnink Besloten Vennootschap v J Townend & Sons (Hull) Ltd* [1979] AC 731. These were:

(1) a misrepresentation, (2) made by a trader in the course of trade, (3) to prospective customers of his or ultimate customers of goods or services supplied by him, (4) which is calculated to injure the business, or goodwill, of another trader (in the sense that it is a reasonably foreseeable consequence) and (5) which causes actual damage to the business or goodwill of the trader by whom the action is brought or (in a quia timet action) will probably do so (at 742).

These five requirements were reduced to three in *Reckitt & Colman Products Ltd v Borden Inc (No 3)* [1990] 1 All ER 873, by Lord Oliver as: (a) the existence of plaintiff's goodwill, (b) a misrepresentation and (c) damage (or likely damage) to the plaintiff's goodwill or reputation. This test was adopted in *Consorzio del Prosciutto di Parma v Marks & Spencer plc* [1991] RPC 351.

11.5 The claimant's goodwill

The claimant must establish goodwill associated with the goods or their get-up. Goodwill has been defined in *Trego v Hunt* [1895] AC 7 as:

The whole advantage, wherever it may be, of the reputation and connection of the firm which have been built up by years of honest work or gained by lavish expenditure of money.

In other words, it is the likelihood that consumers will continue to return, because of the quality and reputation of the goods or service provided by the trader. This suggests a reputation built up over time, so a claimant who has just started trading is unlikely to succeed in a passing off action. However, in *Stannard v Reay* [1967] RPC 589, three weeks was held to be sufficient time to build up goodwill in the name 'Mr Chippy' for a mobile fish-and-chip van.

Each case will depend on the circumstances. If, for example, there has been an intensive advertising campaign, goodwill can be acquired in a relatively short period of time, even if the goods or services to which it relates are not yet available, as happened in *Elida Gibbs Ltd v Colgate Palmolive Ltd* [1983] FSR 94.

Although goodwill suggests trade, passing off can be used to protect non-commercial activities. In *British Diabetic Association (The) v The Diabetic Society* [1996] FSR 1, the plaintiff charity was able to restrain the defendants (another charity) from using the name 'Diabetic Society'. The court was convinced that, as a result of the likely confusion, charitable contributions and support intended for the plaintiff charity might be diverted to the defendant.

In *Richard Burge & Another v John Bernard Haycock & Another* [2001] EWCA Civ 900, members of the Countryside Alliance, a pressure group set up to pursue the interests of those living in the countryside, successfully restrained a former member of the British National Party from standing in an election under a Countryside Alliance banner.

The claimant will need to prove that the goodwill existed at the time that the defendant commenced his activity rather than at the time of the action. See *Inter Lotto (UK) Ltd v Camelot Group plc* [2003] EWCA Civ 1132; [2004] RPC 9.

How long can goodwill last? *See Kevin Floyd Sutherland & ors v V2 Music Ltd & ors* [2002] EWHC 14 (Ch).

11.5.1 Goodwill and geographical considerations

Goodwill can be localised. For example, a hairdresser in Derby, operating under the name 'Clippers', may not be able to stop another hairdresser using the same name in Reading. In *Francis Geoffrey Bignall (t/a Just Employment a firm) v Just Employment Law Ltd* [2007] EWHC 2203, referred to in Chapter 9, the claimant operated an employment law practice in Guildford, mainly representing employees. The defendant operated mainly in Glasgow with an office in London. The defendant stated that the claimant's goodwill was limited to Guildford. However, if the business has a national or international reputation, then a successful action in passing off is more likely. In *Sheraton Corp of America v Sheraton Motels* [1964] RPC 202, Sheraton had a successful chain of hotels, but there were none in the UK. Despite this, the court held that there was a tangible connection, as it was possible to walk into a travel agent in the UK and book a room in a Sheraton anywhere in the world. In *Maxim's Ltd v Dye* [1977] 1 WLR 1155, the plaintiff owned a restaurant in Paris known as 'Maxim's'. The defendant opened a restaurant in Norwich calling it 'Maxim's'. As the plaintiff may have wanted to open a restaurant in the UK using the same name, it was held that he should be able to rely on the goodwill he had acquired in connection with that name to prevent the defendant from trading under that name.

The above cases contrast with *Bernadin v Pavillion Properties* [1967] RPC 581, where the owners of the 'Crazy Horse' nightclub in Paris were unable to stop the defendants using the name for a club in London. In *Anheuser-Busch Inc v Budejovicky Budvar* [1984] FSR 413, the fact that the plaintiff's beer had only been made available in the UK to US diplomats and servicemen meant that it had not established sufficient goodwill in the UK, even though it had a good reputation and goodwill in the United States from where there had been spill-over advertising.

The position of foreign plaintiffs was considered by the High Court in *Jian Tools for Sales Inc v Roderick Manhattan Group Ltd & Another* [1995] FSR 924. Jian Tools had established goodwill in the United States for the 'BizPlan Builder' software for the preparation of business plans. The defendants introduced a product performing the same functions called the 'Business Plan Builder'. The plaintiff claimed ownership of both 'BizPlan Builder' and 'Business Plan Builder' and sought an injunction for passing off. Both parties accepted that a foreign plaintiff, suing in passing off, had to establish goodwill in the UK. Sales of the 'BizPlan Builder' in Britain had reached 127 units. A number of sales were the result of advertising in American publications that were available in the UK, others were the result of recommendations from American friends or colleagues. Two advertisements were placed in British publications and those generated ten sales. Knox J felt that this provided the plaintiff with an arguable case for passing off. It was established that the plaintiff had customers in the UK. The purchases in the UK were not to be disregarded simply because they were generated from foreign sources, unless they were purchases that no member of the general public would make.

Medgen Inc v Passion for Life Products Ltd [2001] FSR 496 concerned a passing off dispute in relation to a natural health care product to prevent snoring, 'Snorenz'. The claimants had developed the product in the United States, and appointed PFL as its exclusive distributors in the UK. PFL, who marketed the product for 18 months, had designed the product's packaging which carried its own name and not that of Medgen. When the parties could not agree terms on which to renew the exclusive distributorship, PFL developed a similar product, which it marketed under its registered trade mark

'Snoreez'. The packaging used was practically the same as that used for 'Snorenz'. It was common ground that 'Snorenz' and its packaging had established a substantial goodwill, but the question was: to whom did that goodwill belong? The marketing and sales of 'Snorenz' had been undertaken by PFL in its own name. Wholesalers, retailers and ultimately consumers would only have known PFL as the source of the product. Medgen did not operate in the UK and there was no reference to Medgen on the product's packaging. Thus on the evidence, the goodwill was said to belong to PFL.

In *Plentyoffish Media Inc v Plenty More LLP* [2011] EWHC 2568; [2012] RPC 5 (a case on Trade Marks Act 1994, s 5(4)a), it was held that having a business reputation in the United Kingdom was not sufficient to support a finding of goodwill in a trading name. Evidence of actual customers was required.

11.6 Misrepresentation

The misrepresentation need not be intentional for a passing off action to succeed, and innocence of a misrepresentation is no defence. However, the defendant's state of mind may influence the remedy awarded by the court.

The misrepresentation may be in respect of the origin of the goods, their quality, or even the way in which they are made. Most of the cases concern misrepresentation as to origin and quality. In *Coombe International v Scholl* [1977] RPC 1, the plaintiff manufactured insoles called 'Odor Eaters', which contained activated charcoal. The defendant, who was a well-known manufacturer of footwear, also produced odour eaters. These were packaged in the same way. An injunction was granted on the basis that there was a misrepresentation as to the origin of the defendant's product, which was found to be inferior. *Spalding (A G) & Bros v Gammage (A W) Ltd* (1915) 84 LJ Ch 449 is an example of misrepresentation as to the quality of the goods. *Wilkinson Sword Ltd v Cripps & Lee Ltd* [1982] FSR 16 is another. The defendant imported blades from the United States called 'Wilkinson blades'. The plaintiff had an established reputation in the UK for its blades under the name 'Wilkinson Sword'. The imported blades were inferior. When the defendant brought the inferior goods into the UK market they created a false impression as to their quality. The defendant had applied to strike out the plaintiff's claim as having no reasonable cause of action but the court held that the plaintiffs did, indeed, have a reasonable cause of action.

11.6.1 Misrepresentation and confusion

Case law would indicate that the misrepresentation should lead, or be likely to lead, to confusion on the part of consumers. This is illustrated by *Morning Star v Express Newspapers* [1979] FSR 113, where the defendant intended to publish a newspaper called the *Daily Star*, a tabloid which would be sold through newsagents. The plaintiff was the publisher of the *Morning Star*, a weekly paper of the Communist Party. Foster J was of the opinion, having looked at the two papers side by side, that there would be no confusion as to the origin of the newspapers. His view was that 'only a moron in a hurry' would confuse the two! This suggests that the test is that of the 'reasonable consumer'. However, there is no uniform standard. In *Reckitt & Colman Products Ltd v Borden Inc (No 3)* [1990] 1 All ER 873, Lord Oliver was of the opinion that customers have to be taken as found: it is no argument to suggest that they would not have been deceived had they been 'more careful, more literate or more perspicuous'. The case of *United Biscuits (UK) Ltd v Asda Stores Ltd* [1997] RPC 513 relied on the statement in *European (The) v The Economist Newspaper* [1996] FSR 431 that, in a case of this kind, the judge should form his own view and decided that the judge's 'judicial first impression [was] of some importance' on the issue of confusion.

In *Alan Kenneth McKenzie Clark v Associated Newspapers Ltd* [1998] RPC 261, the plaintiff, Alan Clark, was a well-known Member of Parliament who had published his diaries. A deal to contribute articles in the form of diary entries to one of the defendant's newspapers, the *Evening Standard*, did not materialise. Instead the newspaper published a weekly spoof of Alan Clark's diaries based on what the journalist imagined Alan Clark would record in his diary. The column was headed 'Alan Clark's Secret Political Diaries' and included a picture of Alan Clark. The journalist was identified as the author, and the basis for the column was also explained. The defendant was held liable for both passing off and false attribution of authorship under copyright law. To be actionable as passing off, the deception had to be more than momentary and inconsequential. In cases where there were mixed messages, the dominant message is what matters and it is not sufficient to claim that a careful sensible reader would not have been misled.

If the likelihood of confusion is marginal, claimants will need actual evidence of confusion. This was confirmed by the Court of Appeal in *Neutrogena Corp & Another v Golden Ltd & Another* [1996] RPC 473. The plaintiff sold a range of hypoallergenic products for the skin and hair under the name NEUTROGENA. The defendant started marketing a similar, but narrower, range of skin and hair products under the name NEUTRALIA. The plaintiff argued that use of the prefix 'NEUTR' led to confusion. At trial, the plaintiff brought varied evidence of confusion. This included complaints received about a NEUTRALIA advertisement, which the complainants had taken to be for NEUTROGENA; members of the public who had been interviewed having picked up the products from shops that had advertised a special offer for NEUTROGENA; and the staff at the plaintiff's solicitors who had responded to an internal e-mail asking whether they had heard of or used NEUTRALIA products. The Court of Appeal held that the legal test on the issue of deception was whether, on a balance of probabilities, a substantial number of members of the public would be misled into purchasing the defendant's product in the belief that it was the plaintiff's. The court felt that the evidence produced (in particular the complaints about the advertisement) demonstrated confusion caused by the defendant's mark.

In *Kimberly-Clark v Ford Sterling* [1997] FSR 877, the judge stated that in a case concerning consumer products in a highly competitive market, damages were bound to follow deception and could almost be assumed. In this case, the manufacturers of Nouvelle toilet paper offered customers who were not satisfied with the Nouvelle product a free pack of Andrex toilet paper (Andrex being the product made and sold by one of Kimberly-Clark's competitors). The reference to the Andrex product on the Nouvelle packaging in order to publicise this offer was held to constitute passing off.

11.6.2 Confusion and common fields of activity

Traditionally there was a need for the claimant and defendant to be in the same field of business activity before it was considered likely that there would be confusion leading to injury to goodwill. This qualification has prevented some individuals from stopping the unauthorised use of their name. In *McCulloch v May* [1947] 2 All ER 845, the plaintiff was a well-known children's broadcaster who used the name 'Uncle Mac'. The defendant sold cereal under the name 'Uncle Mac', alluding to some of the plaintiff's characteristics, without his permission. The plaintiff failed in his action in passing off because he was not involved in the making or marketing of cereals. According to Wynn-Parry J, there had to be a 'common field of activity' in which, however remotely, both plaintiff and defendant are engaged. If the plaintiff and defendant are operating in dissimilar trades, it is thought unlikely that consumers will be misled in a way which would harm the plaintiff.

In *Stringfellow v McCain Foods* [1984] RPC 501, the plaintiff owned a nightclub called 'Stringfellows'. He took action against the manufacturers of oven chips, who had named one of their brands 'Stringfellows' because of their long thin appearance. Their advertising campaign included young people dancing in the kitchen as if in a discotheque. The Court of Appeal considered whether there would be confusion because the plaintiff also served food, and, if so, whether the plaintiff had suffered, or was likely to suffer, damage. The court found that even though some evidence of confusion was shown, this was unlikely to result in any damage to the plaintiff. By contrast, in *Annabels (Berkeley Square) v Schock* [1972] RPC 838, the court felt that there was a possibility of confusion between a nightclub and an escort agency operating under similar names because both could be considered night-time activities.

If the plaintiff has an outstanding reputation, nationally or internationally, then passing off can be shown even where the plaintiff and the defendant are involved in different fields of activity. This is illustrated by *Lego Systems A/S v Lego M. Lemelstrich Ltd* [1983] FSR 155. The plaintiff made coloured plastic construction bricks for children. The defendant used the plaintiff's name (LEGO) on plastic irrigation and gardening equipment outside the UK and planned to use it in the UK. The House of Lords held that the plaintiff's bricks had become so well known in the UK, as had the name LEGO, that confusion was extremely likely merely as a result of use of the same name. However, in *Harrods Ltd v Harrodian School* [1996] RPC 697 there was said to be no confusion where the defendants called their preparatory school 'The Harrodian'. They had purchased the premises from Harrods, who had previously used it as a sports club for their staff. It had been known as 'The Harrodian' since 1929. The Court of Appeal did not accept the plaintiff's argument that the defendants were seeking to take advantage of a perceived connection with Harrods. Kerr LJ dissented. In his view, if the sports club had been called 'The Harrods Club' and the defendants had called their school 'The Harrods School', an injunction would not have been refused.

The need for a common field of activity to prove damage has had a detrimental effect on the commercial practice of character merchandising, as well as preventing well-known personalities from controlling the use of their names and images, as indicated by the 'Uncle Mac' case. This is where the names or pictures of famous characters, whether real or fictional, are applied to everyday goods to make them more marketable. In *Lynstad v Anabas Products Ltd* [1977] FSR 62, the members of the pop group Abba were unable to stop their pictures being applied to T-shirts because they were in the entertainment business and not in the same field as manufacturers of clothing. However, the courts have been moving away from this strict approach in the field of character merchandising. See, for example, *Mirage Studios v Counter-Feat Clothing Co Ltd* [1991] FSR 145 and *Edmund Irvine & Another v Talksport Ltd* [2002] EWCH 367(Ch).

Certain fields of activity may have been traditionally distinct but in the minds of consumers there is a trade connection and the courts appreciate this. In *NAD Electronics Inc v NAD Computer Systems Ltd* [1997] FSR 380, Ferris J held that the fields of audio hi-fi and computers were converging and were not sufficiently distinct to negate confusion in the minds of the public.

11.7 Damage

The claimant must show damage or a probability of damage. The damage need not necessarily be tangible. For example, in *Taittinger SA v Allbev Ltd* [1993] FSR 641, the Court of Appeal accepted that use of the word 'champagne' by those not entitled to use it would diminish the goodwill associated with that name. In *Chocosuisse Union des Fabricants Suisse de Chocolat & ors v Cadbury Ltd* [1998] RPC 117 the defendants were the UK's leading chocolate confectionery manufacturers. They produced a new range of chocolate bars called 'Swiss Chalet'. The claimant successfully argued that the exclusivity of the designation 'Swiss Chocolate', descriptive of chocolate made in Switzerland, would suffer. Laddie J accepted that while the number of people confused into thinking that the defendants' product belonged to a group of products made in Switzerland was smaller than the number for whom there was no confusion, those confused were still likely to have been a substantial number. This was affirmed by the Court of Appeal ([1999] RPC 826).

Certain products associated with particular places are also protected by EC regulations. For example, Council Regulation 1576/89/EEC restricts the use of geographical names for spirits such as whisky. In *Gloag (Matthew) & Sons Ltd v Welsh Distillers Ltd* [1998] FSR 718, the defendant bought Scotch whisky and marketed it under the name Welsh whisky. Laddie J held that there had been an arguable case for passing off and the plaintiff also had a private right under the regulation.

Case C-108/01, *Consorzio del Prosciutto di Parma v ASDA Stores Ltd* [2002] FSR 37, concerned Council Regulation 2081/92/EEC, which restricts designations of origin and geographical indications for agricultural products and Parma ham which comes from the Parma region of Italy. ASDA was selling ham which was sliced and packaged outside the region. The lower courts had found in ASDA's favour. The High Court had decided that as Council Regulation 2081/92/EEC did not directly refer to the slicing and packaging, the defendant was not in contravention. Differing views were expressed in the House of Lords. Lord Hoffmann was of the opinion that a valid Community right that was directly enforceable in a domestic court was being infringed. Lord Scott, on the other hand, was of the view that the consortium's supervisory role to ensure that only the genuine product was sold as Parma ham was discharged once the product left the local processors or packers. In its response to the House of Lords' reference, the European Court of Justice (ECJ) agreed with Lord Hoffmann. The ECJ was of the opinion that in order to maintain the quality and reputation of Parma ham, it should only bear that name if it has been sliced and packed in Parma itself under the supervision of members of the consortium.

In *Harrods Ltd v Harrodian School* [1996] RPC 697 (discussed in Section 11.6.2), the Court of Appeal did not accept that use of the word 'Harrodian' by the school would dilute the good name of Harrods.

A claimant may employ a range of methods to prove confusion leading to lost sales or dilution of reputation. One method is the use of surveys. However, the courts are not usually impressed by this as a means of obtaining evidence. If surveys are used, they should be properly carried out, otherwise the results may be discredited by the court. Guidance on this was provided in *Imperial Group Ltd v Philip Morris & Co Ltd* [1984] RPC

293. The plaintiff made John Player Specials (JPS) cigarettes, which were packaged in black with gold lettering and a gold monogram. The defendant used black-and-gold packets for 'Raffles' cigarettes. The plaintiff used surveys to show that there was a high degree of association between the colours black and gold and the JPS cigarette.

In considering the results of the survey, Whitford J set the following guidelines:

(a) persons interviewed must be selected to represent a relevant cross-section of the public;
(b) the sample size must be statistically significant;
(c) the survey must be conducted fairly;
(d) all surveys carried out must be disclosed in full (that is, warts and all);
(e) all answers given must be disclosed and made available to the defendant;
(f) no leading questions must be asked of interviewees;
(g) interviewees must not be led to embark on a field of speculation they would not otherwise have considered;
(h) instructions to interviewees must be disclosed;
(i) if the answers are to be coded for computer input, the coding instructions must also be disclosed.

Therefore, good statistical methods must be coupled with openness and disclosure. Claimants can also make use of trap orders. This is where they place orders for genuine goods in the hope that the defendant will supply other goods instead.

11.8 Domain names

Domain names are the internet addresses registered by users of the internet to enable e-mails to be sent to them or their websites to be accessed. Ideally, for businesses, the domain name should indicate who they are and in that respect they perform similar functions to trade marks. However, the domain name system is far less flexible than that for the registration of trade marks. Each name given is unique, so there is little scope for having the same name for a number of differing businesses, all of whom may legitimately wish to use it. There can, for example, be only one BBC.com although it is also possible to have BBC.co.uk. The system is not yet as comprehensively regulated as that for trade marks, thus leaving it open to abuse by speculators registering domain names that they have no intention of using. The courts have shown a willingness to allow actions for passing off and trade mark infringement under section 10(3). In *British Telecommunications plc v One in a Million Ltd & ors* [1999] FSR 1, the defendants had registered a large number of domain names comprising the names or trade marks of well-known enterprises without their consent. None were in use as active sites. The defendants had registered them with a view to making a profit either by selling them to the owners of the goodwill or to collectors. Among the brands concerned were Marks & Spencer, Sainsbury, Ladbrokes, Virgin and British Telecom, and all these companies sued the defendants alleging passing off and trade mark infringement. In Marks & Spencer's case, the Court of Appeal was of the opinion that the registration of the domain name made a false representation that the defendants were associated or connected with Marks & Spencer plc. The other cases were slightly different in that there were people called 'Sainsbury' and 'Ladbroke', and there were other companies with the name 'Virgin' and also people or firms with the initials BT. However Aldous LJ believed that for the same reasons expressed in the Marks & Spencer action, passing off and threatened passing off had been demonstrated.

On the trade mark issue, the domain names were registered to take advantage of the distinctive character and reputation of the marks. This was unfair and detrimental. It therefore amounted to infringement under section 10(3) of the Trade Marks Act 1994. See also *Phones 4U Ltd (2) Caudwell Holdings Ltd v (1) Phone4U.co.uk Internet Ltd (2) Abdul Heykali (3) New World Communications Ltd* [2006] EWCA Civ 244.

11.9   Injurious falsehood

In between the torts of defamation and passing off, there is injurious falsehood. The action is sometimes referred to as malicious falsehood or trade libel. It is linked to passing off because it is another form of protection for a trader's goodwill. And it is a form of defamation because the defendant has allegedly libelled the business of another trader.

Injurious falsehood actions can be brought by legally aided plaintiffs, whereas defamation actions cannot. Where there is overlap, it is perfectly acceptable for the claimant to found an action in injurious falsehood and thus benefit from legal aid. See *Joyce v Sengupta* [1993] 1 WLR 337; [1993] All ER 897.

To succeed, the claimant must show that the defendant maliciously made false statements about the claimant's goods or services, which were calculated to cause damage. Mere advertising puffs, suggesting that the claimant's product is slightly better than the plaintiff's product, are not usually sufficient.

11.9.1   Falsehood

If the defendant's statement about the claimant's goods is true, there is no action; the onus is on the claimant to prove that the statement is false. We already know that selling one quality of the claimant's goods as those of another quality amounts to passing off, as illustrated by *Spalding (A G) & Bros v Gammage (A W) Ltd* (1915) 84 LJ Ch 449. This can also amount to injurious falsehood. In *Wilts United Dairies Ltd v Thomas Robinson Sons & Co Ltd* [1958] RPC 94, the Ministry of Food sold off quantities of the plaintiff's old condensed milk on condition that it should not be used for human consumption, because it had been kept during the Second World War and had deteriorated with age. The defendant obtained large quantities of the milk and sold it for human consumption. The defendant was held to have passed off one class of the plaintiff's goods as another and its activities amounted to injurious falsehood as such activities harmed the plaintiff's reputation.

The action has also been used, on the whole unsuccessfully, where a defendant has engaged in comparative advertising. In *McDonald's Hamburgers Ltd v Burger King (UK) Ltd* [1986] FSR 45, Burger King advertised its hamburger, the 'Whopper', by referring to McDonald's 'Big Mac'. The injurious falsehood action failed but the advertisement was said to have led to confusion and the defendant was therefore liable in passing off.

In *British Airways plc v Ryanair Ltd* [2001] FSR 541, the claimant had sued for injurious falsehood as well as trade mark infringement. Jacob J stated that a higher standard of liability was required.

According to Carty (2002 EIPR 294), it would appear that the action would only really succeed where the attack on claimants is a personal one that affects their economic interest: see *Joyce v Sengupta* [1993] 1WLR 337; [1993] All ER 897.

11.9.2   Damage

Traditionally the plaintiff had to prove special damage, such as a fall in trade. Proof of a significant fall in turnover was enough. In *Ratcliffe v Evans* [1892] 2 QB 524, the defendant suggested in its local weekly newspaper that the plaintiff had gone out of business. The plaintiff, whose business was within the area of the paper's circulation, suffered a fall in trade. The court held that this amounted to injurious falsehood. In *Timothy White v Mellin* [1895] AC 154, the plaintiff's infant foods were sold with labels attached to the wrappers that indicated that another product was more nutritious and healthier. The court in that case held that there was no evidence that the statement was false or that it had caused special damage.

The need to show special damage has been modified by section 3 of the Defamation Act 1952. There is no need for the plaintiff to show special damage if the defendant's statement was calculated to cause pecuniary damage to the plaintiff and was published in writing or another permanent form or was calculated to cause pecuniary damage to the plaintiff in respect of any office, profession, calling, trade or business held by the plaintiff at the time of the publication.

11.10 Remedies

Damages are available in a passing off action. These are usually based on the actual loss suffered as far as that can be calculated. Damages may also be calculated on a royalty basis, in other words, the amount that the defendant would have paid if he had applied for a licence to use the claimant's name or mark. In practice, the claimant would prefer an injunction to restrain the defendant's activities and the most effective type of injunction is an interlocutory injunction (in other words, an injunction applied for before the main issues are decided). If this is the case, the court will follow Lord Diplock's guidance from *American Cyanamid Co v Ethicon Ltd* [1975] AC 396 on interlocutory injunctions. See also *Macmillan Magazines Ltd v RCN Publishing Co Ltd* [1998] FSR 9.

Character merchandising

Character merchandising involves attaching the name or image of a popular character to otherwise mundane everyday products. Examples would include U2 on T-shirts, or bedding featuring any of Walt Disney's animated princesses. Personality merchandising is: 'the practice whereby celebrities use their names and images to endorse and associate themselves with products and services ...' (Bentley and Sherman, 2006). Both character and personality merchandising are multi-million-pound activities.

In theory such activities take place with the authority of the personality or the owner of the character concerned, usually in the form of a licence agreement. However, in many cases, characters are attached to merchandise without such agreements and the images of well-known personalities used without their authority. Traders who fail to obtain such licences avoid paying the fees and can, therefore, afford to sell their goods at a lower price than licensed traders. The result is a possible loss of custom for those trading legitimately. Further, unlicensed traders will not have any responsibilities as regards quality. Consumers, therefore, risk being supplied with inferior goods.

Legal protection against the unauthorised use of characters is haphazard, to say the least. In passing off, protection has been hampered by the need to establish a common field of activity between the owner of the character and the person using it. Judges were only prepared to grant protection on the basis that members of the public were aware of this form of commercial exploitation. Whereas the judges tended to deny that such public awareness existed, it was argued that the public were aware of character merchandising. They simply did not know it by that phrase (see Bainbridge, 2009).

Defamation

In some cases, a real person can stop unauthorised use of their character by suing in defamation. An example of such an action is that of *Tolley v Fry* [1931] AC 333. The plaintiff was an amateur golfer. His picture was used by the defendant to advertise its chocolate without his consent, and was sued for libel. The plaintiff successfully claimed that anyone seeing his picture would think that he had compromised his amateur status by accepting money from advertising. Tolley was only able to succeed because the defendant had published '*a false statement which lowered him in the estimation of right thinking members of society*' [our italics]. The advertisement suggested that he had compromised his amateur status and so fell within the standard definition of defamation.

Members of the public are now fully aware that personalities allow their names to be used to endorse all manner of goods and services and this is generally accepted. Defamation would only be a viable action if the name has been used to endorse something undesirable. Otherwise publication is unlikely to lower the esteem of a personality in the eyes of right-thinking members of society, so we cannot see how a real character would succeed. In *Sim v H J Heinz Co Ltd* [1959] 1 All ER 547, the defendant used the voice of one actor to mimic that of another actor, who was the plaintiff. It was held that there was no evidence of damage to the plaintiff's reputation.

Copyright

Copyright offers some protection. Section 1(1)(a) of the Copyright, Designs and Patents Act 1988 states that copyright subsists in 'original literary, dramatic, musical or artistic works'. So the owners of a character can protect its image, under the Act, as an artistic work. Under section 4, photographs and drawings are included as artistic works. Anybody making a copy of the work, or issuing copies of it to the public without the copyright owner's permission, is guilty of infringement according to sections 17 and 18. So putting an unauthorised copy of a cartoon onto a T-shirt would amount to infringement, as would selling the T-shirt bearing the copy of that cartoon. Further, a two-dimensional artistic work can be infringed by a three-dimensional representation. In *King Features Syndicate Inc v O & M Kleeman Ltd* [1941] 2 All ER 403, Popeye dolls and brooches were held to infringe the plaintiff's copyright in the comic-strip character.

Copyright does have its limitations. There are difficulties where only the name of the character is used, as there is no copyright in names or titles, no matter how distinctive (see *Exxon Corp & ors v Exxon Insurance Consultants International Ltd* [1982] RPC 69). Even if a picture of a character is used, the copyright owner must show that the representation is an exact or substantial copy, as copyright protects the expression of an idea and not the idea itself (see *BBC Worldwide Ltd & Another v Pally Screen Printing Ltd & ors* [1998] FSR 665). However, in *Mirage Studios v Counter-Feat Clothing Co Ltd* [1991] FSR 145, the defendant took the concept of humanoid turtles and produced its own designs. Browne-Wilkinson VC, nevertheless, took the view that there was an arguable case of copyright infringement. Where the representation is a photograph of a real personality, the personality will only be able to use copyright to protect his image if the copyright in the photograph has been assigned to him, since the copyright in a photograph usually belongs to the person taking it. In *Lynstad v Anabas Products Ltd* [1977] FSR 62, the defendant obtained a licence from the copyright owners of photographs of the group Abba. When such photographs were reproduced on T-shirts, the group could not sue for copyright infringement and so sued in passing off and failed for reasons we discuss later. An interesting attempt to use copyright to protect a personality's 'features' is the case of

Merchandising Corp of America v Harpbond [1983] FSR 32. This case concerned the pop group Adam and the Ants and, in particular, the distinctive face make-up worn by the lead singer (Adam Ant). The plaintiff sued the defendant for reproducing pictures of Adam Ant with his distinctive make-up, claiming that the make-up was a copyright work (that is, a painting). This argument was rejected by the court.

Registered trade marks

Registering the name of the personality or character is also a possibility but not without its problems. The *Elvis Presley* case (*Elvis Presley Trade Marks* [1999] RPC 567) has made some interesting observations in this field. In particular, Laddie J said that in his view the name 'Elvis' did not satisfy the requirements of distinctiveness necessary to satisfy the test of registrability under sections 9 and 10 of the Trade Marks Act 1938. In fact the more famous the celebrity or character, the less likely they are going to be to establish distinctiveness. In *Linkin Park LL's Trade Mark Application* (unreported, 7 February 2005), the application by the rock group Linkin Park to register its name in respect of printed matter, posters and poster books was refused as devoid of distinctive character. Although the word was an invented word, by the date of the application it had become so well known as to be descriptive of the subject matter, that is, the goods to which it would be applied. This paradox appears to be endorsed by the opinion of A-G Colomer in *Picasso v OHIM* (Case C-361/04), 8 September 2005. He advised that although a famous person may have a reputation in a certain area, this would not afford enhanced distinctiveness where the mark is applied for or licensed for different goods or services typically because the marks would not be seen as designating the commercial origin of the goods or services. If this is the case, how can the decision in *Arsenal Football Club v Reed* (Case C-206/01) [2002] ECR I-10273 be reconciled? The difference between *Arsenal* and *Linkin Park* appears to be that Arsenal had already registered its mark for the merchandise concerned and the decision concerned infringement. In *Linkin Park*, reference was made to *Tarzan Trade Mark* [1970] FSR 245, which had been refused registration under the 1938 Act. Had Tarzan and Linkin Park been registered before they became well known, they would not have become descriptive of the goods to which they were attached. So what can personalities and owners of characters do? Macleod and Wood (2006: 44–6) suggest that personalities can try to create an alter ego or something surrounding their most famous exploits. The examples quoted include the registration by jockey Frankie Dettori of a stylised drawing of himself jumping in the air, or David Beckham's registration of a stylised logo of himself taking a free kick.

Passing off

The use of passing off as a form of protection has been hindered by Wynn-Parry J's statement in *McCulloch v May* [1947] 2 All ER 845, that there has to be a 'common field of activity' in which both the plaintiff and defendant are engaged. In *Lynstad v Anabas Products Ltd* [1977] FSR 62, Abba were unable to stop the unauthorised use of their photographs on T-shirts and souvenirs because they were in the business of making records, even though they were involved in the marketing of goods with their image.

This need for a 'common field of activity' failed to take account of the fact that character owners will not be in the same field as those taking advantage of the character. The Beatles made music, not T-shirts. More importantly, it failed to take account of the fact that character merchandising existed as a distinct commercial activity. Bainbridge (2009) points out that the law was failing to recognise that well-known personalities, in particular, may license others to manufacture products bearing their names. This failure to recognise the practice is illustrated in a number of cases.

Wombles Ltd v Wombles Skips Ltd [1977] RPC 99 concerned the Wombles, who were fictitious animals from a television series and were well known for cleaning up litter. The plaintiff owned the copyright in the books and in the drawings of the Wombles. Its main business was to grant licences in respect of the characters. The defendant formed a company to lease builders' skips and, recalling the Wombles' reputation for tidy habits, decided to call the company 'Wombles Skips Ltd'. It was argued that such use of the name would give the impression that the defendant's business was connected with the plaintiff in some way. A 'common field of activity' was claimed because the plaintiff had granted a licence to reproduce the Wombles on wastepaper baskets. The court disagreed. There was no common field of activity. The similarity between marketing wastepaper baskets and hiring out builders' skips was simply not strong enough.

Taverner Rutledge v Trexa-palm Ltd [1977] RPC 275 concerned the famous television detective Kojak, known for sucking lollipops. The plaintiff made lollipops similar in shape to those used by the character and called them 'Kojak pops'. It quickly established goodwill in the name for the products, yet had not sought a licence from the television company responsible for the series. The defendant company started making similar lollies called 'Kojak lollies', under a licence agreement from the owners of the rights in the television series. The plaintiff sued for passing off. Although it was argued that the defendant's licence, with its terms on quality control, illustrated a connection in the course of trade between the defendant and the owners of the name, in other words a common field of activity, this argument, and with it the defence, failed because there was no actual or potential common field of activity between the owners of the television series and the defendant's business, there being no evidence of any exercise of quality control by the owners of the television series. According to Walton J, the defendant would have to show that the practice of character merchandising had become so well known that as soon as anybody in the street realised that a product was licensed by the owners of some series, like *Kojak*, he would say to himself not only 'this must have been licensed by them', but also 'and that is a guarantee of its quality'. In the event, the plaintiff's lollies were of better value and quality and the defendant's product would have harmed the plaintiff's reputation.

The reference to quality control indicates a way to get around the 'common field of activity' problem. Stricter quality control exercised through the terms of a licence would indicate an active interest in the type of goods being produced and thereby form the necessary connection in the course of trade. An Australian decision indicates that this is a solution. In *Children's T Workshop Inc v Woolworths (NSW) Pty Ltd* [1981] RPC 187, a licence agreement for soft toys of Muppet characters incorporated detailed quality control provisions. This was enough to establish a connection in the course of trade.

The decision in *Mirage* illustrates judicial recognition that the public are well aware of the practice of character merchandising. The plaintiff created the 'Teenage Mutant Ninja Turtle' characters. It also made and marketed cartoons, films and videos containing these characters. Part of the plaintiff's business involved licensing the reproduction of the characters on goods sold by licensees. Without the plaintiff's permission, the defendant made drawings of humanoid turtle characters, which were similar in appearance to the plaintiff's characters but were not exact reproductions. The defendant licensed these drawings to garment manufacturers to reproduce on T-shirts and other goods. In granting an injunction against the defendant, Browne-Wilkinson VC adopted the classic passing off test from *Erven Warnink Besloten Vennootschap v J Townend & Sons (Hull) Ltd* [1979] AC 731. A misrepresentation had taken place because there was evidence to show that a substantial number of the buying public expected, and knew, that where a famous cartoon or television character was reproduced on goods, that reproduction was the result of a licence granted by the owner of the copyright or owner of other rights in that character. The defendant had, therefore, misrepresented that the goods bearing their turtles were produced under licence from the plaintiff:

> Since the public associated the goods with the creator of the characters, the depreciation of the image by fixing the Turtle picture to inferior goods and inferior materials might seriously reduce the value of the licensing rights (at 156).

The decision has been welcomed by practitioners and academics alike. It is obviously welcomed by honest traders. Does it affect the decisions in the Wombles, Kojak or Abba cases? We believe it is distinguishable because only a name was involved in those cases, not a drawing. Further there was, according to Browne-Wilknson VC, an arguable case of copyright infringement in Mirage Studios. However, *Mirage* finally establishes that judges are aware of character merchandising and, more importantly, that they know that members of the public are aware of it, which assists in satisfying the 'course of trade' requirement. For further reading, see Chong and Maniatis (1991: 253).

It is yet to be seen whether this approach will be applied to cases of personality merchandising. In *Stringfellow v McCain Foods* [1984] RPC 501, Peter Stringfellow failed to convince the court that use of his name by the defendant was actionable by him. In the case of *Elvis Presley Trade Marks*, the estate of Elvis Presley did not argue its case on the grounds of personality merchandising, but the court made the interesting observation that, in its view, the purchaser of souvenirs bearing a particular personality's name or likeness 'was likely to be indifferent as to its source' (see above for discussion of both of these cases).

In *Edmund Irvine & Another* v *Talksport Ltd* [2002] EWCH 367 (Ch), Laddie J distinguished *Elvis* from cases which suggest that a sports (or other) personality has expressly endorsed a product or service in exchange for payment. This compares with *Tolley v Fry*, where, as stated, the personality concerned sued in defamation. No doubt that option was also open to the Formula One racing driver popularly known as 'Eddie Irvine', whose photograph had been altered to make it appear that he was enjoying and thereby endorsing the defendant's radio programme. His Lordship also appeared to reject the 'common field of activity' as a requirement. (Note that Irvine's appeal against the damages awarded was also successful in the Court of Appeal: see *Irvine v Talksport Ltd* [2003] EWCA Civ 423.) It would be tempting to see this as extending the tort of passing off, but *Irvine v Talksport* is a false endorsement case rather than one of character merchandising. It is more in line with *Tolley v Fry* than the other cases. It is argued that real characters at least should be protected by a 'right of personality' in line with the United States (see Bains, 2007).

Law of confidence and human rights

It is also suggested that following the decision in *Douglas v Hello! Ltd* (see Chapter 7) the law of confidence incorporating aspects from the Human Rights Act 1998 could also be used by personalities to control the use of their images. That such rights could be extended to a third party with whom the celebrity has entered a contract is confirmed in *Douglas v Hello! Ltd (No 3)* [2007] UKHL 21.

Summary

▶ Passing off is the practice of giving consumers the impression that goods or services of one trader come from another trader who has established goodwill.

▶ Goodwill is the likelihood that customers will return.

▶ The claimant must show that the defendant's misrepresentation will damage, or is likely to damage, his goodwill.

▶ Recent cases suggest that the claimant's misrepresentation must lead, or be likely to lead, to customer confusion about the source of the goods or services.

▶ The claimant must prove damage or probability of damage.

Summary cont'd

▶ Character merchandising involves attaching popular names or images to products.

▶ The Trade Marks Act 1994 has made it easier to register character names and images as trade marks.

▶ The tort of passing off has been of limited use because judges in the UK do not, on the whole, appreciate public awareness of character merchandising.

Exercises

11.1 Outline the elements required for a passing off action.

11.2 Consider whether the following have goodwill:

(a) A Bros, who have had the same market pitch in Leicester market for 25 years;

(b) B Co. Ltd, which owns a string of hotels on the French Riviera;

(c) 'Josie the talking elephant', a children's toy launched in the shops seven days ago and sold out in all major toy shops.

11.3 In January 1995, A wrote a children's book called *Josie In the Jungle*. The main character is a gentle elephant called Josie who teaches her friends to protect themselves against evil ivory hunters. The book is now an international bestseller and has been turned into a full-length cartoon film, which is also a success.

The rights in *Josie* have been assigned to B Ltd, who intends to exploit the characters in Europe.

C, a well-known Spanish stationery company, has acquired the first licence from B Ltd and has made preparations to market *Josie* stationery in the UK. To date, no sales have taken place.

B and C have discovered that two companies are using 'Josie' in the course of their business. One is a company calling itself 'Josie's Tissues' which produces and sells paper tissues. Its packaging has a picture of a fierce-looking elephant. The other is D Co. Ltd, which is manufacturing and selling children's T-shirts with the words 'I'm a friend of Josie' printed in bold letters.

Advise B and C.

Further reading and references

Bainbridge, *Intellectual Property Law* (7th edn, Pitman Longman, 2009).

Bains, 'Personality Rights: Should the uk Grant Celebrities a Propriety Right in Their Personalities?' Part 1 [2007] Ent LR 18(5), 165.

Bentley and Sherman, *Intellectual Property Law* (2nd edn, Oxford University Press, 2006).

Carty, 'Registered Trade Marks and Comparative Advertising' [2002] EIPR 294.

Chong and Maniatis, 'The Teenage Mutant Hero Turtles Case: "Zapping" English Law on Character Merchandising Past the "Embryonic" Stage' [1991] 7 EIPR, 253.

Macleod and Wood, 'The *Picasso* Case, Famous Names and Branding Celebrity' [2006] Ent LR 17(1), 44.

Part III

Copyright and designs

Chapter 12
Copyright

12.1 What is copyright?

The law of copyright is governed by the Copyright, Designs and Patents Act 1988 (hereafter the 1988 Act). As the word suggests, copyright is the right to prevent others from copying, or reproducing, your work. A distinction that is often discussed in the context of copyright is the distinction between ideas and expression. Copyright protects the expression of an idea, not the idea itself. If I have an idea for a story, that idea, while still in my head, or communicated to someone else in speech, will not be a copyright work; once it is committed to paper or some other fixed form, whether by me or someone else, it becomes a work in which copyright can subsist.

If I have copyright in a written expression of my idea, what can I stop others from doing? I can stop anyone from directly or indirectly copying the whole or a substantial part of my copyright work. I cannot stop someone from borrowing my idea and I cannot stop someone who, independently, and without reference to my work, produces an extremely similar or identical work. However, the courts have acknowledged that it is difficult to draw the line between protecting ideas and expression (see, for example: *University of London Press Ltd v University Tutorial Press Ltd* [1916] 2 Ch 601; *Plix Products Ltd v Winstone (FrankM) (Merchants)* [1986] FSR 608; *Designers Guild Ltd v Russell Williams (Textiles)* [2001] FSR 11; *Nova Productions Ltd v Mazooma Games Ltd* [2006] EWHC 24; and *Nova Productions Ltd v Bell Fruit Games Ltd* [2007] EWCA Civ 219). If an idea is expressed in detail in the work, then copying the idea may involve copying the expression; in such cases, copyright will, in effect, protect copying of the idea as well as the expression (*Ibcos Computers Ltd v Barclays Mercantile Highland Finance Ltd* [1994] FSR 275).

12.2 How does copyright arise?

Copyright is a right that arises automatically upon the creation of a work which qualifies for copyright protection. There is no registration process. This means that there is no registration certificate to prove ownership of copyright. To prove ownership, the author will need to produce evidence of the creation of the work and proof of authorship. The author will also need to show that he is a qualifying person or that the work was first published in a Convention country.

12.3 Qualifying person

To be a qualifying person (1988 Act, s 154) the author must have been, at the material time, a British citizen, subject or protected person, a British overseas territories citizen, a British national (overseas) or a British overseas citizen, or must have been resident or domiciled in a Convention country at the material time. In addition, a body incorporated under the law of a part of the UK or another Convention country can also be a qualifying person. The material time is when an unpublished work was created or when a published work was first published (if the author dies before publication, the material time is just before his death). A Convention country is any country which is a signatory to either the Universal Copyright Convention or the Berne Copyright Convention. Broadly speaking, this covers most countries of the world. A work is first published when copies of the work, made with the permission of the copyright owner, are issued to the public.

12.3.1 Types of work protected by copyright

The works that may qualify for copyright protection are defined in section 1 of the 1988 Act. These are: (a) original literary, dramatic, musical and artistic works; (b) sound recordings, films and broadcasts; and (c) typographical arrangements of published editions. Although the broad categories of copyright work in the 1988 Act are the same as those in the Copyright Act 1956, the definitions of the specific works that fall within each of those categories have changed. This change has partly come about because of technological developments and also to reflect decisions reached by the courts over the period between 1956 and 1988. A further change introduced by the Copyright and Related Rights Regulations 2003, SI 2003/2498 (hereafter the 2003 Regulations) is the removal of cable programmes as a distinct category of copyright work and the redefinition of a broadcast to mean a transmission by any electronic means (not just wireless telegraphy) which is transmitted either for simultaneous reception by members of the public or is transmitted for presentation to members of the public at a time determined solely by the person making the transmission. The new definition of broadcast excludes internet transmissions other than those comprising live transmissions or transmissions of recorded material scheduled by the person responsible for making the transmission or those which are being transmitted simultaneously on the internet and by other means.

12.4 Historical background

Copyright has its roots in the sixteenth century. Initially the courts recognised a need for some form of protection for books. In the 1550s, a compulsory system of registration of books with the Stationers' Company was established with the aim of affording protection for authors. This registration system became optional after the 1911 Act. If an author registered a book with the Stationers' Company, it purported to give them a perpetual right to reproduce the book and, consequently, prevent reproduction by anyone else. It was argued by publishers that there existed a common law right of copyright, but it is far from clear whether such a law existed. However, the first copyright Act adopted by Parliament was known as the Statute of Anne 1709, and was introduced following calls for greater protection of authors. This gave an exclusive printing right of 14 years, followed by a further period of 14 years to be enjoyed by the author, if living. In 1734, the Engraving Copyright Act was passed, which gave copyright protection to engravings. Gradually, over the next 150 years, a number of Acts were passed extending copyright protection to musical, dramatic and artistic works. By the 1800s, there were around 14 copyright-related Acts on the statute books. A consolidating Act was needed to pull all the strands together.

In 1875, a Royal Commission looked into the position and recommended that a clear and consistent approach to all the various forms of copyright protection be incorporated into one Act. This did not happen, however, until after Great Britain had signed the Berne Copyright Convention in 1885. The Berne Copyright Convention provided for international protection of copyright for the works of nationals of all countries who signed the Convention. It required each Member Country to extend minimum standards of protection to nationals of all other Member Countries. At that time, the law of the UK did not meet these minimum standards and so the UK was forced to implement the 1911 Copyright Act, which repealed and replaced a number of the existing Acts and abolished common law copyright which had previously extended an indefinite term of copyright for unpublished literary works.

Further changes to the Berne Copyright Convention in 1951 again prompted the UK to amend its copyright law and to introduce the Copyright Act 1956. This Act brought copyright law to a point very close to where we find it today. A number of amending statutes then followed that were necessary to reflect the technological advances being made, in particular in the field of computers and microchip technology.

In 1973, the Whitford Committee was appointed to review the state of copyright law. The Committee reported in 1977, suggesting changes to the law to deal with technological advances and recommending that the UK legislate to implement various changes to copyright law as required by the international conventions to which it was party. The result was a Green Paper in 1981, 'Reform of the Law Relating to Copyright, Designs and Performers' Protection' (Cmnd 8302), and subsequently the White Paper 'Intellectual Property and Innovation' (Cmnd 9712). These led to the 1988 Act, which consolidated the amendments made by legislation subsequent to the 1956 Act and implemented changes in the law that, according to a number of case decisions, were long overdue.

Since the 1988 Act came into force, on 1 August 1989, there have been a number of amending Regulations dealing with matters such as implementation of European Community (EC) Directives on rights to reproduce copyright software as is necessary for lawful use, protection of semiconductor chip topography rights, harmonisation of copyright duration and the introduction of several new rights such as the communication to the public right under the 2003 Regulations. These Regulations came into force on 31 October 2003 to implement the Copyright Directive 2001/29/EC on the harmonisation of certain aspects of copyright and related rights in the information society. The Copyright Directive's aim was to bring national copyright laws into the twenty-first century so that they could deal adequately with the challenges presented by multimedia, digitisation and the internet, and to achieve a degree of harmonisation of copyright protection across the European Union (EU).

Another influence on UK copyright law is the Agreement on Trade Related Aspects of Intellectual Property Rights (TRIPS), which was signed on 15 April 1994. One of the basic principles of TRIPS is to establish minimum standards for protection and enforcement of intellectual property rights (including copyright). In broad terms, TRIPS follows the Berne Convention as a starting point and builds on it. Article 9.1 of TRIPS states that members should comply with articles 1–21 of the Berne Convention, which deal with copyright. Article 10 of TRIPS extended copyright protection to computer programs in object code or source code form. This is now reflected in both UK and EU legislation. Protection of databases and rental rights may also be attributed to TRIPS.

12.5 The need for change?

Prior to implementation of the 2003 Regulations, in theory, the existing law of copyright was probably already capable of dealing with the new developing information technology world. The digitisation of artistic and literary works does not mean that they cease to be copyright works and the transmission of images, data and sound across the internet still constitutes reproduction that requires the same licences as any other form of reproduction or transmission of those copyright works. The real problem was that, as it became easier to reproduce these works and spread unlawful copies across the world and as it became more and more difficult to trace the source of such copies, the enforcement of existing copyright law was becoming almost impossible. The 2003 Regulations were intended to go some way to easing this situation. However, in recent years the UK has seen a series of consultations and reviews of intellectual property laws, with a particular focus on copyright. Rights owners are concerned over the ease at which their works can be exploited over the internet without their consent or control. However, users of digital devices and the businesses seeking to service them are concerned that existing copyright laws are too restrictive and render infringing acts which are part and parcel of accessing and using copyright protected works on digital devices such as mobile phones, personal computers, web browsers etc. The Gowers Review of Intellectual Property in December 2006 was followed by the Hargreaves Review of Intellectual Property in May 2011. The UK Government has now announced its intention to implement some of the recommendations made in these reviews. These issues are discussed further in the following chapters.

Summary

▶ Copyright is an automatic right which entitles the owner to prevent others from copying their work.

▶ The works protected by copyright are original literary, dramatic, musical and artistic works, sound recordings, films, broadcasts and typographical arrangements of published editions.

▶ While each country will have its own copyright law, attempts have been made over the years to harmonise the laws to some degree through international conventions such as the Berne Convention.

Exercises

12.1 How does an individual obtain copyright in a work?

12.2 What is the idea–expression dichotomy?

12.3 Why is the nationality of the person creating the work so important?

13.1 The subject matter protected

As we have already seen, copyright protects expression, rather than ideas, but the dividing line is blurred. A further complication to this area is that a single item may be protected by a number of copyrights, which can sometimes be owned by different people.

A song comprises words and music and each of these will have its own copyright protection. It is quite possible that those elements will have been written by two or more different people. If that song is recorded, the resulting sound recording will be protected by copyright and the underlying copyright in the words and music will continue to be protected separately as copyright works. The sleeve of a compact disc will probably have a photo or design on it that will be a protected artistic work, and any written commentary about the music or song will be a literary work (as well as there being separate copyright protection for the typographical arrangement of the printed words).

Understanding the different rights that may exist in something such as a compact disc requires an understanding of what can be protected as a copyright work.

13.2 Literary works

A literary work is defined in section 1 of the 1988 Act as 'any work, other than a dramatic or musical work, which is written, spoken or sung'. The Act goes on to say that this includes a table or compilation, a computer program and preparatory design material for a computer program and a database.

The inclusion of computer programs is as a result of consolidation of the Copyright (Computer Software) Amendment Act 1985, which implemented into statute what the courts had begun to indicate, namely, that a computer program, being something that is initially written down in a programming language, is a literary work. In *Thrustcode v W W Computing Ltd* [1983] FSR 502, the court had already held under the Copyright Act 1956 that computer programs were capable of protection as literary works. The inclusion of preparatory design material for a computer program is as a result of the Copyright (Computer Programs) Regulations 1992 (SI 1992 No. 3233), which implemented Council Directive 91/250/EEC on the legal protection of computer programs into UK law.

The interpretation of this directive was considered in *SAS Institute Inc v World Programming Ltd* [2012] 3 CMLR 4. The ECJ reflected the stance taken in *Navitaire Inc v EasyJet Airline Co Ltd* (No. 3) [2004] EWHC 1725 (Ch) that the Directive protects the design and underlying code of computer software, but does not go so far as to protect its programming language or its functionality. The point is discussed in more detail in Chapter 15 (see p 171).

The former copyright treatment of databases was changed by the introduction of the Copyright and Rights in Databases Regulations 1997 which amended certain sections of the 1988 Act (see Chapter 18 for a more detailed discussion about the protection of databases).

'Literary' is, perhaps, an unfortunate word to use as a description of the type of work protected because it suggests that the work must have some literary merit. Books, magazines, articles and poems are all obvious literary works, but less obvious examples have also been considered by the courts to merit copyright protection as literary works, provided that they satisfy the condition of originality. For example: a football coupon (*Ladbroke (Football) Ltd v William Hill (Football) Ltd* [1964] 1 WLR 273); rules for a game (*Caley (A J) & Son Ltd v Garnett (G) & Sons Ltd* [1936–45] Mac. CC); instructions on the packaging for weedkiller (*Elanco Products Ltd v Mandops (Agrochemical Specialists) Ltd* [1980] RPC 213), an interim injunction application); and some newspaper headlines (*The Newspaper Licensing Agency Ltd v Meltwater Holdings BV* [2012] RPC 1).

Tables and compilations are perhaps strange examples of literary works – is a table written or drawn? If a table is drawn, does it cease to be a table and become a graphic work (which is part of the definition of an artistic work), or can it be both? A compilation is not defined in the 1988 Act but the dictionary definition is 'that which is compiled. A literary work or the like formed by compilation', and to compile is defined as 'to put together and collect' and 'to construct (a written or printed work) out of materials collected from various sources'. As there is no corresponding category within the definition of artistic works, the courts have considered the possibility of a compilation of drawings or photographs being treated as literary works. In *Express Newspapers v Liverpool Daily Post and Echo plc* [1983] FSR 306, the court held that a grid and set of five letter sequences (as appearing on a scratch card) qualified as a literary work, being a compilation. A significant factor was the skill and labour that had been employed in producing these works.

A particularly complex example of the overlapping of literary and artistic works arises in relation to circuit diagrams. This interrelationship was considered in the case of *Aubrey Max Sandman v Panasonic UK Ltd & Another* [1998] FSR 651. As this case was just an application to strike out, a final decision was not reached on whether infringement had taken place, but Pumfrey J made the point that there was 'a surprising lack of law in relation to copyright in circuit diagrams', although he did refer to the case of *Electronic Techniques (Anglia) Ltd v Critchley Components Ltd* [1997] FSR 401. While the question of infringement was not decided in this case, Pumfrey J felt there was no reason why both artistic and literary copyright could not exist in the same work (namely a circuit diagram).

Although literary works include works which are spoken or sung, section 3(2) of the 1988 Act says that copyright will not subsist in a literary work (or indeed in a dramatic or musical work – see below) until it has been recorded, in writing or otherwise. If I recite a poem of my own composition, which I have never previously recorded in any permanent form, the poem will not attract copyright protection until it is recorded (either by me or someone else). If it is recorded, the poem will, at that point, attract copyright protection as a literary work and the recording will itself attract copyright protection as a sound recording. The question of who owns the two copyrights (which were both triggered by the same event (that is, the recording) and have the same subject matter) is dealt with in Chapter 17.

The word 'original' appears as a qualification to literary, dramatic, musical and artistic works, whereas it does not for sound recordings, films, broadcasts or typographical arrangements of published editions. The relevant sections concerning sound recordings, films and typographical arrangements do state that copies are not protected, and the sections concerning broadcasts state that no copyright will subsist in a broadcast which infringes the copyright of another broadcast. What is intended by the word 'original' is that the work should not be a pure copy of another work. The threshold is low – provided that the work was not copied from a previous work, it can attract its own copyright protection, even though there may be other works already in existence which are very similar to it.

In *University of London Press Ltd v University Tutorial Press Ltd* [1916] 2 Ch 601, the defendant issued a publication which reproduced certain examination papers in which the claimant claimed copyright. In considering the claim, the court expanded on the meaning of originality for the purposes of copyright. The idea expressed in the work need not be original; it is the expression which must be original. If independent skill and labour have been applied in creating a work, this will suggest a new work which attracts copyright protection even if an existing work has been used as a reference point. In *Sawkins v Hyperion Records Ltd* [2005] EWCA Civ 565, Mummery LJ found that Dr Sawkins, the editor of four fragmented and incomplete works by the French composer Lalande (1657–1726), had employed such considerable 'effort, skill and time' in rendering the works capable of performance that (as the High Court had already held) he owned the copyright in the resulting scores as original musical works. However, pure copying, even if it involves considerable skill and labour, will not satisfy the test of originality.

13.3 Dramatic works

Original dramatic works are not defined in section 1 of the 1988 Act save that they include 'a work of dance or mime'. The courts have expanded on the statutory provision by deciding that the word 'dramatic' requires an element of performance accompanied by action.

A case which considered the definition of 'a dramatic work' was *Norowzian v Arks Ltd (No 2)* [2000] FSR 363. This concerned the Guinness advertisement called 'Anticipation', featuring a man performing a jerky dance while waiting for his pint of Guinness to settle. Mr Norowzian, a film director, complained that this advertisement infringed copyright in his film known as *Joy*. The two films appeared similar to the viewer in that they both made use of distinctive 'jump-cutting' techniques, although the steps and the context of the two films were different. In the High Court, the judge held that *Joy* was not a dramatic work because the dance in question was not capable of being performed. However, the Court of Appeal overturned that decision by deciding that the film could itself be protected as a dramatic work, defining such a work as 'a work of action with or without words or music which is capable of being performed before an audience'. Since the film could be performed before an audience, it was entitled to protection as a dramatic work. In the event, however, it was held that the defendant had not copied a substantial part of *Joy* and Mr Norowzian's appeal therefore failed.

The above definition was applied by the judge in *Nova Productions Ltd v Mazooma Games Ltd & ors* [2006] EWHC 24 (the issue was not one appealed in *Nova Productions Ltd v Mazooma Games Ltd, Nova Productions Ltd v Bell Fruit Games Ltd* [2007]) when he had to consider whether the screen displays on a coin-operated video game could constitute a dramatic work. He concluded that it was not a dramatic work because, since it was a game, the sequence of images would change from game to game as it was played, so that it was not capable of performance.

In *Brighton v Jones* [2005] FSR 16, it was decided that the director of a play was not a joint author of the play by virtue of suggestions that she had made during rehearsals to changes in the script and how it would be performed. These amounted to contributions to the interpretation and theatrical presentation of the dramatic work, rather than to its creation.

A recital of a poem or the singing of a song without action and the impromptu 'gags' of a performer (for instance, in a game show) will not be dramatic works (although they may be performances of literary or musical works). To attract copyright protection, a dramatic work must be recorded in some form – the mere performance (without a record) will only be protected by performance rights.

13.4 Musical works

An original musical work is defined in section 1 as 'a work consisting of music, exclusive of any words or action intended to be sung, spoken or performed with the music'. The dictionary definition of 'music' as given in the *Oxford English Dictionary* is the 'art or science of combining vocal and/or instrumental sounds to produce beauty of form, harmony, melody, rhythm, expressive content, etc.'. Again, the musical work must be recorded in some fixed form for copyright to subsist. In *Lawson v Dundas* (Ch D, 12 June 1985, unreported) the four bars of the Channel 4 'Signature' were held to merit protection as a musical work – either the musical notes (as opposed to the words to a song) must be recorded in some final form or the music recorded. The definition of music was considered in *Sawkins v Hyperion Records Ltd* [2005] EWCA Civ 565. There it was found that the sound produced by the musicians when playing the musical score created by the claimant was influenced by the performing indications, tempo and performance practice indicators which he had added to his new edition of an old musical composition, and that his skill and effort in producing the new edition were sufficient to attract copyright protection.

Musical works are often the result of collaboration between several individuals, and interesting questions can arise over the ownership of copyright in the resulting work. The High Court in the case *Fisher v Brooker* [2006] EWHC 3239, involving the band Procul Harum, considered whether former band member Matthew Fisher's contribution to the song 'A Whiter Shade of Pale' was significant enough to entitle him to a declaration that he was co-author of the work, and concluded that it was. However, the High Court (and subsequently the Court of Appeal in *Fisher v Brooker* [2008] EMLR 13 and the House of Lords in *Fisher v Brooker* [2009] UKHL 41) also had to consider the effect of a 40-year delay on Fisher's entitlement to claim an interest in the copyright and a share in the royalties generated by sales of the song (see Chapter 16 for a detailed discussion of this case).

There has even been a copyright dispute relating to a piece of 'music' called '4′33′ by John Cage. The whole piece is simply silence, but when Mike Batt included a track on The Planet's album called 'A Minute's Silence', he settled a legal dispute with John Cage's publishers by paying them a sum of money.

13.5 Artistic works

Artistic works are defined in section 4(1) as being '(a) a graphic work, photograph, sculpture or collage, irrespective of artistic quality, (b) a work of architecture being a building or a model for a building, or (c) a work of artistic craftsmanship'. 'Graphic work' is further defined (s 4(2)) as *including* '(a) any painting, drawing, diagram, map, chart or plan, and (b) any engraving, etching, lithograph, woodcut or similar work' (note that this definition is not exhaustive). The 1988 Act makes clear that a still from a film is not a 'photograph' and will instead be protected as a film.

The first category of artistic works (that is, graphic work, photograph, collage or sculpture) is capable of protection 'irrespective of artistic quality'. This means that a very simple drawing will be protected by copyright, provided that it is original. The case of *Kenrick & Co v Lawrence & Co* [1890] 25 QBD 99 reminds us that it is expression and not idea which is protected. In that case, the work in question was a very simple drawing of a hand pointing to the voting box on a polling card. The court held that if copyright did protect such a drawing, it would only have prevented others from making a virtually identical copy of it – it would not have prevented people from creating their own drawings using the idea of a hand as an indicator of where voters should put their crosses.

In a case involving the band Oasis (*Creation Records Ltd v News Group Newspapers Ltd* [1997] EMLR 444), an attempt was made to claim copyright in the scene featured in the photograph to be used on the cover of their *Be Here Now* album, in order to prevent *The Sun* from printing an unauthorised photograph taken at the photo shoot. However, it was held that the actual arrangement of the members of the group by a swimming pool did not constitute an artistic work. The scene was not a work of artistic craftsmanship because there was no craftsmanship, and it was not a collage because it only existed for a few hours and did not involve sticking anything. This is to be compared with the situation regarding somebody using an existing photograph (which is a copyright work) to recreate a specific arrangement as photographed for the purposes of taking a separate photograph and thereby possibly indirectly infringing copyright in the original photograph.

There are certain types of artistic work which are particularly problematic, namely three-dimensional designs, particularly sculptures, engravings, works of artistic craftsmanship and designs which fall within the protection afforded by both copyright and design right.

13.5.1 Three-dimensional designs

The definition of 'sculpture' includes a cast or model made for the purposes of sculpture. In *Wham-O Manufacturing Co v Lincoln Industries Ltd* [1985] RPC 127, a plastic frisbee, displaying concentric ridges, was held to be a copyright work on the basis that it was an engraving. In that case, the court was not prepared to say that the resulting frisbees produced from injection moulding were sculptures, but the original wooden models used to create the moulds were sculptures. In another case, *Breville Europe plc v Thorn EMI Domestic Appliances Ltd* (1985) [1995] FSR 77, the court found that the plaster shapes of toasted sandwiches created to form the mould for a toasted sandwich maker could be protected as artistic works (being casts for a sculpture). Even the pattern of the underside of a rubber car mat has been protected from copying by relying on the copyright found to subsist in metal plates used to make the mats, and in the resulting mats, as engravings – *Hi-Tech Autoparts Ltd v Towergate Two Ltd* [2002] FSR 254; [2002] FSR 270. However, in *Metix (UK) Ltd & Another v G H Maughan (Plastics) Ltd & Another* [1997] FSR 718, the Patents Court in an interim hearing said that a mould produced in that case as a means for making a functional article should not be treated as a work in which sculpture copyright subsists.

The position regarding the protection of moulds and the resulting products made from them will now be influenced by the courts' decisions in *Lucasfilm Ltd v Ainsworth* [2008] ECDR 17; [2010] EMLR 12; [2011] ECDR 21, considered later in this chapter, such that it will be much harder to obtain copyright protection for functional articles.

Another difficult area is what constitutes an artistic work which is protected as a work of artistic craftsmanship, because a subjective judgment is often involved. Items of furniture have been brought before the courts to determine whether they are works of artistic craftsmanship. In *Hensher (George) Ltd v Restawile Upholstery (Lancs)* [1976] AC 64, the court was not convinced that a prototype for a suite of furniture was a work of artistic craftsmanship. Originality is one hurdle which has to be overcome, but even if original, in order to qualify for protection, the work must also be of artistic value and be a work of craftsmanship. The courts have indicated that the intention of the craftsman or creator is an important factor when considering artistic value. In *Merlet v Mothercare* [1986] RPC 115, the intention of the claimant in making a baby hood was to serve a practical purpose and the style and design of the hood was of secondary consideration, so the design did not qualify as a work of artistic craftsmanship.

A particularly interesting issue in this area is whether haute couture or designer dresses can constitute works of artistic craftsmanship. In a case concerning a dress design, *Burke and Margot Burke Ltd v Spicers Designs* [1936] 1 Ch 400, the designer of a one-off dress design had shown her sketch to her seamstresses who made a dress to the design. The court found that the dress was not protected as a work of artistic craftsmanship because the artistic qualities came from the designer, whereas the craftsmanship came from the seamstresses. Since almost all fashion designers work in the same way, if this decision was followed, it would suggest that none of their designs would be protected by copyright. However, in a later case also concerning dress designs, *Radley Gowns Ltd v Costas Spyrou* [1975] FSR 455, the judge said that he did not consider the decision in *Burke* to be conclusive on the point regarding separate contributions towards the craftsmanship and artistic elements. He was also not convinced that just because a dress was mass-produced meant that it could not be a work of artistic craftsmanship. Two further cases, one in Australia and one in New Zealand, decided that there was no problem where the artist and the craftsperson were different people, so it is hoped that that position will be adopted in future cases in the UK. For a review of all the cases concerning works of artistic craftsmanship up to 2000, see Clark (2000).

In the first-instance case of *Guild v Eskandaar Ltd* [2001] FSR 38, which concerned the design of three fashion garments (a shirt, a sweater and a cardigan), all being 'very wide, unstructured garments inspired from ethnic or "peasant" dress', the court decided that such garments did not qualify as works of artistic craftsmanship (and only the design right issue was appealed to the Court of Appeal). The court reached this decision because the garments were machine-made as prototypes for mass production (which meant that they could not reasonably be regarded as works of craftsmanship) and there was no evidence that the designer intended to create works of art or saw herself as an artist.

The cat was thrown among the pigeons by the Court of Appeal's decision in *Lambretta Clothing Co. Ltd v Teddy Smith (UK) Ltd* [2005] RPC 6. Lambretta had brought copyright infringement proceedings against both Next and Teddy Smith for selling alleged copies of a tracksuit top. The top was of a generic shape, but Lambretta relied on copyright in its design drawing showing the positioning of the colour segments on the top (namely, red sleeves and blue body with a white zip). Before this case, it had been widely considered that the three-dimensional shape (if original) would be protected by unregistered design right, and the surface decoration (the colour layouts and any pattern on the fabric) would be protected by copyright in the design drawing showing them, in exactly the same way that copyright protects paintings, drawings, photographs and other works of a two-dimensional nature. However, the Court of Appeal held that there was no copyright protection in the colour patterns in the Lambretta top. It was a majority decision, with two of the three judges concluding that copyright is not enforceable in any aspects of a design drawing for an article which consist of three-dimensional features falling within the sphere of design right protection, as a result of the wording of section 51 of the 1988 Act. In this case, the outline shape of the top (an aspect of the article which could have fallen within design right) was shown on the design drawing which also showed the positioning of the colours. Unfortunately, the shape of the top was not original and design right protection was therefore denied for that. This therefore also meant that the claimant could not enforce copyright in what were effectively two-dimensional colour patterns. This case could remove copyright protection for most designs which are a combination of two-dimensional and three-dimensional aspects, such as fashion and furniture designs (although protection may be available for more recent designs under the Community design rights) – see Chapters 21 and 22). For further discussion of this case and how it has been distinguished in a more recent case, see Section 16.3.15.

In *Lucasfilm Ltd v Ainsworth* [2008] ECDR 17 Mann J had to decide whether the design of a Stormtrooper helmet from the first *Star Wars* film (now confusingly called *Star Wars Episode IV: A New Hope*) and other parts of the Stormtrooper uniform could be protected either as sculptures or works of artistic craftsmanship.

Dealing firstly with the sculpture issue, although the question whether a work has artistic merit is irrelevant for sculptures under section 4 of the Act, Mann J was firmly of the view that the product which is alleged to be a sculpture must have some appeal to artistic sensibility. That was not in conflict with the fact that artistic merit is irrelevant because, he said, provided that one of the purposes of the product was to provide some visual appeal, no judgment would be made about its artistic worth. One of the key factors is therefore the ultimate purpose of the product. Where the primary purpose of an article is purely a stage in a manufacturing process to create a utilitarian article, it will not be protected by copyright as a sculpture. On the other hand, where the end product is primarily designed to have some aesthetic appeal to the end user, there is a good case for allowing it to benefit from copyright protection.

Mann J gave as an example a pile of bricks. A pile of bricks in Tate Modern could be protected as a sculpture because its purpose was some type of visual, artistic statement, irrespective of whether in fact it had artistic merit. On the other hand, a pile of bricks at the end of the judge's driveway could not be a sculpture as it had no artistic purpose. This means that the same object may be protected by copyright in one situation but not another, depending on its purpose (it is difficult to think of another type of copyright work where the same could be said).

Applying this test to the Stormtrooper helmet and other costumes in *Star Wars*, unfortunately for Lucasfilm, Mann J decided that they were conceived as part of character portrayal in a film, that therefore their primary purpose was utilitarian and so they were not protected as sculptures.

Mann J applied a similar assessment when determining the meaning of work of artistic craftsmanship, saying that the intention of the creator was of 'real relevance'. He found that, while the helmets and armour were works of craftsmanship, they were not works of artistic craftsmanship, saying that their purpose was 'not to appeal to the aesthetic at all', but simply to give a particular impression in a film.

The Court of Appeal [2010] EMLR 12 upheld Mann J's arguments in relation to sculpture, saying that it was not possible to devise a comprehensive or exclusive definition of 'sculpture'. However, the judge had been right to point to the existence of what could loosely be described as a work of art as the key to identifying a work of sculpture. He was therefore entitled to conclude that the helmet and armour were not sculptures.

The Supreme Court also upheld the judge's conclusion [2011] ECDR 21. Although imagination had gone into the Stormtrooper helmet, it was the film that was the work of art. The helmet was purely utilitarian because it was an element in the process of production of the film.

While the decision may be bad news for costume designers, it may still be good news for many other designers. For example, furniture designers who create high-quality modern furniture designs which are designed both to act as pieces of furniture and also to be visually appealing may still be able to rely on copyright protection as a sculpture.

For a more detailed discussion on the case, see Clark, 'Star Wars: New Hope or Lost Cause?' [2010] *Copyright World*, March and Clark, '*Lucasfilm Ltd v Ainsworth*: The Force of Copyright Protection for Three-Dimensional Designs as Sculptures or Works of Artistic Craftsmanship' [2009] *European Intellectual Property Review*, Issue 7.

13.5.2 Photographs

In *Antiquesportfolio.com plc v Rodney Fitch* [2001] FSR 23, the court addressed the question 'is a photograph of a static object protected by copyright?' The judges found that there was no direct authority on this point, so they looked initially to certain commentaries, including US works, for guidance. The conclusion that the court reached was that almost all photographs will qualify as copyright works because of the photographer's skill in the selection of subject matter, lighting, positioning and camera angle. In this case, the photographs were of three-dimensional objects and had been taken in such a way as to exhibit certain colours and qualities of the objects – so the court concluded that they were copyright works. The case left open the possibility that a purely representational photograph (for example of another photograph or picture) might not qualify as a copyright work.

The European Court of Justice (ECJ) has recently had to consider the question in respect of portrait photographs in *Painer v Standard Verlags GmbH* [2012] ECDR 6. The case concerned a portrait photograph of Natascha Kampusch, the Austrian schoolgirl who was abducted when she was 10 years old and held in a cellar for eight years before she escaped. The claimant was a photographer who had taken a portrait photograph of the schoolgirl before she was abducted. The photographer sued various newspapers for copyright infringement when they published the photograph without her consent when reporting the story. The court held that a portrait photograph could be protected by copyright if it was an intellectual creation of the author reflecting his personality and expressing his free and creative choices in the production of the photograph. Portrait photographs should be treated no differently from any other photographic works. Accordingly, by making various creative choices such as the background, the subject's pose, the lighting, the framing, the angle of view etc., the author can stamp their creativity and personality on the work.

13.6 Originality after Infopaq

The question of 'originality' has been given an alternative interpretation by the European Court of Justice in *Infopaq International A/S v Danske Dagblades Forening* [2012] Bus LR 102. The Danish Court referred several questions to the ECJ relating to the issue of whether copyright could subsist in and be infringed by copying 11 words of text copied from a newspaper article as part of a media monitoring process. The ECJ noted from the Berne Convention, and in particular articles 2(5) and (8), that the protection of certain subject matters as artistic or literary works presupposes that they are intellectual creations. Similarly, it noted that under articles 1(3) of Directive 91/250, 3(1) of Directive 96/9 and 6 of Directive 2006/116, works such as computer programs, databases and photographs are protected by copyright only if they are original in the sense that they are their author's own intellectual creation, and similar wording appears in the recitals to Directive 2001/29. Accordingly, the ECJ concluded that copyright will only protect a work which is original in the sense that it is its author's own intellectual creation.

Commentators are divided as to whether this decision introduces a more onerous test for originality than that previously applied by the courts in the UK. However, Arnold J's references to the case in *SAS Institute Inc v World Programming Ltd* [2010] EWHC 1829 suggest that he considered the ECJ to be taking the same approach as that previously adopted by the UK courts. Furthermore, in the Court of Appeal in *Newspaper Licensing Agency Ltd v Meltwater Holdings BV* [2012] RPC 1 the Chancellor said: 'I do not understand the decision of the European Court of Justice in *Infopaq* to have qualified the long standing test established by the authorities referred [to the Court]'.

Apart from originality, prior to *Infopaq* there was another qualification that a written, spoken or sung work had to meet in order to be a literary work. Although nothing is said in the 1988 Act, the courts for some time made it clear that a literary work must impart some instruction, information or pleasure (*Hollinrake v Truswell* [1894] 3 Ch 420). Using this reasoning the courts were not prepared to extend copyright protection to single words (as was shown by *Exxon Corp & ors v Exxon Insurance Consultants International Ltd* [1982] RPC 69) nor to titles of books or films (*Francis, Day & Hunter Ltd v Twentieth Century Fox Corp Ltd* [1940] AC 112), although in *Ladbroke (Football) Ltd v William Hill (Football) Ltd* [1964] 1 WLR 273 there was found to be sufficient skill, judgment and labour in the selection and presentation of bets in the form of a football-betting coupon, including in particular the headings, to attract copyright protection.

In *Newspaper Licensing Agency v Meltwater Holding BV* [2011] EWCA Civ 890, it was held that some newspaper headlines alone can constitute independent literary works capable of copyright protection. The judge said:

> In most cases the text extract (and in particular the headline and opening text) are not merely isolated words or clauses which in themselves convey no meaning. They provide the tone of the article and generally have the special function of drawing the reader in to the work as a whole.

It remains to be seen, post *Infopaq*, whether the courts still refer to this requirement.

Summary

▶ The 1988 Act protects a range of works from literary works to sound recordings.

▶ Literary works include football coupons, instructions on weedkiller packaging and compilations, in addition to more traditional literary works such as novels and magazines.

▶ 'Original' in the context of copyright works means that the work originates from the author and has not been copied. Originality must also be considered in the sense that it is the author's own intellectual creation.

▶ A dramatic work includes a work of dance or mime.

▶ A musical work consists of music without lyrics.

▶ Artistic quality is not a criterion for copyright protection of an artistic work unless the claimant is claiming copyright for a work of artistic craftsmanship.

Further reading and references

Headdon, 'Life After Infopaq: The Court of Appeal Ruling in *NLA v Meltwater*' [2011] *Intellectual Property Magazine*, September.

Clark, 'Star Wars: New Hope or Lost Cause?' [2010] *Copyright World*, March.

Clark, '*Lucasfilm Ltd v Ainsworth*: The Force of Copyright Protection for Three-Dimensional Designs as Sculptures or Works of Artistic Craftsmanship' [2009] *European Intellectual Property Review*, Issue 7.

Clark, 'What Is a Work of Artistic Craftsmanship?' [2000] *Copyright World*, November.

Chapter 14

Subsistence (2)

14.1 Sound recordings

A sound recording is defined in section 1 as 'a recording of sounds from which the sounds may be reproduced; or a recording of the whole or any part of a literary dramatic or musical work, from which sounds reproducing the work or part may be produced', regardless of the medium on which the recording is made or the method by which the sounds are reproduced or produced.

Although there is no 'originality' requirement for sound recordings, the 1988 Act specifically says that a sound recording which is just a copy taken from a previous sound recording will not be protected by copyright. This means that in the case of mass production of a CD, only the original recording will be a copyright work. However, if anyone copies any of the CDs that are sold, this would be an indirect infringement of the original sound recording (see Chapter 15).

The Duration of Copyright and Rights in Performances Regulations 1995 amended section 5 of the 1988 Act so that the soundtrack accompanying a film is now to be treated as part of the film and will be protected as part of the film, where the film is a copyright work. However, where the sound recording is played separately from the film, it will be protected as a sound recording. This avoids double protection for soundtrack rights when the soundtrack is really just part of the film performance and would be protected as such. Sound recordings will cover music recordings, soundtracks of films (when played separately from the film) and audio CDs (such as language courses and narrated stories). It is sound, and not just music, which is the subject matter of a sound recording.

14.2 Films

A film is defined as 'a recording on any medium from which a moving image may by any means be produced' (s 5B(1)). A film will cover video, television and movies. It will also include stills that are produced from a moving film, even though they appear to be photographs; stills are specifically excluded from protection as artistic works. The digitisation of artistic works on computer in a way that enables moving images to be produced will constitute a film.

In the previous chapter we looked at the case of *Norowzian v Arks Ltd (No 2)* [2000] FSR 363, where the Court of Appeal held that a film could constitute a dramatic work under section 3. This would be in addition to the separate copyright which protected the film itself as a film under section 5B. The film will usually incorporate a soundtrack, which as well as forming part of the film (s 5B(2)) could also, as we have just noted, be protected as a sound recording under section 5A (noting the provisions of s 5B(3)). Furthermore, the film will contain various underlying copyright works such as the script (a literary work), the musical works featured in the soundtrack and the set designs.

14.3 Broadcasts

A broadcast is defined in section 6 of the 1988 Act as any non-interactive 'electronic transmission of visual images, sounds or other information' that is either transmitted for simultaneous public reception in such a way that the public can lawfully receive it (for example, by means of legitimate decoding equipment if the transmission is encoded) or at a time determined solely by the broadcaster for presentation to the public. Prior to the 2003 Regulations, the 1988 Act dealt with broadcasts and 'cable programmes' as distinct categories of work, the former being concerned only with transmission by wireless telegraphy, the latter with transmission by telecommunications systems other than wireless telegraphy. The new definition of broadcast does away with both of the old terms, although it clearly does not encompass all types of transmission, particularly 'on-demand' services. Internet transmissions (other than live webcasts, as to which see *UEFA v Briscomb* [2006] EWHC 1268, discussed in Chapter 15, and simulcasts or transmissions starting at times scheduled by the broadcaster) are excluded from the definition of broadcast. The works transmitted in such a service are themselves protected as copyright works (for example, literary works, artistic works, music, sound recordings, films and so on). Furthermore, owners of rights in such works would have a remedy in case of infringement over the internet by virtue of the two rights granted by the 2003 Regulations to both copyright owners and performers enabling them to prevent the communication of a work to the public (see Chapters 15 and 19).

The Broadcasting Acts of 1990 and 1996 impose specific requirements in relation to both digital and analogue broadcasting, covering satellite broadcasts, terrestrial television and radio.

The ECJ recently considered the existence of copyright in Premier League football match broadcasts. Both *Football Association Premier League v QC Leisure and ors* and *Murphy v Media Protection Services* (joint cases – C-403/08 and C-429/08) [2012] 1 CMLR 29) concerned pub landlords who had used foreign decoders to receive and re-broadcast coverage of Premier League football matches at their pubs, while at the same time avoiding payment of the high licence fees demanded by Sky.

The ECJ, considering the cases together, held that while copyright does not subsist in the *matches* being broadcast, as these were not original dramatic works, copyright may subsist in broadcast 'overlay', that is to say, various other things which were transmitted with the broadcast, specifically logos, anthems and edited highlights sequences. (The ECJ also considered the right of communication to the public in the context of re-broadcasts, further details of which can be found in Chapter 15, p 174.)

14.4 Published editions

Section 1 of the 1988 Act provides that copyright may subsist in 'the typographical arrangement of published editions'. 'Published edition' is defined in section 8 as a published edition of either the whole or part of any literary, dramatic or musical work. The typographical arrangement is made up of various elements: the style of the printed letters, their size, and the way in which they are laid out on the page. The typographical arrangement of a published edition will only be protected by copyright if it is new. If it simply reproduces the typographical arrangement of the previous edition of the work then copyright will not subsist in it. The section is intended to protect the effort expended in setting out the literary, dramatic or musical work. There is no such effort where a publisher is simply reproducing an old edition. The practical consequence of section 8 is that if you photocopy an extract from a book, you may be infringing at least two copyrights – copyright of the author of the text (if it is still within copyright) and the publisher's copyright in the typographical arrangement of the text.

Summary

- Sound recordings need not be original to attract copyright protection but not should not simply be a copy taken from another sound recording.

- The definition of 'film' covers video, television and movies.

- The definition of 'broadcast' covers any 'electronic transmission of visual images, sounds or other information' which is transmitted for simultaneous reception at a time determined solely by the broadcaster.

- Since the 2003 Regulations, cable programmes are no longer considered as a distinct category of work from broadcasts.

- Transmissions on the internet and other on-demand services are subject to rights to prevent the making available to the public of certain copyright works by electronic transmission.

- The typographical arrangement of a literary, dramatic or musical work is also protected by copyright.

Exercise

State whether the following are protected by copyright, and the level of protection given:

(a) the latest CD by a popular band;

(b) the first showing on British television of the latest Batman film;

(c) a politician's speech at his or her party's annual conference;

(d) a recording of a child's first words;

(e) the handouts prepared by a college tutor;

(f) a photograph of a boy band taken by a fan;

(g) *Agnes Grey* by Anne Bronte;

(h) Microsoft Word;

(i) a One Direction band member doll;

(j) *Later with Jools Holland*;

(k) a passport photograph of a child carried in his mother's purse;

(l) the movements from *Dancing On Ice*.

Chapter 15

Infringement

15.1 Introduction

The owner of copyright in a work has the exclusive right to do certain specified acts in respect of that work. This means that the owner has the right to prevent others from doing those acts. The owner can either grant a licence (or permission) to a third party to perform those acts or bring an action for infringement against any unauthorised performance of those acts.

The acts which the copyright owner can control in this way in respect of his copyright work are copying, issuing copies to the public, renting or lending the work to the public, performing, showing or playing the work in public and communicating the work to the public. These restricted acts extend to any adaptation of the work. An adaptation will itself be protected as an original copyright work. There are also various acts known as secondary infringements, all of which are subject to an additional knowledge requirement. These are discussed later in this chapter.

15.2 Direct and indirect infringement

The restricted acts will constitute copyright infringement whether committed directly or indirectly. It is irrelevant, in the case of indirect infringement, whether the intervening act infringes copyright. If A writes a book in which A owns copyright, and licenses B to produce a French translation of that book (this would be an adaptation and would be an infringement of A's work if done without A's permission), B's translation will not be an infringement. However, if C, without A's permission, uses B's French translation (with B's permission) to write a Spanish translation, C's work (or adaptation) will be an infringement of A's copyright (done indirectly through B's work) (*King Features Syndicate Inc v O & M Kleeman Ltd* [1941] 2 All ER 403). So, for example, if a photographer uses an existing photograph as a reference point from which to set up a substantially similar or identical 'shoot' reproducing the particular composition of features selected and photographed by the photographer of the original work, his photograph may well be an infringement of the original photograph even though taken independently. In the case of *Baumann v Fussell* [1978] RPC 485, the claimant had photographed two cockerels, but since their positioning in the photograph was a matter of 'luck', the defendant's copy of the subject matter (as distinct from the photograph) did not infringe.

15.2.1 The substantial part test

The restricted acts will only constitute infringement if they are done in relation to the whole or a substantial part of the protected work. Many infringement cases will not involve reproduction of the entire copyright work but just a substantial part. This means working out what constitutes a substantial part. This should not be confused with finding that a substantial part of the infringed work comprises a part of the original work. Even if the defendant has added a great deal of material so that the copied work only forms a small proportion of the defendant's work, it will still be an infringement of the claimant's work if a substantial part of the claimant's work has been reproduced in the small section of the defendant's work. Substantiality is to be judged qualitatively and not just quantitatively. There is no general test and the facts of each case will determine the final decision (the test that you can make five changes to avoid infringement, often quoted, is pure myth). In *Hawkes & Son (London) Ltd v Paramount Film Service Ltd* [1934] Ch 593, twenty-eight bars of a musical piece were held to be a reproduction of a substantial part of that musical piece because those twenty-eight bars were so recognisable. In the case of *Designers Guild Ltd v Russell Williams (Textiles) Ltd* [2001] FSR 11, the House of Lords provided some guidance as to how to decide whether a substantial part of a copyright work has been copied, although with four of the five Law Lords giving separate judgments, it is far from clear-cut. The case involved a copy of a fabric design which featured a background of two different coloured stripes, overlaid with several impressionistic-style flowers scattered across the design. The trial judge found that there had been copying, and this issue was not appealed to the Court of Appeal, who therefore only had to decide whether a substantial part of the original design had been copied. The Court of Appeal concluded that the copy fabric adopted the same ideas and some of the same techniques as the original, but that the resulting visual result was different, and so there was no infringement. The House of Lords overturned this decision, unanimously finding that a substantial part had been copied (although not all for the same reasons). Millett LJ said that the first stage was to identify those features which had been taken from the original and reproduced in the copy. When this list of elements had been compiled, there was no longer any need to consider the copy, but rather to ask whether that list of elements, taken together, amounted to an important part of the original design. If it did, then a substantial part had been copied. This means that it is possible for an infringing copy to appear quite different from the original design, provided that an important part of the original has been reproduced in the copy. This decision was applied in *Nouveau Fabrics v Voyage Decoration Ltd & Dunelm Soft Furnishings Ltd* [2004] EWHC 895 and *Temple Island Collections Ltd v New English Teas Ltd* [2012] ECDR 11.

The issue of substantiality was again explored in a high-profile Court of Appeal judgment concerning the best-selling Dan Brown novel, *The Da Vinci Code* (*Baigent v The Random House Group Ltd* [2007] FSR 24). The claimants were two of the authors of the book *The Holy Blood and The Holy Grail* and submitted that Dan Brown had copied the 'central theme' of their own book and in doing so had reproduced a substantial part of the work. They relied upon an abstract that they had prepared for the purposes of the litigation and which they alleged represented the central theme of their book. At first instance the judge had concluded that the abstract did not in fact represent the central theme expressed by the claimants' book, but rather was no more than 'an artificial contrivance designed to create an illusion of the Central Theme' for the purposes of alleging infringement of the copyright in their work. On appeal the claimants argued that it was legitimate for them to rely on an abstract that had been put together for the purposes of litigation, arguing that if they had put forward a complete précis or summary of the work it would have contained a great deal of information that was irrelevant to the claim, and which would have had to have been ignored. However, the Court of Appeal said that the trial judge was right in holding that the claimants could not rely on a summary which 'is not fairly drawn from the work as a whole, but is conditioned by reference to what is said to have been copied by the Defendant'. The trial judge was also correct in rejecting the claimants' contention that the central theme was a substantial part of *The Holy Blood and The Holy Grail*. To the extent that a central theme was in the original work, it was no more than 'an expression of a number of facts and ideas at a very general level' which did not amount to a substantial part of the claimants' novel (or alternatively was not capable of copyright protection at all). The case confirmed the Court of Appeal's reluctance in most cases to interfere with a trial judge's finding on the issue of substantiality.

The case was applied in *Allen v Bloomsbury Publishing plc* [2010] EWHC 2560 (Ch), when the High Court refused to grant summary judgment to a claim by the estate of a deceased author that J. K. Rowling had copied a substantial part of his book in writing *Harry Potter and the Goblet of Fire*. The court held that the similarities which the claimant sought to rely on actually constituted rather abstract ideas with a high level of generality and therefore did not form the expression of the ideas themselves. The court was therefore not persuaded that it was sufficiently clear that a substantial part of the author's actual work had been copied and therefore could not grant summary judgment.

The issue of substantiality arose again in the European Court of Justice (ECJ) in *Infopaq International A/S v Danske Dagblades Forening* [2012] Bus LR 102 (discussed in Chapter 13). The claimant was a media monitoring organisation which summarised Danish newspaper articles. In the process of doing so it copied and stored an 11-word extract of each article. The court considered whether the 11-word extract could constitute a 'reproduction in part' under Directive 2001/29 (the wording 'substantial part' only appears in the UK legislation). The court held that certain isolated sentences could constitute a reproduction in part if the extract contained an element of the work which expressed the intellectual creation of the author. In this case, the court found that 11 words could be sufficient to constitute a reproduction in part if the national court decided that they satisfied that test.

This reasoning was applied by the High Court in *NLA v Meltwater* [2010] EWHC 3099. In that case, the claimants argued that the publishing of extracts of up to 256 characters which had been copied from newspaper articles appearing on newspaper websites would amount to copying a substantial part of each article. The extracts consisted of the headline, part or all of the opening sentence or sentences and a few words either side of a particular search term chosen by the user of Meltwater's online press monitoring service. The court reiterated that the test for substantiality was a question of the quality of the extracted part, rather than the quantity, and therefore provided that the extract was an expression of the author's intellectual creation, the extract could amount to a substantial part. The court also held that it was not necessary for the extract to convey the attitude, position or meaning of the underlying article (as was argued by the defendant). The court held that some of the published extracts were capable of being a substantial part of an article because they did contain elements that were the expression of the intellectual creation of the author of the article. The judge said that that was the case whether one applied the test of whether there had been an unfair appropriation of the author's skill and labour which went into the creation of the original article (e.g. the traditional UK test) or whether the parts of sentences which made up the extract 'may be suitable for conveying to the reader the originality of the publication such as a newspaper article, by communicating to that reader an element which is, in itself, the expression of the intellectual creation of the author' (e.g. the test taken from the ECJ *Infopaq* judgment). On appeal, the Court of Appeal upheld the ruling of the High Court ([2012] RPC 1).

15.2.2 No copyright in slavish copies

Infringing works will themselves only be copyright works if skill and effort have been expended, but not if they are just slavish copies. So, if B copies A's work slavishly, B's work will be an infringement of A's work but will not be a copyright work in itself. If C then copies B's work, that will not be an infringement of B's work (because B had no copyright) but it would be an indirect infringement of A's work (see *The Bridgeman Art Library Ltd v Corel Corp*, 1999 US Dist LEXIS 1731, 97 Civ 6232 (LAK), an American case, for an example of this in practice.)

15.3 Primary infringement

Primary infringement occurs when the acts restricted by copyright set out in the introduction to this chapter (found in the 1988 Act, ss 16–21) are, without the licence of the copyright owner, committed or authorised (1988 Act, s 16(2)).

15.3.1 Copying

Copyright infringement by 'copying' applies to all types of copyright work but clearly the scope for reproduction of different works varies. In relation to artistic, literary, dramatic and musical works, copying means reproduction in any material form (including by storing in any medium by electronic means – so scanned images or digitised sound will be copies for these purposes).

One common misconception is that reproduction in any material form includes carrying out the instructions in a literary work. To make a recipe from a recipe book is not reproduction of that recipe as a literary work (*Davis (J and S) (Holdings) Ltd v Wright Health Group Ltd* [1988] RPC 403), nor is knitting a jumper to a knitting guide reproduction of that guide (*Brigid Foley Ltd v Elliott* [1982] RPC 433). However, a design drawing for an intricate jumper could be infringed by the knitting of a jumper that reproduced that intricate pattern. This issue was considered in the case of *Jo-Y-Jo v Matalan Retail Ltd & Another* [2000] ECDR 178, where the defendants had produced jumpers which the claimant claimed infringed copyright and design right in the drawings of the claimant's garments. Since the allegedly infringing garments did not reproduce any of the embroidery on the original garments, the copyright claim failed. However, as we saw in Chapter 13, there is, following the decision in the *Lambretta* case, some doubt over the extent to which copyright can be enforced in the design drawings for a garment.

Artistic works may be infringed by reproducing a two-dimensional work in three dimensions and vice versa (1988 Act, s 17(3)) – however, in Chapter 16 we shall see that there are some specific acts within this category which are now not actionable as copyright infringement. In the case of architects' plans, it is an infringement to copy the plan by reproducing the plan or by building the building, and it would be an infringement of a work of architecture to make another work of architecture to the same design. However, it would not be an infringement to make a graphic two-dimensional work (drawing or photograph) of a building or of a sculpture, a model for a building or a work of artistic craftsmanship in a public place, because section 62 of the 1988 Act specifically says as much.

It is worth remembering that a dramatic work is defined as including 'a work of dance or mime' and that it is distinct from any literary or musical work that may be performed in the dramatic work. This is important for the question of infringement – a dramatic work may be infringed even if the language and/or the music is not copied.

15.4 Facsimile copies

Copying films or broadcasts is said by the 1988 Act to include photographing any image in these works (s 17(4)). Copying a typographic arrangement of a published edition means making a facsimile copy, by which is meant not a transmission via a fax machine but rather, as the *Oxford English Dictionary* defines facsimile, making 'an exact copy, counterpart or representation' (s 17(5)). The 1988 Act provides that a reduced or enlarged copy will also constitute a facsimile copy. In the House of Lords' decision in the case of *Newspaper Licensing Agency Ltd v Marks & Spencer plc* [2003] 1 AC 551, the court held that Marks & Spencer had not infringed copyright in typographical arrangements by virtue of making further copies and circulating newspaper cuttings received from a press cuttings agency. The court held that in the case of a typographical arrangement, 'nothing short of a facsimile copy would suffice' for infringement purposes and that in order for there to be copying of a substantial part of a published edition, nothing less than reproduction of a layout of a page of a newspaper would be sufficient. Since Marks & Spencer's cuttings did not reproduce whole pages but merely individual articles, Marks & Spencer were found not to have infringed the typographical arrangement of the published newspapers concerned.

15.5 Copying of computer programs

In cases concerning infringement of computer programs, determining copying has been made more difficult by the possibility of programmers using different computer languages to write programs, thus making a direct comparison difficult. In *Ibcos Computers Ltd v Barclays Mercantile Highland Finance Ltd* [1994] FSR 275, copying was proved by the existence of marked and unexplained similarities between the claimant's and the defendant's code – for instance, spelling mistakes and unused lines of code. The judge set out the test of copyright infringement in a case of non-literal copying as being:

(a) is there a work?
(b) is it original?
(c) has there been copying? and, if so,
(d) was this of a substantial part?

He said that it was not only right to consider 'literal similarities' but also the program structure and design features.

The case of *Navitaire Inc v easyJet Airline Co Ltd* [2004] EWHC 1725 concerned the issue of whether a software program which produced a very similar-looking online flight-booking system to the original program infringed copyright. The judge referred to the recitals from Council Directive (91/250/EC) on the legal protection of computer programs (the 'Software Directive'), which has subsequently been amended and codified by Council Directive 2009/24/EC. These said that only the expression of a computer program is protected and that ideas and principles which underlie its interfaces are not protected by copyright. He therefore found that easyJet had not infringed the copyright in the main software for its online flight-bookings program which had been written for it by the claimant, when easyJet commissioned another software company to write a new program which, although it did not copy the source code of the original program, produced a system which looked very similar and worked in a very similar way to the original program. It was therefore possible for two completely different computer programs to produce an identical result without infringing copyright, because copyright protected the embodiment of the functional effects in the software, rather than the functional effects themselves.

The Court of Appeal in the case of *Nova Productions Ltd v Mazooma Games Ltd and Bell Fruit Games Ltd* [2007] EWCA Civ 219 upheld the High Court's decision which followed the judgment in *Navitaire*. The claimant in this case was a designer and manufacturer of arcade video games and claimed that the two defendants had produced games which infringed the copyright in its own game, 'Pocket Money'. The court accepted that Nova was the owner of artistic copyright in the graphics and frames displayed to the user, and literary copyright in the computer program and the design notes for the game. However, the court upheld the High Court judge's decision to dismiss Nova's claims for infringement of such copyright. The court agreed with the first instance judge that there had been no appropriation of the artistic or literary skill and effort expended by Nova. Instead, what had been taken was a combination of a limited number of generalised ideas reflected in the output of the computer program. The Court of Appeal also said that 'Pumfrey J was quite right to say that merely making a program which will emulate another but which in no way involves copying the program code or any of the program's graphics is legitimate'.

This approach has now been endorsed by the ECJ in *SAS Institute Inc v World Programming Ltd* [2012] 3 CMLR 4 where it confirmed that copyright does not protect the functionality of a computer program or its programming language.

15.6 Linking

If a website provides a hyperlink to material on another website, it is open to debate whether this constitutes copyright infringement. The website has not reproduced any content of the other website on its web server – it merely facilitates access to it by the internet user who will, usually, have an implied licence at least to make a transitory copy for the purpose of accessing the other website. If the user does not have such an implied licence, or does not otherwise have a defence under the 1988 Act, that user will infringe copyright by reproducing the content in question and the linking website owner may be liable for authorising such infringement. However, the law in this area remains somewhat unsettled with different countries adopting different approaches. In the UK, as a practical matter, liability for copyright infringement will usually turn upon the scope of the implied licence of the user to reproduce content from the target website. The text of the hyperlink or the uniform (or universal) resource locator (URL) may or may not constitute an original literary work which would benefit from copyright protection following the Court of Appeal's decision in *The Newspaper Licensing Agency v Meltwater BV* [2012] RPC 1. Frequently, website operators include prohibitions on linking to their website in their terms and conditions, although it is not entirely clear whether such prohibitions would be enforceable as a matter of contract law (where it would be necessary to demonstrate the usual elements of a contract, including consideration).

There are, however, other types of web linking apart from ordinary hyperlinking which present their own set of problems and which copyright law might or might not be apt to address. There is so-called 'deep linking' whereby the link provided directs the user towards an underlying page of another website (rather than the home page). Technically, a deep link is indistinguishable from an ordinary hyperlink but the use of deep links is a practice which has posed a threat to the business models of certain website operators – in particular, those who rely on a large number of users visiting their home page to maximise advertising revenues. 'Inline linking' is a practice whereby the user's browser is instructed by a coded command on the visited website to collect and load onto the user's computer images or material from another website. In this case, the user does not click on any link and does not visit anyone else's website. The advantage for the visited website is that it is not required to store potentially infringing content on its own web server – it is the user who activates the command and to whose computer the images are sent directly. 'Framing' is another practice: frames are essentially a navigational tool employed by website designers and, when used on a single website, are uncontroversial. It is when a frame is used to access another website that problems arise: for example, website A or an advertiser on website A may take issue with website B if the latter provides links to website A but when the user clicks on those links, the content of website A remains framed by website B. From a copyright perspective, 'framing' is not dissimilar to ordinary hyperlinking but other rights are also likely to be relied upon (e.g. passing off).

There is a defence under section 28A of the 1988 Act which applies to certain temporary copies made as part of a technological process, and by the time this edition is published the Supreme Court may well have decided whether or not hyperlinks fall within this exception in the appeal on this single issue of the Court of Appeal's judgment in the *NLA v Meltwater* case (see Section 16.3 for further details).

Copyright may also have a role to play in other activities relating to the internet. One obvious example is the use of 'spider' programs to extract content. These programs conduct automated searches (and usually extract data) of other websites. They have been used to create lists of deep links and in the practice of so-called 'web scraping' (for example, to obtain data for use on price comparison websites). Some of these issues are considered in more detail in Chapter 16.

15.7 Issuing copies, performances in public and communicating to the public

All copyright works may be infringed by the issue of copies to the public (s 18). 'Issuing' means putting into circulation copies of a work not previously put into circulation anywhere in the European Economic Area (EEA). This means that once a copy of a work has legitimately been put into circulation in any country within the EEA (either by the copyright owner or with the copyright owner's permission) the copyright owner cannot prevent subsequent circulation (whether by sale, loan, hire or distribution) of that copy. However, the copyright owner still has the right to prevent the making of other copies of that one legitimately circulated copy. Even though the copyright owner cannot prevent the sale or other issue of any legitimately made copies, he can prevent the unauthorised rental of copies of such works to the public (this is discussed further below).

A case concerning a claim brought against online CD retailer CD Wow by a group of music manufacturers and suppliers confirmed that for internet sellers 'issuing copies to the public' takes place when the product that they are selling is delivered to the end customer through the national postal system (*Independiente Ltd v Music Trading On-Line (HK) Ltd* [2007] EMLR 25). The defendant had submitted that 'delivery' took place when, property in the relevant product having passed to the consumer under contractual arrangements with the latter, it was delivered to the Hong Kong postal authorities for onward transmission. They contended that this meant that the CDs were not 'issued to the public' in the UK by CD Wow, but rather by the consumer – who would not be guilty of infringement because he did so for his private use. The court rejected this argument, relying on section 32(4) of the Sale of Goods Act 1979 which provides that in sale contracts where a buyer is dealing as a consumer and a seller is required to send the goods to the buyer, 'delivery of the goods to the carrier is not delivery of the goods to the buyer'. Therefore delivery took place when the postal service delivered the products to the UK buyers, meaning that CD Wow had issued the copies to the public, thus infringing the claimants' copyright.

The ECJ's decision in *Football DataCo v Sportradar GmbH* [2013] 1 CMLR 29 concerning where acts of reutilisation take place for the purposes of infringement of the database right may also be applicable to the making available right. This case is discussed in Chapter 18.

Performing, showing and playing of works in public are also acts of infringement if done without licence (s 19). Performance, which means 'any form of visual or acoustic presentation', relates to literary, dramatic and musical works, and showing or playing relates to sound recordings, films and broadcasts. The performance must be in public to be an infringement. What constitutes 'in public' will be a question of fact and degree (and common sense) but examples of what have been held to comprise public performances are music played over a loudspeaker system to workers in their place of work (*Ernest Turner etc Ltd v Performing Right Society Ltd* [1943] Ch 167) and playing of music by a shop which is trying to sell the records being played (*Performing Right Society v Harlequin Record Shops* [1979] FSR 233).

In each of these cases, when the performance or playing or showing is done by means of an apparatus for receiving the images or sounds, the sender of the images or sounds and the performers will not be guilty of infringement; the person responsible for operating the relevant apparatus is the primary infringer.

It is also an infringement of most copyright works to communicate the work to the public by electronic transmission, including by broadcasting and by inclusion in an on-demand or other interactive service (that is, 'in such a way that members of the public may access it from a place and at a time individually chosen by them') (s 20).

The unauthorised online streaming of live sporting events was held to constitute communication to the public of copyright works, in the case of *Union des Associations Européennes de Football, British Sky Broadcasting Group plc, British Sky Broadcasting Ltd v Briscomb, Freeman, Rushby* [2006] EWHC 1268 (Ch). In that case, UEFA and BskyB obtained summary judgment against a group of individuals who were operating a website which disseminated sporting broadcasts over the internet, including UEFA Champions League matches. UEFA owned the copyright in the live broadcast of such matches on Sky or ITV channels.

In *Sociedad General de Autores y Editores de Espana (SGAE) v Rafael Hoteles SL* (Case C-306/05) [2007] ECDR 2, the ECJ provided some further clarification of the meaning of communicating works to the public, at least for the purposes of the Copyright Directive, suggesting that 'the public' should be interpreted broadly for these purposes. It ruled that by transmitting television broadcasts received by the hotel by means of television sets installed in guests' rooms, the hotel was communicating such broadcasts to the public. It made no difference that the television sets were in guests' private rooms and may not have been turned on by a particular guest. In *Phonographic Performance (Ireland) Ltd v Ireland* [2012] 2 CMLR 29, the ECJ followed this decision in finding that hotel operators were responsible for communicating works to the public, namely their customers, because those customers were targeted by the hotel operators to receive the communication. The broadcasting of phonograms was said to be of a profit-making nature as it provided an additional service to customers and was likely to attract additional guests. Compare this with the ECJ's decision in *Societa Consortile Fonografici (SCF) v Del Cosso* [2012] ECDR 16, decided on the same day, where background music played in private dental practices did not constitute a communication to the public. The patients were insignificant in number and were not 'persons in general', and so did not constitute 'the public'. Further, the broadcasts were not profit-making and in themselves would not have had an impact on the dentists' income. Accordingly, a communication to the public requires some form of benefit to the communicator, such as the ability to charge more for a hotel room or to attract more customers to a pub. In *Football Association Premier League v QC Leisure* [2012] CMLR 29 (see p 181 for more detail) the ECJ held that showing football matches to customers in a pub was a communication to the public. It confirmed that the term should be interpreted broadly. The ECJ defined 'communication' as meaning any transmission of the protected works irrespective of the technical process used and said that 'public' meant a 'new public' beyond the original viewing public which was in the mind of the creator of the work. In this case, the 'original public' were private television set owners and the 'new public' were the patrons of the pub.

15.8 Adaptation

This act of infringement only relates to literary, dramatic and musical works (s 21). 'Adaptation' means a translation of a literary or dramatic work, the conversion of a dramatic work into a non-dramatic form (and vice versa), the reproduction of a literary or dramatic work in a form whereby the story is conveyed by pictures suitable for inclusion in a book, magazine or periodical and, in relation to a musical work, an arrangement or transcription. Adaptation also includes conversion of a computer program from one computer language to another (from object code to source code, or from FORTRAN to COBOL). As a result of the Software Directive, implemented into English law through sections 50(A)-(C) of the 1988 Act, a lawful acquirer of software has an implied licence to copy to the extent necessary for lawful use of the software.

15.8.1 Rental or lending

Section 18A provides that the rental or lending of a literary, dramatic or musical work, an artistic work other than a work of architecture or applied art, a film or a sound recording is an infringement if done without the copyright owner's consent. 'Rental' is defined in section 18A(2)(a) as an arrangement where, for 'direct or indirect economic or commercial advantage', use is allowed on terms that the copy of the work will, or may, be returned. 'Rental' and 'lending' do not include, among other exceptions, making available for public performance, playing, showing or communicating to the public.

15.8.2   Authorisation

It is also an infringement for someone, without permission of the copyright owner, to authorise another to do an infringing act (s 16(2)). In *Moorhouse v University of New South Wales* [1975] RPC 454, photocopying machines were available in the university library for use by students and other library users, and one such user made two copies of a story from the claimant's book. The decision turned on whether or not the university could be said to have authorised students to copy literary works without licence and whether, therefore, the university authorised an infringement. Notices in library guides and on the photocopiers were held not to be adequate warnings against unlawful copying as they were not a clear enough statement. The court said that indifference as to whether an infringement occurred could reach a degree from which authorisation could be inferred. However, in the case of *CBS Songs Ltd v Amstrad Consumer Electronics plc & Another* [1988] 2 All ER 484, Amstrad was found not to have authorised the making of infringing copies by advertising and selling twin-deck double-speed tape recorders. In that case, it was relevant that the tape recorder did have a number of lawful, as well as unlawful, uses and that Amstrad could not be said to have any influence or control over the activities of those who purchased, and subsequently used, the tape recorders. In this context, in *CBS Inc v Ames Records & Tapes Ltd* [1982] Ch 91, it was said that authorisation

> can only come from someone having or purporting to have authority, and … an act is not authorised by someone who merely enables or possibly assists or even encourages another to do that act, but does not purport to have any authority which he can grant to justify the doing of the act.

In *Twentieth Century Fox Film Corp v Newzbin Ltd* [2010] EWHC 608 (Ch) ('*Newzbin 1*'), various major film studios brought a claim for copyright infringement against the Newzbin website which provided a searching and indexing facility which aided users in downloading the claimant's copyright works. The court held that the term 'authorise' in section 16 of the CDPA 1988 meant the 'grant or purported grant of the right to do the act complained of' and did not extend to mere enablement assistance, or even encouragement. In the case of Newzbin, the sophistication of the search and index functions and the lack of any filtering system for copyright works was enough that a reasonable member of the website would deduce that Newzbin had the authority to grant the right to download the films. The website was therefore liable for authorising infringement.

Liability of intermediaries

One of the most contentious copyright issues which has arisen in relation to the internet is whether an intermediary service provider (such as a website host) can be liable for storing and making available copyright-infringing content provided by its users.

As we have seen, under the 1988 Act such a party could potentially be liable for reproducing and/or issuing unauthorised copies of a work to the public, for making such works available to the public or for showing or playing a work in public. Further, such a party could be liable for authorising acts of copyright infringement by its users. It is also possible that an intermediary service provider could be liable with a user as a joint tortfeasor engaged in a common design or where it otherwise procures the user to infringe copyright. However, and in any event, the Electronic Commerce (EC Directive) Regulations 2002 (SI 2002 No 2013) provide immunity from any financial and criminal liability (but not liability for infringement itself) for intermediary service providers engaging in certain specified acts (namely, acting as a 'mere conduit', 'caching' and 'hosting').

In the late 1990s new file-sharing technologies emerged which reduced the role of intermediary service providers while enabling users to conduct searches and share files with each other (peer-to-peer). At that time, the record industry (and in particular the Recording Industry Association of America (RIAA) in the US) recognised that pursuing individual file sharers would be time-consuming, expensive and potentially damaging to the industry's reputation. The industry therefore decided to pursue the parties that they believed bore overall responsibility for the acts of the individual file sharers.

The battleground was marked out and the first strike was made in *A & M Records Inc v Napster Inc* USDC ND Cal, 114 F Supp 2d 896 10 August 2000. Napster made peer-to-peer software available on its website which enabled its users to share its compressed MP3 music files with each other online. Napster also provided other functions for its users on its own central web server, such as indexing and search functions. Following A & M's application for a preliminary injunction, the court found that on the evidence it was likely that A & M would establish that Napster knew or had a reason to believe that its users were engaging in acts of copyright infringement, making it contributorily liable for such infringement. Similarly, the court found it was likely that Napster would also be vicariously liable for having failed to police its users properly and having gained financial benefit from its activities.

The second strike came in *MGM Studios, Inc v Grokster Ltd* 125 S Ct 2764 (2005). By now, peer-to-peer technology had moved on and had dispensed with the central functions offered by Napster to which the court had previously pinned liability. Furthermore, a previous Supreme Court decision in *Sony Corp of America v Universal City Studios* 464 US 417 Supreme Court 1984 (the 'Betamax case') had established that if a product was distributed which was capable of substantial non-infringing uses, the distributor would not be liable for infringing uses. The *Grokster* case therefore provided the Supreme Court with an opportunity to revisit this authority in the context of the internet environment. The Supreme Court decided, however, that Grokster and the other defendant Streamcast were liable for acts of copyright infringement by users of the peer-to-peer software that they distributed on the basis that they had induced the infringements – in other words, Grokster and Streamcast had distributed the software with the clear objective of promoting its use to infringe copyright.

The concept of 'inducement' in *Grokster* was also referred to by the House of Lords in the *Amstrad* case where Templeman LJ stated that 'A defendant may procure an infringement by inducement, incitement or persuasion'(at 496), although on the facts in that case, Amstrad was not so liable. The concept of inducement in the UK, however, appears to be narrower than that articulated by the Supreme Court in *Grokster* and so it remains unclear as to whether a court in the UK would arrive at the same conclusion as the Supreme Court if faced with a similar case.

We discussed above (see p 175) the decision in *Twentieth Century Fox Film Corp v Newzbin Ltd* [2010] EWHC 608 (Ch) (*'Newzbin 1'*) where the internet site Newzbin was found liable for copyright infringement. Soon after that decision, the Newzbin site was resurrected, this time hosted from the Seychelles. The claimants therefore set their sights on the internet service provider. In *Twentieth Century Fox Film Corp v British Telecommunications plc* [2011] EWHC 1981 (Ch) (*'Newzbin 2'*), the court issued an injunction ordering BT to block access to the new Newzbin website. The court held that the more information BT was given about the infringements, the more likely it was that it would have had actual knowledge of the infringements. Receipt of a detailed notice relating to the infringements, and a reasonable opportunity to deal with them, would be sufficient to give the service provider reasonable notice.

The courts need to take care when determining the scope of relief against internet service providers. In *Scarlet Extended SA v Société Belge des Auteurs, Compositeurs et Editeurs SCRL (SABAM)* [2012] ECDR 4, the ECJ held that national courts could order intermediaries to take measures not only aimed at ceasing existing infringements, but also at preventing further infringements. However, the national courts had to take into account article 15(1) of Directive 2000/31 (the e-Commerce Directive) which prevented intermediaries from being required to carry out general monitoring of the information transmitted on their networks. In *Belgische Vereniging van Auteurs, Componisten en Uitgevers CVBA (SABAM) v Netlog NV* [2012] 2 CMLR 18, the ECJ held that granting an injunction against an internet service provider in that case would have been contrary to article 15(1) because it would have had to have installed an expensive computer system to actively monitor all of its customers' data for future infringements. In the *Newzbin 2* case, BT already had suitable screening systems in place. Blocking injunctions are likely to become increasingly common as a potentially effective way of overcoming jurisdictional issues where the original infringer is based overseas – see for example, *Dramatico Entertainment Ltd v British Sky Broadcasting Ltd* [2012] 3 CMLR 15, where the High Court ordered a blocking injunction preventing access to The Pirate Bay peer-to-peer file-sharing website through the defendant internet service providers, who held a 94% market share of UK internet users. In addition, the courts are prepared to order internet service providers to disclose the names of their customers who may have been involved in illegal file-sharing activities – see for example *Golden Eye (International) Ltd v Telefonica UK Ltd* [2012] EWCA Civ 1740.

The Digital Economy Act 2010 also allows rights owners to require internet service providers to send letters to copyright infringers, and if three such letters are sent to the same customer within a 12-month period, to then require the internet service provider to disclose details of that customer to the rights owner so that further action can be taken against them. However, although the Act is required to be implemented by 2014 this is looking increasingly unlikely as it has been met with a series of obstacles concerning its proposed operation, including in particular regarding the wording of the Ofcom Obligations Code and the costs of setting up the new regime.

15.9 Secondary infringement

Acts of secondary infringement are dealt with in sections 22–26 of the 1988 Act and are the acts committed by persons dealing in infringing copies. The secondary infringer is one step removed from the act of unlawful reproduction or performance.

Secondary infringement requires some level of knowledge or reason to believe that the works dealt in are infringing.

The acts of secondary infringement under the Act commence with:

- importing into the UK (otherwise than for private and domestic use);
- selling, letting for hire or offering or exposing for sale or hire;
- possessing, exhibiting or distributing in the course of a business; and
- distributing other than in the course of a business to an extent that will prejudicially affect the owner of a copyright (so if a private individual distributes copies of infringing software over the internet as freeware, this will not be in the course of a

business, but will prejudicially affect the copyright owner who is licensing the software for a licence fee commercially).

Sections 24, 25 and 26 are concerned with the actions of providing the means or the premises or the apparatus to enable an infringing act to be committed. Section 24(1) prohibits the making, importing, possessing in the course of business or the selling, or hiring or exposing for sale or hire of any item that is designed or adapted for making copies of a particular copyright work, if the person believes, or has reason to believe, that the item will be used to make infringing copies of that work. The position on copying works by faxing them or transmitting them by means of a telecommunications system (otherwise than by communication to the public), to a machine where a copy will be produced for the recipient is specifically covered by section 24(2).

15.10 Knowledge

The level of knowledge or suspicion required for secondary infringement was addressed in the case of *Hutchison Personal Communications Ltd v Hook Advertising Ltd* [1995] FSR 365. In that case, knowledge of allegations of infringement, the facts of which had yet to be proved, was held not to be sufficient to constitute knowledge of infringement for the purposes of secondary infringement. However, in the case of *Vermaat and Powell v Boncrest Ltd* [2002] FSR 21, the judge stated that for there to be sufficient knowledge for secondary infringement, the defendant must have reason to believe that there is an infringement rather than just a suspicion. The judge expanded on this by stating that the person must have notice of the facts, with sufficient information identifying the copyright work (with a copy of the work or access to view the copyright work) and that such information must be given sufficiently in advance that he can have time to 'evaluate the facts and convert them into a reasonable belief'.

The question of when an alleged infringer will have the requisite knowledge or reason to believe was considered in the case of *Nouveau Fabrics Ltd v Voyage Decoration Ltd and Dunelm Soft Furnishings Ltd* [2004] EWHC 895. In that case, Voyage, an importer and distributor of fabrics, was accused of importing and selling an infringing copy of Nouveau's fabric design which was protected by copyright. Voyage denied that it was aware at the time it began importing the fabric that it might infringe Nouveau's copyright and relied upon evidence from its Italian supplier of the fabric of the independent creation of the fabric design by the supplier as a reason for defending Nouveau's infringement claims. It was held that Voyage ought to have known that the fabric had been copied from Nouveau's design when it became clear, after pressure from Nouveau to disclose this information, that the Italian supplier could not provide satisfactory evidence of the origin of the allegedly infringing fabric design. Accordingly, it is possible to be found to have the requisite reason to believe by not taking sufficient steps to discover the true origins of an allegedly infringing article, having been made aware of a potential infringement.

15.11 Copy protection devices, electronic rights management information and decoders

In an effort to prevent acts of infringement, devices are constantly being created to make unlawful copying more difficult. Copy protection devices can, of course, be overridden or incapacitated and therefore if the legal protections offered by the 1988 Act against infringements are to be effective, these devices need to be offered protection under the law.

Under section 296 of the 1988 Act, if someone issues or communicates to the public (with the permission of the copyright owner) a computer program which is protected by some form of copy protection device or system, they will have the same rights as the copyright owner has against infringers, against anyone who makes, imports, distributes, sells, hires etc. means to get around the copy protection device or who publishes information enabling someone to get around the copy protection device. Originally, section 296 applied to all copyright works but the 2003 Regulations amended it so that it now applies just to computer programs, and then added further provisions (sections 296ZA–296ZD) to offer equivalent protection for all other copyright works to which effective technological measures have been applied. An effective technological measure is 'any technology, device or component which is designed, in the normal course of its operation, to protect a copyright work other than a computer program' from infringement and which is controlled by the copyright owner through some means such as 'encryption, scrambling or other transformation of the work' (see s 296ZF). It is now a criminal offence to make, import, sell, hire, offer or expose for sale or hire, advertise, possess in the course of business or distribute (whether in the course of business or otherwise to such an extent as to prejudice the copyright owner) any 'device, product or component which is primarily designed, produced or adapted for the purpose of enabling or facilitating the circumvention of effective technological measures'. Equally, it is a criminal offence to provide, promote, advertise or market any service the purpose of which is to enable or facilitate the circumvention of effective technological measures. It is, however, a defence that the defendant did not know or have reason to believe that the device or service could enable avoidance of effective technological measures.

Section 296ZE provides for a situation where certain permitted acts in relation to copyright works are being prevented by an effective technological measure. This applies to all copyright works other than computer programs. In such a case someone who wishes to exercise one of the permitted acts in relation to that copyright work may serve a notice of complaint on the Secretary of State who will then require the copyright owner or exclusive licensee to provide the required access (unless there are already arrangements in place, such as a licensing agreement, allowing such access). The complaint notice route is not available where the copyright work in question is available via an on-demand service or where the complainant has already obtained the copyright work unlawfully.

In *Kabushiki Kaisha Sony Computer Entertainment Inc v Ball* [2005] EWHC 1522 (Ch) Sony made an application for summary judgment claiming copyright infringement under section 296 (both before and after its amendment by the 2003 Regulations). Sony claimed that Mr Ball manufactured and offered for sale electronic chips which were capable of being fitted into Sony's Playstation2 and which circumvented the copy prevention measures within the consoles. Summary judgment was refused in part because to infringe under section 296 before it was amended, Mr Ball had to know or believe that the chips would assist copyright infringement. Since acts of exportation of the chips out of the UK would not be an infringement of copyright in the UK, Mr Ball would only have the requisite knowledge of an infringing act in the UK in respect of chips which he imported into the UK to meet orders from UK customers. This question could not be determined by a summary application.

The 2003 Regulations also introduced protection for electronic rights management information – this is information concerning the identity of the author, the work and terms and conditions of use of the work. Anyone who 'knowingly and without authority, removes or alters electronic rights management information' or who 'distributes, imports for distribution or communicates to the public copies of a copyright work from which electronic rights management information ... has been removed or altered without authority' when they know or have reason to believe that by doing so an infringement will be committed or concealed or made easier, will be open to an action for infringement by the copyright owner or exclusive licensee of the work to which the electronic rights management information relates.

There are also provisions in the 1988 Act concerning reception of broadcasts where recipients avoid payment of charges applicable to the reception, and concerning distribution, manufacture and possession of unauthorised decoders (that is, devices which unscramble any form of encryption, password and so on which is intended to prevent viewing of broadcasts unless appropriate payments have been made).

The case of *R v Mainwaring* [2002] FSR 20 concerned a criminal prosecution for breach of section 297 of the 1988 Act (as amended by the Conditional Access (Unauthorised Decoders) Regulations 2000). The court stated that 'unauthorised' in relation to a decoder meant that the decoder allowed an encrypted transmission to be received in intelligible form without payment of the fee which the broadcaster usually charges. In this case, the broadcast in question was not intended to be received in the UK and so the broadcaster had not made arrangements to collect fees from potential recipients. But the court said that this made no difference, otherwise the legislation (which emanates from a Directive) could be avoided merely by selling decoders in countries other than the country where the broadcast was intended to be received. This would defeat the purpose of the European Directive aimed at removing geographic barriers.

The meaning of 'dishonestly receiving a programme included in a broadcasting or cable programme service provided from a place in the United Kingdom' for the purposes of section 297(1) was considered in detail in the case of *Murphy v Media Protection Services* [2008] FSR 15; [2008] FSR 33. The defendant, a pub landlady, screened live English Premier League matches in her pub, which she received by subscribing cheaply to a Greek broadcaster. She thereby avoided paying licence fees to BskyB which was exclusively licensed by the UK Premier League to broadcast such matches in the UK. She argued that because the satellite feed she received was first sent by the Premier League to the Greek broadcaster, which added its own content to the feed before transmitting it to its subscribers, she was not receiving a programme included in a broadcasting service 'provided from a place in the UK'. She argued that the court was required to consider the effect of section 6(4) of the 1988 Act which defines the place from where a broadcast is made as 'the place where, under the control and responsibility of the person making the broadcast, the programme-carrying signals are introduced into an uninterrupted chain of communication'. The court held that this was not correct. Instead, it was necessary to identify the programme that had been received and then determine where the 'broadcasting service' in which the programme was included had been provided from, which was the place where the initial transmission of the programme for the ultimate reception by the public had taken place – namely, the UK. It was irrelevant that the Greek broadcaster had added content to the programme before transmitting it to its subscribers. However, the court allowed the defendant to restore the appeal in order to argue certain further points of defence based on European

Union (EU) free movement and competition laws, and the defendant's appeal resulted in the court making a reference to the ECJ on a number of points of law.

The ECJ heard the reference in *Murphy* alongside a similar reference in *Football Association Premier League Ltd v QC Leisure* [2008] EWHC 1411 (Ch). These two cases considered the use of foreign decoder cards in the UK in connection with the screening of live matches. The Premier League claimed that QC Leisure's dealing in, and use of, such cards involved an infringement of their rights under section 298 of the 1988 Act, which gives broadcast rights holders rights equivalent to copyright owners. One of the issues referred to the ECJ was whether the Premier League's prohibition on foreign broadcasters' supply of decoder cards for use in the UK was contrary to article 81(1) of the EC Treaty, which prohibits anti-competitive agreements, and whether a restriction on the use of the decoders amounted to a quantitative restriction on trade contrary to article 28.

In the combined reference [2012] 1 CMLR 29, the court held that restriction on the use of foreign decoders was only justifiable where it served the public interest and did not go beyond what was necessary to achieve this. The court held that article 56 of the Treaty on the Functioning of the European Union required the abolition of all restrictions on the freedom to provide services unless there was justification, and that such restrictions had to be in the public interest and should not go beyond what was necessary. The foreign decoder card was not an 'illicit device' under article 2 of Directive 98/84 and so section 297(1) could not be applied to the use of foreign decoder cards. The territorial restriction imposed on the use of such cards was therefore unlawful under EU law. In the light of this decision, the case was returned to the High Court to reconsider the case against Ms Murphy, resulting in the conviction against her being quashed (*Murphy v Media Protection Services Ltd* [2012] 3 CMLR 2). The ECJ decision is discussed in more detail in Chapter 23.

Additional provisions allowing for search warrants and forfeiture of unauthorised decoders were added by the Copyright, etc and Trade Marks (Offences and Enforcement) Act 2002 which came into force on 20 November 2002.

15.12 Infringing copy

Obviously, an infringing copy is any copy of a copyright work that has been made without the permission of the copyright owner. It also includes copies of works that were made legitimately outside the UK (for example, with the permission of the owner of the copyright in another country, who may be a different person from the copyright owner in the UK) but were then imported or proposed to be imported into the UK, when the making of such copy in the UK would have been an infringing act or a breach of an exclusive licence agreement (s 27).

This provision of the 1988 Act is subject to the operation of EU competition law. In particular, section 27(5) protects any enforceable EU right (such as freedom of movement of goods). This conflict between competition law and the exercise of copyright is considered in more detail in Chapter 23.

15.13 Remedies

The remedies available to a copyright owner for copyright infringement are:

▶ to bring a civil action (for damages, an account of profits, an injunction, delivery up or destruction of the copies, disclosure of the names of suppliers and sometimes customers, legal costs and interest); and/or

▶ to prompt a criminal prosecution either privately or by the enforcement authorities (commonly Trading Standards) for one or more of the criminal offences under the 1988 Act;

▶ under section 100 of the 1988 Act, which gives the copyright owner or a person authorised by him or her the right to seize and detain infringing copies which are openly on sale, subject to certain conditions.

In proceedings relating to copyright infringement, there are a number of presumptions laid down by the 1988 Act (in sections 27(4), 93A, 104, 105 and 106) that allow certain issues to be assumed and that shift the burden of proof to the other party.

Although it is beyond the scope of this book to cover in detail jurisdictional issues and justiciability issues relating to the enforcement of intellectual property rights between different countries, there has been an apparent willingness by the courts to enable the enforcement of overseas intellectual property rights in national states. Some intellectual property rights are EU-wide rights, such as the Community trade mark and Community design rights, so that decisions of a national court which is sitting as a Community court, such as was the case with the UK High Court in *Samsung Electronics UK Ltd v Apple Inc* [2012] EWCA Civ 1339, are binding across the EU (see further *DHL Express France SAS v Chronopost SA* [2011] ETMR 33 for an ECJ ruling relating to Community trade marks). In *Lucasfilm Ltd v Ainsworth* [2012] EMLR 3 the Supreme Court ruled that a UK court could determine issues of US copyright law. See also *Wintersteiger AG v Products 4U Sondermaschinenbau GmbH* [2012] ETMR 31.

15.13.1 Injunctions

An injunction is a court order preventing the infringer from continuing to commit the infringing acts complained of. Failure to comply with the order can be a contempt of court, punishable by imprisonment or a fine, depending upon the severity of the breach. In some cases, a claimant may wish to apply for an interim injunction, because the continued infringement pending a full hearing could put the copyright owner out of business or be highly prejudicial in some other way to the copyright owner. It is customary to seek undertakings from the infringer first and apply to the court for an interim injunction where the infringer fails to provide them. The matters that must be proved for the grant of an interim injunction were established in the case of *American Cyanamid Co v Ethicon Ltd* [1975] AC 396 and endorsed in *Series 5 Software Ltd v Philip Clarke & ors* [1996] FSR 273.

In the case of *Microsoft Corp v Plato Technology Ltd* [1999] FSR 834, the innocence of the defendant, who was found to have been dealing in counterfeit copies of Microsoft software, was found by the court to be a justification for limiting the scope of the injunction granted to the claimant.

European legislation states that Member States must allow rights holders to apply for injunctions against intermediaries whose services are used by a third party to infringe intellectual property. This is dealt with in article 8(3) of the InfoSoc Directive (2001/29) and in article 11 of the Enforcement Directive (2004/48). The UK has not taken any specific action to implement this legislation as the view has been taken that existing UK law already makes provision for this in that injunctions can be granted when it is 'just and convenient to do so' (Senior Courts Act 1981, s 37(1)). An example of an injunction granted against an intermediary is the blocking injunction granted in *Newzbin 2* (see p 176).

15.13.2   Damages

In the case of infringing articles which are commercially exploited, the basis of a damages award is often the loss of profit which would have been made by the copyright owner on the same quantity of sales of its own products that it would have sold had the copies not been on the market. For the principles relating to the calculation of damages, see Chapter 20.

Under section 97(2), the court has the power to award additional damages if the infringement was flagrant or the infringer benefited substantially from the infringement. Such damages are not frequently awarded (although see Section 15.13.6).

15.13.3   Account of profits

An account of profits is a discretionary remedy, but it is available in most cases as an alternative to damages. It can be useful in a case where the infringer's profit is much greater than the profit that the copyright owner would have made, where the royalty method of assessing damages applies or where the infringer is able to rely upon the innocence defence. Under section 97, if an alleged infringer can prove that it was not aware that copyright subsisted in the work alleged to have been copied, it will escape liability for damages. This does not, however, prevent the copyright owner from seeking an account of profits or any of the other remedies.

For the principles relating to the calculation of relevant profits, disclosure of names of suppliers/importers/others and costs and interest, see Section 15.8.2 and Chapter 20.

15.13.4   Limitation period

The limitation period for making a claim for infringement of copyright is six years from the act of infringement committed (with each new act of infringement having its own corresponding limitation period).

15.13.5   Trading Standards' powers

Section 107A of the 1988 Act gives Trading Standards officers the power to make test purchases and to enter premises to inspect and seize goods and documents. Amendments to the Enterprise Act 2002 which came into force in October 2007 (see s 241A) now enable intellectual property rights holders greater access to information held by Trading Standards to assist them to bring civil proceedings against counterfeiters.

15.13.6   Enforcement Directive

Directive 2004/48/EC of the European Parliament and of the Council of 29 April 2004 on the enforcement of intellectual property rights (the Enforcement Directive) is designed to harmonise sanctions and remedies across the EU and signal to Member States certain measures (such as the publication of judicial decisions and the development of professional codes of conduct) that would contribute to the fight against counterfeiting and piracy. The Directive includes procedures covering evidence and provisional measures, such as injunctions and seizure. Remedies available to rights holders include the destruction, recall or permanent removal from the market of illegal goods, as well as financial compensation, injunctions and damages. It also includes a right of information allowing judges to order people to reveal the names and addresses of those involved in distributing the illegal goods or services, together with details of the quantities and prices involved. The Intellectual Property (Enforcement, etc.) Regulations 2006 (SI 2006/1028) which implement the Enforcement Directive came into force on 29 April 2006. These provide that damages shall be appropriate to the actual prejudice that the claimant suffered as a result of the infringement when assessing compensation in the case of infringers of intellectual property rights who know or have reasonable grounds to believe that they are infringing an intellectual property right. This gives the courts greater scope for making more punitive awards in favour of successful claimants in intellectual property right actions and might therefore lead to more awards for additional damages.

The Directive's provisions regarding the publication of judgments only refer to publicity of judgments where the intellectual property rights holder has been successful. Accordingly, a defendant found to have infringed an intellectual property right could be ordered to pay for adverts in national newspapers reporting the judgment made against them. However, in *Samsung Electronics (UK) Ltd v Apple Inc* [2012] ECDR 2 the Court of Appeal held that the court also has jurisdiction in appropriate cases to require a rights owner to publish a declaration of non-infringement obtained by a successful applicant. In that case, Apple was ordered to publish a statement on the home page of its website saying that Samsung had not infringed its registered design following a dispute concerning the parties' respective tablet computer designs.

15.14 Criminal offences

Broadly speaking, most of the acts constituting infringement of copyright are also criminal offences if the requisite knowledge can be shown. Now that the 2003 Regulations have introduced a new criminal offence of communicating a copyright work to the public in the course of a business or in circumstances prejudicial to the owner, service providers are also liable to prosecution. This is in addition to the fact that the 2003 Regulations now give the High Court the power to grant injunctions against service providers where the service provider has actual knowledge of another person using their service to infringe copyright. Where an infringement constituting a criminal offence is committed by a company, the directors, managers, secretary and similar officers could also be guilty of an offence if the act was committed with that person's 'consent or connivance'. The presumptions referred to above do not apply in criminal proceedings (except s 27(4)) because the burden of proof in criminal proceedings is different from that in civil proceedings. Conviction for criminal offences under the Act can result in imprisonment or a fine or both. In addition, there can be an order for delivery up of infringing copies, which can be enforced by Trading Standards. Trading Standards officers, HM Revenue & Customs and the police have rights under the 1988 Act (as amended by the Copyright, etc and Trade Marks (Offences and Enforcement) Act 2002) and other legislation to search for and seize infringing material and seek orders for delivery up and forfeiture of infringing material in connection with offences under the 1988 Act.

At a European level, a second Enforcement Directive was proposed in 2005 to strengthen the criminal framework for dealing with intellectual property infringements. If introduced, the directive would have required Member States to ensure that intentional infringements of an intellectual property right on a commercial scale were treated as criminal offences. An early draft of the proposal for the directive included all forms of intellectual property infringement, drawing significant criticism from many quarters, including the Law Society of England and Wales, which questioned the broad scope of the proposed directive and doubted whether there was a public interest in the EU for adopting such measures. The European Commission withdrew the proposal for the directive in 2010. Instead, the Commission has announced its intention to revise the Enforcement Directive, in particular to meet the specific challenges of the digital environment and to adopt a new Customs Regulation.

15.15 Remedies available to licensees

An exclusive copyright licensee will have the same rights as the copyright owner in respect of an infringement committed after the granting of his licence. Except for the application for interim relief, which the exclusive licensee may bring on his own, all other infringement actions brought by the exclusive licensee must also involve the copyright owner. Either the claimant licensee will get the copyright owner's agreement to be joined as co-claimant or the exclusive licensee will join the copyright owner as a second defendant. In the latter case, the copyright owner is not liable for any costs awarded in the case unless he takes part in the proceedings.

A non-exclusive licensee now has the right to bring an action for copyright infringement where the infringing act was directly connected to a prior licensed act of the licensee (s 101A, introduced by the 2003 Regulations). As with an exclusive licence, it must be in writing and signed by the copyright owner, but must also expressly grant the right of action under section 101A. The non-exclusive licensee then has the same rights and remedies as the copyright owner would have had.

Summary

- The copyright owner is the only person entitled to deal in the copyright work unless another person has a licence from the copyright owner. Anyone else copying, issuing copies to the public, performing etc. a substantial part of the work without the owner's authority infringes the copyright. 'Substantial' is judged qualitatively and not quantitatively.

- Issuing copies of the work means making a work available to the public that was not previously in circulation anywhere in the EEA.

- Any translation of a copyright work is an adaptation and amounts to infringement if done without the owner's authority.

- The copyright owner's consent is needed before a copyright work can be rented out for profit.

- Dealing in infringing goods (for example, importing) amounts to secondary infringement provided that the person dealing with the goods has the requisite knowledge.

- Infringing copies include works legitimately made outside the UK but then imported into the UK, when making the works in the UK would have amounted to infringement or breach of an exclusive licence.

- A range of remedies is available that includes damages, injunctions and delivery up or destruction of the copies.

- The activities that fall under secondary infringement are also criminal offences.

Exercises

15.1 Consider whether the following are likely to lead to successful copyright infringement proceedings:

(a) Six bars in the refrain of a chart-topping song are identical to an extract from a piece of classical music composed in 1788.

(b) A Co. Ltd produces dining chairs of an unusual shape with African carvings on the backrest. These are available for sale in limited numbers at £2,000 each. B Co. Ltd starts producing chairs of a similar shape but decorated with different artwork and of generally inferior quality, to be sold at £200 each.

(c) C Co. Ltd is the UK copyright owners of Wordplan 7, a word-processing program. It has come to its attention that D Co. Ltd is importing Wordplan 7 from India.

15.2 E is the Student Housing Officer for F University. As part of her job, she is required to provide information for new students about travelling and living in the locality.

Each summer, she spends time consulting rail and bus timetables, as well as investigating cheap but decent accommodation. When the information is collated, she writes a series of articles for the university's student journal with extracts from bus and rail timetables, adding useful hints on dealing with difficult landladies. The articles are usually published in *Fresher's Week* and are always an immediate success.

Last autumn, G collected the articles. She spent a few hours in the library extracting the main timetables and then added a list of cheap guest houses obtained from the university telephone directories. She also listed a few cheap places to eat in town. The result was one long article on where to go in the area surrounding F University.

Advise E, who objects to G's activities.

Further reading and references

Samsung Electronics (UK) Ltd v Apple Inc [2013] FSR 10, which dealt with the inadequacy of the original notice published by Apple on its website following the decision referred to in Section 15.13.6.

'Beyond Liability: on the Availability and Scope of Injunctions against Online Intermediaries after *L'Oreal V Ebay*' By Toby Headdon http://www.blplaw.com/media/2012_EIPR_Issue_3_Headdon.pdf

Chapter 16

Defences

16.1 Introduction

In an action for infringement of copyright, there are a number of approaches that the defendant can adopt:

(a) challenge the existence of copyright or the claimant's ownership of copyright;
(b) deny the infringement;
(c) claim to have been entitled, because of a permission granted, to do the act in question, or argue that it is within one of the statutory fair dealing exemptions or claim public interest or European Union (EU) competition law rights.

A claim of ignorance of the law, either as to the fact that copyright subsisted in the claimant's work or that the act committed constituted infringement of that copyright, will not work as a defence to liability (*Mansell v Valley Printing Co* [1908] 2 Ch 441).

Ignorance of subsistence of copyright is, however, relevant as to damages. If the person charged with infringement can satisfy the court that he did not realise that copyright subsisted in the work that has been copied, then damages will not be awarded in respect of that period of ignorance (s 97(1) and the discussion in the previous chapter). In the case of secondary infringement, as already discussed, an element of knowledge is required for the infringement to be actionable in the first place. The infringement only occurs if the person 'knows or has reason to believe' that he is dealing with an infringing copy of a copyright work.

16.2 Acts permitted by licence

An infringement is the doing of any of the acts restricted by copyright 'without the licence of the copyright owner'. Although assignments of copyright must be in writing signed by the copyright owner, there are no such formal requirements for the granting of licences of copyright (s 90). There are, however, special rights granted to an exclusive and non-exclusive licensee of copyright to pursue infringers, and to benefit from such rights the licensee must have been granted the licence in writing signed by the copyright owner (s 92 and s 101A). In the case of *Biotrading v Biohit Ltd* and *Labsystems v Biohit Ltd* [1998] FSR 109, the definition of an exclusive licensee for the purposes of section 92 was considered and the case made clear that all that was required was that somebody should be given the exclusive right to 'exercise a right'; therefore, in that case, the second claimant had been granted an exclusive right to import the products in question and was held by the court to be an exclusive licensee for the purposes of section 92 and entitled to bring an action for infringement in its own name.

A licence can be granted expressly in writing or orally or can, in certain cases, be implied (but as seen above, before the licensee takes court action, the licence will have to be recorded in writing, and an assignment of past rights of action will have to be entered into with the copyright owner if damages are to be recovered for any acts committed before the licence in writing was signed). In the case of *Film Investors Overseas Services SA& Another v Home Video Channel Ltd (trading as the Adult Channel)* [1997] EMLR 347, an action for copyright infringement failed because the court found that the claimants knew, or strongly suspected, for several years that the defendants were carrying on the activity complained of and had, as a result, consented to or acquiesced in the activity.

Courts have implied licences of copyright in respect of commissioned copyright works for value. In a number of cases the courts have implied a limited licence to the commissioner to give effect to the obvious intention of the contract of commission. In *Cala Homes (South) Ltd v Alfred McAlpine Homes East Ltd* [1995] FSR 1818, the court found sufficient involvement by the commissioner in the drawing of plans to find joint ownership. The judge said that, had he not found sufficient involvement, he would have found an exclusive licence implied in favour of the commissioner. In the case of *Pasterfield v Denham & Another* [1999] FSR 168, although the judge found a transfer of equitable ownership from the designer to the commissioner, he said that, had that not been his finding, he would have found an implied licence since the designer was aware of the commissioner's intentions to use the commissioned design in a promotional leaflet.

In *Griggs v Evans* [2005] FSR 31 the court had to decide whether the designer of a new logo for Dr Martens footwear had retained the copyright in the logo for uses beyond use as point of sale material in the UK. The owners of Dr Martens footwear argued that there was an express or an implied term in their contract with the designer that they would own all the copyright in the new logo. In this case, the court found that it would never have been contemplated that the designer would retain the copyright in the logo and ordered the copyright to be assigned to the footwear company. The case sets out useful guidance as to when a licence will be implied and when an assignment of copyright will be implied.

These kinds of dispute are unfortunately all too common, and yet could easily be avoided by the parties entering into written contracts at the outset, setting out who will own the copyright in the designs to be created. The problem with implied licences and, to some extent, oral licences is establishing their exact terms. What is the duration and extent of the licence, to whom did it extend, were any royalties payable, and in what circumstances could it be brought to an end by the licensor?

Provided that the defendant in an infringement action can prove to the satisfaction of the court that the allegedly infringing act was covered by a valid licence, the claim of infringement will fail.

In the context of internet content, the worldwide organisation Creative Commons (established in the United States in 2001) provides licensing schemes which seek to allow copyright owners a range of 'middle ground' solutions between maintaining full copyright control and ceding all rights over their works to allow these to be freely exploited with no restrictions. A great deal of digital content is currently licensed through Creative Commons licensing schemes, facilitating the re-use and exploitation of such content by third parties, without the risk of copyright infringement. Creative Commons schemes aim to give copyright holders greater freedom of choice to permit the use by third parties of their work, whilst retaining as much control over such use as they wish.

The Creative Commons movement was generally well received when it was first established. However, it attracted some negative attention from several different quarters, in particular in the United States, where it was inaugurated, when a Dallas family filed a lawsuit against Virgin Mobile in which Creative Commons was initially included as a co-defendant.

The background to the lawsuit commenced when Virgin Mobile obtained a photograph of American minor Alison Chang through the photo-sharing website Flickr. The photographer had uploaded Alison's photograph onto the site and had selected for his work the Creative Commons 'Attribution' licence which broadly permits commercial re-use of the work provided that the photographer is credited appropriately. Virgin used the photograph as part of a series of photos in an advertising campaign called 'Are you with us or what?' The advert in question featured a picture of Alison alongside the slogan 'Dump your pen-friend' and highlighted the availability of free texts between Virgin Mobile customers. Alison's family objected to such a use of her photograph and issued proceedings against Virgin Mobile claiming damages for the grief and humiliation they allege that she suffered through the invasion of her privacy and damage to her reputation. Initially, Creative Commons was also dragged into the frame as a co-defendant. This was because the photographer, a co-claimant in the lawsuit, claimed that he was not adequately educated by Creative Commons about the implications of licensing his photographs through a Creative Commons Attribution Licence.

The claimants subsequently dismissed Creative Commons from the lawsuit. However, the case highlights that while companies may rely on Creative Commons licences to access and exploit freely a greater range of digital content, such companies still need to exercise caution when dealing with works licensed in this way. In particular, when re-using photographs such companies must consider the rights of the subjects of photographs in addition to those of copyright owners. A spokesperson for Creative Commons said on its website that: 'now that this lawsuit has received so much attention, if you've released a photo of a person under a CC license (or under no license at all), you could reasonably expect that no [company] would consider using that photo commercially without making sure the person pictured in the photo is OK with that'.

This case arguably gives greater ammunition to those critics of Creative Commons who perceive the movement as undermining copyright owners' rights, being difficult to understand or as primarily benefiting big corporate entities. However, Creative Commons also has many supporters who see the movement as generally striking a good balance between private owners' rights and the public interest.

16.3 Permitted acts

The 1988 Act contains statutory permissions, or exceptions, to the exclusive rights of the copyright owner. Many of these have come about as a result of case decisions over the years that acknowledged the need for certain, fair exceptions. A number of changes were implemented by the 2003 Regulations to comply with the Copyright Directive.

16.3.1 Section 28A – making of temporary copies

When copyright-protected works are transmitted over the internet a number of temporary copies of those works or parts of them are often made to facilitate the transmission. For example, when a work is transmitted from the web server on which it is hosted to an end-user's computer running a web browser, a number of temporary copies will be made on intermediate servers to facilitate that transmission. Section 28A of the 1988 Act sets out how copyright law deals with these temporary copies and applies into UK law article 5(1) of Directive 2001/29/EC (the 'InfoSoc Directive').

The remainder of Section 16.3.1 will refer to article 5(1), since the majority of the case law interprets the Directive rather than the 1988 Act. In practice, the wording of the provisions has the same effect.

16.3.1(a) The general rule on temporary copies

Article 9(1) of the Berne Convention prescribes for authors of literary and artistic works the exclusive right to authorise their reproduction 'in any manner or form', although it does not explicitly state whether this includes temporary copies. In the EU, the rule is in article 2 of the InfoSoc Directive. The owner of the reproduction right in a copyright-protected work has the exclusive right to authorise copies, including temporary copies. In the UK, section 17(6) of the 1988 Act states that copying includes 'transient' copying.

16.3.1(b) Strictness of the exemption

The European Court of Justice (ECJ) appears to have adopted the understanding that the temporary copying exception is to be applied restrictively. In *Infopaq International A/S v Danske Dagblades Forening* [2012] Bus LR 102, the first case before the ECJ to consider the article 5(1) exception, it observed that 'provisions of a Directive which derogate from a general principle established by that Directive must be interpreted strictly'.

16.3.1(c) The article 5(1) exception

Article 5(1) states:

1. Temporary acts of reproduction referred to in Article 2, which are transient or incidental [and] an integral and essential part of a technological process and whose sole purpose is to enable:

   (a) a transmission in a network between third parties by an intermediary, or
   (b) a lawful use

   of a work or other subject matter to be made, and which have no independent economic significance, shall be exempted from the reproduction right provided for in Article 2.

In *Infopaq*, the ECJ identified within article 5(1) five conditions, all of which must be fulfilled for the exception to apply. Each condition is considered in more detail below.

16.3.1(c)(i) The act must be temporary

Conceptually, it is very difficult to determine what is meant by 'temporary', which perhaps explains the absence of any attempt to define it in the InfoSoc Directive. In one sense, everything that is not infinite in duration is temporary. At one end of that spectrum of possibility, most people would agree that a copy made on an intermediate server in the course of a transmission that subsists for only a fraction of a second is a 'temporary' copy.

The concept of 'temporary' does not operate in the abstract under article 5(1) for at least two reasons. Firstly, it is supplemented by the other conditions under article 5(1) including the concept of 'transience' (see further below). Secondly, it is given life when considered in a particular context. So, for example, recital 33 to the InfoSoc Directive states that, provided all the conditions are met, the article 5(1) exception 'should include acts which enable browsing as well as acts of caching to take place....'. This at least suggests that copies which 'enable' browsing or caching may, in principle, be temporary copies, offering some assistance, but also prompting further lines of enquiry.

For example, do such copies include only the copies made in the RAM of a computer or do they also include the copies on an end-user's computer screen?

16.3.1(c)(ii) The act must be transient or incidental

In *Infopaq*, the ECJ stated that 'an act can be held to be "transient" within the meaning of the second condition laid down in article 5(1) of Directive 2001/29 only if its duration is limited to what is necessary for the proper completion of the technological process in question, it being understood that that process must be automated so that it deletes that act automatically, without human intervention, once its function of enabling the completion of such a process has come to an end'.

When is an act of temporary copying 'incidental'? Presumably when it is ancillary to and made in pursuance of some other main purpose. For example, a temporary copy made in the RAM of a computer to enable browsing may be regarded as incidental to the purpose of browsing. Conversely, the further copy made on the end-user's computer screen might not be regarded as incidental; it is the copy which is browsed and therefore is not incidental to the purpose of browsing.

16.3.1(c)(iii) The act must be an integral and essential part of a technological process

A 'technological process', while not defined, will cover processes which are effected by technological means. This begs the question – what are technological means? This will need to be addressed on a case-by-case basis. In some cases it will be fairly clear (for example, something that goes on inside your computer). Examples of a 'technological process' include a data-capture process operated by a media monitoring organisation (*Infopaq*) and streaming of content of broadcasts to subscribers of a broadcast service (*ITV Broadcasting v TV Catchup* [2010] EWHC 3063 (Ch)). In *NLA v Meltwater* [2010] EWHC 3099, the High Court held that a copy of a monitoring report shown on the computer screen of the end-user to whom it is sent by e-mail was not part of a technological process because it was generated by the volition of that end-user and was in fact the 'end' that the process itself was designed to achieve. Thus, we might conclude that where the temporary copy is volitional, in the sense that it is made as a result of the application of human will, it cannot be part of a technological process. However, in *Infopaq International A/S v Danske Dagblades Forening* (C-302/10) (known as '*Infopaq II*') the ECJ appeared to find that a similar process but which included the manual scanning of newspaper articles could be a technological process.

To be 'integral', the act of making the temporary copy must be integrated within the technological process. Put another way, the act must be one in a sequence of actions which the technological process is made up of. To be 'essential' the successful operation of the technological process must be dependent upon the making of the temporary copy.

16.3.1(c)(iv) The sole purpose of the process must be to enable a transmission of the work in a network between third parties by an intermediary or a lawful use of the work

There are two alternative 'sole purposes' here.

The first concerns the making of a temporary copy for the sole purpose of enabling the transmission of a work by an intermediary between third parties in a network. Thus, it is aimed at providing an intermediary with some comfort in relation to the numerous 'invisible' temporary copies that it will inevitably make to facilitate transmissions over the internet and other networks. These would include some of the copies referred to in recital 33 that 'enable' browsing and caching to take place.

The second concerns use. Subject to fulfilment of the other conditions, temporary copying that enables lawful use of a work is permitted. Recital 33 states that 'A use should be considered lawful where it is authorised by the rightholder or not restricted by law.'

If a use is 'restricted by law', then the article 5(1) exception should not apply. This could refer to any law, not just copyright law. A use 'not restricted by law' might include the 'fair dealing' provisions under sections 29 and 30 of the CDPA 1988 (see Sections 16.3.2 and 16.3.3). However, there is a suggestion in the ECJ's judgment in *Football Association Premier League Ltd v QC Leisure* [2012] 1 CMLR 29 that the phrase 'restricted by law' must be interpreted as a reference to legislation not including copyright legislation, on the apparent basis that because article 5(1) is an exception to copyright infringement copyright law should be ignored in order to avoid the exception becoming circular. So in that case the ECJ concluded that the reception of a television broadcast in private circles was a lawful use.

16.3.1(c)(v) The act must have no independent, economic significance

The temporary copy itself must have no independent, economic significance if it is to benefit from the article 5(1) exception. Recital 33 to the InfoSoc Directive puts it this way: 'The acts of reproduction concerned should have no economic value on their own.' This condition has attracted the most attention in the case law to date.

In *NLA v Meltwater* [2011] ECDR 10, the High Court (upheld in the Court of Appeal) held that the copy of the monitoring report shown on the computer screen of the end-user to whom it is sent by e-mail did have independent, economic significance since it was the very thing that the end-user was paying for. This appears to reflect the view of Advocate General Kokott in her Opinion in *FAPL v QC Leisure* [2012] FSR 12, that fragments of digital video created on a television screen (and fragments of the accompanying soundtrack) had independent, economic significance because they were the subject matter of the exploitation of a broadcast, regardless of whether its reception was paid for by a subscriber, through advertising or from a national budget. (In contrast, she found that the frames of digital video and audio created in the memory of a decoder in the course of a broadcast transmission did not have independent, economic significance; their economic significance was dependent upon the proposed exploitation.)

However, the ECJ declined to follow this approach in *FAPL v QC Leisure*, instead deciding that both the copies in the decoder memory and on the television screen did not have independent, economic significance. They said that the economic advantage had to be 'independent in the sense that it goes beyond the advantage derived from the mere picking up of the broadcast and its visual display'. The ECJ stated that the copies in the case formed 'an inseparable and non-autonomous part of the process of reception of the broadcasts transmitted containing the works in question ... they are performed without influence, or even awareness, on the part of the persons thereby having access to the protected works'. It is not at all clear why the ECJ departed from the view of the Advocate General concerning temporary copies which are made on a television screen and which are clearly for consumption. There is a suggestion in its judgment that to require television viewers to obtain authorisation to view copyright-protected content would impede and paralyse the spread and contribution of new technologies. However, television viewers often pay to watch programmes, or in the case of the BBC, a licence fee. Broadcasters often receive advertising revenue off the back of them. Where viewers do not pay a subscription, they no doubt have an implied licence of any copyright to make the required temporary copies, making it neither necessary nor appropriate for the article 5(1) exception to play any role. The problem with the ECJ's decision is that it has made the exception the rule.

Nevertheless, the ECJ concluded, applying their reasoning discussed above, that the temporary screen copies were not capable of generating an additional economic advantage going beyond the advantage derived from mere reception of the broadcasts. Similarly, in *Infopaq* II the ECJ found that that a data capture process such as the one in that case would not have independent economic significance provided that the acts of temporary reproduction did not enable the generation of an additional profit and that they did not lead to a modification of the work.

16.3.1(d) Where the article 5(1) exception does not apply

Article 5(5) states:

> The exceptions and limitations provided for in paragraphs 1, 2, 3 and 4 shall only be applied in certain special cases which do not conflict with a normal exploitation of the work or other subject-matter and do not unreasonably prejudice the legitimate interests of the rightholder.

Therefore, in order for the article 5(1) exemption to be relied upon, the temporary acts of copying must also fulfil the following conditions, which are often referred to as the 'three step test' and also appear in international copyright treaties such as the Berne Convention (article 9(2)).

16.3.1(d)(i) In certain special cases

This essentially means that there are special circumstances which justify the making of an exception. In this respect, it is reasonable to suppose that the legislature has already identified the circumstances envisaged in Article 5(1) as a certain special case.

16.3.1(d)(ii) No conflict with a normal exploitation of the work

In *NLA v Meltwater*, the newspaper publishers argued that the normal exploitation of their works involved granting a licence for commercial use of their content in return for payment from users, and that if section 28A of the 1988 Act were to operate so as to, in effect, license such use and exploitation of their copyright works, there would plainly be a conflict. Neither the High Court nor the Court of Appeal expressly referred to article 5(5), although the article 5(1) exception was found not to apply by both.

16.3.1(d)(iii) No unreasonable prejudice to the legitimate interest of the rightholder

An example of unreasonable prejudice might be where the owner suffers a serious loss of profit.

It is difficult to find any reasoning given by the ECJ in *Football Association Premier League Ltd v QC Leisure* [2012] 1 CMLR 29 as to why these conditions were fulfilled – the court appeared to suggest that they were automatically fulfilled for the same reasons that applied to the five criteria under article 5(1). In *Infopaq* II, the ECJ followed the ECJ decision in FAPL, saying that in a process such as the one in issue in *Infopaq* II, article 5(5) would always be satisfied. If that will always be the case, it would appear to render article 5(5) redundant for the purposes of article 5(1).

16.3.1(e) The NLA v Meltwater appeal to the Supreme Court

All of the issues discussed above concerning article 5(1) were the subject of the appeal to the Supreme Court in the *NLA v Meltwater* litigation to be heard in February 2013, so it will be interesting to see how the Supreme Court decides the issue of the application of the temporary copies exception to images of websites which appear on an end-user's screen when browsing the internet.

16.3.2   Section 29 – research and private study

Anyone may make a copy of a literary, dramatic, musical or artistic work for the purpose of private study or for research for a non-commercial purpose provided that, in both cases, it is 'fair dealing' and, in respect of research, that it is accompanied by a sufficient acknowledgement (unless that would be impossible for reasons of practicality or otherwise). The 2003 Regulations added specific references to acts relating to the observing, studying and testing of the functionality of a computer program which will not amount to fair dealing unless they fall within the acts permitted under section 50BA.

'Fair dealing' is not defined in the 1988 Act but case law suggests that the following will be relevant factors:

(a)   whether the copying deprives the copyright owner of a sale which would otherwise have been made;
(b)   the size or proportion of the piece copied; and
(c)   whether the copier will obtain a substantial financial benefit from the copying.

Discussions of what constitutes fair dealing can be found in the cases of *Beloff v Pressdram Ltd* [1973] RPC 765 and *Hubbard v Vosper* [1972] 2 QB 84. *Hubbard v Vosper* concerned a critical book about Scientology written and published by the defendant. This book included extracts from the claimant's books, bulletins and letters about Scientology. It was found by the Court of Appeal that, even though a substantial taking was shown, this could amount to 'fair dealing'. Fair dealing is a question of fact and impression. Lord Denning held that relevant factors to be considered could include the number and extent of extracts and the use made of the extracts. If the extracts are used as the basis for comment, review and criticism, that may be fair dealing. If they are used to convey the same information as the author, for a rival purpose, that may be unfair. Another relevant factor was the proportion of the copied part in relation to the comment added. The extent to which the work has been circulated will also be a relevant factor.

The section also exempts copying carried out by someone (other than the person who will be carrying out the research or study) on that person's behalf (including by a librarian) but makes clear that, in such cases, multiple copies are not permitted. Other forms of copying by librarians which are exempted are covered by sections 37–44.

16.3.3   Section 30 – criticism, review and news reporting

Reproduction of a copyright work for the purpose of criticism or review is permitted, provided that it is fair dealing, that there is a sufficient acknowledgement of the work and that the work has been made available to the public. Making available to the public can be by any means, including by means of an electronic retrieval system, by rental or lending, or by communicating the work to the public. However, unauthorised acts resulting in the making available will not count for the purposes of this permitted act. Fair dealing for the purposes of reporting a current event will not infringe the copyright in any work, other than a photograph, provided that there is a sufficient acknowledgement.

In *Associated Newspapers Ltd v His Royal Highness the Prince of Wales* [2006] EWCA Civ 1776, *The Mail on Sunday* could not rely on this defence to escape liability for copyright infringement for publishing extracts of a private journal written by the Prince of Wales. The newspaper had argued that the extracts were published for the purpose of reporting on a topical story about the Prince's recent failure to attend a banquet at Buckingham Palace for the Chinese state visit. But the appeal court held that much of the published article had no bearing on current events and could not criticise the judge at first instance's conclusions following his finding that the quotations 'had been chosen for the purpose of reporting on the revelation of the contents of the journal as itself an event of interest and not for the purpose of reporting on current events'. Note that with sound recordings, films or broadcasts, an acknowledgement will not be necessary if it would be impossible for reasons of practicality or otherwise. The exclusion of photographs must not be forgotten – this means that a newspaper, for example, should always obtain prior permission to use a photograph before going to press.

In *Newspaper Licensing Agency Ltd v Marks & Spencer plc* [1999] RPC 536, Marks & Spencer's claim that it was entitled to distribute newspaper cuttings to its staff without a licence from the Newspaper Licensing Agency (NLA), on the basis that it benefited from the defence in section 30(2) of reporting current events, failed. In that case Lightman J found that the daily programme of circulating and distributing cuttings of articles of interest to Marks & Spencer did not fall within the language of section 30(2), namely 'reporting current events'. Furthermore, the course followed by Marks & Spencer did not constitute 'fair dealing', since there was wholesale copying of material which went far beyond what was necessary to report current events. As discussed in Chapter 15, this decision was overturned on appeal on other grounds.

In *Fraser-Woodward Ltd v BBC* [2005] EWHC 472 a photographer sued the BBC for unauthorised use of his photographs of Victoria Beckham in a programme called *Tabloid Tales*. The BBC successfully ran a fair dealing defence on the grounds that it used the photographs to criticise and review celebrity journalism. Some of the criticism related to the photographs themselves – namely, whether photographs taken of the Beckhams apparently off their guard were in fact pre-arranged with them – but the court held that the criticism could extend to the underlying philosophy or ideas of the work being criticised. In that case, the criticism was of a certain style of journalism.

In *Newspaper Licensing Agency Ltd v Meltwater Holding BV* [2012] Bus LR 53 Meltwater argued that they had given a sufficient acknowledgement of the author of a newspaper article in the form of a hyperlink to the newspaper's website where the full article, including the author's name, appeared. The Court of Appeal rejected this as a sufficient acknowledgement because it did not identify the author. It was no better than citing the title of a book together with an indication of where the book may be found, because if the reader did not go to find the book, he would not be able to identify the author.

16.3.4 Section 31 – incidental inclusion of copyright material

Incidental inclusion of a copyright work in an artistic work, sound recording, film or broadcast will not be an infringement and neither will the issue to the public, playing, showing or communicating to the public of the result of that incidental inclusion be an infringement. Incidental, but deliberate, inclusion of music will be an infringement. The wording of the 1988 Act suggests that, in the case of all other works, whether the incidental inclusion is deliberate or not is irrelevant.

The question of what comprises 'incidental inclusion' was considered in the case of *IPC Magazines Ltd v MGN Ltd* [1998] FSR 431. This case concerned a television advertisement for the *Sunday Mirror* and a free women's supplement. That free supplement was compared with the claimant's magazine *Woman* and in the television advertisement the magazine cover of *Woman* was displayed. Richard McCombe QC said in this case that 'incidental' must be given its normal meaning (since it is not defined in the 1988 Act), which means casual, inessential, subordinate or merely background. He decided that the inclusion of the magazine cover of *Woman* in the *Sunday Mirror* advertisement had been an essential part of the advertisement for the *Sunday Mirror* free women's supplement.

In the case of *Football Association Premier League Ltd & ors v Panini UK Ltd* [2003] EWCA Civ 995, the inclusion of Football Association badges and logos in photographs taken by a company for use on football cards for sticker albums was argued by the defendants to be 'incidental' and therefore allowed by virtue of section 31. The Court of Appeal held that the appearance of the badges and logos on the football cards was not incidental. In deciding whether the use was incidental, it was proper to ask why the work in question had been included, considering commercial and aesthetic reasons. Here, the use of the team and the logos in the stickers was not incidental.

16.3.5 Sections 31A–F (inclusive) – visual impairment

The 2003 Regulations introduced various new provisions providing exceptions to copyright infringement concerning use in relation to the visually impaired.

16.3.6 Section 32 – things done for instruction or examination

Literary, artistic, dramatic and musical works may be copied or performed by a person giving or receiving instruction but not if done by reprographic process (for example, on a photocopier) – but see also Section 36 below. The exception which most students would rely upon for photocopying relevant extracts and articles is section 29 (but that requires fair dealing to be shown as well). Section 32 is aimed at allowing a teacher to reproduce a literary work by writing it up on a whiteboard or projector and allowing the students to transcribe from the whiteboard or direct from the literary work in question. The 2003 Regulations introduced conditions that copies be accompanied by sufficient acknowledgement, unless it would be impossible to do so, and that the instruction was for a non-commercial purpose. If that literary, dramatic, musical or artistic work has been made available to the public, then it can be copied for instruction or preparation of instruction on the same terms as above, save that it must be fair dealing with the work, but there is no requirement that it be for a non-commercial purpose.

Films, sound recordings and broadcasts may be copied in a film or soundtrack (by the instructor or student) for the purpose of instruction on the subject of the making of films and/or soundtracks. In each case, the 2003 Regulations introduced conditions of there being a sufficient acknowledgement (unless impossible) and the instruction being provided for a non-commercial purpose.

Anything done for the purpose of examination (for example, setting the questions and communicating them to the candidates) will not be a copyright infringement (although the 1988 Act specifically prohibits the photocopying of a musical work for use by an examination candidate to perform the work). The 2003 Regulations introduced a requirement for sufficient acknowledgement to accompany the questions (unless impossible). If a copy of a copyright work made under this section is subsequently dealt with (for example, sold or hired), the subsequent act will be an infringement.

16.3.7 Section 33 – anthologies for educational use

It is permissible to include a short passage from a published literary or dramatic work (which is not intended for educational use) in a collection of similar works that is intended for use in an educational establishment provided that the collection consists mainly of material in which no copyright subsists and subject to limitations on the number of excerpts from works by the same author.

There must be sufficient acknowledgement of the copyright owner of the copied work.

16.3.8 Section 34 – playing, showing or performing in an educational establishment

Teachers and pupils (and anyone else at a school for the purpose of instruction) may perform musical, literary and dramatic works without permission. The performance must be before teachers and pupils and anyone else 'directly connected with the activities of the establishment' (governor of school or inspector) but specifically excludes performances before parents. It is for this reason that school plays open to the public (that is, parents and friends) require the licence of the owner of copyright in the play being performed.

This section also provides that the showing of films, sound recordings and broadcasts to teachers, pupils and persons directly connected with the activities of the establishment, for purposes of instruction, is not a performance in public and, therefore, not an infringement under section 19.

16.3.9 Section 35 – recordings by educational establishments

An educational establishment can make, or have made for it, a recording of a broadcast, but only for educational purposes. This exception does not apply to any broadcasts that are being licensed by a certified statutory licensing scheme. The 2003 Regulations introduced the requirement of a sufficient acknowledgement and that the educational purposes are non-commercial.

16.3.10 Section 36 – reprographic copying by educational establishments

An educational establishment may make photocopies of published literary, dramatic and musical works for the purposes of instruction provided that no more than one per cent of any work is copied in any three-month period; the 2003 Regulations introduced new conditions of sufficient acknowledgement (unless such acknowledgement would be impossible) and that the instruction is for a non-commercial purpose. If licences are available for copying of the works in question, this section will not apply.

16.3.11 Sections 37–44 (inclusive) – libraries and archives

The libraries and archives covered by these sections must fall within the statutory definition. A library in a company or firm will not be covered by all of these sections. The acts that a librarian may do under these sections without infringing copyright are broadly the following:

(a) provide a copy of an article from a periodical or a copy of a reasonable proportion of a published work (provided that the person to whom the copy is supplied satisfies the librarian that it will be used only for research for a non-commercial purpose or private study, a charge is made to cover cost of production, not more than one copy is made, and the librarian is satisfied that the request is not one of several related requests for such a copy);

(b) provide a copy of an article from a periodical or the whole or part of a published work to another library (provided that, in the case of a published work, the receiving library is not able to find the person who could grant the proper licence to make such a copy);

(c) make a copy of a published work to replace a missing or damaged permanent library copy in that or a separate collection (provided that it is not reasonably practicable to buy such a replacement or additional copy);

(d) make copies of previously unpublished works (subject to similar conditions as apply to (a) above) unless the copyright owner has prohibited copying and the librarian ought to have been aware of the fact; and

(e) make copies of a work where a copy of the work needs to be deposited in a library or archive as a condition of export of the original work.

16.3.12 Section 44A – legal deposit libraries

The Legal Deposit Libraries Act 2003 introduced provisions allowing for copying of a work from the internet by a legal deposit library subject to certain conditions.

16.3.13 Sections 45–50 (inclusive) – public administration

Section 45 provides that anything done 'for the purposes of judicial proceedings' will not be copyright infringement; there is no 'fair dealing' requirement and multiple copies are not prohibited.

The Controller of HM's Stationery Office v Green Amps Ltd [2007] EWHC 2755 (Ch) was an action against Green Amps Limited for infringing Crown copyright in Ordnance Survey mapping data. Green Amps was a provider of wind turbines, and as part of that business had to deal with planning applications for wind turbine sites. It had made use of the Ordnance Survey's map database, which it did not have a licence to use. Green Amps unsuccessfully relied upon the 'fair dealing for the purposes of private research or study' defence described above. The court held that the defence did not apply because the use was for commercial purposes (while it was for research, that research was for commercial purposes) and it was not fair dealing in light of the amount which had been copied.

Section 47 permits copying with the authority of the appropriate person of any material that is open to inspection by statute provided that it is not intended to issue those copies to the public (although issuing copies to the public, purely for the purposes of facilitating the right of public inspection, is permitted).

16.3.14 Sections 50A–D (inclusive) – lawful users of computer programs and databases

These sections were added to the 1988 Act by the Copyright (Computer Programs) Regulations 1992 (SI 1992 No. 3233) and the Copyright and Rights in Databases Regulations 1997 (SI 1997 No. 3032). Sections 50A–C (introduced by SI 1992 No. 3233) essentially provide that a lawful acquirer of a computer program has certain rights to copy, adapt, decompile and make back-up copies of that program as is necessary for lawful of that computer program. Certain of these rights cannot be excluded by contract between the licensor and licensee of the computer program and any clause attempting to exclude these provisions would be void.

Section 50BA was added by the 2003 Regulations and provides that it is not an infringement of copyright in a computer program to observe, study or test the functioning of the program in order to determine the ideas and principles which underlie any element of the program, provided that it is done so by performing lawful acts (that is, running, loading, storing, etc., the program). Again, this right cannot be excluded by contract.

In *SAS Institute Inc v World Programming Ltd* [2012] ECDR 22 the ECJ held that the purpose of article 5(3) of Directive 91/250, from where this wording was derived, was to ensure that ideas and principles were not protected by a copyright owner by means of a licence agreement, such that the licensee was entitled to observe, study and test the behaviour of the software in order to determine its underlying ideas and principles. However, a user cannot use the decompilation exception (under art 6(2)(c)) to use information obtained through decompilation to develop a substantially similar program.

Section 50D (introduced by SI 1997 No. 3032) provides that it is not an infringement of copyright in a database for a lawful user of any part of the database to do anything necessary for the purposes of access to or use of the contents of that database; again in such a situation any contractual clause which tries to prevent the act which would otherwise be an infringement of copyright is void.

16.3.15 Sections 51–53 (inclusive) – designs

The Copyright Act 1956 and the Design Copyright Act 1968 provided that a design which was capable of protection as a registered design and which had been applied industrially would not also be protected as an artistic copyright work after the period of 15 years from when the article in question was first offered for sale or hire. However, what those Acts did not deal with specifically was industrially applied designs which were not capable of registration – such designs, which did not satisfy the Registered Designs Act 1949 requirements of, say, aesthetic appeal, perhaps because they were purely functional, could still claim full-term copyright protection if there was an underlying two-dimensional artistic work (e.g. a design drawing). The result was that some purely functional designs obtained longer protection under copyright law than more deserving, aesthetically appealing designs which were capable of registration.

In *British Leyland Motor Corp v Armstrong Patents Co Ltd* [1986] RPC 279, the House of Lords decided that, although an independent supplier of car exhausts designed to fit a particular British Leyland (BL) car had infringed BL's copyright in the design drawings for those exhausts, BL could not assert its copyright against the supplier because car owners had an inherent and overriding right to repair their cars in the most economical way possible by buying the cheapest available spare parts. The case highlighted the need for a change in the law. The result was a new right in designs, namely the unregistered design right (UDR) created by the 1988 Act, which protects aspects of shape and configuration of articles and was aimed at the protection of works of an industrial or functional nature. At the same time, the ability to rely on the copyright subsisting in design drawings of functional articles was removed, so that designers of such articles would have to rely on the new design right.

Section 51 of the 1988 Act deals with the overlap between copyright and design right. It provides that it is not an infringement of any copyright in a 'design document' for a design to make an article to the design shown in the design document (this means reproducing a two-dimensional work in three-dimensional form). Similarly, it is not an infringement of any copyright in a design document for a design to copy an article made to the design shown in the design document (which means reproducing a three-dimensional article in three-dimensional form). As discussed, it might, of course, amount to an infringement of the unregistered design right in the design. Section 51 does not take away the copyright which subsists in a design document – it simply prevents that copyright from being enforced in certain circumstances by providing a defence to infringement. The intention when creating unregistered design right was to prevent long-term monopolies arising in the design of functional articles, such as spare parts.

An article made within the ambit of section 51 can also be issued or communicated to the public or included in a film without an infringement of the copyright occurring.

Section 51 was successfully used as a defence to a claim of copyright infringement in the *Star Wars* dispute (*Lucasfilm Ltd v Ainsworth* [2008] ECDR 17; see Chapter 13). Lucasfilm brought an action against Ainsworth for infringement of UK copyright claiming that its 'Stormtrooper' helmets and armour were artistic works and that Ainsworth had infringed Lucasfilm's copyright by producing replica items from the original moulds. Section 51 expressly does not apply to designs for artistic works (for example, the design drawing for a sculpture), for a typeface or for surface decoration. In those cases, copyright in the design drawing can still be enforced. Ainsworth argued that he had a defence to copyright infringement under section 51 because the designs were not for artistic works.

Mann J considered that the designs did not amount to works of artistic craftsmanship or sculpture, and so section 51 operated in Ainsworth's favour. They were designs for functional articles which would have been protected by design right (had they been created more recently). This decision was upheld by both the Court of Appeal and the Supreme Court ([2010] ECDR 6 and [2011] ECDR 21).

In *BBC Worldwide Ltd & Another v Pally Screen Printing Ltd & ors* [1998] FSR 665, a summary judgment application which concerned the 'Teletubby' characters, the defendant had manufactured various garments with pictures of the Teletubbies displayed on them. It was found that these copies had been made from the *Teletubbies* television programmes and from comics. The defendant argued that they had not infringed any copyright the claimant might own in the images of the Teletubby characters in their three-dimensional form (e.g. the costumes worn by the actors playing the Teletubbies). Since section 51 says that it is not an infringement of the copyright in a qualifying design drawing to copy an article made to the design, there could be no infringement of copyright. The defendant said that what had been copied were the Teletubbies as seen in the programme, which were made to designs falling within section 51, namely drawings for the design of the Teletubbies. The judge therefore refused the application for summary judgment, on the basis that there was an arguable defence under section 51 because the images used on the garments amounted to indirect copies of the design documents which fell within the wording of section 51.

Two cases in particular highlight the confusion which surrounds the application of section 51 of the 1988 Act. The main intention of section 51 was to prevent owners of copyright in design drawings for articles which deserved a shorter period of protection from suing for infringement of copyright anyone who made an article to the design drawings. Designers were instead supposed to rely on their unregistered design right which subsists in the designs shown in the drawings. The section is not very well worded and the decision in *Lambretta Clothing Co Ltd v Teddy Smith (UK) Ltd* [2005] RPC 88 muddied the waters even further. The decision also appeared to take away copyright protection for features of articles in which copyright had traditionally been the appropriate form of protection, simply because they were recorded in the same document as aspects of shape and configuration.

The *Lambretta* case concerned a claim of copying of the design for a tracksuit top which was made up of a combination of coloured body panels and piping. Lambretta claimed rights in the choice and arrangement of colours in the top (since the shape was just a commonplace track top design). The issue which needed to be decided was how section 51 applies to a design drawing which features aspects of surface decoration (or other types of artistic work to which copyright applies) as well as aspects of shape and configuration (to which design right applies).

Understandably, Lambretta's design drawings showed both the design of the shape of the garment and the colour scheme. The Court of Appeal (by majority) decided that section 51 would apply to the whole design drawing not just the aspects of shape and configuration contained within it. Therefore, although Teddy Smith had indeed copied the Lambretta top, section 51 meant that Lambretta could not enforce any copyright which subsisted in their drawing.

This is how the court came to that conclusion:

▶ Firstly, the court ruled that Lambretta had no design right in the shape of the top because it was commonplace.

▶ Secondly, Lambretta had no design right in the colour arrangement, since that was surface decoration and therefore expressly excluded from design right protection by section 51.

▶ Although surface decoration would usually be protected by copyright, the fact that the colour arrangement had no conceptual independence from the top as drawn in the design document (e.g. it could not appear on another surface material in the same way that a logo could) led to the finding that section 51 operated and the copyright in the drawing could not be enforced. The suggested reason for this conclusion is that because the drawing showed some aspects of shape and configuration (the outline shape of the tracksuit top) as well as some aspects of surface decoration, the design document still fell within section 51 because if artistic copyright were to be enforced in the design document, it would be enforced in respect of the whole of the document, which was not allowed by section 51 because it included elements of shape and configuration.

It is submitted that the court's interpretation of section 51 was awkward. A more satisfactory result would have been for the section to have applied only to the aspects of shape and configuration so that copyright could still have been enforced in the design for the colour scheme (which was arguably a design for a graphic work which is untouched by section 51). After all, did Lambretta really create a design document for a commonplace tracksuit top? The evidence of the designer was that he took an existing Lambretta top shape and created a new design by combining and arranging a series of coloured panels and piping. His drawing was therefore arguably a graphic work within section 4 of the 1988 Act and not a design document within section 51 at all. If the court had taken that approach, it would have avoided the awkwardness of saying that the copyright aspects of the design had no independent existence from the aspects of shape and configuration because the coloured panels were defined by the shape of the garment.

The judgment appeared to say that any two-dimensional artwork featured in a design drawing caught by section 51 – that is, any design drawing bearing 'any aspect of shape or configuration' – would effectively be stripped of copyright protection from copiers of the three-dimensional product, regardless of whether there were aspects of the design which would usually be protected by copyright.

However, the decision in *The Flashing Badges Co Ltd v Brian David Groves (t/a Flashing Badges by Virgo and Virgo Distribution)* [2007] ECDR 17, although only a first instance decision, may have 'reinstated' copyright protection for articles in cases which fall outside the particular facts in *Lambretta Clothing Co Ltd v Teddy Smith (UK) Ltd* [2005] RPC 88.

In *Flashing Badges Co Ltd v Brian David Groves (t/a Flashing Badges by Virgo and Virgo Distribution)* [2007] ECDR 17, the High Court took a different approach. It distinguished *Lambretta Clothing Co Ltd v Teddy Smith (UK) Ltd* [2005] RPC 88, saying that the case seemed to turn on its special facts. The claimant had designed decorative badges in various shapes and bearing flashing lights. The shape of each badge was determined by the outline of the decoration on the front of each badge. The outline also determined the position of the flashing lights. The defendant argued that because the shape of the badges followed the same outline as the artistic design for the decoration appearing on them, that decoration was part of the shape and configuration of the badges and therefore fell within section 51 (i.e. following *Lambretta*). Therefore, the defendant argued that it had a defence to the allegations of copyright infringement.

The claimant argued that its two-dimensional designs were 'artistic works' in the nature of surface decoration which had been created and subsequently applied to the badges and that it did not matter that the badges were the same shape as those designs. The original design drawings for the badges, it claimed, therefore did not fall within section 51 because they were not records of designs for something 'other than an artistic work'; they were artistic works. The defendant countered that (citing *Lambretta*) the design document for each badge was not for an artistic work, but was for a badge and that, since a badge was not an artistic work, it fell within section 51.

Finding for the claimant, Mr Justice Rimer ruled that the design drawings contained both designs for artistic works *and* designs for badges and that section 51 could not provide a defence to copying the artwork. Mr Justice Rimer distinguished his judgment from the Court of Appeal decision in *Lambretta*, arguing that that case turned on its 'special facts' – namely that the colour arrangement on the tops 'could not be divorced from the design of the shape of the article' and was therefore not capable of independent existence.

Crucially, unlike in *Lambretta*, in which the colourways applied to the track top were said not to be able to exist physically or conceptually apart from the shape of the article, the judge in *Flashing Badges* felt that this was a case in which the relevant design could be applied to any other substrate. The design of the artistic work was for a particular shape, which the outline of the badge itself happened to follow. It is submitted that distinguishing *Lambretta* was a convenient, albeit sensible, approach in *Flashing Badges*, but that the *Lambretta* decision still poses serious problems for any design drawing which may illustrate an extremely valuable commercial design for an article – be it a garment, a toy, a piece of furniture, etc. – which has been designed around the shape of the article to which it will be applied.

16.3.16 Section 52

Section 52 provides that (subject to some excepted works) if an artistic work (which may be three-dimensional or two-dimensional) is industrially produced, the period of its copyright protection will be reduced to 25 years from the end of the year in which it was first marketed. Several types of works are excluded from the scope of section 52 by virtue of an order enacted under section 52(4). These include wall plaques, medals, calendars and trade advertisements. The case of *Jules Rimet Cup Ltd v The Football Association Ltd* [2007] EWHC 2376 (CH) confirmed that even where section 52 applies to reduce the life of the copyright in a particular artistic work as exploited, it will not affect the duration of the copyright in the work in respect of articles which are excluded from the ambit of section 52. In respect of such articles, the full period of copyright protection survives.

In *Lucasfilm*, Ainsworth also argued successfully that he had an additional defence under section 52 in that the designs of the costumes had been exploited industrially for the purposes of the section. Although, ultimately, the case was decided under section 10 of the Copyright Act 1956, which provided for a 15-year reduced period of protection, because of the time at which the designs were exploited, it would have been decided in the same way under section 52. It made no difference that the industrial production had taken place outside of the UK.

However, in 2012 the government announced that it was proposing to repeal section 52 in the Enterprise and Regulatory Reform Bill so that the shorter period of protection would no longer apply to industrially exploited artistic works, which in future would retain their full period of protection of the life of the designer plus 70 years. The justification given for the repeal is an ECJ ruling in *Flos SpA v Semeraro Casa e Famiglia SpA*, Case C-168/09. Essentially, the government is concerned that section 52 may breach the UK's obligations under the Copyright Term Directive 2006/116/EC to afford copyright protection to works of applied art for life plus 70 years. The original purpose of section 52 was to bring the period of protection for industrially exploited artistic works into line with the same 25-year period of protection available if those works were registered as registered designs. However, it remains to be seen in practice whether it will have much of an impact because the UK courts have traditionally been reluctant to recognise copyright protection for many three-dimensional works such as furniture designs. If no copyright protection subsists in such articles, then the lengthening of any copyright protection will have no effect on them. Further, articles such as greeting cards, calendars etc. were already excluded from section 52 and so have always benefited from the full period of protection.

16.3.17 Registered designs

It is possible that a copyright work will also have been registered as a registered design. If that is so, then the proper exercise of those registered design rights will form a defence against any claim of copyright infringement in respect of the same work (s 53).

16.3.18 No right to repair

In the case of *Mars UK Ltd v Teknowledge Ltd* [2000] FSR 138, the defendant had reverse-engineered a 'discriminator' used in coin-operated machines which allowed the recalibration of such machines to accept different coinage. This discriminator was protected by confidential information, copyright and database right. The defendant claimed that it was entitled to reverse-engineer the discriminator by virtue of a common law 'right to repair' or 'spare parts defence'. The court found that although a limited spare parts defence was set out in the 1988 Act in relation to design right, such a defence was not available in relation to copyright in computer programs or database rights.

16.3.19 Sections 54 and 55 – typefaces

Typeface designs can be copyright artistic works. However, it is not an infringement to use a typeface in the ordinary course of typing, printing or typesetting, or to possess an article for such use, or to do anything with the work produced. Making, importing or dealing in articles designed to produce the typeface in question will not, however, be exempted.

16.3.20 Section 56 – works in electronic form

Section 56 allows the use of computer programs (or other works in electronic form, such as CD-ROMs) by a subsequent purchaser of the same copy of that work, without the need for the copyright owner's consent – but this is subject to any provisions prohibiting transfer or bringing the original licence to an end on transfer of the licence.

The rights which the purchaser acquires are the same rights which the original purchaser had, either by express or implied licence or by rule of law. Rule of law would include sections 50A–D of the 1988 Act.

16.3.21 Sections 57–75 (inclusive) – miscellaneous

There are exceptions relating to: reproduction of works of unknown authors; use of written or recorded speeches in reports of current events and broadcasts; the public performance and/or broadcasting of extracts read from published works; reproduction of abstracts to technical or scientific articles; recordings of folksongs; reproduction of any buildings, sculptures, public works of artistic craftsmanship in a graphic work, photograph or broadcast; advertising of an artistic work for sale; reproduction of part of an artistic work by the artist (when no longer owning copyright in the original copyright work); and reconstruction of a building.

The Secretary of State may order the lending to the public of copies of certain works, subject to payment of a reasonable fee (s 66). Copyright in a film will not be infringed if it was reasonable to assume that the copyright in it had expired and the identity of the key personnel could not be ascertained (s 66A).

On 4 October 2012 the European Council adopted the Orphan Works Directive 2012/28/EU. An orphan work is one where, whilst copyright subsists in it, it is not possible to identify or trace the author. The Directive is designed to allow the digital use of such works for non-commercial purposes. The government has also expressed its approval of a proposal made in the Hargreaves Review of Intellectual Property (see Section 16.6) to set up a Digital Copyright Exchange to streamline the process of copyright licensing. Since this idea is still in its very early stages, we do not propose to discuss it further in this edition.

Non-profit-making clubs and societies can play sound recordings in public without the consent of the copyright owner (s 67). Incidental copying for the purpose of broadcasting is permitted, as is recording by the BBC for the purposes of supervision and control.

Section 70 is the one that permits you to record television and radio programmes so that you can watch or listen to them later, although it is more limited than many think, and has been amended by the 2003 Regulations. The recording must now be made in 'domestic premises' for private and domestic use, and solely for the purpose of viewing it or listening to it at a more convenient time. In *Sony Music Entertainment (UK) Ltd & ors v Easyinternetcafé Ltd* [2003] EWHC 62, Easyinternetcafé operated an internet café where it offered a CD-burning service to customers so that they could retain a copy of any material which they had downloaded from the internet while using the computers at the internet café. Easyinternetcafé claimed that they were not liable for any possible infringement because, among other things, the copies were made for the customers' private and domestic use to enable them to view the material at a more convenient time. The court held that there was no evidence to this effect and, in any event, the copying was carried out by Easyinternetcafé, which was a commercial entity charging for the CD-burning service, and that the copying was certainly not for Easyinternetcafé's private and domestic use.

It is also permissible to make a photograph from a broadcast image, again solely for private and domestic use and in domestic premises. Broadcasts, certain sound recordings and films may be played in public without infringement as long as the audience is not charged for viewing (s 72). This section was relied on by the publicans in *Football Association Premier League Ltd v QC Leisure* [2012] EWCA Civ 1708 as a defence to their alleged acts of infringement by showing live Premier League football matches in their pubs without charge using foreign decoder cards. The Court of Appeal held that section 72 did give them a defence both to their acts of showing the film works in public contrary to section 19, and to communicating film works to the public contrary to section 20. The FAPL had tried to argue that section 72 should only provide a defence to the acts covered by section 19, namely showing a work in public, and that it was never intended to cover acts which were equivalent to broadcasting, which fell within section 20. However, whilst accepting that the Copyright Directive did not permit such a defence to acts of communication to the public, the government in error had clearly drafted section 72 in such a way that acts of broadcasting fell within it. Unless and until the wording of the section 72 defence is amended, it does provide a defence to acts falling within section 20 as well as section 19.

Section 73, relating to the reception and retransmission of wireless broadcasts by cable, has been amended by the 2003 Regulations and a new section 73(A) added relating to royalties. Broadcasts may be copied for the purpose of adding subtitles or other modifications to assist handicapped viewers and listeners and reissued to the public without infringing rights in the broadcast (s 74). Recordings are also permitted for archiving purposes (s 75).

It should be noted that the government has announced its intention to introduce additional or amended copyright exceptions to widen their scope. These are discussed further at Section 16.6.

16.3.22 Estoppel, acquiescence and laches

In the case of *Fisher v Brooker* [2007] EMLR 9, the former organist in the band Procol Harum, Matthew Fisher, brought a claim against his former band members for declarations that he was a joint author and owner of the copyright in the song 'A Whiter Shade of Pale', for which he had composed the organ solo. The claim was brought after a delay of nearly 40 years after the release of the record. Fisher also claimed a share of royalties. The High Court upheld the claim in 2006. The judge said that 'of itself, delay provides no defence'. It was necessary for the defendants to show that 'it would be unconscionable for the other party to be permitted to deny what he has allowed or encouraged the first party to assume to his detriment'. The judge said that in the absence of the defendants being able to establish any detriment arising from the claimant's delay in asserting his rights, the estoppel argument must fail.

The Court of Appeal in *Fisher v Brooker* [2008] EWCA Civ 287 partially allowed the defendants' appeal, upholding the declaration as to authorship, but denying Mr Fisher a declaration as to joint ownership and any restitutionary relief due to his excessive and inexcusable delay in bringing the action and for having acquiesced in the commercial exploitation of the song for 38 years after its release. The Court of Appeal said that it was unjust that the claimant should be permitted to succeed in his claim to a joint interest in the work and that the implied licence to exploit the work had become irrevocable by virtue of such acquiescence. As a result, the claimant was not entitled to any damages for copyright infringement or to any share of royalties to be received from the future exploitation of the song.

However, on a further appeal to the House of Lords ([2009] UKHL 41), the organist argued that there had been no implied assignment at the time the song was recorded. The House of Lords agreed, stating that there could only have been an implied licence if it had been obvious to the parties at the time. The Lords also held that mere passage of time itself could not undermine the organist's claim and that the doctrine of laches could only bar equitable relief, not a declaration relating to a long-term property right.

16.4 Public interest defence and the Human Rights Act 1998

There is no statutory public interest defence as such, but public interest is a defence, along with claims of national security, which can be claimed successfully in certain cases (see, for example, *Beloff v Pressdram Ltd* [1973] RPC 765 and *Cambridge Nutrition*

Ltd v BBC [1990] 3 All ER 523, although in *Beloff*, the claimant's case failed because she did not own the copyright in the relevant work). The defence is set out in section 171(3) of the 1988 Act.

In *Hyde Park Residence Ltd v Yelland* [2000] RPC 604, a newspaper, which had used security camera footage of Diana, Princess of Wales and Dodi Al Fayed taken the day before their fatal accident, failed in its argument that it was entitled to publish those photographs without permission, on the basis that such publication was in the public interest. In denying its application, the court said that although the stills were arguably of public interest, their publication was unnecessary because the information contained in the photographs could have been conveyed in a way which did not involve infringing the copyright in the photographs.

In *Ashdown v Telegraph Group Ltd* [2002] Ch D 149, Paddy Ashdown MP claimed copyright infringement against the Telegraph Group when it published excerpts from confidential diaries and records in its newspaper. The Telegraph Group claimed various defences, including under the Human Rights Act 1998 on the basis that article 10 of the European Convention for the Protection of Human Rights and Fundamental Freedoms (which was implemented by the Human Rights Act) entitled the newspaper to protection for its right of freedom of expression. The Court of Appeal held that there could be rare circumstances where the right to freedom of expression might override copyright and in which section 171(3) could provide a public interest defence. However, such circumstances were not capable of precise categorisation or definition. In this case, the publication was not justified by public interest considerations because the newspaper had published for essentially commercial purposes.

16.5 Competition or Euro defence

The conflict between intellectual property rights (essentially monopoly rights) and rights of free competition is a tension which is common to all intellectual property rights. This issue is dealt with in Chapter 23.

16.6 Proposed new exceptions to copyright infringement (the Hargreaves Review)

In his Review of Intellectual Property and Growth in May 2011, Professor Ian Hargreaves recommended making a number of additions to the exceptions in the 1988 Act. In response to this the government has published a white paper setting out those areas where it intends to expand the copyright exceptions. The legislative changes are expected to start coming into force towards the end of 2013. Some of these proposed exceptions are summarised below.

16.6.1 Private copying exception

Under UK law, there is currently no exception to copyright allowing private copying of copyright works (other than the fair dealing exceptions discussed previously). Even so-called 'format shifting' of music – for example by transferring music from a CD onto an MP3 player – is technically an illegal act. As the Hargreaves Review noted, 'The UK has a thriving market for personal media devices which rely on private copying'. The white paper proposes a private copying exception which will allow individuals to copy works onto other media for their personal use (but not extending to their family or friends). It also permits service providers to offer limited private cloud storage services without infringing copyright.

The government response to the Hargreaves Review indicated that it intended to bring forward proposals for a limited private copying exception.

16.6.2 Enabling new research tools

The use of text mining tools to carry out computerised searches and analysis for research does not currently receive the benefit of the 'fair dealing' exception. The Hargreaves Review stated that 'Research scientists, including medical researchers, are today being hampered from using computerised search and analysis techniques on data and text because copyright law can forbid and restrict such usage'. As such technologies become more routine, it suggested that copyright law is essentially restricting innovation. The report recommended that, in the interim, the government introduce a new UK exception under the current non-commercial research exception whilst at the same time lobbying the EU to provide for an exception for mining and data analytics for commercial use. It also recommended that the research exception should be modernised to cover a full range of media. The white paper proposes widening the exception for non-commercial research to allow computer analysis where researchers have lawful access to copyright works, as well as expanding the research and private study exception to include sound recordings, films and broadcasts.

16.6.3 Caricature, parody or pastiche exception

Presently there is no copyright exception for parody or caricature. In theory, a comical, exaggerated imitation of an author's work could infringe the copyright in the original work, provided that it incorporates a substantial element of that work. Despite this, the UK has a strong tradition of creating parodies and caricatures. The Hargreaves Review did not make any definitive recommendation on introducing a new exception relating to this point as it stated that issues of freedom of expression fell outside its remit. However, it did note one or two cases of parodies being restricted by current copyright laws, including the well-publicised 'Newport State of Mind' music video. The white paper introduces an exception for parody, subject to the 'fair dealing' criteria.

16.6.4 Quotations

The current exception permitting quotations for the purposes of criticism and review and reporting current events will be expanded to cover any fair purpose provided that it is accompanied by a sufficient acknowledgement (save that photographs will still be excluded from the reporting current events exception).

16.6.5 Libraries and digital content

The existing exceptions do not allow libraries to archive audio-visual works and sound recordings. The Hargreaves Review notes that 'it should be uncontroversial to deliver the necessary change by extending the archiving exception, including to cover fully audio visual works and sound recordings'. The report therefore recommends introducing such an exception. The white paper proposes widening the exception for archiving and preservation by libraries, museums, galleries and the like.

16.6.6 Exclusion of exceptions by contract

As far as it is legally possible to, the government has also proposed that it shall change the law so that it will not be possible to override the application of the exceptions by contractual terms. It remains to be seen what the details will look like, but it may well have implications in the online environment where websites currently seek to restrict the extent to which their content can be used or reproduced through their website terms and conditions. The extent to which the government can broaden the scope of copyright exceptions is limited by its need to comply with EU law and the 'three step test' (under the Berne Convention and other international copyright treaties) which requires exceptions to copyright to be limited to certain defined areas. (See Section 16.3.1(d).)

Summary

- ▶ A defendant may avoid liability for infringement by showing that his activities fall within a licence agreement. Such agreements need not be in writing, and they can be implied in certain circumstances.

- ▶ The Copyright, Designs and Patents Act 1988 provides for a number of permitted acts.

- ▶ Copies of copyright works may be made for a number of reasons provided that there is fair dealing in the sense that the owner is acknowledged and that the copying has not taken place to enrich the defendant.

- ▶ The common law recognises the defence of public interest. The Human Rights Act 1998 is also a relevant consideration in copyright infringement cases.

- ▶ A defence is available if the copyright owner's rights conflict with EU competition law.

Exercise

A and B became well known after they were captured by rebels and kept in a remote part of Eritrea for five years. On their release back to the UK, they were approached by *C News*, a daily newspaper, for a series of articles on their experiences. A fee of £25,000 each was agreed.

During the interviews A and B recounted their experiences to D, a reporter. Everything was recorded on her tape recorder. Afterwards D spent considerable time editing the recordings, entering details into her computer and producing a number of articles based on the interviews. These were published by *C News*.

(a) ETV uses a substantial amount of the material from the articles as part of its news programme without acknowledging the source.

(b) F was also captured by the rebels. He knows that A and B were held for only two years. After that they had joined the rebels in looting campaigns. He writes an article for a competing newspaper disputing their story, making substantial use of the material in the articles published by *C News*.

(c) G, a research student engaged in a Ph.D. thesis on rebel groups, uses material from the articles for her thesis. H, a political history teacher, photocopies the articles for his pupils.

Advise ETV, F, G and H of their legal liabilities and the defences available, if any.

Further reading and references

For a discussion of the arguments surrounding the proposed repeal of section 52, see www.ipkitten.blogspot.co.uk/2013/01/go-with-the-flos-aippi-debates-copyright -in.html

Chapter 17

Ownership and duration of copyright, moral rights and artist's resale right

17.1 Ownership of copyright

Copyright in a work is first owned by the author of that work. In the case of literary, dramatic, musical and artistic works, the author is just who you would imagine it to be. In the case of other types of work, the author may be the producer (for sound recordings), the producer and principal director (for films), the person who made the arrangements necessary for the creation of the work (in the case of computer-generated works), the person making the broadcast, or the publisher (in the case of typographical arrangements). The first owner of copyright in films and sound recordings was, until 31 December 1996 when the Copyright and Related Rights Regulations 1996 came into force, the person who made the arrangements necessary for the creation of the work.

17.2 Employees

The general rule about ownership of copyright vesting in the author is subject to one important statutory exception. If a literary, artistic, dramatic or musical work or a film is created by an employee in the course of his employment, the employer will be the first owner of any copyright in the work which would otherwise have been owned by the employee.

This statutory exception did not apply to films until the Copyright and Related Rights Regulations 1996 came into force. Definitions of 'employee' and 'in the course of employment' are not provided in the 1988 Act, although section 263 states that reference to an 'employee' or 'employment' is to be read as a reference to employment under a 'contract of service' or apprenticeship. This is distinct from a 'contract for services', which is essentially an arrangement between two people for the provision of services by one to the other, for example consultancy services.

The question whether a person is under a contract of service is increasingly becoming a question of fact resolved by consideration of the details of the relationship. The courts will consider the contract between the parties, oral or written, as a whole to identify if it is indicative of one form of relationship or another. See for example *Ready-Mixed Concrete (South East) Limited v the Minister of Pensions and National Insurance* [1968] 2 QB 497, *Market Investigations Limited v Minister of Social Security* [1952] 69 RPC 10 and *ABC News International Inc v Gizbert* Employment Appeal Tribunal 21 August 2006.

Once it has been decided that the author of a copyright work is an employee, the question has to be asked whether the copyright work has also been created in the course of employment. The answer to that question will depend upon the nature of the employment and the nature of the copyright work. There is usually little difficulty in finding that it was where the employee's job is specifically to design copyright works of the type in issue. However, the question whether the work was carried out in the course of employment is often more difficult to answer. The following cases give some guidance.

▶ In *Stephenson Jordan & Harrison Ltd v MacDonald & Evans* [1952] RPC 10, a former employee of the claimant had written a book and had purported to assign the copyright in it to his publishers. The book was made up partly of lectures which had been written and presented publicly by him while he was working for the claimant and partly based on information acquired by him while on an assignment for a client of the claimant. The court held that the material based on public lectures did not fall within his contract of employment, but the work for the particular client did.

▶ *Ultra Marketing (UK) Limited and Thomas Alexander Scott v Universal Components Ltd* [2002] EWHC 2285 involved issues of ownership of copyright in drawings, one of which was produced by the defendant when he was a director of the claimant. This aspect of the case was decided under the 1956 Act because the relevant drawing was drawn in 1976. The judge's decision that copyright vested in the author, Mr Scott, rather than the company, was based on a number of factors: (a) the company did not deal in the type of frames for which the drawing was a design; (b) there was some doubt that Mr Scott was employed by the company at the relevant time under a contract of service; and (c) Mr Scott did not work on the drawings during the working day or at the company's premises.

▶ In the case of *Vitof Limited v Antony John Altoft* [2006] EWHC 1678 (Ch), Vitof claimed it owned the copyright in a source code created by Mr Altoft before, but in anticipation of, the incorporation of the company and his being a director of that company. The court, granting summary judgment, found that Mr Altoft held the copyright on trust for the company.

17.2.1 Commissioned works

Under the Copyright Act 1956, there was another exception to the first-owner rule. The commissioner for money or money's worth of a photograph, sound recording, engraving or portrait was treated as the first owner (1956 Act, ss 4(3) and 12(4)). Under the 1988 Act, commissioners of copyright works do not own the copyright in the resulting work. However, because the general intention in contracts of commission is that the commissioner should obtain some rights of use, if not ownership, case law has developed over time to give commissioners certain rights. Those rights are often granted by a licence to use the copyright work in the way in which the parties anticipated it would be used at the time of the commission.

The case of *Robin Ray v Classic FM* [1998] FSR 622 set out the principle that, when required, the courts should only imply the minimum necessary term in order to give effect to the commercial intentions of the parties. The application of this principle in later cases has varied according to the facts of each case.

In *Meridian International Services Ltd v Richardson and ors* [2008] EWCA Civ 609, the court refused to imply a term into a software agreement that copyright in the software should be assigned to the claimant; the copyright was therefore retained by the developer. (See also *Lucasfilm Ltd v Ainsworth* [2008] ECDR 17, and *Griggs v Evans* (discussed in Chapter 16) for further examples of the courts' approach to implied rights.)

As a result of the uncertainty in this area, the question of ownership of copyright between commissioner and author should always be provided for in any contract for a commission.

17.2.2 Joint ownership

The courts have made it clear that they will only find that there is joint ownership of copyright when each party has contributed to the act of authorship of the work in question (*Fylde Microsystems Ltd v Key Radio Systems Ltd* [1998] FSR 449; *Robin Ray v Classic FM plc* [1998] FSR 622; *Pierce v Promco SA and ors* [1999] ITCLR 233; *Hadley & ors v Kemp & Another* [1999] EMLR 589; and *Robert James Beckingham v Robert Hodgens & ors* [2003] EMLR Civ 18). The principle which emerges from these cases is that in order for there to be joint ownership, the claimant has to show that it made 'a significant and original contribution' to the creation of the work 'which approximated to penmanship: a direct responsibility for what actually appeared on the page'. It should be noted that there is no requirement that before a work can be regarded as a work of joint authorship, there has to have been a joint intention to create a joint work.

In the case of *Cala Homes (South) Ltd v Alfred McAlpine Homes East Ltd* [1995] FSR 1818, the court found that, as a result of the involvement of the commissioner in the creation of the work, there was joint ownership. The court added that, if it had not held that the commissioner was a joint owner, it would have found an implied term that the drawings were made exclusively for the commissioner. In the case of *Fisher v Brooker* [2008] EWCA Civ 287 the Court of Appeal held that an organ solo which the claimant had developed for incorporation into the song 'A Whiter Shade of Pale' amounted to a creative contribution to the piece and that the claimant was entitled to a declaration of authorship in order to satisfy his claim to be entitled to attribution for his share of the work. The Court of Appeal refused to grant the claimant a declaration of co-ownership of the work, which would have entitled him to a share in the musical copyright and in the proceeds from the work. That appears to have been motivated by the financial prejudice which the Court of Appeal perceived such a declaration would have caused to the defendant, given the claimant's 38-year delay in bringing the claim. The House of Lords, however, granted the claimant's appeal and re-instated the declarations of co-authorship and co-ownership of the musical copyright which the High Court had awarded. The claimant's interest in the musical copyright gave him (it was decided) a 40 per cent share. The House of Lords was of the view that there would be no financial prejudice to the other co-owners of the musical copyright, since they had benefited from the delay (they had enjoyed the fruits of the copyright interest without having to account for any part of them to the claimant).

17.2.3 Crown copyright

There are specific provisions in the 1988 Act on ownership of Crown copyright, parliamentary copyright and copyright of international organisations. Copyright in any works created by an officer of the Crown or under the direction or control of the House of Lords or House of Commons, or by an officer or employee of an international organisation will, generally speaking, vest in the relevant directing or controlling body (ss 163, 164 and 168).

17.3 Moral rights

The moral rights of the author or creator of a copyright work, as distinct from the rights of ownership of the copyright, are: (a) the right to be identified as the author (the 'paternity right') in section 77; (b) the right to object to derogatory treatment of the work (the 'integrity right') in section 80; and (c) the right not to have a work falsely attributed in section 84. These rights may be waived in writing by the person entitled to the right, either generally or specifically and either conditionally or unconditionally, and a waiver may be expressed to be revocable at any time. Even although the 1988 Act requires a waiver to be in writing, the common law on waiver and estoppel still applies in this area.

The owner of the copyright in a work may not always be the same person as the owner of the moral rights in that work. Copyright is an economic-based right, whereas moral rights protect the artistic rights of the creator.

Moral rights apply in respect of the whole or a substantial part of a copyright work, but in the case of the false attribution right and the integrity right, any part of a copyright work (even if not substantial) is protected.

There are now also moral rights for performers. These are discussed in Chapter 19.

17.4 Paternity right

This is the right of the author of a literary, dramatic, musical or artistic work and the right of a director of a film to be identified as such whenever, generally speaking, the work is performed in public, issued or communicated to the public, or commercially exploited. For the right to exist, it must be asserted by the person entitled to the right. An assertion must be made in an assignment of the copyright in the work or in some other written document. An architect also has the right to be identified on their buildings. The right of paternity does not apply to computer programs, typefaces and computer-generated works (s 79). Where a third party has been licensed by the owner of copyright in cases where the work was created by an employee and the copyright vested in his employer by operation of law, then the employee (who will be the owner of any moral rights in that work) will not be entitled to exercise his moral rights against that third party (s 79).

There are also other specific exceptions to the enforcement of the paternity right in relation to publication in newspapers, magazines, and so on (ss 79(5) and 79(6)) and in relation to any activities which broadly correspond to the copyright permitted acts (see Chapter 16).

17.5 Integrity right

This right arises automatically and does not need to be asserted. It applies to the same copyright works as the paternity right. 'Derogatory treatment' is an 'addition to, deletion from or alteration to or adaptation' of a copyright work which distorts or mutilates the work or which is in any way prejudicial to the honour or reputation of the author. A translation is not a 'treatment' for these purposes and neither is a change in the key or register of a musical work.

The same exceptions apply to this right as with the paternity right (although the design of a typeface is not specifically excepted), plus a few more (ss 81 and 82). Also, in relation to derogatory treatment of a work of architecture in the form of a building, the architect's rights are limited to having their name removed from the building (s 80(5)). The right does not apply in circumstances where the copyright in a work created by an individual is vested in the employer, the Crown, Parliament or an international organisation by operation of law and the owner of the copyright has given his authority for the particular treatment of the work, unless the identity of the author was made known at the time of publication or any earlier publication, in which case a sufficient disclaimer is required (s 82).

17.6 False attribution

The right not to have work falsely attributed is also an automatic moral right and applies to literary, artistic, musical and dramatic works and films. It is the right not to be falsely attributed as the author or the director of the work in question. It is also an infringement of this right falsely to attribute an artistic work as the unaltered work of the author when the work has been altered.

In *Clark (Alan) v Associated Newspapers Ltd* [1998] 1 All ER 959, Lightman J said that for section 84 to be infringed, it had to be shown that there was, in relation to the work in question, a false attribution of ownership and not merely something which was or might be understood by some or more people to be a false attribution.

17.7 Rights of privacy in photographs and films

This specific right is to protect private commissioners of photographs and films (most typically, the wedding couple). Under the 1956 Act, a commissioner of photographs who paid for the commission was the owner of copyright in those photographs. Under the 1988 Act, all commissioned copyright works (including photographs) are owned by the author. This would have left the private consumer who commissions photographs of essentially private events (weddings, christenings, bar mitzvahs etc) unprotected from commercial exploitation of those photos. Section 85 reinstates some protection by leaving the copyright with the photographer but giving the commissioner in these cases a moral right to prevent the photographs being issued to or communicated to the public, or exhibited in public.

17.8 Dealings in copyright and moral rights

Copyright must be assigned in writing, signed by the assignor (s 90(3)). Assignments may be made of limited rights (such as of certain of the exclusive rights only) and it is also possible to assign future copyright (in other words, copyright in works still to be created).

Moral rights cannot be assigned; they attach to the first author of a work and can only be asserted or waived by that person. Moral rights can, however, pass under a testamentary disposition (save for false attribution, which remains with the personal representatives of the deceased) and can be bequeathed independently of the ownership of copyright in the work to which they relate (s 95). If no specific, independent disposition is made of the moral rights, they will automatically transfer with the copyright relating to the work in question. If the copyright work is bequeathed to two or more persons, any related moral rights will be split accordingly. If no disposition of the copyright in the work is made, the personal representatives will be entitled to exercise the moral rights.

Moral rights owned by more than one person are exercisable severally; in other words, each person who is entitled to assert, waive or exercise a moral right can do so independently (s 95(3)). A waiver of moral rights by one joint owner does not act as a waiver for the other owners. When passing by testamentary disposition, moral rights will bind the persons inheriting with any prior waivers or consents. Any damages recovered by a person inheriting moral rights will be treated as part of the estate of the original owner of the moral rights.

17.9 Duration of copyright

For most works, copyright lasts for 70 years from the end of the year in which the author (who may be a different person from the first owner) dies. Until 1 January 1996, the period from death was 50 years but the Duration of Copyright and Rights in Performances Regulations 1995 (SI 1995 No. 3297) (the 1995 Regulations) has brought the UK into line with the rest of Europe with the harmonised term of 70 years. This extension of the duration of copyright (which only applies to literary, dramatic, musical and artistic works and films) means that certain works whose copyright had expired are again within copyright protection. Moral rights relating to such copyright works were also revived by the 1995 Regulations. To deal with the obvious problems, there are transitional provisions covering works already published while outside copyright protection, including the right for such a work to be reproduced subject to payment of a reasonable royalty (Regulation 24).

In the case of works of joint authorship, the duration of copyright protection runs from the death of the last surviving author (s 12(8)(a)(i)). In the case of works of unknown authorship, the period runs from the end of the year in which the work was first made or, if during that period the work was made available to the public, the period of 70 years will run from the end of the year in which it was so made available. For a work to have been made available for the purposes of duration of copyright, it must have been made available with the permission of the copyright owner.

In the case of films, under the Copyright Act 1956, in general terms, copyright lasted for 50 years from the end of the year in which the film was registered under the Cinematograph Films Act 1938 or, if later, released. However, the 1995 Regulations not only extended the 50-year period for film copyright to 70 years but also changed the rules governing duration of copyright in films. Copyright in such works now lasts for 70 years from the end of the year in which the last of the principal director, author of the screenplay, author of the dialogue or composer of the music specific to the film dies. Special provisions apply in cases where one or more of the contributors is unknown. Where there is no-one falling within the category of persons by reference to whom duration of copyright is measured, copyright in a film will last for 70 years from the end of the year in which the film is made or, if later, released.

Copyright in computer-generated works still lasts for only 50 years from the end of the year in which the work is made.

Copyright in a sound recording currently lasts for 50 years from the end of the year in which it is made or, if during that period the sound recording is released, 50 years from the end of the year in which it is released (with the permission of the copyright owner). However, the European Parliament has recently passed Directive 2011/77/EU which extends the period of copyright protection for sound recordings from 50 to 70 years.

This must be implemented by 1 November 2013. The European Parliament's decision to make the change came despite severe criticism of the proposal by the Gowers Review and, later, the Hargreaves Review, both of which argued that such an extension would not benefit most performers, as most of the royalties would go to the record labels under their contract with the performers, and that an extension would have a negative impact on the balance of trade. The Directive also provides that the duration of protection for a musical composition with words is 70 years after the death of the last to die of the lyricist or the composer, whether or not they were designated as joint authors.

Generally speaking, copyright in broadcasts lasts for 50 years from the end of the year in which the broadcast is made. Copyright in typographic arrangements lasts for 25 years from the end of the year in which they are first published. There is currently an important section (1988 Act, s 52) which limits the duration of protection of artistic works which have been industrially exploited. This provides that at the end of 25 years from the end of the year in which articles made by an industrial process were first marketed, then articles of any design can be made to the design without infringing the copyright in it. The Copyright (Industrial Process and Excluded Articles) (No 2) Order 1989 defines what amounts to making by an industrial process, which generally speaking means that either more than 50 articles have been made, or any quantity has been made if the goods are made in lengths or pieces, but are not handmade goods. So, for example, a fabric design which has been made in lengths would only be protected by copyright for 25 years from the end of the year in which the first length was made. The Order also excludes certain articles from the effects of section 52, such as works of sculpture, and printed matter primarily of a literary or artistic character (for example, greetings cards). In *Fearns (t/a Autopaint International) v Anglo-Dutch Paint and Chemical Co Ltd* 2007 EWHC 955 (Ch) the court took the view that the printed-matter exception did not apply to the design and logo on paint tins (which at first featured stuck-on labels and were later lithographed) because what was being marketed was a tin, not just printed matter. Therefore the tins were subject to the limited copyright protection under section 52.

However, as discussed in more detail in Section 16.3.16, this section is to be repealed, so that artistic works which currently have their period of copyright protection reduced to 25 years will revert to the full period of protection of life of the creator plus 70 years.

17.10 Duration of moral rights

The various moral rights last for as long as the copyright in the work to which they relate lasts, except for the false attribution right, which lasts until 20 years after the death of the person entitled to that right.

17.11 Artist's resale right

As a result of the approval of European Directive 2001/84/EC, the Artist's Resale Right Regulations 2006 (the 2006 Regulations) came into force in the UK on 14 February 2006. The right, also known as *droit de suite,* is arguably the most important development in copyright law for artists for some time and entitles the author of the original work of art to a royalty on resale.

The resale right applies so long as copyright subsists in the work and to any works of graphic or plastic art, such as pictures, paintings, photographs and sculptures, provided that the work is only produced in limited numbers (including one-offs). The obligation to pay the royalty applies only to those resales of €1,000 and over.

The right will not apply to the first sale of the work, nor will it apply to works which fall outside the definition of works referred to above and set out in the 2006 Regulations. Private resales between individuals are exempt from the obligation to pay a royalty and a sale for not more than €10,000 by a seller who acquired the work directly from the author less than three years before the resale is also exempt. Furthermore, resale rights are only exercisable by certain nationalities, notably to the exclusion of US nationals, and the 2006 Regulations do not extend to sales which precede 14 February 2006.

The royalty to be paid is based on the resale price itself, net of the tax payable on that resale. A percentage scale is set out in Schedule 1 to the 2006 Regulations, the highest being 4 per cent, but there is a limit on the total amount of royalties payable on any such resale of €12,500.

The royalty becomes payable upon completion of the sale, the seller and the buyer (or agent) being jointly responsible for payment, and may be withheld until evidence of entitlement to the royalty is produced. A collecting society will manage the collection of royalties.

The UK took advantage of a derogation in the Directive which allowed Member States to exclude works of deceased authors from the scope of the resale right. This derogation expired on 1 January 2012. The European Commission is due to report on a review of the resale right in 2014.

Summary

▶ Moral rights protect the artistic rights of the creator of the work, who may not always be the same person as the copyright owner.

▶ In the case of original literary, dramatic, artistic or musical works, the copyright is owned by the creator unless the work was created by an employee in the course of employment.

▶ When a literary, dramatic, musical or artistic work is commercially exploited or performed in public, the author has the right to be identified. This right must be asserted.

▶ The author can object to his work being distorted or mutilated in a way that will affect his reputation. This is an automatic right.

▶ It is also an automatic right not to have work falsely attributed.

▶ Since the 1988 Act the commissioner of photographs for private and domestic purposes is no longer the copyright owner, but has the right to prevent photographs being issued or exhibited in public.

▶ Moral rights cannot be assigned but can be bequeathed to one or more persons.

▶ The rights generally run for 70 years from the end of the year in which the author died, but for computer-generated works and broadcasts, the period runs to 50 years from the end of the year in which the work was made or released (whichever is later). Sound recordings will soon be protected for 70 years, whereas copyright in the underlying musical work lasts for the life of the songwriter plus 70 years. The period for typographic arrangements is 25 years from the end of the year of first publication. Artistic works which have been industrially exploited currently have their copyright protection period reduced to 25 years from the end of the year of first marketing, subject to exceptions, although this limitation is due to be repealed.

▶ An artist can benefit from a royalty on every subsequent sale of one of their works, subject to various conditions.

Exercises

17.1 In 1987, students at D University organised a series of lectures and invited leading socialist politicians to speak. One of these was A. In part of his speech he said: 'If the budget permits, the next socialist government will ensure that each child over the age of six months will be entitled to free nursery education.' A delivered his speech without the use of notes. B, an enthusiastic student, attended the lecture and recorded A's speech. B, who is now a journalist for a right-of-centre newspaper, writes a series of articles based on the recordings that he made as a student. He quotes A as maintaining: 'Each child over the age of six months will be entitled to free nursery education!'

Advise A, who is now a member of a socialist cabinet which cannot afford to provide free nursery education.

17.2 D, a reporter from *C News*, recorded a verbatim account of A's and B's experiences following their release by rebels in Eritrea (see Exercise in Chapter 16). She spent considerable time working on a series of articles for *C News*. In her spare time, D also wrote a book on rebel groups using material which she obtained from A and B.

Advise the following:

(a)   A and B who are in the process of writing their memoirs and want to stop D's publication;

(b)   *C News* which wants to claim copyright in the book written by D.

Chapter 18
Database rights

Introduction

Prior to 1998, databases in their various forms were protected as copyright works. Under the 1988 Act, a database was treated as falling within the definition of a 'compilation', being a collection of materials or data from various sources, and was thus protected like any other literary work and benefited from the low threshold of originality required for copyright protection to arise. However, this form of protection was for some time regarded as inappropriate for some forms of database. For example, the law resulted in some databases of limited originality being protected against copying for too long a period of time and yet the protection offered did not prevent certain types of commercial use of the contents of the database. Further, the treatment and protection of databases had developed along different lines in the various countries of the European Union (EU) and as databases have become more vital to business, it has become even more important that databases are given consistent treatment throughout the EU to ensure the free movement of goods and services.

Database right and database copyright

These issues led to an EU Directive (the European Parliament and Council Directive on the legal protection of databases, 96/9/EC) which was implemented into English law by the Copyright and Rights in Databases Regulations 1997 (SI 1997/3032) ('the Databases Regulations'). The Databases Regulations came into force on 1 January 1998 and, as well as creating a new database right, they amended provisions in the 1988 Act regarding the copyright protection of databases.

Two parallel rights came into existence. These were (i) the *sui generis* right (the 'database right'); and (ii) copyright in databases ('database copyright'). The database right subsists in a database 'if there has been a substantial investment in obtaining, verifying or presenting the contents of the database' (Regulation 13(1)). Database copyright subsists in an original database, which means that, by reason of the selection or arrangement of its contents, it constitutes 'the author's own intellectual creation' (1988 Act, s 3A(2)). A database is defined as 'a collection of independent works, data or other materials which (a) are arranged in a systematic or methodical way and (b) are individually accessible by electronic or other means' (1988 Act, s 3A(1) and Regulation 6).

The Directive aims to give protection to the structure of the database, rather than to its contents, which can result in certain databases being protected by both database right and database copyright in parallel. In addition, each of the independent works, data or materials comprised in the database might itself attract separate copyright protection.

The effect of the legislation was the loss of the right to protection of a database as a compilation (s 3(1)(d)) and the need to achieve a higher standard of originality for copyright protection to arise.

18.3 Subsistence and duration

18.3.1 Subsistence and duration – database right

Database right comes into existence automatically as soon as a database meeting the relevant requirements has been created. Database right lasts for 15 years from the end of the year of creation of the database but if a database undergoes substantial change (including by the accumulation of possibly insubstantial changes) the 'new' database is protected for a further 15 years from the end of the year in which such change was made. Where a database is made available to the public during the 15-year period, database right in the database will expire 15 years from the end of the calendar year in which the database was first made available to the public (Regulation 17).

In determining whether there has been 'a substantial investment in obtaining, verifying or presenting the contents of the database' (Regulation 13), substantiality is measured in terms of quantity or quality or a combination of both (Regulation 12). A substantial investment may be in any one or more of obtaining, verifying or presenting the contents of the database.

Database right will only subsist in a database if, when the database was made, the maker (or in the case of joint makers, one of the makers) was a state national of the European Economic Area (EEA) or habitually resident there or, in the case of a company or partnership, had the required link with an EEA state (Regulation 18). The residency requirements have been extended to include the Isle of Man.

The Databases Regulations apply retrospectively so that databases created between 1 January 1983 and 31 December 1997 will generally be protected by database rights for 15 years from 1 January 1998 (Regulation 30).

18.3.2 Interpretation of the database right

British Horseracing Board Ltd & ors v William Hill Organisation Ltd (Case C-203/02) was the first UK database right case and is, together with the Fixtures Marketing Ltd cases referred to below, a leading authority on the interpretation of the database right.

The British Horseracing Board (BHB) maintained a database containing information on horses, riders, races and so on. BHB expended considerable time, effort and cost in keeping this database up to date and accurate. BHB licensed the database to a number of information service providers who in turn were allowed to transmit the data to their subscribers. William Hill was licensed through one of BHB's licensees to use the database information in its betting shops. However, William Hill also used that information in its online betting business (for which it was not licensed). BHB sued, seeking an injunction. The High Court judge decided that William Hill's use of BHB's racing information infringed BHB's database right because it took advantage of the investment that BHB had made in obtaining, verifying and presenting the contents.

William Hill appealed this decision claiming, among other things, that in giving his judgment the judge had misinterpreted the Database Directive by giving too wide a definition of database right and what it protects. The Court of Appeal referred this point to the European Court of Justice (ECJ) for interpretation.

The ECJ gave a narrow interpretation of the scope of the database right, resulting in no database right subsisting in the BHB's databases. The ECJ said that investment in obtaining the contents of the database had to be investment in seeking out independently existing data and compiling the data into a database and that investment in verification of the contents of the database meant checking and correcting the already existing data. Investment in the creation of the data in the first place does not count, nor does verifying its correctness as part of the creation process. The ECJ also said that although William Hill had extracted and re-utilised a part of the database, it was not a substantial part of the database, because the data had not been the subject of the required investment in obtaining, verifying or presenting it. Moreover, even though William Hill had repeatedly and systematically extracted and re-utilised insubstantial parts of the database, there would be no infringement because the cumulative effect of these acts did not reconstitute the whole or a substantial part of the database.

At the same time as giving judgment in the BHB case, the ECJ gave judgment in three cases involving database rights in lists of football fixtures. The fixture lists were created by the football leagues in England and Scotland, a process which involved selecting the dates and times of matches and the teams that would play, and were licensed to the claimant, Fixtures Marketing Limited ('Fixtures'). Fixtures sued three entities (*Fixtures Marketing Ltd v Organismos prognostikon agonon podosfairou*, Case C-444/02; *Fixtures Marketing Ltd v Svenska Spel AB*, Case C-338/02; *Fixtures Marketing Ltd v Oy Veikkaus Ab*, Case C-46/02) for use of the fixtures information on a website (in the first case mentioned) and on pools coupons (in the latter two cases).

In judgments that reflected those in the BHB case, the ECJ held that no database rights subsisted in the fixtures lists because the investment that the leagues had made was as part of the creation of the data in the first place, not as part of a separate process of obtaining, verifying or presenting that data. In the first case, the ECJ also gave its opinion as to what constituted a relevant database, stating that the collection must have a fixed basis, it must include some means to allow retrieval of the individual data elements (for example, an index, table of contents or particular method of classification) and that the individual data elements must be separable without the value (whether informative, literary, artistic, musical or other) of their contents being affected.

18.3.3 Subsistence and duration – database copyright

The Databases Regulations withdrew copyright protection from certain types of database, but a database will still be protected as a copyright work (and hence protected for a longer period, namely 70 years after death of the creator of the database or 50 years after creation of a computer-generated database) if it meets the new, stricter test, namely that the selection or arrangement of the database amounts to the intellectual creation of the author (1988 Act, s 3 as amended by Regulation 6). This phrase is clearly intended to exclude from copyright protection databases which are collected in a mundane way and arranged, say, alphabetically.

Databases created before 28 March 1996 (the publication date of the underlying Directive), which were protected by copyright before the Databases Regulations came into force, will continue to be protected as copyright works in accordance with the existing law even if they would not qualify for copyright protection under the Databases Regulations. However, databases created between 28 March 1996 and 31 December 1997, even if formerly protected by copyright, lost copyright protection with effect from 1 January 1998 if they did not meet the Databases Regulations' new 'intellectual creation' test (Regulation 29).

18.3.4 Interpretation of database copyright

The phrase 'intellectual creation of the author' has caused much debate. The issue was brought to a head in *Football DataCo Ltd v Brittens Pools Ltd (Chancery Division)* [2010] EWHC 841 (Ch). The dispute surrounds the use by Yahoo! and others of football fixture lists to provide news and information and to organise betting facilities. They did not pay Football DataCo ('DataCo'), the body which owned the rights to the fixture timetable for English and Scottish football matches, for the use of its fixtures lists. Understandably, DataCo demanded that they did.

In its original claim, DataCo claimed protection under both database right and database copyright. The English High Court ruled out database right protection, relying on the ECJ's rulings in *British Horseracing Board Ltd & ors v William Hill Organisation Ltd* (Case C-203/02) and *Fixtures Marketing*.

The defendants admitted that the fixture lists were databases. They merely denied that, even as databases, they qualified for copyright protection. The High Court accepted that the fixture lists were databases (as the ECJ had done in *Fixtures Marketing*) and held that they were entitled to database copyright protection. Both DataCo and the defendants appealed that decision (DataCo on the database right and the defendants on database copyright).

Whilst rejecting the appeal on the database right issue, saying that the position was already clear from the *Fixtures* Marketing cases, the Court of Appeal decided to refer questions to the ECJ ([2011] ECDR 9). It could see the force of the arguments on either side. On the one hand, on DataCo's analysis, there was data consisting of all the matches to be played (dates, times, teams, venues) and that data was selected and arranged, using what the court considered to be very significant labour and skill in satisfying the multitude of often competing requirements of the clubs and rules, into fixture lists. That process was not mechanical and did not automatically determine who would play whom and when. At each stage, the Court of Appeal said that there was scope for the application of judgment and skill.

On the other hand, the court sympathised with the defendants' proposition that deciding on a date for a match was creating data, not selecting or arranging it, and database copyright was not concerned with the protection of the contents of a database. The defendants said that it was intellectual skill applied to the selection or arrangement of pre-existing data which counted towards protection.

In *Football DataCo Ltd v Yahoo! UK Ltd* [2012] 2 CMLR 24 the ECJ held that intellectual skill and effort in creating data was irrelevant. The phrase 'selection and arrangement' referred to the selection and arrangement of data through which the author gave the database its structure. The author's own intellectual creation related to the originality requirement, which would be satisfied if the author expressed his creative ability in an original manner by making free and creative choices, thereby stamping his 'personal touch' on the way in which the data were selected and arranged. As such, the addition of important significance to the data was irrelevant, as was the fact that significant skill and effort was required to set up the database if the result did not express any originality in the selection or arrangement. It is therefore likely that the Court of Appeal, when applying these criteria to the facts, will conclude that no database copyright subsisted in the database because the author was constrained by technical considerations and rules which left no room for creative freedom.

18.4 Ownership and dealings

The rules concerning ownership of database right and of copyright in a database do not coincide, which means that it is quite possible that, if both copyright and database right exist in a database, those rights will be owned by different people.

18.4.1 Ownership – database right

The first owner of the database right is the maker of the database (Regulation 15). The 'maker' is defined as 'the person who takes the initiative in obtaining, verifying or presenting the contents of the database and assumes the risk of investing in that obtaining, verification or presentation' (Regulation 14). As a result, there will be many situations where the initiator and the investor will be different people and these people will then be joint owners of the relevant database right. However, where a database is made by an employee in the course of his employment, the employer will be treated as the maker and, therefore, first owner of the database (Regulation 14(2)). In *Cureton v Mark Insulations Ltd* [2006] EWHC 2279 (QB), an agent for an insulation company was held to be the owner of a database of the company's customers that he had built up while acting as its agent.

18.4.2 Ownership – database copyright

As explained in Chapter 17, copyright is first owned by the author (except in the case of employees) and that is so even where a third party has invested heavily in the creation of the work by means of a commission.

18.4.3 Assignment and licensing

The provisions of the 1988 Act relating to assignment and licensing of copyright and the special rights accorded to exclusive licensees of copyright apply equally to database rights and exclusive licensees of database rights. There are special provisions in Schedule 2 of the Databases Regulations regarding licensing schemes operated by licensing bodies in relation to the grant of licences of various databases.

18.5 Infringement, defences and remedies

18.5.1 Infringement and defences – database right

Database right entitles the owner of that right to prevent others from extracting or re-utilising all or a substantial part of the database (Regulation 16). For these purposes 'extraction' is defined as the 'permanent or temporary transfer of the contents of a database to another medium by any means or in any form' and 're-utilisation' means 'making the contents of the database available to the public by any means'.

In *Crowson Fabrics Ltd v Rider* [2007] EWHC 2942(Ch) two of Crowson's employees left to form their own company. While employed by Crowson, they had created a spreadsheet with details of suppliers, contact details, agents' details and costs of transactions. Before they left, they copied this spreadsheet for use by their new company, and e-mailed the company a list of Crowson's customers' e-mail addresses. The High

Court agreed that Crowson owned database rights in the spreadsheet and the e-mail list, and that the transfer to the defendants' company was an infringing 'extraction'. It was irrelevant whether the defendants or their company made any subsequent use of the extracted data.

In *Directmedia Publishing GmbH v Albert-Ludwigs-Universität Freiburg* (Case C-304/07), a team at the university had spent two and a half years researching German poems. They consulted anthologies of poems and listed all those which were mentioned in three or more anthologies, the result of which was the creation of a collection of poems entitled *The 1,100 Most Important Poems in German Literature between 1730 and 1900.*

Directmedia later marketed a CD-ROM entitled '1,000 Poems Everyone Should Have'. On this CD-ROM, of the 876 poems written between 1720 and 1900, 856 appeared in the university's list. Directmedia created the CD-ROM by consulting the university's list, considering each poem on it, and then including or discarding it depending on Directmedia's assessment, and adding in others as it saw fit. The texts of the poems were obtained from Directmedia's own sources.

The German courts held that database rights subsisted in the university's list, but made a reference to the ECJ on the question of what sort of extraction constituted infringement. The ECJ held that 'extraction' is to be given a wide interpretation. In particular, there can be infringement by extraction regardless of: whether the copier had exercised its own skill and judgment in choosing which parts of the data to take; the method of extraction (whether 'manual' as here, or automated electronic copying); and the purpose of the extraction (e.g. whether or not it was to be used to create another database). Directmedia was also held to have infringed the copyright in the university's list.

More recently, in *Football DataCo v Sportradar GmbH* [2011] EWCA 1 Civ 330, DataCo accused the German company Sportradar of copying its database of football statistics and relaying this to customers across Europe, including in the UK. The Court of Appeal held that such use of the statistics did not infringe DataCo's database copyright because the information that had been copied was mere factual data, the recording of which had involved no creative skill. However, it decided to refer to the ECJ the question whether Sportradar was, in principle, liable in the UK as a joint tortfeasor for any acts of infringement of the database right by UK-based users who access information from Sportradar's servers in Austria and Germany. In other words, would the mere transmission of the data from servers abroad to users' computers in the UK constitute an act of 'extraction' or 're-utilisation' as set out in the Database Directive and therefore infringe the *sui generis* database right which DataCo might have in its database? The answer from the ECJ was that such a transmission to users in the UK could amount to an act of re-utilisation if there was evidence to show that the website owner intended to target the UK public (a question referred back to the UK Court of Appeal to decide) ([2013] 1 CMLR 29).

In relation to the question of what amounts to a 'substantive part' of a database, the BHB case made it clear that a 'qualitatively' substantial part has been extracted/re-utilised if the amount of investment in obtaining/verifying/presenting that part was significant, even if the amount extracted was quantitatively not significant. Whether a 'quantitatively' substantial part has been extracted/re-utilised is to be judged by comparing the amount taken in relation to the contents of the entire database. The part taken must fulfil both requirements to be substantial. In the case *Apis-Hristovich EOOD v Lakorda AD* (Case C-545/07), a database was composed of several separate modules or sub-databases. The ECJ held that if an individual module is substantial enough to count as a protectable database in its own right, the question of whether a 'quantitatively' substantial part had been extracted/re-utilised could be judged by comparing the part taken to the individual module, rather than to the entire database.

Repeated and systematic extraction or re-utilisation of insubstantial parts of the database can also amount to infringement of the database right (Regulation 16(2)). However, if someone has been allowed to use a database which has been made available to the public, that person cannot be prevented from extracting and re-utilising insubstantial parts of the database for any purpose (Regulation 19(2)). Where a database has been made available to the public, it is not an infringement of the database right for a lawful user of the database to extract a substantial part of the database for fair dealing purposes provided: (a) such extraction is for the purpose of instruction or research and not for any commercial purpose; and (b) the source is indicated (Regulation 20). There is, in certain circumstances, an exception for database right infringement in respect of the copying of work from the internet by authorised deposit libraries (Regulation 20A). There is also a list of other permitted acts in Schedule 1 of the Databases Regulations.

Anything done after 1 January 1998 in relation to a database pursuant to an agreement entered into before that date will not generally constitute infringement of the database right.

If at any time it is not reasonably possible to establish the identity of the maker of the database and it is reasonable to assume that the database right has expired, it will not be an infringement of the database right to extract or re-utilise a substantial part of the database (Regulation 21).

18.5.2 Infringement and defences – copyright in databases

Copyright in a database is infringed by any of the activities which amount to infringement of other copyright works. An adaptation of a database, for the purposes of infringement of copyright by making an adaptation, means an arrangement or altered version of the database or any translation of it.

The general exceptions to copyright infringement of literary works apply to databases. It is also not an infringement of copyright in a database for a person who has a right to use the database to do any act which is necessary for access to and use of the database, and any contractual provisions purporting to undermine this right will be void (1988 Act, s 50D – see Chapter 16).

18.5.3 Remedies

Remedies for infringement of copyright and database right are the same and are as set out in sections 96–102 of the 1988 Act. The presumptions laid down in the 1988 Act in relation to copyright works apply in almost identical terms to database rights (Regulation 22).

Summary

▶ A database will only be protected as a copyright work if the selection or arrangement of the database amounts to an intellectual creation of the author.

▶ A database may be protected by both copyright and database right.

▶ The database right lasts for 15 years from the end of the year of creation of the database, or the end of the year of first marketing where applicable, and protects against unauthorised extraction or re-utilisation of all or substantial parts of the database.

▶ The investment in a database must be in seeking out already existing independent data and compiling it into a database, rather than in creating that data.

Exercise

Consider the protection available to the following:

(a)   an alphabetical list of names and addresses of customers of a mail-order business;

(b)   a comprehensive audit of all IT systems used by a business and compiled by its IT manager;

(c)   an index for a medical journal; and

(d)   a directory of solicitors practising in England and Wales.

Chapter 19

Performance rights

19.1 Introduction

As we have seen in earlier chapters, copyright protects the results of artistic, literary, musical and dramatic effort. It requires the existence of a work that has been recorded in some form. So, if someone speaks a poem, without it having been written down or recorded in some other fixed form, no copyright will arise to protect the poem.

There is, however, clearly 'work' worthy of protection in any live performance, as distinct from any underlying copyright works which are being performed. Live performances are regularly recorded or transmitted in one form or another and, arguably, it should be the performer or performers who decide by whom and for what purpose such recordings and transmissions are made. This is particularly so where the performer has made a significant contribution to the work. However, because many performers are in a relatively weak bargaining position, these rights need to be entrenched in statute law as automatically arising and not depending on contract.

Before the Copyright, Designs and Patents Act 1988, a number of specific legislative measures had been implemented, starting with the Dramatic and Musical Performers' Protection Act 1925 and culminating with the Performers' Protection Act 1972. The position under statute law in the early 1980s was that performers' rights were protected through criminal measures, which gave the performers no means of private redress or compensation beyond those that a performer was able to negotiate in any contract. The state of the law also left certain categories of performers unprotected (namely, variety and circus artists) and gave no recognition to those to whom recording rights had been granted. During the 1980s, this area of the law developed through case decisions. In *Rickless v United Artists Corp* [1988] QB 40, the court confirmed that performers and their successors should have a civil right of action to protect performers' rights.

The 1988 Act substantially improved the position of performers and those who have entered into exclusive recording contracts with performers, giving civil rights of action against persons doing certain acts in relation to a live performance (including recording that performance) without consent. The position of performers was further improved by the introduction of additional rights under the Copyright and Related Rights Regulations 1996 (SI 1996 No. 2967) ('the 1996 Regulations') which implemented European Directive 92/100 ('the Rental and Lending Directive') and, more recently the Copyright and Related Rights Regulations 2003, SI 2003/2498 ('the 2003 Regulations'). These regulations came into effect on 1 December 1996 and 31 October 2003 respectively and include certain rights which bring the performers' rights more closely in line with copyright protection. These rights are subject to exclusions which are similar to the permitted acts allowed in respect of copyright works. Finally, the Performances (Moral Rights, etc.) Regulations 2006, which entered into force on 1 February 2006, created moral rights for performers, which, together with the Copyright Directive, implemented the UK's obligations in relation to performances under the World Intellectual Property Organisation (WIPO) Performances and Phonograms Treaty.

19.2 Subsistence

The 1988 Act provides for rights in performances which may be held by the performer or group of performers themselves, and by those who have recording rights in a performance.

19.2.1 Performers' rights

The 1988 Act creates two distinct categories of performers' rights: 'property rights' and 'non-property rights'. These rights allow the performer to control various aspects of the performance and any recordings or broadcasts made of that performance. The distinction between the two categories of rights and the different requirements for the infringement of each of them is explored in greater detail below. In addition to the property and non-property rights, the performer will also be entitled to 'equitable remuneration' where a commercially published sound recording is played in public or communicated to the public (other than by making available through an on-demand service).

19.2.2 Persons with recording rights

Rights will also subsist for those who have recording rights in a performance. For a person to come within the definition of a person having recording rights in a performance, that person must be a qualifying person who has been granted exclusive recording rights by the performer. The 1988 Act defines exclusive recording rights as the right to record a performance for commercial exploitation to the exclusion of everyone including the performer. If the person who has been granted the exclusive recording rights is not a qualifying person, but their licensee or assignee of the rights is a qualifying person, the licensee or assignee will be the person with the recording rights under the 1988 Act.

19.2.3 Qualifying performances

The 1988 Act defines those performances that give rise to performers' rights and rights held by those with recording rights as being dramatic performances (including dance and mime), musical performances, readings and recitations of literary works and variety act performances or similar presentations (s 180(2)). This definition is broad enough to cover the variety acts and circus acts that were not protected under previous statutes and would undoubtedly include comedy acts. There are still areas of doubt and potential dispute that one can imagine being argued in future cases. For instance, certain sports or Olympic events could arguably fall within the term 'dramatic performance' (for example, floor exercises, gymnastics and ice skating).

To be a qualifying performance, and thus be protected under the 1988 Act, the performance must be a live performance and must take place in a qualifying country, or must be performed by a qualifying person (generally an individual who is a citizen of or a resident in a qualifying country, or a legal body, for example, a company constituted under the laws of a qualifying country and having an established and real place of business in a qualifying country) (s 181). There is no definition in the 1988 Act of the term 'live' in relation to performances.

The rights conferred by the 1988 Act also protect performances that took place before August 1989 (including where the performer has died before the 1988 Act came into force – see *Experience Hendrix LLC v Purple Haze Records Ltd & ors* [2007] EWCA Civ 501, 24 May 2007), but the infringing acts under the Act must have taken place after that date to be actionable.

The rights of performers and those with recording rights exist separately from any copyright or moral rights arising in respect of the works that are performed or the works that result from the exercise of recording rights (that is, in any sound recordings or films of the performance). This means that a performer, or person with recording rights, can be liable for copyright infringement if he or she has not obtained the necessary licences from the owner of the copyright in a song, piece of music or dramatic work. It also means that the rights in a final sound recording of a performance will possibly belong to a different person from the person who was granted the recording rights.

19.2.4   Duration

The performer's rights (and the rights of a person with recording rights) currently last for 50 years from the end of the year of performance or for 50 years from the end of the year of release, if that occurs within the first period (s 191). This could mean that the term of protection may be extended where a release of a performance does not take place within the same year as a performance ('release' means first published, played or shown in public or communicated to the public, with authority). Directive 2011/77/EU extends the term of protection for a performer's rights in sound recordings to 70 years, and must be implemented by 1 November 2013.

The Directive also introduces a 'use it or lost it' right, allowing performers to terminate contracts with producers of sound recordings if 'insufficient' copies of the recording have been made available for sale, or if the recording has not been made available to the public by the producer, within 50 years of its publication or communication to the public. This right cannot be waived. There will also be a requirement for the producer to pay the performer an annual supplementary payment each year after the 50-year period has expired, which cannot be waived by the performer. This payment should represent 20% of the annual revenue from the reproduction, distribution and making available of the sound recording.

19.3   Infringement

19.3.1   Performer's property rights

The performer's property rights may be infringed by certain acts done in respect of recordings of a performance. The legislation gives the performer property rights in relation to recordings of qualifying performances. The four property rights given are: (a) the right to copy recordings of a performance ('the Reproduction Right'); (b) the right to issue copies of a recording to the public ('the Distribution Right'); (c) the right to rent and lend copies of the recording to the public ('the Rental and Lending Right'); and (d) the right to authorise and prohibit the making available to the public of a recording of a qualifying performance ('the Making Available Right').

The performer's Reproduction and Distribution Rights will be infringed by anyone who, without his or her consent, copies (which includes indirect or transient copying), or issues to the public copies of, the whole or any substantial part of a recording of a qualifying performance. There will be no infringement of the Distribution Right where copies of the recording are issued to the public if the copy of the recording has been first put into circulation in the European Economic Area (EEA) with the performer's consent.

Where a performer (or assignee) with property rights has granted a licence in relation to any of the acts requiring the performer's licence, then this licence will be binding on any successor in title to the interest in the rights, apart from a bona fide purchaser for value without notice of the licence.

19.3.2 Performer's non-property rights

The performer's non-property rights are infringed by anyone who, without his or her consent, records a live performance, broadcasts live or makes a recording directly from a broadcast of the whole or a substantial part of the qualifying performance. These non-property rights of the performer give rise to a right to take action for breach of statutory duty.

A performer's non-property rights are also infringed by anyone who, without his or her consent, shows or plays in public or communicates to the public the whole or a substantial part of a recording of a qualifying performance knowing, or having reason to believe, that the recording was made without the performer's consent or who imports into the UK (other than for domestic or private use) or possesses or deals in a business with an illicit recording, believing, or having reason to believe, that the recording is illicit.

Consent can be given to do certain acts (that is, to record or to broadcast) in respect of a specific performance or any particular type of performance or performances generally and may be given for past or future performances.

If a performer has given consent in respect of any of the acts requiring consent under the performer's non-property rights, anyone acquiring rights from the performer takes those rights subject to the consent (regardless of whether they are aware of the consent). It is, therefore, important in all cases where such rights are assigned or granted that the person acquiring the rights obtains full, contractual warranties from the grantor or assignor so that, if it turns out that consents have previously been granted, the person acquiring the rights can make a contractual claim against the grantor or assignor.

19.3.3 Persons with recording rights

The rights of a person having recording rights are infringed by anyone who, without that person's consent or the consent of the performer, makes a recording of the whole or a substantial part of the performance. Similarly, those rights will also be infringed by anyone who, without the consent of the person having recording rights in the performance, or (where the recording is of a qualifying performance) without the consent of the performer, shows or plays in public or communicates to the public the whole or a substantial part of a recording of the performance or imports into the UK (other than for private use) or, in the course of business, possesses or deals in a recording of the performance.

However, the infringement relies on the infringer knowing or having reason to believe that the recording was made without the consent of the performer or the person or persons having exclusive recording rights in respect of the performance or, in the case of importing, possessing or dealing with, that the recording was an illicit recording.

If a performer or a person having recording rights has given consent in respect of any of the acts requiring consent set out above, then any person having recording rights takes those rights subject to that consent (regardless of whether they are aware of it). As with non-property rights (above), it is important in all cases where such recording rights are assigned or granted that the person acquiring the rights obtains full contractual warranties from the grantor or assignor.

19.4 Dealing in the rights

19.4.1 Performer's property rights

The performer's property rights may be assigned (like copyright) and the assignment may be partial or total. The assignment will not be effective unless it is in writing and signed by or on behalf of the assignor.

In a case involving the band Busted, the High Court confirmed that performers' property rights could become the property of a partnership, such as a band of which the performer is a member, but that individual members would retain their individual performer's property rights (and the power to assign such rights) ((1) *James Bourne (2) Universal-Island Records Ltd (3) Mercury Records Ltd v Brandon Davis (t/a Brandon Davis Publishing* [2006] EWCH 1567 (Ch), 15 June 2006). The court clarified that the 1988 Act provides performers' property rights to each individual performer in a band, rather than a single, jointly shared performer's property right, so that while the performer's property rights could perhaps become partnership property, individual performers retained their individual interest, and would be entitled to assign such interest as required.

19.4.2 Performer's non-property rights

The performer's non-property rights cannot be assigned but can be transmitted on the death of the performer.

19.4.3 Performer's equitable right to remuneration

Where a performer assigns his Rental Right in relation to a sound recording or a film to the producer of the sound recording or film, he retains an equitable right to remuneration for the rental. The equitable right to remuneration may not be assigned by the performer, except to a collecting society to enable it to enforce the performer's right on his or her behalf.

19.4.4 Persons with recording rights

Although the rights conferred on a person with recording rights by the 1988 Act are not assignable or transmissible on death, the benefit of the exclusive recording contract by which a person has recording rights is assignable.

19.5 Moral rights

The Performances (Moral Rights, etc.) Regulations 2006 created moral rights for performers in relation to the whole or a substantial part of their performances, thus aligning rights in performances with copyright.

A performer now has a right to be identified as such where a person produces or puts on a qualifying performance in public, broadcasts a qualifying performance, or communicates to the public a sound recording of, or issues to the public copies of a recording of, a qualifying performance. The Regulations prescribe the manner in which the performer is to be identified in relation to live performances, live broadcasts and sound recordings. The right to be identified must be asserted by the performer in order to be binding – this is generally done by an instrument in writing by or on behalf of the performer. The Regulations prescribe a number of exceptions to the performer's right to be identified (for example, where it is not reasonably practicable to identify the author or where the performance is given for the purposes of reporting current events).

A performer also has the right to object to derogatory treatment in relation to live broadcasts and in relation to sound recordings which are played in public or communicated to the public. A 'derogatory treatment' is any distortion, mutilation or other modification which is prejudicial to the performer's reputation. As with the right to be identified, there are a number of exceptions to the right to object to derogatory treatment (for example, modifications consistent with normal editorial or production practice). The right is also infringed by a person who possesses in the course of business or deals in an article which he knows or has reason to believe is an 'infringing article'. An 'infringing article' is a sound recording of a qualifying performance which has been subjected to a derogatory treatment.

These moral rights last for the duration of the performer's rights in the performance. A performer's moral rights can be waived in writing but cannot be assigned.

The new right only applies to performances after 1 February 2006.

19.6 Defences and exceptions

19.6.1 Performer's property rights

Where a property right of the performer is infringed, knowledge or constructive knowledge on the part of the infringer is not required before infringement can be said to have taken place. If the infringer did not know, or had no reason to believe, that the performer had rights in the recording, damages will not be awarded against him. However, the court is free to award any other remedy, for example an injunction or an account of profits, against the infringing party.

19.6.2 Performer's non-property rights

In cases concerning those performer's non-property rights (under s 182) where knowledge is not required, if the infringer can show that at the time of the infringing act he believed that the consent of the relevant person had been given, damages will not be awarded against the infringer. The availability of other remedies is not mentioned in the 1988 Act, but infringements of a performer's non-property rights are actionable as a breach of statutory duty (see below).

In the case of the infringements involving importing, possessing or dealing in illicit recordings, if the infringer can show that he acquired the recordings in circumstances where he did not know, and did not have reason to believe, they were illicit, the only remedy to be awarded against him will be damages not exceeding a reasonable payment in respect of the infringing act. A recording that is made for 'private purposes' is not an 'illicit recording'.

19.6.3　Persons with recording rights

The remedies available for infringements of recording rights involving importing, possessing or dealing in illicit recordings are limited in the same way as the equivalent performer's non-property rights (see above) if the infringer did not know, and did not have reason to believe, that the recordings were illicit.

19.6.4　Other defences

In addition, there are a number of specific acts that may be done in respect of performances and recordings, without infringing the rights of the performer or the person having recording rights. These acts are set out in Schedule 2 to the 1988 Act and are broadly parallel to the permitted acts in respect of copyright works. The Copyright Tribunal has jurisdiction in respect of certain matters relating to the exploitation of the various non-property and property rights of performers or other persons entitled to record or to exploit recordings of performances.

19.7　Criminal offences

As well as the civil infringements of performance and recording rights which are now actionable under the 1988 Copyright Act and the 1996 and 2003 Regulations, there are a number of criminal offences in the 1988 Act arising out of certain acts involving illicit recordings. It is a criminal offence for a person, without sufficient consent, to do any of the following in respect of a recording which he knows or has reason to believe is an illicit recording:

(a) make for sale or hire;
(b) import into the UK (except for private and domestic use);
(c) possess such recordings in order to commit an infringing act or deal in such recordings in the course of a business.

Furthermore, it is a criminal offence for a person to infringe a performer's Making Available Right, either in the course of business or otherwise in a way which is prejudicial to the owner of that right, if he knows or has a reason to believe that he is infringing the right in the recording.

It is also a criminal offence to cause a recording of a performance (made without sufficient consent) to be shown or played in public, or communicated to the public, knowing or having reason to believe that the rights of the performer or the person having recording rights will be infringed by such act.

If any of these acts would be exempted from civil action by the permitted acts in Schedule 2 of the 1988 Act, they will not be a criminal offence.

Other criminal offences under this part of the 1988 Act include falsely representing the authority to give consent in relation to a performance (without having reasonable grounds for believing that such authority exists), and being a director, manager, secretary or similar officer of a body corporate convicted of a criminal offence who has consented to or connived in an offence.

There are specific provisions under the Act as to what can be done with illicit recordings which are delivered up or seized and the time limit for making applications to the court for destruction or forfeiture of recordings which have been delivered up or seized.

The criminal offences committed under this part of the Act are punishable by fines and/or imprisonment, depending on whether the conviction is summary or on an indictment.

19.8   Remedies and penalties

19.8.1   Performer's property rights

Infringement of a performer's property rights will entitle the holder of those rights to sue for damages, injunctions, an account of profits and any other remedy available for infringement of any other property right. Furthermore, the rights holder may also seek an injunction against an internet service provider where that service provider has 'actual knowledge' of another person using their service to infringe the performer's property rights. 'Actual knowledge' will be determined by the court depending on the particular facts at hand, but the court will pay attention to whether the service provider has been given notice of an infringement.

19.8.2   Performer's non-property rights and persons with recording rights

Rather than specifying the remedies available to the holders of performers' non-property and recording rights, the 1988 Act provides that infringement of a performer's non-property rights and of a person's recording rights are actionable by those persons as a breach of statutory duty. Breach of statutory duty entitles a person to claim damages and/or injunctive relief, in addition to interim relief remedies. The Act also provides for delivery up, upon an order of the court, of illicit recordings that are in a person's possession in the course of a business. This order may be applied for by the performer or person with recording rights as part of the civil action for breach of statutory duty, or it may be instigated by the relevant authorities as part of a criminal action. The performer or person with recording rights is also entitled to seize and detain illicit recordings if they are exposed for immediate sale or hire. The right may only be exercised if notice has been given to a local police station, access to the place where seizure will take place is available to the public, the illicit recordings are not at a person's permanent or regular place of business, no force is used, and, at the time of seizure, a notice is left containing the prescribed information about who seized the goods, on whose authority and on what grounds.

Summary

- ▶ Performers and persons with recording rights have similar protection to the rights of copyright owners, particularly since the 1996 and 2003 Regulations and the 2006 Moral Rights Regulations.

- ▶ The rights of performers are, however, more akin to those of copyright owners, as they protect the artistic creation, whereas the rights of the person with a recording right are purely economic rights created by contract. In order to have full protection for its rights, the holder of recording

Summary cont'd

rights will need the contractual warranties of the performer as well as the rights granted by the Copyright, Designs and Patents Act 1988.

▶ There are also particular practical threats to performers' rights posed by developing digital technology. The advances in this area mean that works of performers may be copied, many times over, with little reduction in quality. The 1996 and 2003 Regulations have gone some way towards addressing this issue.

Exercise

On 17 March 1997, A University Students' Union engaged the legendary Cameroonian poet Z to recite her work at one of their functions. Z, who composes her work with audience participation, improvised a number of new poems. The entire reading was taped by Y.

Y subsequently played the tape at a number of Students' Union functions. On each occasion he was paid a fee, which he donated to the Afro-Caribbean Society.

Z has a publishing contract with X Ltd, who are based in Paris. X Ltd have already published two collections of her poems, the first winning a literary prize, the second selling a total of 7 million copies worldwide.

On 1 May 1997, Z committed to paper the poems she had constructed at the Students' Union function on 17 March 1997 for X Ltd to publish.

Y's activities have come to the attention of Z and X Ltd, both of whom would like to put a stop to them.

Advise Z and X Ltd.

Chapter 20

United Kingdom unregistered design right

20.1　Introduction

Until the Copyright, Designs and Patents Act 1988, protection for designs, whether artistic or functional, was dealt with by copyright and registered designs (and, to a lesser extent, patents). The duration of copyright protection was felt inappropriate for functional and commercially exploited articles and this was addressed to a certain extent by the Design Copyright Act 1968 (see Chapter 16). The registered design system was seen as a little too stringent and too formalistic to be of real commercial use to an industrial concern which produces thousands of designs requiring some level of protection.

The need for a change in the law in this area was highlighted by the decision in *British Leyland Motor Corp v Armstrong Patents Co Ltd* [1986] RPC 279 (see Chapter 16) and the decision in *LB (Plastics) v Swish Products* [1979] FSR 145. Following heavy lobbying, the issue was finally addressed in the Copyright, Designs and Patents Act 1988 by the creation of a new, hybrid design right known as unregistered design right.

The position has been confused somewhat by the introduction of the unregistered Community design right. References in this chapter to 'unregistered design' or 'design right' are references to the UK unregistered design right under the 1988 Act. All references to the unregistered Community design right will be expressed in full.

20.2　What design right protects

Design right arises automatically, like copyright, and subsists in the shape and configuration of the whole or part of an article, the design of which is original. Originality is dealt with in detail below.

An 'article' is not defined in the Act. However, there is case law which has described an article as applying equally to living and formerly living things as well as to inanimate things (see *Ocular Sciences Ltd and Another v Aspect Vision Care Ltd* [1997] RPC 289 where the human eye was held to be an 'article'). Provided that the subsistence criteria are met, design right will subsist in any three-dimensional article (that is, an article which has aspects of shape and configuration), whether that design is functional or decorative. In *Rolawn Ltd and Rolawn (Turf Growers) Ltd v Turfmech Ltd* [2008] EWHC 989 (Pat), the High Court rejected the claimants' claim saying that they sought to rely on the underlying design concepts, such as the concept of a folding arm of a lawn mower, rather than the physical manifestation of their designs.

20.2.1　Exclusions from design right protection

There are various exclusions which prevent design right from arising in certain articles which are designed to interface with other articles so that one or other article can perform the function which it was designed to perform or match the appearance of other articles.

Design right is also excluded in the case of designs which are methods or principles of construction of an article. Nor does it subsist in surface decoration.

20.2.2   'Must fit'

Design right will not subsist in features of shape or configuration which enable the article to be connected to, or placed in, around or against, another article so that either article may perform its function (the so-called 'must fit' or 'interface' exclusion) (s 213(3)(b)(i)). The way in which this section is worded means that the exclusion will apply to features of shape or configuration of an article which feature the characteristics described, even if they also bear other characteristics, such as performing a decorative function. This means that it is also irrelevant that the designer could have found alternative ways of designing an article to achieve the interface (see *Ocular Sciences Ltd and Another v Aspect Vision Care Ltd* [1997] RPC 289; *Ultraframe v Fielding* [2003] RPC 435; and *Dyson Ltd v Qualtex (UK) Ltd* [2006] EWCA Civ 166). In the *Ocular Sciences* case, the parts of a contact lens that were shaped to fit a human eye were excluded from design right protection, even though there were other possible shapes of contact lens, since they had to be shaped in a particular way so that they interfaced with an eye.

The ability to rely upon design right in not only the whole of an article but also the individual parts of an article can cause this exclusion to arise in relation to different parts of the *same* article. In the case of *Baby Dan AS v Brevi SRL* [1999] FSR 377, for example, a stair-gate designed to prevent young children from going up or down stairs was the subject of scrutiny under this section of the Act. The claimant in the case had relied upon design right in the whole of the stair-gate as well as in individual parts of the stair-gate which it claimed the defendant had copied. The defendant argued that design right could not subsist in various aspects of the stair-gate, first, because it was designed to fit against a wall or banisters and, second, because its numerous component parts were designed to interface with each other to enable the stair-gate to work. The court agreed that certain aspects of the design were designed to interface with a wall or banisters and held that design right did not subsist in those aspects of the design. However, the court rejected the argument that numerous parts of the design could be eliminated on the basis that those parts were designed to interface with each other. If this were the way the law applied, no design right would subsist in articles which were made up of component parts because they all have to fit together.

The claimant in that case had claimed design right protection in the *whole* of its design. It was therefore the *whole* of the stair-gate which constituted the 'article' for the purposes of applying the exclusion to design right protection. It was only appropriate to consider excluding design right protection in individual parts of the design where design right protection was claimed in such parts of the stair-gate *individually*, since then each of those parts (however such parts were defined for the purposes of the claim) would be a separate 'article' which was designed to interface with another 'article' (another part of the design).

20.2.3   'Must match'

Design right does not subsist in features of shape or configuration of an article which are dependent on the appearance of another article of which the article is intended by the designer to form an integral part (the so-called 'must match' exclusion) (s 213(3)(b)(ii)).

A typical example of a design which will fall within the exclusion is the design of a replacement body panel for a car, since its appearance must match the rest of the car so that the car's appearance returns to how it was before the panel was damaged.

This is intended to prevent a monopoly arising in favour of the manufacturer of a product for the provision of spare parts for their product. However, this does not mean that a manufacturer can never prevent a competitor from supplying spare parts for its products, because the exclusion will not apply where an alternative design can be used which is consistent with the design of the main article. See, for example, the case of *Dyson Ltd v Qualtex (UK) Ltd* [2006] EWCA Civ 166, in which the Court of Appeal upheld the trial judge's refusal to exclude design right protection in parts of the design of a vacuum cleaner where he considered on the evidence before him that it was not necessary to reproduce the features of certain parts in order to provide suitable replacement parts – i.e. there was not the sort of dependence which the wording of the section anticipates. The trial judge had decided that certain parts of the Dyson cleaner could be replaced with spare parts of a different appearance without radically altering the look of the whole article, so the appearance of those parts was not 'dependent'.

The same issues will arise in relation to the application of this exclusion from protection as arise in relation to the 'must fit' exception in the case of connecting parts of a product when it is sought to enforce design right in respect of those parts individually.

20.2.4 Method or principle of construction

As noted above, design right does not subsist in a design for something which is a method or principle of construction (s 213(3)(a)) – for example, the concept of a dovetail joint in the construction of a drawer. However, such a feature might be used in order to add decoration to the design of a piece of furniture and, when viewed in combination with other aspects of the design, might in that sense be treated as an aspect of the design protected by design right. In the case of *Landor & Hawa International Ltd v Azure Designs Ltd* [2006] EWCA Civ 1285, a case involving an expanding mechanism for a suitcase, the court held that unregistered design right can exist in something which has function as long as a design is also present. In that case, there was a combination of zips and piping of different sizes. While the concept of the expanding mechanism was too general to amount to a design capable of design right protection, the particular combination of zips and piping on the design in issue was protectable. Otherwise, designs which have exclusively aesthetic features would be favoured over those with both aesthetic and functional features. In *Elite Angling Products v RAGS* [2007] FSR 10, the court held that a fishing net was not protected by design right because its appearance was generated by a stitching method and amounted to a method or principle of construction. To give design right protection to something which is construed at a very general level would create a monopoly in a method or principle of construction (see *Rolawn Ltd and Rolawn (Turf Growers) Ltd v Turfmech Ltd* [2008] EWHC 989 (Pat)).

20.2.5 Surface decoration

Surface decoration is also specifically excluded from design right protection by section 213(3)(c) and by the definition of 'design' in section 51(3) of the 1988 Act. Therefore, all designs for features of an article which decorate the surface of that article should be protected by copyright or Community design right, rather than UK unregistered design right. Surface decoration has been defined as not only including decorative additions to the surface of an article, such as embroidery or a painted pattern applied to the surface of an article, but also to design features which quite literally decorate the surface, even although they might be applied in the manufacture of the article. For example, in the case of *Mark Wilkinson Furniture Ltd v Woodcraft Designs (Radcliffe) Ltd* [1998] FSR 63, it was held that decorative grooves cut into and decorative cock-beading on the door panels of kitchen units would amount to surface decoration since they were there to decorate the surface of the doors and did not amount to aspects of shape or configuration of the kitchen units.

In the case of *Lambretta Clothing Co v Teddy Smith plc & Next Retail Ltd* [2004] EWCA Civ 886, the Court of Appeal held that the design for coloured panels and sleeves on a tracksuit top amounted to surface decoration, saying that surface decoration could be a thin layer applied to the surface of a material, or it could be dye that ran right through it. See Chapter 16 for further details about this case and the subsequent position adopted by the court in *The Flashing Badges Co Ltd v Brian David Groves (t/a Flashing Badges by Virgo and Virgo Distribution)* [2007] ECDR 17.

20.2.6 Can copyright and design right both subsist in a design?

Where a design falls to be protected under both the copyright and design right provisions of the 1988 Act because it fulfils the criteria for both types of protection, both rights will subsist. In many cases, the copyright will not be enforceable because of the operation of section 51 – see Chapter 16 where this is discussed in more detail. However, where it does arise because, for example, an article which is potentially protected by design right is also a sculpture and therefore an artistic work protected by copyright, section 236 prevents the designer from enforcing the design right in the design. In other words, copyright takes precedence. However, this does not prevent a claim of infringement of both design right and copyright being made in infringement proceedings should one of the claims fail.

20.3 Criteria for the subsistence of design right

There are two criteria which must be fulfilled for design right to arise. First, a design must be 'original'. This means that it has not been copied from another design – that is, it is the result of the independent skill and labour of the designer. Second, a design must not be 'commonplace' in the design field in question at the time the design was created. This means that it is necessary to look at the relevant design field at the time that the design was created in order to confirm that there were no other identical or very similar designs. This includes old designs which are still present in the marketplace (see *Scholes Windows Ltd v Magnet Ltd* [2002] FSR 10).

The relevant design field is an issue which the courts have had to consider in several cases. The tendency is for the courts to prefer a fairly broad definition of the relevant design field (see Jacob LJ's judgment in *Lambretta Clothing Co v Teddy Smith plc & Next Retail Ltd* [2004] EWCA Civ 886). For example, in the *Scholes Windows* case, it was held that the relevant design field to be considered was the field of window designs generally and not a special, narrower category of 'UPVC windows' and in *Rolawn Ltd and Rolawn (Turf Growers) Ltd v Turfmech Ltd* [2008] EWHC 989 (Pat) it was agricultural machinery, not mowers.

20.4 How design right arises

20.4.1 Design drawings

As mentioned above, design right is an automatic right, and arises as soon as a design is created by either producing design drawings or making a first prototype recording or embodying the design. In *Società Esplosivi Industriali SpA v Ordnance Technologies Ltd (formerly SEI (UK) Ltd and ors)* [2004] EWHC 48 (Ch), Lewison J was willing to define 'design drawings' widely in this context. He held that while final production drawings would attract design right protection, so could sketched concept drawings where detail is only developed later in the design process.

20.4.2 Qualification

There is also a qualification criterion which must be fulfilled. This can be fulfilled in one of three ways, each of which is considered below.

The first is that the creator of the design must be a 'qualifying individual' (1988 Act, s 218), the same principle which arises in relation to copyright. The rules on qualification and the countries to which design right protection extend are, however, different from the copyright provisions and are set out in section 217. Design right is not granted to citizens of all the countries to which copyright protection is granted. Since there are some countries which do not have an unregistered design right system, the UK has no reciprocal protection arrangements with them. This means that a US citizen, for example, cannot have design right protection for a design under the first qualification criterion.

In the case of joint designers, the design qualifies for protection as long as one of the joint designers is a qualifying individual, but only that individual is entitled to design right.

The second way is where a design has been commissioned or created by an employee and the commissioner or employer is a qualifying person (ss 217 and 219).

The third criterion is the 'qualification by reference to first marketing' in section 220. This is that the design was first marketed in the European Economic Area (EEA) or another country with reciprocal protection by a qualifying person who is exclusively authorised to put the articles on the market in the UK (for example, they have an exclusive licence for the UK).

20.5 Who owns design right?

The first owner of design right will be one of four people: the creator, the creator's employer, the person who commissioned the design or the person who first marketed the articles under section 220.

20.5.1 Employees

If a design is created in the course of the designer's employment, the designer's employer will automatically be the owner of the design right. The meaning of 'in the course of employment' has been considered in several cases involving a variety of circumstances. The cases vary as to what is treated as being 'in the course of employment'.

If someone creates a design during working hours and the creation of that design falls within that person's job description, the design will usually be deemed to be the employer's property. However, if an employee creates a design outside normal hours of work but using the employer's resources, it is questionable whether the design is the property of the employer or the designer. The position is even less clear in the case of an employee who is not employed as a designer, but who creates a design during working hours. It seems logical that if the designer uses his employer's resources, the employer should own the design right in the design. Where the employee has not used his employer's resources, however, the answer might be different.

What is clear is that an employee who creates a design in his own time using his own resources will own the design right in the design, even though he might be employed as a designer at other times. The meaning of 'in the course of employment' is considered in more detail in Chapter 17.

20.5.2 Commissions

A commission arises where someone engages a designer to create a design in return for valuable consideration. The consideration need not be money, but it has to represent something of value. However, commissioning someone to design and manufacture a product in return for an agreement to buy the finished products from that person may not amount to sufficient consideration for a commission to arise (see Chapter 17 and Clark (2002), for a review of the cases on this issue).

20.6 Duration of design right

Design right lasts for a maximum of 15 years from the end of the year of creation of the design. However, in the case of a design which is commercially exploited, the design right period is reduced to ten years from the end of the year in which the design is first made available for sale. In the *Dyson* case, the Court of Appeal approved the trial judge's finding that a design is not made available for sale when products made to the design are advertised, or even when orders are taken for those products, but only when products are actually delivered pursuant to orders which have been taken. In addition, during the last five years of protection, anyone can copy the design, subject to taking a licence from the design right owner and paying a reasonable royalty. This is known as a 'licence of right'. This has consequences for the remedies available for the infringement of the design right in a design which is within the licence of right period (see below).

If someone offers to take a licence of right during the last five-year period, the design right owner cannot refuse to grant the licence. If the terms of the licence cannot be agreed between the parties, they will be determined by the Comptroller of Patents at the Intellectual Property Office.

20.7 Infringement

Design right is infringed when a design is copied so as to produce articles 'exactly or substantially' to the design. An 'infringing article' is defined accordingly in section 228. An article will also be treated as an infringing article if it has been made outside the UK (and is therefore not technically an infringing article), but is subsequently imported into the UK and it would have been an infringement to make the article in the UK (s 228(3)).

20.7.1 Copying

Design right is not a monopoly right and it is therefore necessary to show, as with copyright, that copying has taken place before an infringement will be established. Copying might be inferred by demonstrating that the person accused of copying the design has had the opportunity to copy the design and that there is a substantial similarity between the alleged infringing article and the design said to have been copied. Copying can also take place subconsciously – that is, a design is reproduced exactly or substantially by subconscious recollection of an earlier design in which design right subsists. It is also irrelevant whether design right is infringed directly by copying the original design or indirectly by copying some other representation of the design (such as a photograph in a magazine), including another infringing article.

20.7.2 Primary and secondary infringement

As with copyright, the acts of infringement for which someone can be liable are divided into 'primary' and 'secondary' acts. Primary infringement covers: manufacturing, making of a design document to enable the manufacture of an infringing article, or authorising another to do such acts. Secondary infringement covers: importing for commercial purposes, offering or exposing for sale or hire in the course of a business, selling, letting or hiring in the course of a business, or possessing for commercial purposes an infringing article.

Acts done in relation to an article for 'commercial purposes' are defined in section 263(3) as being done with a view to the article being sold or hired in the course of a business. Therefore, mere use in the course of a business is not enough (for example, the use of an infringing chair design in a hotel lobby).

The difference between primary and secondary infringement is that, for primary infringement, there is no need to show that the infringer knew that the article being made was an infringing copy. For the acts of secondary infringement, a claimant must show that the defendant knew or had reason to believe that the article with which it was dealing was an infringing article. See Chapter 15 for a discussion of when a defendant will be deemed to have the requisite knowledge.

20.7.3 Where the infringement is committed

In order to be actionable in the UK, the act of infringement has to take place in the UK. It will not be possible to take action against someone for authorising the manufacture of potentially infringing articles from the UK if the manufacture of those articles takes place outside the UK. This is an increasingly prevalent problem with the quantity of articles which are made in the Far East. It will therefore be necessary to find an alternative act of infringement, such as importing the infringing articles into the UK or making a 'design document' recording the design for the purpose of enabling articles (in this case the infringing articles) to be made to the design. Making such a document for this purpose is an act which is reserved exclusively to the design right owner by section 226(1)(b). 'Design documents' are defined in section 263 as 'any record of a design, whether in the form of a drawing, a written description, a photograph, data stored in a computer or otherwise'. It would therefore be an infringement of the design right in an article to take a photograph of it for the purpose of enabling a manufacturer to make a copy of the article.

It should be noted that in *Società Esplosivi Industriali SpA v Ordnance Technologies (UK) Ltd* [2007] EWHC 2875, Lindsay J held that a successful allegation of section 226(1)(b) infringement could only occur where it was proved that the alleged infringer had intended that articles should be made – whether or not articles were actually made – to the design document he made or authorised to be made.

20.7.4 Joint liability

More than one person can be liable for the same acts of infringement of design right in a design. This can arise where two or more persons are said to be acting towards a 'common purpose' of carrying out acts which prove to be an infringement of the design right owner's rights (see *Unilever plc v Gillette (UK) Ltd* [1989] RPC 583).

Directors can be made liable for the infringing acts of companies in which they are involved. Whether they are held liable depends upon the extent of their involvement in the particular acts complained of. In *Re Mitsubishi Corp* (10 June 2005), an interim injunction application to prevent the infringement of a trade mark, the court permitted the sole director of a company to be joined to the action and to be made a party to the injunction order on the basis that he was the sole director of the company and it was clear that any tort committed by the defendant company must have been committed on his instructions. In *MCA Records v Charly Records* [2002] FSR 26, a copyright case, the court held that a director could be liable for the acts of the company of which he was a director where he did not commit the infringing act himself if he had procured or induced the company to do those acts or if he had joined with the company in a concerted action to see that those acts were done. It was necessary to show some personal involvement in the release of the infringing product. This case was relied upon in *Società Esplosivi Industriali SpA v Ordinance Technologies (UK) Ltd* [2007] EWHC 2875 in which a sole director and shareholder was found liable for facilitating an infringement which he must have known would occur.

20.8 Remedies for infringement

The following are the usual remedies available for the infringement of design right:

(1) an injunction preventing the continuation or further commission of infringing acts;
(2) damages for the design right owner's lost profits or an account of the profits made by the infringer;
(3) delivery up or destruction of infringing articles in the possession or control of the infringer;
(4) disclosure of the identity of the supplier of the infringing articles, where relevant; and
(5) interest and costs.

An injunction is a final order preventing the infringer from continuing to commit the infringing acts complained of. Failure to comply with the order can be a contempt of court, punishable by imprisonment or a fine, depending upon the severity of the breach.

Where a design is subject to a licence of right and the infringer undertakes to take a licence in the course of court proceedings, the court will not order an injunction (1988 Act, s 239(a)).

20.8.1 Damages and accounts of profits

Section 229 provides for damages or an account of profits.

20.8.2 Damages

In the case of infringing articles which are commercially exploited, the basis of a damages award is often the loss of profit which would have been made by the design right owner on the same quantity of sales of its own products that it would have sold had the copies not been on the market. Lost profits are assessed by working out what the design right owner's profit less 'direct expenses' of producing and selling that quantity of products would have been (see *Gerber Garment Technology Inc v Lectra Systems Ltd* [1997] RPC 443 CA). Direct expenses are all the expenses that are attributable only to the production and sale of the actual products in question. It is therefore irrelevant to consider, for example, what the design right owner's general overheads of running its business would be. The obvious direct expense for a wholesaler of a product is the cost of buying stock. With regard to other relevant direct expenses, if the design right owner had to employ extra staff in order to handle the copied products specifically because they could not be handled using existing resources, this would constitute an additional or 'direct' expense which would be deductible in arriving at a lost profit figure. Similarly, if the design right owner had to make special deliveries of its products because those orders could not be fitted in with other deliveries to customers buying its products, this would be a deductible expense.

However, it cannot always be shown that the claimant would have sold one of its original articles had the copies not been on the market, for example where the copies were much cheaper than the originals. In that case, the claimant's damages on those sales by the defendant will be equivalent to a reasonable royalty, as if the parties had a licence agreement between them (see further Section 20.8.6).

20.8.3 Account of profits

In the case of an account of profits, because it is the profit that the infringer made which is being considered, it will be relevant to deduct an appropriate proportion of the infringer's general business overheads ('indirect expenses'), as well as any other expenses which have the effect of reducing its profit on the infringing articles sold, albeit in the appropriate proportion to the infringer's overall business (see *Celanese International Corp v BP Chemicals Ltd* [1999] RPC 203). An account of profits is a discretionary remedy, but it is available in most cases as an alternative to damages. It can be useful in a case where the infringer's profit is much greater than the profit that the design right owner would have made, where the royalty method of assessing damages applies or where the infringer is able to rely upon the innocence defence. Under section 233, if an alleged infringer can prove that it was not aware that design right subsisted in the design alleged to have been copied, it will escape liability for damages. This does not, however, prevent the design right owner from seeking an account of profits or any of the other remedies.

20.8.4 The Enforcement Regulations

The Intellectual Property (Enforcement, etc.) Regulations 2006 ('the Enforcement Regulations'), which came into force on 29 April 2006, provide that damages shall be appropriate to the actual prejudice that the claimant suffered as a result of the infringement. The court is required to take into account other factors, such as the moral prejudice caused to the claimant by the infringement, when assessing compensation in the case of infringers of intellectual property rights who know or have reasonable grounds to believe that they are infringing an intellectual property right. This gives the courts greater scope for making more punitive awards in favour of successful claimants in intellectual property right actions and might therefore lead to greater use of section 229(3) (see Section 20.8.7), although in practice there has been little noticeable change in the courts' orders.

20.8.5 Damages and secondary infringement

Someone accused of infringing design right by committing an act of secondary infringement will not be ordered to pay the design right owner damages in relation to any articles sold which he did not know or have reason to believe were infringing articles at the time he acquired them. This is in contrast to the position regarding infringement of unregistered Community design right, where there is no knowledge requirement (see Section 21.10). The design right owner may be entitled to an injunction to prevent the infringer from acquiring any more of the infringing items, but the infringer will be allowed to sell off its remaining stock of the infringing products, subject to paying the design right owner a reasonable royalty (s 233(2)).

20.8.6 Damages where a licence of right is available

Where a design is within the licence of right period of design right, it will usually only be possible to obtain damages equal to up to twice the amount of a reasonable royalty based on the numbers of infringing articles which the infringer has sold during that period (s 239(1)(c)). This provision only applies if in proceedings for infringement of design right, the alleged infringer undertakes to the design right owner at any time before trial to take a licence of right in the event that the design right owner is successful in its claim. If the alleged infringer does not give such an undertaking, the design right owner will be able to claim damages in full.

This does not affect the damages available for infringing acts committed prior to the licence of right period. In addition, if the infringer wishes to sell off its remaining stock of infringing articles, it will have to agree the terms of a licence of right with the design right owner.

The royalty payable will be a reasonable market royalty which will need to be assessed using evidence of comparable licences granted by the design right owner, where possible, or other similar licences if the design right owner has not itself granted any. If this is not possible, the assessment will be as described below in Section 20.8.12, since the approach will be the same as if a royalty rate were being assessed outside the context of litigation.

20.8.7 Additional damages

Under section 229(3), the court has the power to award additional damages if the infringement was flagrant or the infringer benefited substantially from the infringement. However, such damages are very rarely awarded.

20.8.8 Delivery up/destruction

Delivery up is an equitable remedy and is therefore subject to the discretion of the court. The court will not order infringing articles to be delivered up to the design right owner under section 230 unless it is also prepared to make an order for the disposal of those articles under section 231.

The court will not order someone to deliver up infringing articles where the design is subject to a licence of right and the infringer undertakes to take a licence (s 239(1)(b)).

There is a limitation period of six years from the date the infringing article was made on the entitlement to seek delivery up, subject to limited exceptions (s 230(3)).

20.8.9 Disclosure of names of suppliers/importers/others

Under the principle set out in the case of *Norwich Pharmacal v Comrs of Customs and Excise* [1973] FSR 365, the successful claimant in an action is entitled to the disclosure of the names of all other parties which have committed an infringing act in respect of the same articles, from manufacturers to importers. The rationale for this is that it is inequitable for the infringer to withhold information about an infringement of an intellectual property right.

It is possible to obtain such information in an application to the court for pre-action disclosure where the rights owner seeks to obtain information from a party which is not an infringer itself, but which is in possession of such information. This is to enable the rights owner to pursue the party which is infringing its rights. The costs of such an application, including the defendant's costs, will usually have to be borne by the party seeking the information. The remedy is an equitable one and therefore within the discretion of the court.

20.8.10 Costs and interest

A successful claimant or defendant is also normally entitled to seek payment of its legal costs incurred in the proceedings, together with interest on those costs from the date of the judgment on liability. A successful claimant will also be entitled to payment of interest on the damages awarded or payment ordered under an account of profits. Interest runs from the date of the infringing act(s).

20.8.11 Limitation period

As with the other intellectual property rights, the limitation period for making a claim for infringement of design right is six years from each act of infringement committed. Where design right is being infringed on a continual basis, each new act of infringement will have its own corresponding limitation period.

20.8.12 Licences of right

Failing agreement, the terms of the licence would be determined by the Comptroller of Patents, who would also determine the royalty rate payable on the basis of evidence put forward by each party. In the absence of any evidence of a typical royalty which the design right owner would expect to receive (often the design right owner will not have such evidence because it does not license its designs), one formula which the courts can apply is to calculate what 25 per cent of the licensee's 'available profits' would have been on sales of the infringing product. This principle is set out in *Gerber Garment Technology Inc v Lectra Systems Ltd* [1997] RPC 443 CA.

'Available profits' are the licensee's gross profits on sales of the products in question less the direct expenses incurred in buying, advertising, distributing and selling (see Section 20.8.2 above for the meaning of 'direct expenses'). The licensee's general overheads are not taken into account. The royalty often ranges between about 3 per cent and 10 per cent of the licensee's selling price for its product.

20.9 Who can enforce design right?

Design right is enforceable by the design right owner or an exclusive licensee of the design right owner.

Where an exclusive licensee of the design right owner seeks to enforce design right, it is necessary to join the design right owner to the court proceedings as either a claimant or a defendant (s 235(1)). In the latter case, the design right owner will have no liability for costs to any party to the proceedings (s 235(2)). This approach would be the usual one to adopt if the terms of the licence provided for the licensee to take action to protect the licensed rights or if the design right owner simply did not wish to become involved in the proceedings.

A non-exclusive licensee will need the design right owner to enforce the licensed design right on its behalf or to enter into an agreement with the licensee granting the licensee the right to issue and conduct proceedings in the licensee's own name (or possibly to assign the right to take action for past infringements to the licensee). Suitable indemnity provisions should be included in the agreement to protect the design right owner.

20.10 Relationship with other rights

20.10.1 Copyright

As has been noted already, although both copyright and design right can subsist in a design, it is not possible to enforce design right in a design in which copyright also subsists, where that copyright would be infringed, as a result of section 236.

20.10.2 Unregistered Community design right

The position with the unregistered Community design right is different from the position with copyright, in that UK design right and unregistered Community design right can both subsist and be enforced in a design. This can cause problems because of the different ownership provisions which apply in relation to commissioned designs. Under UK design right, the commissioner owns the design right. There are no such provisions under unregistered Community design right law, which means that the designer will own the unregistered Community design right.

The unregistered Community design right also gives its owner greater powers of enforcement against infringements of the design because of the possibility of infringement of the right through mere use of an infringing article and the absence of a distinction between primary and secondary infringement. The list of infringing acts under design right law is more limited and, in order to prove infringement in the case of acts of secondary infringement, it is also necessary to prove that the alleged infringer knew or had reason to believe that acts were an infringement of design right.

20.11 Groundless threats

The recipient of a groundless threat of court proceedings for the infringement of UK design right, unregistered Community design right and registered UK and Community design right (as well as for trade mark and patent infringement) is entitled to sue for the damage which it suffered as a result of the threat, in addition to an injunction against the making of further threats and a declaration that the threats are unjustifiable. For example, if the recipient of such a threat ceased sales of the allegedly infringing products upon receipt of the threat and thereby lost the profits on the sales which it would otherwise have made, it is entitled to sue the person making the threat to claim compensation for that loss.

It is up to the person making the threats to show that the acts alleged to be infringing did constitute (or, if done, would have constituted) an infringement of the relevant right. A threat will be considered to be groundless if the maker of the threat, for example, had no reasonable grounds for making it, such as when the rights alleged to subsist in the design in question did not in fact subsist, the person making the threats did not own the rights claimed or the allegedly infringing design was found not to infringe the rights. Whether a threat is caught by the groundless threats provisions will depend upon what a reasonable person, in the position of the recipient of the alleged threat, with its knowledge of all the relevant circumstances as at the date the threat was made, would have understood the maker of the threat to have intended, when viewed in the context of the overall communication containing the threat.

There is an exception to the rule in relation to allegations of infringement by the manufacture or importation of infringing products only, which cannot give rise to a groundless threat.

Note that solicitors themselves can be liable for making a groundless threat, by writing a letter making the claims on behalf of their client.

Also note that the use of the internet auction website eBay's 'Verified Rights Owner' (VeRO) programme can amount to a groundless threat (see *Quads 4 Kids v Campbell* [2006] EWHC 2482). VeRO is intended to help owners of intellectual property to enforce their rights in relation to products being sold on eBay. In this case, Campbell used it to allege that quad bikes being sold by Quads 4 Kids on eBay infringed his registered design rights. Quads 4 Kids' goods were then removed from eBay, apparently without eBay checking Campbell's claims. When it became apparent that Campbell did not intend to issue proceedings to protect those rights, the court granted an injunction against him preventing him from making further groundless threats of proceedings.

In *Best Buy Co Inc v Worldwide Sales Corp Espana SL* [2011] Bus LR 1166, the Court of Appeal held that a threat made by a Spanish law firm against a UK company of proceedings in respect of the infringement of a Spanish company's Community trade marks, following the UK company's application for a conflicting Community trade mark, amounted to a threat of proceedings in the UK courts which fell within the groundless threats provisions. The court ruled that a threat included sending a letter which expressly or impliedly threatened proceedings if the recipient did not agree to the proposed settlement terms. This illustrates the risk which both UK and non-UK lawyers and their clients face of contravening UK threats laws. The case of *Carflow Products (UK)*

Ltd v Linwood Securities (Birmingham) Ltd and ors [1998] FSR 691 is worth noting. The defendant claimed for losses arising out of the threats section as a result of the second defendant (Argos) cancelling all orders of the alleged infringing product. This claim was not successful as the judge in that case found that, although a threats letter had been sent to Argos, it was not until the writ was issued that Argos made the decision to withdraw the infringing product from sale. Once the writ had been issued, the court said that the correspondence containing the threats 'was little more than historical interest'.

20.12 Government review of design law

The government conducted a consultation in 2012 on areas of possible reform of UK design law. Many of the possible proposals considered concerned changes designed to align the unregistered design right more closely with Community design right, as well as the more extreme possibility of doing away with unregistered design right altogether (a move which most respondents opposed). The responses to the consultation can be found at http://www.ipo.gov.uk/response-2012-designs-summary.pdf. We now wait to see what the government intends to do to progress any of the proposals.

Summary

▶ Unregistered UK design right arises automatically in the whole and/or part of a qualifying design.

▶ It protects the shape and configuration, but not surface decoration, of any original article which is not commonplace.

▶ It usually lasts for ten years from the end of the year in which articles made to the design were first marketed.

▶ Licences of right are available in the last five years of protection.

▶ An article will infringe design right if it is made to substantially the same design.

Exercise

A, a UK company, commissioned B, an Australian citizen, to create a new table design, and paid B a design fee for doing so. Articles made to the design were first marketed in the UK in 2001. C, a competitor of A, saw that the table was very successful for A and sent a photograph of the table to its Hong Kong manufacturers to copy. A has just discovered that C is selling copies of the table and wants all sales stopped immediately.

Advise A accordingly.

Further reading and references

Clark, 'Commissioned Designs – Who Owns Them?' [2002] *Copyright World*, May.
Clark, 'Design Rights All Wrapped Up: a Case Comment on Albert Packaging Ltd V Nampak Cartons and Healthcare Ltd' http://www.blplaw.com/know-how/expert-updates/wp-content/uploads/2012/10/Design_Rights_All_Wrapped_Up-SCLA-July-12.pdf

Chapter 21

Unregistered Community
design right

21.1 Introduction

The unregistered Community design right is a right created by Council Regulation (EC) No. 6/2002 of 12 December 2001 on Community designs ('the Regulation'). The Regulation also creates the registered Community design right, many of the provisions of which are the same as the unregistered Community design right provisions, including in particular the criteria for subsistence and many of the infringement provisions. The registered Community design right is dealt with in Chapter 22. Both rights apply throughout the European Union (EU).

21.2 What the unregistered Community design right protects

Unregistered Community design right subsists in a design. A design is defined as 'the appearance of the whole or a part of a product resulting from the features of, in particular, the lines, contours, colours, shape, texture and/or materials of the product itself and/or its ornamentation' (art 3(a)).

A product means 'any industrial or handicraft item, including inter alia parts intended to be assembled into a complex product, packaging, get-up, graphic symbols and typographic typefaces, but excluding computer programs' (art 3(b)).

A complex product means 'a product which is composed of multiple components which can be replaced permitting disassembly and re-assembly of the product' (art 3(c)).

21.3 Criteria for the subsistence of unregistered Community design right

In order for a design to qualify for protection as a Community design, it must be 'new' and have 'individual character' (art 4). Provided that the subsistence criteria are met, unregistered Community design right will subsist in any two- or three-dimensional design, whether that design is functional or decorative. There are, however, exclusions from protection based upon aspects of technical function, interface and appearance of a design which are similar to (but not the same as) those which apply to UK design right. These are considered further below.

21.3.1 New

A design is 'new' if no identical design has previously been made available to the public (art 5). Another design will be identical if it differs only in immaterial details from the design seeking protection. It is therefore only necessary for there to be one such previous design for novelty to be destroyed.

Designs must be new in the context of all prior art, and not just in the specific field they have been applied to, if they are to be the subject of enforceable Community design rights. This was made clear in *Green Lane Products Ltd v PMS International Group Ltd and ors* [2008] FSR 28.

The court considered the test for whether a design had already been disclosed and was therefore not novel – namely, whether the design could reasonably have become known in the normal course of business to the circles specialised in the sector concerned (art 7 of the Regulation). The court held that these words did not mean that the search for prior art was limited to the design field in which a later design claimed to sit. It is the sector of the earlier design which is the 'sector concerned'. The decision was upheld on appeal. The result is that all designs can be relevant when assessing novelty.

The case concerned Green Lane's production of spiky plastic balls for use in tumble dryers which they claimed softened clothes and reduced drying time. The company had applied for registered Community designs in August 2004 (although this case involved registered Community designs, the principle is equally applicable to unregistered designs). PMS had been producing spiky plastic balls since 2002, but as massaging devices. When, in late 2006, PMS sought to start marketing its balls for laundry purposes, Green Lane sought to enforce its registered designs.

Green Lane tried to argue that 'the sector concerned', for the purposes of the test, was the sector specified in its registered Community design. The Court of Appeal disagreed, instead agreeing with PMS's argument that the 'relevant sector' was the sector of the earlier design and that Green Lane's registered Community design rights were therefore invalidated by the pre-existence of the PMS massage balls.

There were a number of arguments against Green Lane's logic. Perhaps the strongest was the argument that, if Green Lane were right, astute applicants could indicate a narrow class of products – to narrow the scope of prior art against which the registration may be invalidated – while at the same time enjoying a wider scope of protection, beyond the indicated products, under article 10 of the Community Design Right Regulation. Article 10 gives designers protection against 'any design which does not produce on the informed user a different overall impression', regardless of whether the design has been applied to laundry, massage or any other products. The trial judge had also said that Green Lane must have been wrong because, in the case of unregistered Community design right, there is no registration certificate in which a narrow field of application could be specified.

21.3.2 Individual character

A design has 'individual character' if it creates a different overall impression on the 'informed user' from any design previously made available to the public (art 6). The 'informed user' is someone who has some knowledge of the design field in question but who is not necessarily an expert. This was considered in *Woodhouse UK plc v Architectural Lighting Systems* [2005] ECPCC (Designs) 25, in which 'informed' was held to imply some notion of familiarity beyond the knowledge of the average consumer and to require some knowledge both of market trends and availability of products and of basic technical considerations. It was held not to require any familiarity with the underlying technology, eye appeal being held to be the more important consideration.

In *Karen Millen v Dunnes Stores* [2007] IEHC 449, the Irish court held that the informed user was:

▶ an end user of the product to which the design in question relates;
▶ aware of similar designs which form part of the design corpus;

- ▶ alert to design issues and better informed than the average consumer in trade mark law; and
- ▶ familiar with the functional or technical requirements and limitations of the design or the product for which the design is intended (because the freedom of the designer is relevant to whether the design has individual character).

In *PepsiCo Inc v Grupo Promer Mon-Graphic SA* (C-281/10 P), the first registered design case to go before the European Court of Justice (ECJ), it was held that the informed user was a particularly observant user, either because of their personal experience or their extensive knowledge of the sector in question. The court held that the informed user would be aware of the various designs which exist in the sector concerned and have a degree of knowledge with regard to their features, but will not be a designer or a technical expert.

It is also necessary to take into consideration the nature of the product to which the design is applied or in which it is incorporated, and in particular the industrial sector to which it belongs and the degree of freedom of the designer in developing the design, in deciding whether a design has individual character. In *Dyson Ltd v Vax Ltd* [2010] EWHC 1923 (Pat) (a case concerning a UK registered design), the court held that a large departure from the existing design corpus could be an indication of greater design freedom, which could also entitle the owner to a broad scope of protection. However, the court accepted that this would not be the case if a large departure brought with it new design constraints. The Court of Appeal did not interfere with the judge's decision and dismissed Dyson's appeal against his finding that Vax's design produced a different overall impression on the informed user ([2012] FSR 4). Although this case concerned a UK registered design, the approach of the UK court to design freedom in the context of Community designs would be the same in view of the harmonised nature of UK registered design law.

In *Neuman, Galdeano del Sel* and *OHIM v Baena Grupo – Neuman Joined Cases* C 101/11 P and C 102/11 P, the ECJ held that the 'informed user' lay somewhere between the average consumer applicable in trade mark matters, who need not have any special knowledge and generally makes no comparison between the trade marks in issue, and the sectorial expert with detailed technical expertise. They were therefore particularly observant, but whilst they would make a direct comparison between the respective designs when possible, such a comparison may be impracticable or uncommon in the relevant sector. Accordingly, it concluded that the General Court had made no error by basing its reasoning on the imperfect recollection of the overall impression produced by the respective designs, rather than from a side-by-side comparison.

21.4 Complex products

For designs for component parts of complex products, there are additional requirements that the part remains visible during normal end use of the product and that the visible features of the component part fulfil the novelty and individual character criteria (art 4(2)).

Further, article 110 states that Community design rights shall not exist for a design which constitutes a component part of a complex product used for the purpose of the repair of that complex product so as to restore its original appearance. In *Bayerische Motoren Werke Aktiengesellschaft v Round & Metal Ltd* [2012] ECC 28 the High Court held that article 110 only applied where the design of the component part was dependent on the appearance of the complex product. This was because recital 13 of the Regulation referred to a component part of a complex product *upon whose appearance the design was dependent*, even though those words did not appear in article 110 itself. Accordingly, it held that alloy wheels sold by a third party for use on BMW cars did not fall within the article 110 exception because different designs of alloy wheels could be used on the cars, so that their appearance were not dependent on the design of the car. Further, they were not used to 'repair' the car, but to upgrade it, and they did not restore the car to its original appearance, but improved the appearance of the car.

21.5 Making available to the public

A design is considered to have been made available to the public if it has been disclosed, for example, by publication, exhibition or use in the course of trade (art 7). There is an exception to this rule where such disclosure could not reasonably have become known in the normal course of business to the circles specialised in the sector concerned, operating within the Community. In addition, a design will not be considered to have been disclosed if it is disclosed to a third person under explicit or implicit conditions of confidentiality.

21.6 Exclusions from unregistered Community design right protection

There are exclusions (in art 8) which prevent unregistered Community design right from arising in certain products which are designed to enable them to interface with other products so that one or other product can perform the function which it was designed to perform and in products whose designs are only attributable to the function that they have to perform. Therefore, features of a design which are excluded from protection for one of these reasons are not to be taken into account in assessing whether other features of the design fulfil the requirements for protection.

As noted above, protection is also excluded for component parts or features of a part which are not visible during normal use of a product or which do not fulfil the novelty and individual character requirements. Again, such features are not taken into account in assessing whether other features of the design fulfil the requirements for protection.

The so-called 'must fit' exclusion states that a Community design shall not subsist in features of appearance of a product which must necessarily be reproduced in their exact form and dimensions in order to permit the product in which the design is incorporated or to which it is applied to be mechanically connected to or placed in, around or against another product so that either product may perform its function (art 8(2)). The way in which article 8(2) is worded, in particular the use of the words 'necessarily' and 'exact form', means that the exclusion will probably not apply where there are alternative ways of designing those features to achieve the same function. The ability to rely upon unregistered Community design right in not only the whole of a product but also the individual parts of a product can cause the exclusion to arise in relation to different parts of the same product in the same way as considered in relation to UK design right (see Section 20.2.2), although the same result will probably not be obtained where there are alternative ways of designing interface features. This problem will not arise where it is the whole product that is relied upon in its entirety.

There is no direct equivalent to the so-called 'must match' exception which applies to UK design right.

Community design can subsist in a design serving the purpose of allowing the multiple assembly or connection of mutually interchangeable products within a modular system, for example, a Lego brick (art 8(3)).

A Community design will not subsist in features of appearance of a product which are solely dictated by its technical function (art 8(1)). This exception denies protection to aspects of products the appearance of which is dictated solely by the function that the product has to perform. Accordingly, designs which also have an aesthetic appeal in addition to their functional purpose will still attract protection. A narrow interpretation of article 8(1), such that the exception would only apply if the design was the *sole* way of performing that function, was endorsed by both the Patents County Court and the Court of Appeal in *Landor & Hawa International Ltd v Azure Designs Ltd* [2006] EWCA Civ 1285, referred to in Section 20.2.4. Accordingly, if there was more than one design which would perform the same function, neither would be excluded from protection. However, this approach was criticised in *Dyson Ltd v Vax Ltd* [2010] EWHC 1923 (Pat) (which dealt with a UK registered design). In that case, Arnold J preferred the interpretation of the OHIM Appeals Board in *Lindner Recyclingtech GmbH v Franssons Verkstader AB* [2010] ECDR 1, namely that the configuration of a product would be solely dictated by its technical function if every feature of the design was determined by technical considerations, even if an alternative product configuration could achieve the same function. However, as long as function is not the only relevant factor, so that the aesthetic appeal of the product has some relevance, the design is in principle eligible for protection.

21.7   How unregistered Community design right arises

Unregistered Community design right is an automatic right which arises as soon as a product the design of which meets the subsistence criteria is disclosed by being made available to the public.

There are no further qualification provisions other than that in article 11 that the product must be made available to the public (the concept of which has been discussed above in connection with art 7). In contrast to the position under UK design right, therefore, it is possible for a citizen of a country which does not benefit from UK design right protection (for example, the US) to obtain protection under the unregistered Community design right.

21.8   Who owns unregistered Community design right?

The first owner of unregistered Community design right will be the designer or the designer's employer. If the designer of a product created the design in the course of employment, the employer will automatically be the owner of the unregistered Community design right in the product. The meaning of 'in the course of employment' has already been considered in relation to UK design right (Chapter 20) and copyright (Chapter 17). The same principles are likely to apply to unregistered Community design right.

There are no provisions dealing with commissioned works. There is therefore a potential conflict with UK design right law if both rights fall to be considered in relation to the same design. The position under unregistered Community design right in relation to commissioned works is that the right is owned by the designer, whereas the commissioner will own the UK unregistered design right. As with copyright in relation to commissioned works, there is still the possibility of an equitable right to the unregistered Community design right arising in favour of the commissioner, if, for example, both parties agreed that the commissioner would own the rights.

If two or more people jointly develop a design, the right to the Community design vests in them jointly (art 14(2)).

21.9 Duration of unregistered Community design right

Unregistered Community design right lasts for three years from the date on which the product in which a design has been incorporated or to which a design has been applied is first made available to the public within the Community (art 11).

21.10 Infringement

Unregistered Community design right is infringed when a product which does not produce a different overall impression on the informed user (see art 10) (referred to below as an 'infringing product') is used. You will recognise this as the same test as for subsistence of the right. 'Use' is described in article 19, which also describes the exclusive right which is conferred upon the unregistered Community design right owner.

'Use' has a broad definition and includes making, offering, putting on the market, importing, exporting, stocking for any of those purposes, or otherwise using an infringing product.

Unregistered Community design right is not a monopoly right and it is therefore necessary to show that copying has taken place before an infringement will be established (art 19(2)). As with copyright and UK design right, copying might be inferred by demonstrating that the person accused of copying the design has had the opportunity to copy the design and that there is a substantial similarity between the alleged infringing article and the design said to have been copied.

However, unlike under copyright or UK design right law, there is no requirement to prove knowledge on the part of the infringer. In this respect, liability for infringement is strict. This will have an important effect on retailers who, before the introduction of the Community design, were able to avoid infringement by showing that they did not know or have reason to believe that the article which they were selling was a copy. Since that defence does not apply with the Community design, it is essential for retailers to obtain indemnities from their suppliers so that they can recoup any damages which they may have to pay for stocking a copy. Some legal commentators have argued for the innocent infringement defence available under UK unregistered design right law to apply to the unregistered Community design right and the Community registered design. However, the High Court in *J Choo (Jersey) Ltd v Towerstone Ltd* [2008] FSR 19 held that those limitations on the remedies available for infringement do not apply to the unregistered and registered Community design rights (see further Chapter 22 on this case).

21.11 Place where the acts of infringement take place

An infringement of unregistered Community design right is actionable in any Member State of the EU in which the infringement occurs. The usual rules on jurisdiction apply to determine where proceedings for infringement should be commenced.

21.12 Limitations on the enforcement of the rights conferred by a Community design

Article 20 of the Regulation provides that the rights conferred by the Community design do not extend to the following acts:

- acts done privately and for non-commercial purposes;
- acts done for experimental purposes; and
- acts of reproduction for the purpose of making citations or of teaching, provided that such acts are compatible with fair trade practice and do not unduly prejudice the normal exploitation of the design, and that mention is made of the source.

There are also exclusions relating to equipment on ships and aircraft registered in a third country when these temporarily enter the territory of the Community, the importation into the Community of spare parts and accessories for the purpose of repairing such craft and the execution of repairs on such craft.

Article 21 of the Regulation prevents the Community design right being enforced in respect of a product in which a protected design is incorporated or to which it is applied when it has been put on the market in the Community by the holder of the Community design or with his consent. It is not, therefore, an infringement of the Community design right to buy such a product in the EU and to use it, including, for example, by incorporating it into another product which is subsequently sold. This is referred to as the 'exhaustion of rights' principle.

21.13 Remedies for infringement

These are set out in article 89(1)(a)–(d). The court has the power to make the following orders:

(a) an order prohibiting the defendant from proceeding with the acts that have infringed or would infringe the Community design;
(b) an order to seize the infringing products; and
(c) an order to seize materials and implements predominantly used in order to manufacture the infringing goods, if their owner knew the effect for which such use was intended or if such effect would have been obvious in the circumstances.

Article 89(1)(d) provides that the national law of the Member State in which the acts of infringement or threatened infringement are committed applies in relation to other remedies available for the infringement of the unregistered Community design right. The remedies for infringement and the limitations on those remedies will therefore be similar to those for infringement of UK design right, which were discussed in Chapter 20, except that, as already discussed above, there is no defence of innocent infringement to the unregistered Community design right.

Article 90 provides for applications for interim relief, such as an interim injunction.

The limitation period for making a claim for infringement of unregistered Community design right is six years from each act of infringement committed. Where unregistered Community design right is being infringed on a continual basis, each new act of infringement will have its own corresponding limitation period.

21.14 Licences of right

Licences of right are not available under unregistered Community design right in light of the very short period of protection afforded by the right.

21.15 Dealing with the unregistered Community design right

As with other intellectual property rights, the unregistered Community design right may be assigned or licensed.

Article 32 provides that licences may be granted for the whole or part of the Community and that a licence may be exclusive or non-exclusive. Article 32(2) contemplates licences being granted for particular forms of use of the design, for example. This is in apparent contrast to the position with regard to assignments of the Community design right which must be for the entirety of the right and for the whole area of the Community, according to article 27.

Unless the licence provides otherwise, the licensee may bring proceedings for infringement only if the right holder consents, although the holder of an exclusive licence may bring proceedings if the licensor does not bring infringement proceedings within an appropriate period, having been given notice by the licensee to do so (art 32(3)).

A licensee is entitled to intervene in an infringement action brought by the licensor for the purpose of obtaining compensation for damage which it has suffered (art 32(4)).

21.16 Relationship with other rights

Both copyright and unregistered Community design right can subsist in a design and are both enforceable, which contrasts with the position under UK design right. However, the Regulation gives Member States the option of making their own provisions about the extent of protection, including the level of originality required, so the position might not be the same in all countries (art 96(2)).

In the UK, both unregistered Community design right and UK design right can also subsist and be enforced in a design. As noted in Chapter 20, this can cause problems because of the different ownership provisions that apply in relation to commissioned designs.

21.17 Groundless threats

Chapter 20 sets out the rules on groundless threats, which also apply to the unregistered Community design right.

Summary

▶ Unregistered Community design right will subsist in the whole and/or part of any new design with individual character.

▶ 'Design' includes any aspect of lines, contours, colours, shape, texture and/or materials of the product itself and/or its ornamentation.

▶ The right arises automatically and lasts for three years from the date on which it was made available to the public.

▶ The right can be infringed by using the design and there is no knowledge requirement for liability to arise (as there is for secondary infringements of copyright and UK design right).

Exercises

21.1 Who can own an unregistered Community design?

21.2 When will the right first come into existence?

21.3 Who can infringe an unregistered Community design and how?

Further reading and references

A discussion of the *Neuman* cases by Dr Henning Hartwig at www.bardehle.com/es/news/ip.

Chapter 22

United Kingdom and Community registered designs

22.1 Introduction

Copyright was always available to protect artistic designs, whether in two-dimensional form as graphic works or photographs, or in three-dimensional form as sculptures, works of architecture or works of artistic craftsmanship. Until the Copyright, Designs and Patents Act 1988 (the 1988 Act), the low level of artistic quality required for protection of two-dimensional works, and the possibility of infringement of a two-dimensional work by a three-dimensional representation, meant that functional articles could be protected by copyright existing in underlying design drawings. After August 1989, this form of protection for functional designs and other aspects of shape or configuration was replaced by UK unregistered design right (supplemented more recently by the unregistered Community design as an additional right).

Registered designs have been available as an addition to copyright protection. The 1988 Act made some minor changes to the Registered Designs Act 1949 (RDA). However, since then, more substantive changes have been made to the RDA in order to implement the European Directive 98/71/EC on the legal protection of designs – this Directive aimed to harmonise the requirements for registered design protection across Member States. Accordingly, each Member State should apply the same law to their own national registered design.

However, in addition to national registered designs, Council Regulation of 12 December 2001 on Community Designs (6/2002/EC) ('the Regulation') also introduced a single European Union (EU)-wide design registration, called the Community Registered Design. This is operated by the Office for Harmonisation in the Internal Market (OHIM) in Alicante, Spain. The beauty of this new right is that the subsistence requirements and infringement provisions are virtually identical to those that apply to the national design registrations (unlike, for example, the differing provisions which apply to national and Community trade marks). References to the RDA are to that Act as amended by the 1988 Act and by the Registered Design Regulations 2001 which came into force on 9 December 2001. References to the 'old RDA' are to the RDA before its amendment by the Registered Design Regulations 2001.

The main advantages of a registered design over the unregistered rights are:

(1) there is no need to prove copying for an infringement of a registered design – the registered design owner has a monopoly in that design; and
(2) the registered design can last for up to 25 years, whereas unregistered Community design only lasts for three years, and unregistered UK design right usually only lasts for ten years, with licences of right being available in the last five years.

This chapter therefore considers the registered design rights which exist in the UK and throughout the EU at the Community level. Owing to the harmonisation of UK registered design law with Community registered design law, most of this chapter will refer only to the Community registered design but, in most cases, the same will apply to the UK registered design.

22.2 The UK registered design

The territorial scope of the UK registered design is obviously limited to the UK. The amendment to the RDA also affected registered designs which were in existence prior to the amendments coming into force insofar as enforcement of the right is concerned. The test for infringement of an earlier registered design is now the same as the test for infringement of a design registered under the harmonised system.

Applications for the UK registered design are made to the UK Intellectual Property Office in the UK on payment of a fee.

22.3 The registered Community design

As in the case of the unregistered Community design right, the registered Community design right is a right created by the Regulation. Many of the rules on registered Community designs are therefore the same as the unregistered Community design right provisions, including, in particular, the criteria for subsistence and many of the infringement provisions. These were considered in Chapter 21. Both rights apply throughout the EU.

The registered Community design right is not an automatic right and therefore an application for registration must be filed, which can be done online through OHIM's website, together with payment of a fee.

A registered Community design can be used to protect the aspects of shape, configuration, contours and lines of a design, its texture, ornamentation, colours and even packaging. It can also protect logos, motifs and typefaces, either as stand-alone designs or as decoration on a product or its packaging.

Since it is the design itself that is protected by the registration, once registered, it can be applied to any number of different products.

Since the European Union has now acceded to the Geneva Act of the Hague Agreement (see Council Regulation 1891/2006), applicants wishing to obtain protection for a design both within the EU and throughout the non-EU contracting Member States may do so through the filing of a single international application.

22.4 What are the criteria for registration?

Designs can be registered if they are 'new', which means that they do not differ only in immaterial details from another design already in the marketplace, and have 'individual character', which means that they create a 'different overall impression' from other designs on the 'informed user' of such a design (see the definition of this term in Chapter 21). Novelty and individual character also have the same meanings as in relation to the unregistered Community design right.

In relation to a design having 'individual character' the Court of Appeal in *Procter & Gamble Co v Reckitt Benckiser (UK) Ltd* [2007] EWCA Civ 936 held that a designer seeking protection for his works must pass a different, higher standard in order to obtain a Community design registration than the test that a successful defendant to an enforcement action must pass.

The case concerned two competing designs of domestic air-freshener spray cans. Procter & Gamble accused Reckitt Benckiser of having infringed its registered Community design and, at first instance, the court ruled that it had done so. The court reached this conclusion by applying the same test for infringement as the test that must be passed to obtain a valid registration, which is understandable, since the wording of the two sections is the same (i.e. the 'same overall impression' test).

The Court of Appeal disagreed. It argued that there was a policy reason for applying a higher standard for registration. This policy was apparent from the recitals to the Council Regulation (EC) No. 6/2002 of 12 December 2001 on Community Designs, which state that the overall impression created by a design on an informed user must 'clearly differ' from that produced by the existing body of design. Such a policy was necessary in order to avoid design monopolies which could prevent minor or everyday design alterations. It said that this did not apply to the prevention of infringement. Subsequent designs accused of being copies need only produce a 'different overall impression'.

However, Jacob LJ, who gave the leading judgment in the case, has since accepted in his judgment in *Dyson Ltd v Vax Ltd* [2012] FSR 4 (at [34]) that he was mistaken in making this distinction. He said that the difference in wording was simply down to 'sloppy drafting', citing the following in support of his conclusion: Dr Alexander von Mühlendahl in Design Protection in Europe , 3rd edn (2009), pp. 232–233 (although he said that it would not have affected the result in the Procter & Gamble case). It is therefore now assumed that the correct position is that there is no distinction between the overall impression test when considering both subsistence and infringement.

The same exclusions for functional designs and interface design features apply as they do for unregistered Community design right, discussed in Chapter 21.

A design can be marketed for up to 12 months prior to filing an application in order to test the success of the product in the marketplace without prejudicing the registrability of the design – that is, its novelty will not be affected by the fact that it had already been disclosed, provided that the first disclosure was less than 12 months prior to the date of application.

22.5 What does the registered design cover and for how long?

The registered Community design allows one registration to be filed for all 27 Member States of the EU with the Community designs office. The UK registered design obviously only covers the UK, as noted above. It is also possible to file a registered Community design application for a series of designs in one application for a lower fee than the cost of multiple, separate applications, provided that all the designs are for the same type of product (for example, all lighting designs). It is therefore possible for designers to protect a complete new collection of products in one application. This makes the registered Community design very cost-effective in protecting a wide range of products – for example, a range of cutlery which features a certain handle design.

The duration of a registered design is up to a maximum of 25 years, renewable every five years on payment of a renewal fee to the relevant registered designs office (the UK Intellectual Property Office in the UK and OHIM for the registered Community design).

22.6 What protection does the registered design give?

A registered design will be infringed if a design which does not create a different overall impression on the informed user (the same test as for subsistence) is used without the authorisation of the registered design owner. As in the case of the unregistered Community design right, 'use' includes making, offering for sale, selling, importing and exporting to and from the EU infringing products and stocking such products for the above purposes. It is not necessary to show that a registered design has been copied or that the alleged infringer knew that they were infringing – the registered design creates a monopoly right in this respect.

Much of 2012 was dominated by the high profile dispute between Apple and Samsung in respect of the similar appearance of Apple's iPad tablet computer and Samsung's Galaxy tablet computers. Apple issued proceedings against Samsung in Germany and the Netherlands for infringement of Apple's registered Community design which related to the appearance of a tablet computer which was very similar (but not identical) in appearance to its iPad design (it was presumably filed when still at the prototype stage). In response Samsung applied to OHIM to have the registration declared invalid for lack of novelty, but also commenced proceedings in the UK for a declaration of non-infringement. After an unsuccessful attempt by Apple to stay the proceedings pending the outcome of the invalidation action, the High Court ruled that there had been no infringement (*Samsung Electronics (UK) Ltd v Apple Inc* [2013] ECDR 1). The court had to decide whether the typical user of tablet computers (the relevant 'informed user'), when comparing the iPad design and the Galaxy designs side by side, would have thought that their appearance gave the same overall impression. The judge decided that:

1. whilst the front faces of the respective designs were very similar, there were several other very similar looking products in existence when Apple's design was registered. Since Apple's design and the Galaxy designs all fell within this 'family' of similar looking designs, the judge gave little weight to the similarities of the front face;
2. the Galaxy designs were twice as thin as the Apple design, which was a noticeable difference;
3. the rear of the products were also noticeably different, the Apple design being very simple and plain, whereas the Galaxy designs were more detailed.

Weighing up these three factors, the judge concluded that the Galaxy designs were simply not as 'cool' as the Apple design and therefore gave a different overall impression and so did not infringe.

Given the huge popularity of the iPad, it was not surprising that Apple chose to appeal the decision. However, the Court of Appeal held that the judge had made no error of judgment and rejected the appeal (*Samsung Electronics (UK) Ltd v Apple Inc* [2013] ECDR 2). For the fun and games which followed relating to the publication of the notice announcing the decision on Apple's website, see *Samsung Electronics (UK) Ltd v Apple Inc* [2013] FSR 10.

22.7 Who has the right to register a design?

The position for registered Community designs is the same as with the unregistered Community design right. The person entitled to apply for the registered Community design will therefore be either the designer(s) or their employer.

In relation to the UK registered design, any application to register a design must be made by the owner of the design who can be the author of the design in accordance with section 2 of the RDA, or the owner as a result of assignment, transmission or operation of law. Where unregistered design right subsists in a design which is intended to be registered, the application for registration must be made by the owner of the unregistered UK design right (s 3(2)).

22.8 Dealing with registered Community designs

As with other intellectual property rights, registered Community designs may be assigned or licensed. The provisions are the same for the registered Community design as in relation to the unregistered Community design right considered in Chapter 21, save for the following additional provisions.

Article 28 provides that a transfer of a registered Community design must be entered in the register and published at the request of one of the parties and that until the transfer has been entered in the register, the assignee of the registered Community design may not enforce the rights under the registered Community design.

The grant or transfer of a licence must, at the request of one of the parties, be entered in the register and published (art 32(5)).

22.9 Dealing with UK registered designs

According to section 15B of the RDA, registered design rights or applications for registered design rights are transmissible by assignment, testamentary disposition or operation of law. A proprietor can also grant an exclusive (s 15C) or non-exclusive (s 15B(7)) licence to use a registered design. An exclusive licence must be in writing and signed by or on behalf of the proprietor (s 15C(1)). The licensee under an exclusive licence has the same rights against any successor in title as against the licensor. The person who becomes entitled to a registered design or to an interest in a registered design (such as a licence) must apply to the Registrar to record his interest on the register (subject to provision of proof of title) under section 19(1) RDA.

As a result of the possible interrelationship between registered designs and unregistered design right, the Registrar will not record any disposition in an interest in a registered design unless he is satisfied that the person claiming an interest has acquired an interest in the corresponding unregistered design right (s 19(3A)). In particular, where a person owns a registered design and the unregistered design right in that design, any assignment of the unregistered design right will be presumed to be an assignment of the registered design also, unless the contrary intention is expressed or implied (s 19(3B)).

A registered design may be given as security, as is the case with other proprietary rights.

22.10 Remedies and limitations on enforcement of registered designs

There is an exclusion in article 22 of the Regulation in favour of any third person who can establish prior use (that is, use before the date of application of the registered design or the date of priority if claimed – see Section 22.15). That third party has to show that they have in good faith commenced use within the EU, or have made serious and effective preparations to that end, of a design which is covered by the scope of protection of a registered Community design, which has not been copied from the registered design. The exception creates a limited right to continue exploiting the design. This right cannot be licensed, but it can be transferred with the business in the course of which the prior use was made or preparations for use commenced.

The same limitations also apply as they did with unregistered Community design right where the use is undertaken privately and for non-commercial purposes, etc. – see Chapter 21 and article 20.

As a result of the Intellectual Property (Enforcement, etc.) Regulations 2006 ('the Enforcement Regulations'), the RDA now provides for damages, injunctions, accounts and other remedies as are available in respect of the infringement of any other property right (previously, the RDA was silent on remedies). As noted in Chapter 20, the Enforcement Regulations provide that damages shall be appropriate to the actual prejudice suffered by the right owner. Sections 24C and 24D RDA set out detailed provisions for delivery up and destruction of infringing goods which are similar to the copyright provisions. A defendant who can show that, at the date of the infringing act, he did not know and had no reasonable grounds for supposing that the design was registered, will not have damages or an account of profits awarded against him (see s 24B). The defendant will not be deemed to know, or have had reasonable grounds for believing, the design to be registered, even if the word 'registered' or a similar marking was displayed on an article bearing the design, unless the word or marking was accompanied by the registration number of the design. Obviously, a prudent person would carry out a search of the UK Register, even if only the word 'registered' was displayed, but this section of the RDA suggests that failure to do that would not deprive the defendant of a defence to a damages award. Section 24B of the RDA provides that the court may still grant an injunction in the case of an innocent defendant. Even before the Enforcement Regulations amended the RDA, the approach of the courts was to make awards in registered design infringement cases akin to the remedies granted in respect of the infringement of other intellectual property rights.

The remedies for infringement of the registered Community design are the same as for the infringement of the unregistered Community design right (see Chapter 21). There is no express provision in the Regulation equivalent to section 24B of the RDA for innocent infringement of the right. A case involving high-profile fashion designer Jimmy Choo has highlighted this apparent anomaly in the remedies available for infringement of UK and Community registered designs (*J Choo (Jersey) Ltd v Towerstone Ltd* [2008] FSR 19).

Jimmy Choo brought an action against the owners of an Oxford Street shop, Towerstone Ltd, claiming that the shop was selling copies of Jimmy Choo's 'Ramona' handbag. The Ramona handbag was protected by registered and unregistered Community design rights and Jimmy Choo sought to recover either compensatory damages or an account of the profits made from the sales of the disputed bags.

Towerstone argued that it did not know that it was selling infringing copies and that it was therefore an 'innocent infringer' and not liable to pay any compensation to Jimmy Choo. Towerstone compared the remedies for infringement of Community design rights with the position under UK design law and argued that the remedies for infringement of the Community and UK registered design rights should be the same.

Article 89 of Council Regulation (EC) No. 6/2002 of 12 December 2001 on Community Designs ('the Regulation') sets out some of the sanctions for infringement of Community design rights, but leaves the application of other sanctions to national courts. The Regulation is directly applicable in all EU Member States, so its provisions are automatically binding. However, the Regulation does not prescribe all of the available remedies for infringement of Community design rights. The prescribed sanctions include injunctions preventing infringers from committing infringing acts and orders to seize infringing products. Article 89(1)(d) provides that Community design courts should make

> any order imposing other sanctions appropriate under the circumstances which are provided by the law of the Member State in which the acts of infringement or threatened infringement are committed, including its private international law.

Towerstone therefore relied on section 24B of the Registered Designs Act 1949 ('the Act'), which, as we have seen, states:

> In proceedings for the infringement of the right in a registered design damages shall not be awarded, and no order shall be made for an account of profits, against a defendant who proves that at the date of the infringement he was not aware, and had no reasonable ground for supposing, that the design was registered.

Alleged infringers of UK unregistered design rights are equally exempt from liability for damages if they can show that they did not know and had no reasonable grounds for supposing that the design was protected by design right (Copyright, Designs and Patents Act 1988, s 233).

Some legal commentators have interpreted the combined effect of article 89 of the Regulation and section 24B of the Act as meaning that Member States should not only apply their own laws on financial remedies to cases involving infringement of Community design rights, but also apply any limitations on the availability of such remedies to such cases (for example, see Howe, 2004: 325 ff.). This was the interpretation argued for by Towerstone.

This argument was not accepted by the court. The court said that, while there was no possible policy reason for giving an innocent infringer a defence in respect of a UK registered design right but not in respect of a Community registered design right, that was exactly what the legislature had done. Therefore, no defence of innocent infringement was provided for with respect to registered or unregistered Community design rights.

The government has since announced its intention to change the law as soon as possible to harmonise the remedies available in respect of infringements of UK registered designs and registered and unregistered Community designs. In future, an innocent infringer could be required to pay an account of profits, but not damages.

22.11 Who can enforce a registered design?

Until 2006 the owner of a UK registered design was the only person entitled to enforce the right in a registered design. Unlike the situation under the Patents Act and the 1988 Act, exclusive licensees of registered designs did not have a right to sue for infringement (for example, see *Isaac Oren v Red Box Toy Factory* [1999] FSR 785, a case decided under the old UK law). However, as a result of the Enforcement Regulations, exclusive licensees of registered designs now have the same rights against: (a) subsequent owners of the registered design as against the person granting the licence; and (b) infringers of the registered design as the owner of the registered design has. The provisions for bringing an action in respect of the infringement of a registered design if you are an exclusive licensee (see s 24F) are the same as the provisions for an exclusive licensee of a copyright work.

In an action for infringement, similar to the position under section 229 (2) of the 1988 Act, relief by way of damages, injunctions, accounts or otherwise is available (s 24A), except in the case of an innocent infringer, where neither damages nor an order for an account of profits is available, although an injunction is still available (s 24B) – compare this with section 233 of the 1988 Act for innocent infringement of UK unregistered design right, as discussed in Chapter 20.

The licensee of a registered Community design may bring proceedings in its own name for infringement of a Community design, but only if the right holder consents (or the licence agreement provides for the licensee to do so). However, an exclusive licensee may bring an action for infringement in its own name if the right holder, having been given notice to do so, does not himself bring infringement proceedings within an appropriate period (see art 32(3) of the Regulation). A licensee of a registered Community design is also able, for the purpose of obtaining compensation for damage suffered by him, to intervene in an infringement action brought by the right holder (art 32(4)).

22.12 Groundless threats

Chapter 20 sets out the rules on groundless threats which also apply to registered designs. These provisions are contained in Community Design Regulations 2005 (SI 2005 No. 2339) in relation to the registered Community design and section 26 of the RDA in relation to the UK registered design. Groundless threats provisions are no stranger to the UK registered design and unregistered design right, which have had them for some time. They came into force for the registered Community design and unregistered Community design right on 1 October 2005.

22.13 Deferment of publication of a registered Community design application

Article 50 of the Regulation provides the opportunity to defer the publication of a registered Community design for up to 30 months from the date of filing (or any earlier priority filing date) in case the normal publication following registration could destroy or jeopardise the success of a commercial operation involving the design, or could destroy the novelty of a later patent application by disclosing the design.

22.14 Cancellation procedure

Under the old RDA, once registered, a registered design could be cancelled: (a) on the application of the proprietor without cause; or (b) on the application of any person interested on grounds that the registration should never have been granted; or (c) if the design had a corresponding copyright in subsistence and that copyright had expired. These applications for cancellation would take effect, respectively: (a) immediately; (b) with effect from registration; and (c) on expiry of the corresponding copyright. These provisions are still relevant for UK registered designs granted pursuant to the old RDA.

In relation to all new applications, the provisions for cancellation as far as the UK registered design is concerned were harmonised with Community registered design law by the 2001 Regulations.

A registered design may be cancelled at any time on the application of the proprietor or it may be declared invalid on the application of an interested party or person holding conflicting rights on broadly the following grounds: (a) failure of the application to meet the legal requirements for registration; (b) the applicant not being the proper applicant; or (c) objections by holders of earlier rights or earlier distinctive signs. A cancellation will be effective from the date of the registry's decision (or such other date as the registry directs); a declaration of invalidity will result in the registration being treated as invalid from the registration date (or such other date as the registry directs).

In *Celaya Emparanza y Galdos Internacional SA (Cegasa) v Proyectos Integrales de Balizamiento* SL (C-488/10) [2012] ECDR 17 the ECJ confirmed that an earlier registered design can be relied on in infringement proceedings to stop a third party from using a design which infringes that registered design, despite the fact that the infringer also successfully applied to register their own design at a later date. There is no need for the earlier registered design right owner to apply to invalidate the later registration.

22.15 International provisions

A registered design is a national right providing protection for the design in question only within the country of registration or, in the case of the registered Community design, a right which applies throughout the EU. However, as already explained, an application will fail if the design is not new and does not have individual character, and this is an international test.

The Paris Convention provides rights of priority in respect of registered design applications, in the same way as it does for patents and trade marks. If an application for a registered design has been filed in a Convention country, further applications for the same or a substantially similar design may be filed in other Convention countries within six months of that first application. Those subsequent Convention applications may claim as their priority date the application date of the first application in a Convention country. Since all such applications will be treated as having been filed on the same date, they will not fail the novelty or individual character tests merely because of the existence of corresponding international registrations or applications.

22.16 Criminal offences in relation to UK registered designs

It is a criminal offence to mark an article in a way which suggests that the design applied to it is a registered design when it is not or once the registered design has expired (see RDA, s 35). The penalty for such an offence is a fine. There are specific provisions which enable the Secretary of State to prevent publication and registration of a design if it is considered to be prejudicial to the defence of the realm, and which prohibit an applicant from filing corresponding applications for such a design outside the UK. Failure to comply with any directions given in connection with that provision or filing an application for a design which has been blocked pursuant to that section is a criminal offence punishable by imprisonment and/or a fine. It is also a criminal offence to falsify, or procure falsification of, an entry on the Register of Designs or any documents purporting to be a record of register entries (s 34). This is punishable by imprisonment and/or a fine.

As with most criminal offences involving intellectual property rights, officers who have consented to or connived in the commission of an offence by a corporate body will also be guilty of a criminal offence (s 35A).

However, unlike with copyright and trade marks, there are no criminal provisions for an infringer of any of the registered or unregistered design rights.

22.17 Parallel actions under national and Community registered design laws

Article 95 of the Regulation provides that the court first seized in respect of an action involving the same cause of action and the same parties will have jurisdiction, the later court having to decline jurisdiction or stay any proceedings issued before it if the court's jurisdiction is disputed. For further details on jurisdictional issues, including in particular where in infringement proceedings the defendant has applied for a declaration of invalidity of the registered design relied on, see *Samsung Electronics (UK) Ltd v Apple Inc* [2013] ECDR 1.

Summary

▶ The Registered Community Design provides one design registration which gives protection throughout all Member States of the EU.

▶ The right lasts for an initial period of five years, but can be renewed up to a maximum period of 25 years.

▶ The same tests for subsistence and infringement apply as with the unregistered Community design, save that there is no need to prove copying since the Registered Community Design is a monopoly right.

▶ There is a 12-month grace period within which a valid application can still be filed even though the design has been made available to the public in the preceding 12 months.

▶ Unlike the old UK registered design system, the right protects the design irrespective of the nature of the goods on which it is used.

Exercise

A designs a new watch in his spare time, based on a design he saw in a museum in Peru ten years ago. He discusses it with his boss at the watch manufacturer where he works, and they decide that they should put the watch into production. Advise A as to:

(1) how to protect the new design;

(2) whether the design will be new; and

(3) how to protect his own interests in the design while allowing his employer to exploit it.

Further reading and references

Howe, *Russell-Clarke and Howe on Industrial Designs* (7th edn, Sweet & Maxwell, 2004).

'Too Cool for Law School? Simon Clark Looks at the Lessons to Be Learned from the Community Registered Design Decision in *Samsung v Apple*' http://www.blplaw.com/know-how/expert-updates/wp-content/uploads/2012/09/Too-cool-for-law-school-SCLA-Sept-121.pdf

Part IV

Competition

Chapter 23

Intellectual property and competition law

23.1 Introduction

Intellectual property rights essentially confer total or qualified monopolies. The ownership of an intellectual property right entitles the owner to prevent third parties from exploiting the intellectual property in question, in some cases for an unlimited period. Having the exclusive right to exploit a particular form of intellectual property also gives the owner the potential to license others, for a fee, to exploit the same intellectual property.

In contrast, competition policy is primarily about ensuring freedom of competition between market players. Competition policy imposes on companies in a dominant or monopoly position a 'special responsibility' not to abuse that position by impairing undistorted competition. As a result, although both intellectual property law and competition law share the same fundamental goals of enhancing consumer welfare and promoting innovation, there may be instances where the exercise of an intellectual property right may harm consumer welfare to such an extent that competition law should intervene. The question of when this point is reached in an individual case is often a complex one. The existence of European law on free movement of goods and services, in addition to those regarding competition, adds a further level of complexity.

It is important to note at the outset that the competition law rules do not engage with the validity of ownership or existence of intellectual property rights. Rather, the competition law rules have the potential to bite on the *exercise* of intellectual property rights and the impact that their exercise has on innovation and the relevant markets for products and/or services which benefit from that innovation. In certain limited circumstances, the competition authorities or courts enforcing the competition law rules may require compulsory licensing by a dominant party of its intellectual property rights (for example, if those rights are an 'indispensible' input for downstream competitors of the intellectual property owner).

23.2 European Union law and intellectual property

The key principles of European Union (EU) law on free movement and competition are set down in the following articles of the Treaty on the Functioning of the European Union (TFEU):

Article 34 – Quantitative restrictions on imports and all measures having equivalent effect shall be prohibited between Member States;

Article 35 – Quantitative restrictions on exports and all measures having equivalent effect shall be prohibited between Member States;

Article 36 – The provisions of Article 34 and 35 shall not preclude prohibitions or restrictions on imports, exports or goods in transit justified on grounds of … the protection of industrial and commercial property. Such restrictions shall not, however, constitute a means of arbitrary discrimination or a disguised restriction on trade between Member States;

Article 101 – prohibits agreements and concerted practices which may affect trade between Member States and which have as their object or effect the prevention, restriction or distortion of competition within the internal market, except to the extent that they deliver countervailing economic benefits;

Article 102 – prohibits any abuse of a dominant position within the whole or a substantial part of the internal market; and

Article 345 – This treaty shall in no way prejudice the rules in Member States governing the system of property ownership.

These articles were re-numbered from the previous equivalent articles in the latest consolidated text by the Treaty of Lisbon which came into force in December 2009. For convenience, all references to the previous numbering (for example, when discussing earlier cases) have been changed to refer to the equivalent numbering under the current text.

These Treaty provisions are also supplemented by secondary legislation, case law and published guidance of the competition authorities of the EU.

Intellectual property rights can be used to prevent the free movement of goods or services, can be the subject of an agreement which has an anti-competitive object or effect or can be a relevant factor in the abuse of a dominant position. For this reason, the exploitation of intellectual property rights may be constrained by European law concerning free movement of goods and services and competition. Although these two areas of law are distinct, the ways in which each area of law has been applied to the exploitation of intellectual property have many common aspects and, given the single-market objective underpinning the enforcement of European competition law, developments in one area have often informed another. As a result, both areas are considered in this chapter.

23.3 UK competition law and intellectual property

The Competition Act 1998 mirrors the European competition law framework (see above) within the UK by prohibiting:

(a)   agreements which have as their object or effect the distortion of competition in the UK (the Chapter I prohibition); and

(b)   the abuse of a dominant position in the UK (the Chapter II prohibition).

There are no specific exemptions from the Act in relation to intellectual property licences or other agreements or arrangements involving intellectual property, although agreements that are exempt from article 101 under a European block exemption will also be excluded from the Chapter I prohibition. National courts and competition authorities (in the UK, the Office of Fair Trading and sectoral regulators) are obliged to apply the domestic law (including the Competition Act) in a way which is consistent with European law regarding articles 101 and 102.

23.4 Intellectual property and free movement of goods

The use of intellectual property rights, which remain primarily national rights, to prevent any circulation of goods or services in the European Economic Area (EEA) is prohibited by articles 34 and 35. However, article 36 provides a 'get-out' whereby restrictions can be justified to the extent that they protect the 'specific subject matter' of the intellectual property right in question. Although this will vary according to the right concerned, it will always include the owner's right to put the relevant product into circulation within the EEA for the first time and to prevent infringements of the right by unconnected third parties. The identification of the 'specific subject matter' of a right as a means of distinguishing legitimate measures to protect intellectual property rights from illegitimate restrictions on free movement or competition has now largely supplanted the distinction adopted in earlier cases between the ownership and exercise of rights, which often proved unhelpful in practice.

However, once the owner has put those products into circulation in the EEA, they have exhausted that right and cannot use it to prevent free circulation of those goods. This concept as it applies to trade marks is now enshrined in UK law by section 12 of the Trade Marks Act 1994.

Put simply, if the owner of a trade mark in France manufactures and sells products under that trade mark in France, he cannot then use his corresponding trade mark rights in Italy or Germany to prevent the French goods being resold in Italy or Germany. By putting the goods on the market under his trade mark somewhere in the EEA, the owner has exhausted his right to control distribution of those goods within the EEA. The owner can still, however, prevent a third party applying his trade mark to any other goods.

The doctrine of exhaustion of rights was first applied by the European Court of Justice (ECJ) in the seminal article 101 case of *Consten and Grundig v Commission* [1966] ECR 299 (which concerned the use of trade marks to restrict imports) and was subsequently applied in the context of articles 34 and 36 in the case of *Deutsche Grammophon v Metro* [1971] ECR 487 (a case concerning copyright in sound recordings). The application of the doctrine to trade marks was confirmed in *Centrafarm v Winthrop* [1974] ECR 1183 and to patents in *Centrafarm v Sterling Drug* [1974] ECR 1147. It was subsequently enshrined in the European Trade Marks Directive (89/104), which has been superseded by the revised Trade Mark Directive (2008/95/EC) – see article 7.

The exhaustion doctrine has given rise to a line of interesting cases concerning what happens when a trade mark is owned by different proprietors in different countries. In the case of *Van Zuylen Frères v HAG* [1974] ECR 731 (commonly referred to as HAG I), the HAG coffee business, which had originally been owned by a German enterprise, was divided as a result of the Belgian subsidiary having its assets sequestrated in 1944 for being enemy property. Eventually those assets were sold off and in 1971 the trade mark previously held by the Belgian subsidiary was bought by Van Zuylen. Van Zuylen then sued the German HAG company for infringement of its trade mark when the German company started to sell coffee under the HAG name in Luxembourg. The ECJ held that Van Zuylen could not use its trade mark rights to prevent the import of goods to which the trade mark had been legitimately applied.

This decision was distinguished in the decision in *CNL-Sucal NV SA v HAG GF AG* [1990] 1 ECR 3711 (HAG II), which involved the German trade mark owner bringing an action to prevent the importation of coffee marked by the Benelux trade mark owner. The ECJ said that, because a trade mark is intended to guarantee the identity of the origin, and hence the quality, of the goods, a trade mark owner could only have exhausted his rights in respect of trade marks that were in his ownership or under some form of common control. Where marks were of common origin, but the owner voluntarily split the ownership without exercising any quality control, that owner had given up any right to seek protection against importation of goods marked with that mark. The split of ownership in the case of the HAG marks had not been voluntary because of the sequestration.

In the later case of *IHT Internationale Heiztechnik GmbH v Ideal Standard GmbH* [1994] 3 CMLR 857, which marked the first explicit use of the term 'exhaustion of rights' by the ECJ, the voluntary splitting of ownership of a trade mark was seen as allowing each of the subsequent owners to exercise their trade mark rights to prevent imports of products bearing their trade mark. This principle will only be followed where the transaction that splits ownership of the trade marks is an arm's-length commercial transaction and is not aimed at partitioning the EEA.

One special exception to the exhaustion of rights doctrine, particularly in the area of trade marks, relates to repackaged and relabelled goods. As the underlying purpose of a trade mark is seen as guaranteeing the origin and quality of the goods, a trade mark owner may assert his rights to prevent situations in which the manner in which goods are resold impairs their quality. This can potentially happen when goods are repackaged or relabelled, for example to meet language or regulatory requirements of the importing country. This issue has been considered most frequently in the field of pharmaceuticals, where repackaging is most likely to happen (for example, for regulatory purposes or to enable drugs to be sold in smaller quantities) and where such repackaging could have an impact on the products themselves.

In a series of 1996 decisions before the ECJ (*Bristol-Myers Squibb v Paranova, Eurim-Pharm v Beiersdorf* and *MPA Pharma v Rhone-Poulenc* [1996] FSR 225), it was confirmed that a trade mark owner could not use his rights to prevent importation of products that had been put into circulation in the EU with his consent unless, as a result of relabelling or repackaging, the quality of the goods might be adversely affected. In these cases, the court considered that alteration only to the outer packaging would not impair the goods unless the quality of the replacement outer packaging was such as to undermine the good reputation of the trade mark owner. Also, if during repackaging the goods have been exposed to inappropriate storage conditions (such as high temperature or humidity) or if in any translated or reproduced instructions there are any errors or omissions, this too could impact adversely on the trade mark owner. The list is not exhaustive and it seems that the ECJ is prepared to consider any sensible objection to repackaging, on the grounds that it impairs the quality and reputation of the goods and, hence, the trade mark.

In *Glaxo v Dowelhurst* (Case C-143/00) [2002] FSR 61, the ECJ confirmed that, although repackaging is prima facie harmful to the trade mark owner's rights, the trade mark owner cannot rely on those rights to prevent repackaging if it is objectively necessary to avoid artificially partitioning the market within the EEA. Repackaging, rather than simply relabelling by overstickering the original packaging, will be objectively necessary if a significant proportion of consumers would object to relabelled products. The ECJ also confirmed that the parallel importer must give prior notice to the trade mark owner of any intended repackaging.

The English High Court followed the ECJ in a second judgment in several combined cases on 6 February 2003 ([2003] EWHC 2109 (Pat)). The subsequent appeal to the Court of Appeal resulted in a further reference to the ECJ, on which judgment was handed down on 26 April 2007 (*Boehringer Ingelheim KG and ors v Swingward Ltd and ors* Case C-348/04). The ECJ ruled that parallel importers who repackage by overstickering must show that they have complied with the conditions set out in *Bristol Myers-Squibb* in order to avoid a successful infringement claim. The Court of Appeal applied this ruling in February 2008 (*Boehringer Ingelheim Kg and Another v Swingward Ltd* [2008] EWCA Civ 83 (21 February 2008), holding that the High Court's (Laddie J) conclusion of fact (that the specific de-branding complained of did not damage the claimants' trade marks) had not been shown to be wrong and accordingly had to stand. The Court of Appeal stated that the defendant had complied with one of the key conditions in *Bristol Myers-Squibb*. In particular, the defendant's activities by way of re-boxing and relabelling had not and would not cause damage to the reputation of the claimants' trade marks.

In *Wellcome Foundation Ltd v Paranova Pharmazeutika Handels GmbH* (Case C-276/05, 22 December 2008), the ECJ ruled that, where it is established that repackaging of a pharmaceutical product is necessary to market the product in the Member State which is receiving the product, that repackaging should be assessed only in terms of whether it is likely to bring the trade mark or its owner into disrepute. Furthermore, the ECJ stated that the onus was on the parallel importer to give the trade mark owner enough information to enable the owner to decide whether the repackaging was indeed necessary. The ECJ said that the type of information that was required to make such a decision would vary from case to case.

Despite the clear guidance provided by these cases, and the fact that the ECJ appears to be growing frustrated with the constant flow of references concerning repackaging, the economic incentives for parallel trade in pharmaceuticals, on the one hand, and to resist such trade, on the other, suggest that such cases will continue.

In *Phytheron International SA v Jean Bourdon SA* (Case C-352/95) ECJ, 20 March 1997 [1997] FSR 936, the owner of a French trade mark relating to health products refused to allow the products bearing the trade mark to be imported into France from Germany (being the EU country into which they had originally been sold from Turkey). This refusal was based on French trade mark law. The seller of the products argued that the French law on this point was in breach of EU law and the case was referred to the ECJ. The ECJ confirmed that the doctrine of exhaustion of rights (as contained in revised Trade Marks Directive, art 7) prevented a trade mark owner from stopping the importation into a Member State, from another Member State, of goods to which the trade marks had been applied and put on the market by or with his consent (unless the goods had been subsequently impaired), even if the goods were originally placed on the market of a country outside the EEA.

The position regarding the right to control imports of trademarked goods from outside the EEA was first addressed in the case of *EMI Records Ltd v CBS UK Ltd* (Case C-51/74) [1976] ECR 811 which confirmed that EMI could prevent distribution by CBS of products bearing the 'Columbia' mark within the EU, in circumstances where EMI held the rights to that mark in Europe and CBS in the United States. The question was further considered by the ECJ in *Silhouette International Schmied GmbH and Co KG v Hartlauer Handelsgesellschaft mbH* [1998] FSR 729. In that case, Silhouette objected to the sale in Austria of grey market 'Silhouette' spectacle frames which had initially been offered for sale in Bulgaria (which was at that time not a Member State of the EU). Silhouette argued that the sale in Austria amounted to an infringement of its registered trade mark there, since by selling the frames outside the EEA it had not consented to their sale in Austria. The ECJ held that Silhouette was entitled to object to the sale of the frames in question in Austria, on the basis that the frames had not been put on the market within the EEA with Silhouette's consent, whether explicit or implicit.

The position was further clarified in *Sebago Inc and Ancienne Maison Dubois et Fils SA v GB Unic SA* [1999] 2 CMLR 1317. In that case, Sebago and its Belgian distributor objected to the sale in Belgium of Sebago shoes which had been imported from El Salvador without Sebago's consent. The defendant argued that consent could be implied, because the shoes were identical to others which were sold in Belgium through Sebago's authorised distributor. The ECJ disagreed. It held that a trade mark owner cannot be deemed to have consented to the parallel importation of its branded goods from outside the EEA just because it had itself sold the same type of goods within the EEA. The ECJ held that the rights conferred by a trade mark are exhausted only in respect of the individual items of the product that have been put on the market with the proprietor's consent. As regards other individual items of that product, put on the market without the proprietor's consent, the proprietor may continue to prohibit the use of the trade mark with respect to those items. Consent must therefore relate to each individual item of the product in respect of which exhaustion is pleaded. Taken together, these cases confirmed that the exhaustion of rights doctrine did not extend beyond the EEA. In other words, Community exhaustion excluded any application of international exhaustion.

The English High Court initially appeared to be taking a slightly different approach, which sought to maintain a form of international exhaustion. The case of *Zino Davidoff SA v A & G Imports* [1999] RPC 631 concerned the sale in the UK of bottles of fragrance which had been imported from Singapore. The High Court held that Davidoff could not prevent such sale if it had not expressly prohibited it when it first put the goods on the market in Singapore. Since the fragrance had been sold to Davidoff's distributor in Singapore without any such restriction, the court held that Davidoff could not now prevent its parallel importation into the UK. This case was referred to the ECJ for a further ruling and came up for consideration with the joined cases brought by Levi Strauss against Tesco and Costco (*Zino Davidoff SA v A & G Imports Ltd; Levi Strauss & Co v Costco Wholesale UK Ltd; Levi Strauss & Co v Tesco Stores Ltd* [2002] Ch 109). The ECJ's decision in these cases confirmed that:

(a) implied consent of the trade mark proprietor who has placed his goods on the market outside the EEA to the subsequent marketing of those products within the EEA can be found only if the facts show that the trade mark proprietor has renounced his right to oppose such marketing;

(b) the burden of proof is on the parallel importer to prove such consent by the trade mark proprietor;

(c) just because the trade mark proprietor has not informed all subsequent purchasers of his opposition to subsequent marketing, and the goods do not have any statement on them prohibiting sale in the EEA, and there is no contractual restriction imposed on the purchaser of the goods from the trade mark proprietor on resale in the EEA, implied consent from the trade mark proprietor to sale in the EEA cannot be inferred; and

(d) it does not matter that the parallel importer is not aware of the trade mark proprietor's objections to resale of the products in the EEA.

The issue of copyright in packaging of parallel imported goods was considered in the case of *Parfums Christian Dior SA v Evora BV* (Case C-337/95) [1998] 1 CMLR 737. In this case, Evora (through its subsidiary chemist business) advertised for sale certain Christian Dior perfume products which it had obtained through parallel imports. The advertising included leaflets comprising photographs of the perfume bottles and associated packaging. Christian Dior sued for infringement of its trade marks and copyright claiming that the advertising leaflets contained unauthorised reproductions of the Dior trade marks and of the copyright works comprised in the perfume bottles and packaging. The court decided that the Trade Mark Directive specifically allowed use of trade marks in connection with the resale of goods in the EEA which had been put onto the EEA market by the trade mark owner, and in relation to copyright, similar principles applied as a result of the impact of articles 34 and 36 of the TFEU. See also the case of *Norwegian Government v Astra Norge AS* (Case E-1/98) Advisory Opinion of the ECJ, 24 November 1998 [1998] 1 CMLR 860. However, there is a distinction between copyright works which are reproduced in a physical form (where exhaustion of rights applies in the same way as in relation to trade marks) and copyright works whose value is realised in performance or broadcast of the work (where each separate performance or broadcast requires authorisation and, therefore, any one particular broadcast or performance does not exhaust rights in the copyright work). For decisions on the latter issue, see *Ministère Public v Tournier Civil Party Verney* (Case C-395/87) [1991] FSR 465 and *Warner Bros Inc & Another v Christiansen* (Case C-158/86) [1988] ECR 2605.

This brings us to the interesting position with software licences which are issued online. In *UsedSoft GmbH v Oracle International Corp* [2012] 3 CMLR 44 the ECJ held that a copyright owner had exhausted their rights if they had granted the right to download a copy of the software from the internet and use that copy for an unlimited period in exchange for a fee representing the value of that copy such that the subsequent acquirer(s) of that licence could rely on the exhaustion of rights principle so that they were 'lawful acquirers' for the purposes of article 5(1) of Directive 2009/24.

The ECJ has also considered the application of articles 34 and 36 to patents. In *Merck & Co Inc v Primecrown* (Joined cases C-267/95 and C-268/95) [1997] FSR 237 the patent owner had marketed the patented drugs in Spain and Portugal (once they had joined the EU) at a time when no patent protection was available in those countries. The ECJ held that the products had been put into circulation in the EU by the patent owner (or with his consent) and as a result he had exhausted his rights in the patent. The absence of patent protection in Spain and Portugal was irrelevant. This position was confirmed in *Sandvik Aktiebolag v K R Pfiffner (UK) Ltd* [2000] FSR 17, where the proprietor of a patented product had consented to its marketing in countries in the EU where it had not obtained patent protection.

Although exhaustion of rights has not been considered in case law in the area of designs, the Community Designs Regulation (Council Regulation 6/2002) and the Designs Directive (Directive 98/71/EC of the European Parliament and of the Council) both include specific provision for the exhaustion of rights doctrine. In the UK, the corresponding provisions are set out in the Registered Designs Act 1949, as amended by the Registered Design Regulations 2001 (SI 3949 of 2001).

23.5 Licensing and article 101

As noted above, article 101(1) of the TFEU prohibits agreements and concerted practices which have as their object or effect the prevention, restriction or distortion of competition and which may affect trade between Member States. Intellectual property licences (particularly exclusive licences) may fall within the ambit of article 101(1). If this is the case, and the agreement does not meet the requirements for exemption under article 101(3) – namely, that it: (a) contributes to improving the production or distribution of goods or promotes technical or economic progress; (b) while allowing consumers a fair share of resulting benefit; without (c) imposing unnecessary restrictions; or (d) eliminating competition in respect of a substantial part of the products in question – the agreement (or, if severable, just the anti-competitive provisions) will be void under article 101(2). The parties to an infringing agreement may also be subject to fines of up to 10 per cent of worldwide turnover and damages actions. It was previously possible to apply to the European Commission for an individual exemption under article 101(3). The Modernisation Regulation (Council Regulation 1/2003), which came into force on 1 May 2004, empowered national courts and competition authorities to apply article 101(3) and abolished the system under which parties notified the European Commission of their agreements to gain an individual exemption. Parties to agreements are now required to assess their own agreements to establish whether an agreement will be caught by article 101(1) and, if it is, whether it satisfies the exemption criteria in article 101(3).

23.6 Block Exemption Regulations

The European Commission has the power to enact Regulations (which have direct effect in all EU countries) to disapply article 101(1) from certain categories of agreement which are assumed to meet the requirements of article 101(3). These Regulations are known as Block Exemption Regulations, and essentially take the form that agreements are block exempted provided that the parties to the agreement meet certain market share 'safe harbour' thresholds, and that the agreements do not contain listed 'hard-core' or 'excluded' restrictions which are assumed to be damaging to competition. It is important to note that simply because the safe harbour protection of a Block Exemption Regulation is not available for a particular agreement, that agreement will not necessarily fall foul of the competition law rules. Rather, it will be necessary for the parties to undertake a 'self-assessment' as to whether any restrictions contained in the agreement which may infringe article 101(1) can be justified with reference to efficiencies under article 101(3).

Competition authorities generally recognise that the licensing of intellectual property rights is desirable to ensure exploitation of technological advances for the ultimate benefit of the consumer and that certain restrictions may be necessary to ensure that such licensing takes place. Nevertheless, although there are Block Exemption Regulations which are relevant to certain arrangements involving intellectual property rights (namely those relating to vertical agreements (Regulation 330/2010), specialisation agreements (Regulation 1218/2010) and research and development agreements (Regulation 1217/2010), there is currently only one block exemption specifically relating to intellectual property licences. This is the Technology Transfer Block Exemption (TTBER) (Regulation 772/2004), which covers licences of patents, software copyright and/or know-how for the production of goods or services. In order to determine which of the relevant Block Exemption Regulations apply, it is necessary to consider the terms of the Regulations themselves as well as the 'centre of gravity' of the agreement under consideration. The TTBER came into force with effect from 1 May 2004 and replaced the earlier Technology Transfer Block Exemption (Regulation 240/96), which was more prescriptive in nature. At the same time, the European Commission issued a Notice entitled 'Guidelines on the Application of Article 81 of the EC Treaty [Now Article 101 TFEU] to Technology Transfer Agreements' which, although not binding on the Community courts, provides useful guidance on the interpretation of the TTBER and those forms of common licensing arrangements which do not fall within the TTBER (e.g. multi-party patent pools). The European Commission's recent 'Guidelines on horizontal cooperation agreements' also contains useful guidance in relation to the Commission's current approach to standard setting.

The TTBER introduced new market share limitations for the first time in relation to technology-licensing arrangements. These are calculated by reference to the relevant party's previous year's sales data for the relevant technology and product markets. The TTBER distinguishes between competitors and non-competitors: actual or potential competitors cannot rely on the block exemption if they have a combined share on the relevant market(s) of more than 20 per cent, whereas the market share threshold for non-competitors is 30 per cent for each party. The stricter rule for agreements between competitors is justified on the basis that such agreements are more likely to have anti-competitive effects. The distinction between the treatment of competitors and non-competitors is carried through into separate lists of 'hard-core restrictions' for competitors and non-competitors. Any inclusion of a hard-core restriction (which include, for example, limiting the ability of a licensee to determine its own sales price for the products which exploit the relevant technology) will prevent the entire agreement from benefiting from the TTBER. The TTBER also lists specific restrictions which will not benefit from the block exemption and which will therefore require individual assessment of their anti-competitive and pro-competitive effects (which include, for example, compulsory grant-backs of severable improvements to the licensed technology). If an agreement contains any of these restrictions, the rest of the agreement may still be covered by the block exemption, if the restriction can be severed from the agreement. The European Commission and the national competition authorities in each Member State of the EU can withdraw the benefit of the block exemption if the effect of an agreement will be to restrict access to the market for other technologies or for other potential licensees, or where the licensed technology is not exploited, without a valid reason.

The TTBER may also apply to trade mark, general copyright or design right licences, provided that:

(a) the licence also covers software copyright, patents and/or know-how;
(b) the licence of the other rights does not constitute the primary object of the agreement; and
(c) the licence is also directly related to the application of the licensed technology.

The current TTBER is due to expire on 30 April 2014 and the European Commission commenced a consultation in December 2011 in connection with a revised form, which is still ongoing.

23.7 Copyright licensing

In the area of copyright licensing, a distinction is commonly made between 'non-performance copyrights' (that is, copyright embodied in a physical product) and 'performance copyrights' (that is, copyright subsisting in the performance itself). Agreements relating to the licensing and exploitation of performance copyrights are generally treated more favourably under article 101(1), given the relative difficulty of protecting the owner's interest in such copyrights. A good example of this approach is the judgment of the ECJ in *Coditel SA v Ciné Vog Films SA (No 2)* [1982] ECR 3381, in which the court ruled that an exclusive territorial licence to exhibit a film did not necessarily infringe article 101(1), bearing in mind 'the characteristics of the cinematographic industry'.

Copyright licensing also raises particular issues because of the prevalence of collective rights administration at a national level, by so-called collecting societies, which is based on national monopolies and is often implemented by relatively restrictive terms. The European Commission has sent a clear policy signal that it wishes to create EEA-wide licensing and improve competition on the market for copyright licences in general. In 2005, the European Commission adopted a non-binding recommendation on collective cross-border management of copyright and related rights for legitimate online music services (Commission Recommendation 2005/737, OJ 2005 L276/54). This recommended that Member States should promote the growth of legitimate online services and that these should not be subject to restrictions in terms of territory or customer allocation. It also recommended that Member States should improve regulatory regimes in a number of ways to facilitate the management of copyright and related rights at Community level.

In the *Santiago* case (COMP/C2/38126, COMP/C-2/39152 - *BUMA*, COMP/C-2/39151 - *SABAM*), the European Commission accepted commitments from collective rights managers that, in relation to online music, they would not accept licensing restrictions requiring commercial users to obtain their licences from a particular national collecting society.

In the *IFPI Simulcasting* case (Case COMP/C2/38.014 *IFPI Simulcasting*, decision of 8 October 2002, OJ L107 (30 April 2003), at 58) the European Commission exempted under article 101 agreements between collecting societies to grant 'one-stop-shop' licences covering all the territories of the EEA to broadcasters. These licences were to be granted in respect of 'simulcasting', where radio and television programmes are broadcast via the internet alongside the more traditional media (radio wave, cable, satellite, etc.). This move enabled collecting societies across the EEA to compete to grant licences for the commercial exploitation of copyright, particularly in relation to the fees charged for such licences.

In the *Cannes Extension Agreement* case (COMP/38.772, OJ 2007 L296/27) in October 2006, the European Commission accepted binding commitments which indicated that it rejected attempts by record companies and publishers to impose restrictions on collecting societies. Such restrictions included asking the collecting societies to agree not to enter the publishing or record production markets, and to control price competition in this market (e.g. by imposing conditions on the granting of rebates).

Distribution issues involving internet sales were examined in the *iTunes* case. In April 2007, the European Commission sent a Statement of Objections to major record companies and Apple asserting that agreements between each record company and Apple unlawfully restricted music sales by forcing consumers to buy music only from the iTunes online store in their country of residence. (The iTunes website limited access according to consumers' country of residence by using their credit card details.) In March 2008, the European Commission closed the case, on the basis that the agreements between Apple and the major record companies did not determine how the iTunes store was organised in Europe. Rather, the structure of the iTunes store was chosen by Apple to take into account the country-specific aspects of copyright laws. The European Commission acknowledged that some record companies, publishers and collecting societies still applied licensing practices which made it difficult for iTunes to operate stores accessible for a European consumer anywhere in the EU.

The ongoing *CISAC* proceedings involve the national collecting societies in the individual EU Member States, which (in the context of this case) grant exploitation licences to commercial users of public performance rights for the purposes of music broadcasting via satellite, cable retransmission and internet transmission. In 2006, following complaints from broadcasting group RTL and Music Choice (a UK online music provider), the European Commission became concerned about certain parts of the CISAC model contract and its implementation on a bilateral level by The International Confederation of Authors and Composers Societies ('CISAC') members. The European Commission was specifically concerned about:

(a) the membership restrictions, which obliged authors to transfer their rights only to their own national collecting society (whatever the subsequent exploitations of the rights);

(b) the territorial restrictions, which obliged commercial users to obtain a licence only from the domestic collecting society and limited to the domestic territory; and

(c) the network effects of the agreements.

In July 2008, the European Commission issued a formal decision (COMP/38.698 – *CISAC Agreement*) prohibiting twenty-four European collecting societies from restricting competition by limiting member societies' ability to offer their services to authors and commercial users outside their domestic territory. The prohibited practices consisted of clauses in the reciprocal representation agreements concluded by members of CISAC as well as other concerted practices between those collecting societies. The European Commission held that these practices infringed article 101 and required the collecting societies to end these infringements by modifying their agreements and practices (without imposing any fines). The European Commission argued that:

(a) the removal of these restrictions would allow authors to choose which collecting society managed their copyright (e.g. on the basis of quality of service, efficiency of collection and level of management fees deducted); and

(b) it would also make it easier for users to obtain licences for broadcasting music over the internet, by cable and by satellite in several countries from a single collection society of their choice.

By October 2008, many of the national collecting societies had challenged the European Commission's decision in the General Court (formerly the Court of First Instance). At the time of writing, the outcome of these appeals is awaited.

In July 2012 the European Commission adopted a proposal for a Directive on collective rights management and multi-territorial licensing of rights in musical works for online use.

In a separate development, in June and July 2008, the High Court in London referred a number of questions to the ECJ, having heard two appeals concerning public houses which used cheap foreign satellite-decoder equipment and cards for use in screening live football matches (*Karen Murphy v Media Protection Services Ltd* [2008] EWHC 1666, *Football Association Premier League Ltd & ors v QC Leisure & ors* [2008] EWHC 1411). Using this equipment meant that the publicans had avoided paying fees to BSkyB, which owned the UK rights to live broadcasts of Premier League football matches. The questions put to the ECJ concerned the application of article 101 to exclusive licence agreements which are not only confined to one or more Member States, but which also oblige the licence holder to prevent actively its satellite-decoder cards (which enable reception of the licensed football broadcasts) from being sold outside the particular territory for which they hold a licence. Before it could judge whether such licence agreements infringed article 101, the High Court in London sought guidance on several points, including what legal test it should use to determine this, as well as which circumstances it should take into consideration. The judgment was issued on 4 October 2011 (*Football Association Premier League Ltd v QC Leisure* (Joined Cases – Case C-403/08 and C-429/08) [2012] 1 CMLR 29). The ECJ ruled that:

▶ National law which prohibits the import, sale or use of foreign decoder cards is contrary to the fundamental freedom to provide services and cannot be justified; such decoders are not 'illicit devices', even if bought using a false name and address.

▶ Football matches themselves are not an author's own intellectual creation, so they are not a copyright 'work', but broadcasts of them may include copyright works such as the opening video sequence.

▶ Payment of a premium by broadcasters for absolute territorial exclusivity, and prohibitions on the use of foreign decoders, go beyond what is necessary to ensure appropriate remuneration for the holders of relevant rights. They may result in artificial price differences between different EU Member States. Partitioning the EU in that way is irreconcilable with the fundamental aim of the TFEU.

▶ A system of exclusive licences infringes EU competition law if the agreements prohibit the supply of decoder cards to TV viewers who want to watch the broadcasts outside the Member State for which the licence is granted. Licence agreements giving absolute territorial exclusivity to broadcasters in their Member State eliminate competition between broadcasters for relevant services. They divide the EU along national boundaries, have the object of restricting competition and therefore infringe competition law.

Micro Leader Business v Commission (Case T-198/98) [1999] ECR II 3989 concerned the European Commission's rejection of a complaint against Microsoft by Micro Leader, a French wholesaler. It was alleged that Microsoft's restriction on the import of French language software from Canada to France breached articles 101 and 102. The former Court of First Instance (now the General Court) ruled that the software was copyright protected and as it had not previously been placed on the EU market, there was no breach of article 101 (see Section 23.4 for further details on exhaustion of rights). In relation to article 102, the judgment stated that while the protection of copyright in this way is not in itself a breach of article 102, such enforcement may, in exceptional circumstances, involve abusive conduct.

23.8 Trade mark licensing

In relation to trade mark licensing, the leading cases of *Re the Agreements of Davide Campari-Milano SpA* [1978] FSR 528 and *Moosehead/Whitbread* Commission Decision (90/186/EEC) [1991] 4 CMLR 391 provide helpful guidance on what kinds of restrictions can fall within article 101(1). In the *Campari* case, provisions requiring the licensee to comply with the licensor's manufacturing instructions and to buy secret raw materials from the licensor were held not contrary to article 101(1), as they were necessary to maintain the quality of the goods and hence the goodwill of the trade mark. In *Moosehead*, the Commission noted that an obligation on a licensee not to challenge the validity of the licensor's trade mark could in certain circumstances be caught by article 101(1) where the use of a well-known trade mark would be an important advantage to a company entering or competing in a given market. Since these factors were not present in this case, given the novelty of the Moosehead brand, the agreement was granted an individual exemption under article 101(3).

23.9 Patent licensing

In relation to patent licensing, two cases from the early 1980s offer helpful guidance. The first concerned the extent to which Windsurfing International Inc. (WI) could restrict the activities of its European distributors by relying on its ownership of a German patent (relating to the configuration of a sailboard's rig), the use of which was licensed together with related know-how and trade marks.

Several trade competitors complained to the European Commission about WI's licensing arrangements. The European Commission held that a number of provisions in WI's agreements infringed article 101(1) (Case IV/29.395 – *Windsurfing International*), on the basis that they went beyond what was necessary to protect the specific subject matter of the patent. Concluding that a number of restrictions went beyond this, the European Commission imposed a fine of ECU 50,000 on WI. Less surprisingly, the European Commission objected to export bans in the distribution agreements and fined a number of distributors and dealers lower amounts.

WI appealed the European Commission's decision to the ECJ, which in Case 193/83 *Windsurfing International/Commission* (ECR-1986, p 611, judgment of 25/02/1986) substantially upheld the decision, ruling that the following restrictions did not fall within the specific subject matter of the patent and therefore infringed article 101(1):

(a) quality controls imposed by the licensor, either in respect of products not covered by the patent or which were not based on objective criteria, laid down in advance;

(b) an obligation on the licensee only to sell the patented product in conjunction with a product outside the scope of the patent;

(c) a method of calculating royalties which was based on the selling price of a product which comprised both patented and unpatented products, which induced the licensee to refuse to sell separately a WI product which was not covered by the patent;

(d) an obligation on the licensee to affix a notice of the patent to a product not covered by the patent; and

(e) a no-challenge clause with regard to the licensor's trade marks and patents (preventing licensees from challenging their validity).

This strict approach was slightly relaxed in the ECJ's *Maize Seeds* judgment (Case 258/78 *LC Nungesser KG and Kurt Eisele v Commission* [1982] ECR 2015). The French national agricultural institute (INRA) had granted a German company the exclusive right to propagate and sell certain varieties of hybrid maize seed developed by INRA within what was then West Germany. In September 1978, the European Commission decided that the licence infringed article 101(1) (Case IV/28.824 – *Breeders' rights – maize seed*). On appeal to the ECJ, the challenge was partially upheld. Given the specific nature of the rights in question (namely plant breeders' rights, which are similar to those conferred by a patent), the ECJ held that the restriction on INRA not to license similar rights to any other plant breeder in the licensed territory, or itself to sell or produce seeds in the licensed territory, did not represent a restriction of competition by 'object' (i.e. the object of the agreement was not to restrict competition within the meaning of article 101) and was not therefore automatically caught by article 101(1). The exclusivity obligation was essential to the rights that the licensee acquired; without it, the licence would have lost its commercial substance.

In reaching this conclusion, the ECJ held that article 101(1) did not necessarily apply at all to an 'open exclusive licence', under which the licensee remained free to respond to unsolicited orders from outside the licensed territory, despite the grant of exclusivity. In contrast, a licence conferring absolute territorial protection on a licensee by completely banning imports from other licensed territories would automatically infringe article

101(1), on the basis that this constituted a restriction of competition by 'object'. (It is notable, however, that the TTBER allows for absolute territorial protection in limited circumstances.)

Nungesser is authority for regarding all 'open' exclusive licences of intellectual property rights (i.e. not just plant breeders' rights) as likely to fall outside the scope of article 101, subject to two key provisos:

(a) exclusivity provision may need to be objectively justifiable, e.g. by the level of investment required by the licensor and licensee, the nature of the products concerned, the degree of novelty and the need to ensure a sufficient return for the licensee; and

(b) additional restrictions on the exercise of the licensed rights may bring the licence within the scope of Article 101(1).

23.10 Article 102

As noted above, article 102 of the TFEU prohibits conduct which constitutes an abuse of a dominant position and which has a potential effect on trade between EU Member States. Like article 101(1), an infringer can be subject to fines of up to 10 per cent of worldwide turnover. An infringement may also enable third parties to claim damages or injunctive relief in national courts.

Article 102 is aimed primarily at controlling the activities of a single dominant entity (i.e. unilateral conduct), although in limited circumstances it may be applied to control the conduct of a group of entities which are together collectively dominant. In order for article 102 to apply, a party must be shown to have a dominant position on a relevant market within the EU or a substantial part of it. The definition of the relevant market is therefore crucial in determining dominance and the Commission has defined 'relevant markets' very narrowly in some cases.

Although there is no exact percentage market share above which dominance is proved, it is generally viewed as unlikely if an undertaking's market share is less than 40 per cent and has been presumed at market shares of 50 per cent or more. Whether an undertaking is in fact dominant will depend on a number of factors, in addition to its own market share, including:

(a) the shares held by other participants in the relevant markets;

(b) barriers to entry and expansion; and

(c) countervailing buyer power.

Dominance alone is not prohibited by article 102. Once dominance is established, abuse of that dominance must be shown. The list of activities that constitute an abuse is non-exhaustive. The most common examples, however, are exclusive dealing, refusal to supply, tying/bundling, discriminatory pricing, predatory pricing (that is, setting prices below cost to eliminate competition with a view to then increasing prices) and exclusionary discount and rebate schemes.

It has always been considered that ownership of intellectual property rights could, of itself, confer dominance, although this will be the case only if the relevant products cannot be produced without the specific intellectual property concerned. In other words, ownership of intellectual property rights will not necessarily ensure market power on the markets on which the rights are exploited, as this will depend on the availability of substitute technologies and production methods.

As with article 101, the extent to which article 102 may justify intervention in an owner's intellectual property is often assessed by reference to the specific subject matter of the right concerned. This has led to particular controversy over the question of whether article 102 may be used to require the licensing of intellectual property rights by a dominant entity, given the essential importance of a rights owner to exclude others from using the rights concerned without authorisation. The traditional approach is well illustrated by the case of *Volvo AB v Erik Veng (UK) Ltd* (Case C-238/87) [1988] ECR 6211, in which the ECJ held that a refusal to license intellectual property rights could not in itself be considered abusive, since the right to be the only manufacturer of the protected product in question was part of the specific subject matter of the right concerned.

In the case of *RTE and ITP v Commission (Joined Cases C-241/91 P and C-242/91 P)* [1995] 4 CMLR 718 (*Magill*), the ECJ decided for the first time that a refusal to license intellectual property rights did infringe article 102, on the basis that the ownership of copyright in television programme schedules (which were released to newspapers for publication on a daily basis and used for broadcasters' own weekly listing guides) conferred an effective monopoly over a class of information and that the owners' refusal to supply that information to rivals who wished to publish a weekly guide to all broadcasters' programmes prevented the emergence of a new product and thus prevented an unfulfilled consumer need being met. While the ECJ said that intellectual property rights would only breach article 102 in 'exceptional circumstances', it found that the 'exceptional circumstances' in that case included the fact that the refusal to grant a licence amounted to preventing a new product from coming on the market for which there was a proven consumer demand (see also *Oscar Bronner v Mediaprint* [1998] ECR I-7791 and *IMS Health* (Case C-418/01) [2004] CMLR 28).

In a more recent case (Commission Decision of 24 March 2004, Case COMP/C-3/37.792 – *Microsoft*), Microsoft was fined €497 million by the European Commission for two alleged abuses under article 102, namely tying its Windows Media Player application to its Windows operating system and refusing to supply necessary interface information to rival developers of work group server operating systems. In both cases, the Commission considered that such conduct materially reduced rivals' ability to compete with Microsoft.

On 17 September 2007, the Court of First Instance essentially upheld the European Commission's decision (Case T-201/04 *Microsoft Corp v Commission*). Significantly, the Court of First Instance appeared to water down the requirement (established in *Magill*) that a refusal to license would be abusive only if it prevented the emergence of a new product, by upholding the Commission's finding of an abuse based on the argument that Microsoft's conduct had made the development of better, rather than wholly new, operating systems less likely. Microsoft did not appeal this judgment. The European Commission sent a further 'Statement of Objections' to Microsoft concerning the tying of Internet Explorer to Windows in January 2009. As a result of this investigation, Microsoft gave legally binding commitments to offer a 'choice screen' to users of Windows for five years. The choice screen allows users to choose between Internet Explorer and eleven competing web browsers.

The clear precedent provided by these cases that a refusal to license intellectual property may constitute an infringement of article 102 is noted in the European Commission's article 102 guidance paper on its enforcement priorities in applying article 102 to abusive exclusionary conduct by dominant undertakings (Commission Communication of 9 February 2009). This document states that:

(a) the Commission will view a refusal to supply as an enforcement priority where the refusal relates to a product or service which is objectively necessary to be able to compete effectively on a downstream market;

(b) the refusal is likely to lead to the elimination of effective competition on the downstream market; and

(c) the refusal is likely to lead to consumer harm.

The commercial pressures that have led to protracted litigation between pharmaceutical companies and parallel importers, as noted above in the context of article 101, have also had an impact on article 102 case law. For example, in Joined Cases C 468/06 to C 478/06 *Sot. Lélos kai Sia EE and ors v GlaxoSmithKline AEVE Farmakef-tikon Proïonton* (16 September 2008), the ECJ ruled that a pharmaceuticals company abuses its dominant position if it refuses to meet 'ordinary' orders by wholesalers in order to prevent parallel exports. The ECJ left it to the national courts to ascertain whether orders are 'ordinary' in the light of both the previous business relations between the pharmaceutical company and the wholesalers concerned, and the size of the orders in relation to the requirements of the market in the Member State concerned.

In June 2005, the European Commission fined AstraZeneca €60 million for allegedly misusing the patent system to block or delay market entry for generic competitors to its ulcer drug Losec, which at one stage was the world's bestselling prescription medicine (COMP/37.507 – *Generics/Astra Zeneca*). The European Commission found serious abuses of AstraZeneca's dominant market position, contrary to article 102, including:

(a) giving misleading information to several national patent offices in the EEA, resulting in AstraZeneca gaining extended patent protection for Losec through so-called supplementary protection certificates (SPCs) and;

(b) misusing rules and procedures applied by the national medicines agencies that issue market authorisations for medicines by selectively deregistering the market authorisations for Losec capsules in Denmark, Norway and Sweden with the intent of blocking or delaying entry by generic firms and parallel traders.

On appeal, the General Court largely upheld the European Commission's decision (*Case T-321/05 AstraZeneca v Commission*). However, it found that the European Commission had failed to establish that AstraZeneca's conduct in Denmark and Norway had breached article 102 by preventing or restricting parallel imports in Denmark and Norway when it requested the deregistration of the Losec capsule market authorisations, withdrew Losec capsules from the market and launched new Losec MUPS tablets. The fine was reduced to €52.5 million accordingly.

On 6 December 2012, the ECJ dismissed an appeal lodged by AstraZeneca against the General Court judgment (*Case C-457/10 AstraZeneca v Commission*).

In February 2007, the European Commission initiated proceedings against Boehringer concerning the alleged misuse of the patent system in order to exclude potential competition for the treatment of chronic obstructive pulmonary disease (COPD). The alleged infringements concerned abuses of a dominant position (see Case COMP/B2/39246 – *Boehringer*). The European Commission closed its investigation after Boehringer agreed to remove the alleged blocking positions.

23.11 The EU pharmaceutical sector inquiry

In January 2008, the European Commission further extended its interest in the European pharmaceutical sector by launching an in-depth sector inquiry with an unprecedented round of 'dawn raids'. In November 2008 the European Commission issued its preliminary findings (DG Competition Staff Working Paper, 28 November 2008, at http://ec.europa.eu/competition/sectors/pharmaceuticals/inquiry/preliminary_ report.pdf). The working paper stated that branded pharmaceutical makers ('originators') have deployed a 'toolbox' of tactics to delay the entry of generic drugs onto European markets. In July 2009 the Commission adopted its final report, which reiterated its earlier findings in the working paper and reported shortcomings of the regulatory framework in relation to patents, marketing, authorisation, pricing and reimbursement (Commission communication, 8 July 2009, at http://ec.europa.eu/ competition/sectors/pharmaceuticals/inquiry/communication_en.pdf).

The inquiry found that originators maintain revenue streams, in particular those from 'blockbuster' drugs, for as long as possible, thereby delaying generic entry. This has led to healthcare systems and consumers paying at least €3bn more than they would otherwise have done. Those revenues may represent a considerable opportunity for generic companies.

The Commission highlighted five main areas of concern in relation to originators and generic firms.

23.11.1 Strategic patenting

The European Commission identified patent 'clusters' or 'thickets' as obstacles to the market entry of generic medicines – one blockbuster was apparently protected by up to 1,300 separate filings EU-wide. Divisional patent applications (instruments allowing the applicant to split an initial patent application) are another way to extend the validity of originators' original filings. Given the increasing number of applications, and the limited resources of patent offices, the report might therefore offer generic firms grounds to consider challenging trivial or non-inventions. As the legal costs of both originators and generic companies represent only a small proportion of what is at stake, the report effectively invited generic firms to challenge vigorously any patents to which they object. The benefit of winning such proceedings may be diluted, however, by other 'free rider' producers entering the market once legal action has cleared away the obstacles.

23.11.2 Patent litigation

Where generic firms have litigated patent disputes with originators, the European Commission's report indicated that they won 62 per cent of the cases where a final judgment was given. Generic firms also prevailed in around 75 per cent of final decisions rendered by the European Patent Office involving secondary patents. While the total cost of patent litigation in the period 2000–07 was estimated at €420 million, the figures suggested that, even where the originators initiated proceedings to exploit their 'strong dissuasive effect' on generic entry, it may be worth the generic firms' while to resist. However, these figures may not reflect those cases where generic firms conceded their ground to more powerful originators.

23.11.3 Patent settlements

Originators and generic firms often choose to settle their disputes out of court, thereby saving the costs of lengthy and complex litigation, and avoiding uncertainty. Accompanying 'value transfers' can include direct payments, licences, distribution agreements or 'side deals', all of which can restrict market entry by generic medicines. The European Commission's report detailed over €200 million in direct payments made by originators to generic companies.

On the basis of this report, some generic firms may consider approaching the Commission (or a national competition authority) with evidence of restrictive settlement agreements, and this could ultimately increase generic sales in Europe. However there may be legal risks for generic firms that are party to settlements with originators, if the European Commission subsequently regards those settlement agreements as infringing the competition rules. The European Commission has the power to impose fines, declare agreements unenforceable and issue decisions which can be used by third parties in 'follow-on' damages actions.

23.11.4 Interventions before national regulatory authorities

Originators often intervene against applications by generic firms for marketing authorisations. Some regulatory bodies expand the narrow scope of such assessments by considering arguments by originators that the generic product may infringe the originator's patents ('patent linkage'). The report says that patent linkage is considered 'unlawful' under EU law. On this basis, generic firms could therefore resist arguments regarding the violation of patent rights, which often delay generic market entry by an average of four months. The report stated that, where such cases resulted in litigation, originators won only 2 per cent of cases, indicating that generic firms may have every incentive to counter such arguments.

23.11.5 Life cycle strategies for 'second-generation' products

According to the report's findings, generic firms could react to originators' attempts to launch 'second-generation' medicines by carefully monitoring the originators' marketing and patent filing efforts. The European Commission found that, if generic medicines enter the market before patients are switched to the originators' 'second-generation' products, the originators have difficulties in convincing doctors to prescribe the product and/or obtaining a high price. Generic firms may also be able to challenge second-generation products by arguing that they contribute only a marginal (if any) improvement.

23.11.6 Action after the sector inquiry

In November 2008, Competition Commissioner Kroes warned that 'the Commission will not hesitate to open antitrust cases against companies where there are indications that the antitrust rules may have been breached' (Speech/08/659). To date, the Commission has launched formal proceedings against companies including Teva, Krka, Servier, Lundbeck, Cephalon, Johnson & Johnson and Novartis to establish whether there were pay-for-delay agreements between originator and generic pharmaceutical companies to delay product launches on the European market. The Commission also continues to monitor patent settlements. In April 2011, the Office of Fair Trading (OFT) in the UK fined Reckitt Benckiser £10.2 million for infringing article 102. The fine was levied after Reckitt Benckiser admitted that it had infringed UK and European competition law and agreed to cooperate with the OFT. The OFT found that Reckitt Benckiser had abused its dominant position by withdrawing packs of its Gaviscon Original Liquid Medicine from sale to the National Health Service in the UK after its patent had expired, but before the generic alternative had been introduced. The result was that doctors wrote prescriptions for another of the company's products, Gavison Advance Liquid, which was still patent protected. In addition to the fine by the OFT, the British government has issued proceedings to seek damages from Reckitt Benckiser arising from the abuse of dominance.

23.12 Standard essential patents

More recently, the Commission has opened investigations regarding standard setting and standard essential patents ('SEPs'). 'Standards' define the technical or quality requirements for current or future products, production processes, services or methods. They are often set by standards bodies, such as the European Telecommunications Standards Institute (ETSI), whose members are usually required to commit to license any of their patents that are essential for a standard – otherwise known as SEPs – on fair, reasonable and non-discriminatory ('FRAND') terms. For example, it might be necessary to use patented designs to comply with a standard, in which case the owner of those SEPs would agree in advance to licence them on FRAND terms. This commitment is designed to allow effective access to the standard by limiting the power of the SEP owner and fairly remunerate the SEP holder for the use of its patents.

In January 2012, the Commission began an investigation into Samsung Electronics over allegations that it had breached article 102 by seeking injunctive relief against Apple based on alleged infringements of certain SEPs for 3G mobile devices. The Commission has commented that seeking injunctions could be abusive when the potential licensee of a SEP is willing to agree a licence on FRAND terms. In December 2012, Samsung announced that it would no longer seek injunctions against Apple throughout Europe in relation to SEPs, but would limit its claims to financial relief. However, despite this, a few days later the Commission issued a Statement of Objections against Samsung setting out its preliminary conclusion that Samsung had abused its dominant position by seeking injunctions against Apple.

In April 2012, the Commission initiated similar proceedings against Motorola to investigate whether it infringed article 102 through enforcing injunctions against Apple's and Microsoft's flagship products, such as the iPhone, iPad, Windows and Xbox, for SEPs that it had agreed to licence on FRAND terms. The investigation will also consider allegations that Motorola offered unfair licensing conditions for its SEPs.

Summary

▶ The exercise of intellectual property rights can conflict with competition law in certain instances.

▶ The principles of EU law on free movement of goods and competition can be found in articles 34–36, 101, 102 and 345 of the TFEU.

▶ UK competition law is closely based on the principles of EU competition law.

Summary cont'd

▶ Once the owner of an intellectual property right has freely put products onto the market in one part of the EEA, he cannot use his rights in another part of the EEA to prevent resale of the goods in question unless, for example, in the case of repackaged goods, the quality of the goods might be adversely affected by the repackaging.

▶ Agreements that distort competition in the EEA are controlled by article 101.

▶ Where certain criteria are met, a restrictive agreement will be exempt from article 101(1). The European Commission can make provision for automatic exemption from article 101(1) under a Block Exemption Regulation. To date there is only one block exemption relating specifically to intellectual property licensing – the TTBER.

▶ Article 102 controls activities which amount to an abuse of a dominant position. In certain limited instances, the remedy to an article 102 infringement may be a requirement for compulsory licensing.

Exercises

23.1 How can ownership of an intellectual property right conflict with competition?

23.2 How might an owner of intellectual property abuse his rights so as to distort competition in the EEA? Discuss whether EU competition law is adequate to control such abuse.

23.3 Is there a proper balance in protecting the fruits of creative endeavour and maintaining an effective competition policy?

23.4 Consider the courts' developing attitude towards parallel imports.

Index